BERTRAND de MARGERIE, S.J.

THEOLOGICAL RETREAT

With Some Ignatian Spiritual Exercises

BERTRAND de MARGERIE, S.J.

THEOLOGICAL RETREAT

With Some Ignatian Spiritual Exercises

Translated by A. Owen, S.J.

FRANCISCAN HERALD PRESS

1434 WEST 51st STREET • CHICAGO, 60609

Theological Retreat by Bertrand de Margerie S.J., translated from the French original by A. Owen, S.J., copyright © 1976 by Franciscan Hearld Press, 1434 West 51st St., Chicago, Illinois 60609. All rights reserved.

Library of Congress Cataloging in Publicata Data

Margerie, Bertrand de.
  Theological retreat.

  Bibliography: p. 309
  Includes indexes.
  1. Loyola, Ignacio de, Saint, 1491-1556. Exercitia spiritualia. 2. Spiritual exercises. I. Title.
BX2179.L8M33   242'.1   76-50929
ISBN 0-8199-0656-5

NIHIL OBSTAT:
  Daniel L. Flaherty S.J.
  Provincial, Chicago Province,
  Society of Jesus

IMPRIMATUR:
  Msgr. Richard A. Rosemeyer, J.C.D.
  Vicar General, Archdiocese of Chicago

October 4, 1976

"The Nihil Obstat and the Imprimatur are official declarations that a book or pamphlet is free of doctrinal and moral error. No implication is contained therein that those who have granted the Nihil Obstat and Imprimatur agree with the contents, opinions, or statements expressed.

DEDICATION TO THE MOST GLORIOUS AND BLESSED VIRGIN MARY, OUR SOVEREIGN, MEDIATRIX AND QUEEN[1] OF THE SPIRITUAL EXERCISES.

Mother of Christ,[2] it is from your immaculate hands[3] we have received, with Saint Ignatius, and still receive, the salvific doctrine[4] of the Exercises which the Spirit of your Son wishes to work in us.[5]

At the very moment he was composing the Exercises, you appeared, with your Son to Inigo de Loyola to teach him and to confirm him in their truths. Thus it was that, often invoked and contemplated by him at this period, you exercised a special influence on their composition.[6] You are, then, the mediatrix[7] of the gift of the Exercises, for the greater glory of God, Father, Son and Holy Spirit.

Present at the conception of the Exercises, you also constitute their content, for you are contemplated, invoked,[8] imitated[9] and glorified in each one of the Four Weeks. Be still their end!

Blessed Virgin Mary,[10] Mother of God,[11] most sorrowful of old[12] but now most blessed[13] and glorious,[14] you are our queen[15] and sovereign.[16] In all that this book contains that is true and good, just as the Exercises on which it comments and which it prolongs, there is a gift of your heart, a fruit of your tears.

I offer it in reparation for so many offenses, in supplication for its readers, and that it may be an instrument of your reign and dominion,[17] at the service of the glory of the eternal king, your Son. Through it may they enter more deeply into your immense joy[18] of mother of the King. Turn your eyes of mercy towards us and show us the fruit of your womb, Jesus![19]

NOTES ON THE DEDICATION

1. All these Marian titles, except that of mediatrix, taken from the Spiritual Diary of Saint Ignatius, form part of the Marian vocabulary of the Exercises as the following notes will show.

2. Ex. 63,V (*N.B.* V = Vulgate; A = Autograph.)

3. Pius XII: *Meditantibus Nobis,* AAS,14,(1922) 629: "in his retreat of Manresa, (Ignatius) learned from the Mother of God herself how he ought to combat for the Lord. In some manner he received from her hands this most perfect code of laws every true soldier of Christ is to follow, the Spiritual Exercises, given, it is said, to him from heaven." We shall cite the essential Latin words ". . .*ab ipsa Deipara didicit, cujus tamquam ex manibus illum accepit absolutissimum legum codicem quo quisque bonus miles Christi Jesu utatur oportet. . ."* Cf. note 6 for how this text is to be understood.

4. Ex. 45,V. Observe in passing that this teaching concerns in part the Virgin Mary.

5. It is under the action of the Spirit of the Father and of the Son that the spiritual operations of the Exercises are realized by the retreatant (Ex.1,2).

6. *Cf.* A. Codina, S.J., *Los origines de los Ejercicios espirituales de San Ignacio de Loyola,* Barcelona, 1926, pp. 85-93. There is no need at all to say that the Virgin "dictated the Exercises" for asserting that she exercised a decisive influence on their composition. Much greater, for instance, than that of her instruments, Blessed James. de Voragine, Ludolph the Carthusian, Garcia de Cisneros. No one dreams of denying their role, why then deny Mary's?

7. *Cf.* note 1.

8. Ex. 63, 147, etc.

9. *Cf.* Ex. 248, A: "If he wishes to imitate our Lady. . ."

10. Ex. 243, V, 102, V.

11. Ex. 114 V: The only mention, so far as I know, of the Divine Maternity in the Vulgate. I do not think it is mentioned at all explicitly in A.

12. Ex. 298, V: Ex. 208, V toward the end: "Let him consider, likewise, the desolation of our Lady, her great sorrow and weariness. . ." This point will be covered more throughly in Chapter XV. Saint Ignatius, however, does not repeat explicitly in the Third Week the so suggestive reflection he made in regard to Mary at the circumcision: "They returned the child to his mother who felt compassion for him because of the blood he shed" (Ex. 266), yet this thought may well be taken for granted.

13. The expression "Blessed Virgin" (*Cf.* Lk 1:27,45) seems to be a technical term replacing in the Vulgate (102, 108 etc.) "*Nuestra Senotra,*" of the Spanish Autograph.

14. Ex. 98, V: "In the presence of thy *glorious* virgin mother." (*in conspectu gloriosae virginis martris tuae"*). It is likely that these words of th oblation in the Kingdom are an allusion to the assumption. For other saints are not mentioned with this qualificative adjective, glorious, either in the Vulgate or in the Autograph.

15. The Exercises do not contain this title explicitly, unless there is an allusion to it (Ex. 253) in the prayer "*Salve Regina*" as proposed as subject of prayer according to the second and third ways of prayer (Ex. 258), which brings out clearly furthermore how dear to Saint Ignatius it was and how it fashioned his Marian piety.

16. In this way we translate the expression: *"Domina nostra"* or *"Nuestra Senora."* The Spanish words are the ones which occur most frequently in A, to designate *Mary*, who is so frequently called by this name. The Latin expression is used in the Vulgate (Ex. 63). Saint Ignatius here is influenced by Ludolph the Carthusian and Blessed James de Voragine. This expression, without doubt, also has a profound doctrinal meaning since it accents the dominion of the Mother of God over the world of her Son. This is what we wished to emphasize at the close of our dedication. The concept of "lady," of "sovereign," differs from that of "queen." It not only implies the right to dispose of a person or thing in view of the good of the one who is governed or the common good, but also in view of the particular good of the one who governs. (*Cf.* A. Musters, *La Souveraineté de la Vierge* according to the mariological writings of Barthelemy de Los Rios, O.E.S.A., Gand, 1946, p. 101). Above all it is to be observed that by constantly calling Mary, "our lady," Saint Ignatius is perfectly faithful to the etymological and historical meaning of the name of Mary in the mideastern biblical sense. Ugaritic documents have confirmed that the word means "highest, most exalted." (*Cf.* E. Vogt, S. J., De nominis Mariae etymologia, *Verbum Domini,* 26, 1948, 164–166). In fact, in the times of Joachim and Anna, Hebrew parents attached to this word the same sense given by its etymology: "The intention of the Virgin's parents was to call her lady or princess and we still pray to her under the name of *Notre-Dame"* (Lagrange, *Evangile selon saint Luc.,* Paris, 1927, pp. 27,28). And so modern works but confirm what the fathers and doctors of the Church had already emphasized. Saint Peter Chrysologus in an excellent commentary on Lk 1:30 (Sermo 142; ML, 52, 579); Saint John Damascene (*De fide orthodoxa,* IV, 14; PG, 94, 1158): "Grace (i.e. Anna) engenders the sovereign." Saint Thomas Aquinas: "Rightly the Angel honors the blessed virgin, for she is the Mother of the Lord, and hence sovereign." (Exposition on the Angelical Salutation, X): all try to outdo each other in exalting the meaning, divinely intended, of the name of Mary. Besides, the Old Testament has already shown that Hebrew parents expressed their joy at the coming into the world of a child by giving it a name that was most flattering. The sweet name of Mary is fittingly an expression of the dignity and the glory of Mary the Mother of God, queen of the created universe. She is the exalted one. (*Cf.* R. Kugelman, C.P., *Mariology,* J.B. Carol, Ed. Bk. I, pp. 419, 422, Milwaukee, 1955.) By calling Mary *"Notre-Dame,* our Lady, Saint Ignatius implicitly alluded to the meaning of the name of Mary, to her Divine Maternity and to her universal dominion.

17. *Cf.* A. Musters, *op. cit.* (note 15) pp. 161–74; Pius XII, *Ad Coeli Reginam,* DS, 3917. *Cf.* Chapters XIV and XV of this work.

18. Ex. 221, V.

19. *Cf.* the second part of the "Salve Regina": *Illos tuos misericordes oculos ad nos converte. Jesum. . .nobis post hoc exilium ostende."*

Prefatory Note
by John Hardon S.J.

Theological Retreat is the answer to a real need. It offers priests, religious and the laity a sound theological study of the Spiritual Exercises of St. Ignatius. To be stressed is the soundness of this study in its fidelity to the spirit of St. Ignatius, and in its loyalty to the teachings of the Roman Catholic Church. On both levels, this volume will repay the efforts of its readers, whether as retreatants or retreat directors, or as persons who wish to better understand the meaning of the spiritual life.

Father de Margerie has spared no pains to get to the heart of the real St. Ignatius, in order to share with others the results of his own research. He has carefully analyzed all the available documentary evidence bearing on the Spiritual Exercises. There should be no doubt that what the *Theological Retreat* gives us is based on the most scholarly and authentic Ignatius sources. Today, when there is so much discussion about what did Fr. Ignatius really say, it is good to read someone who makes sure that we first have the mind of Ignatius before we go on to speculate on his thoughts.

Even more important is the author's concern to relate the teachings of the Exercises with the Church's teaching authority. This, then, is a full-scale integration of Ignatian spiritualty with authentic Catholic doctrine. It not only identifies this doctrine, but reflects a great deal of doctrinal development since Ignatius and the Council of Trent. It shows how the Ignatian approach to Christian perfection is both constant and adaptable: constant in its continuity with Catholic tradition down the centuries, and vitally progressive in its adoptability to modern needs.

Thus, in dealing with Ignatius' Norms of Orthodoxy, the author correctly explains that in our century as in Reformation times the faithful look to the hierarchy under Peter for the true interpretation of divinely revealed truth. That is a simple expression of the Church's constancy of doctrine.

At the same time, there has been development of doctrine. The faithful are, indeed, to look to the hierarchy united with Rome for correct interpretation of faith and morals. But they are themselves to seek to grow in their grasp of what they believe, by their own prayerful meditation, studious reflection and affectionate contemplation.

This emphasis on what the Church had always held, but now insists upon with special vigor, places the Exercises of St. Ignatius in a new and welcome light. They are seen as not only powerful means for purifying the will of unruly affections so as to more perfectly serve the will of God. They are recognized as equally effective to enlighten the mind about the mysteries of faith, in order to advance, as the Council bids us, in the possession of revealed truth and to grow in the understanding of the mind of God.

After all, holiness is not only progress in charity. It is progress in faith, hope and charity. And although charity is more noble, faith is more fundamental. We must first know God, and grow in this knowledge, if we are to advance in His love and become more perfect in His service.

Father de Maegerie's reliance on St. Thomas to bring out more fully the meaning of St. Ignatius is consistent with this wise approach to sanctity as supernatural charity, of course, but charity that is grounded and that grows on a strong and progressively deeper faith.

So, too, the author's frequent advertence to the Sacred Heart is no mere pious allusion. It is the awareness that devotion to the Heart of Jesus belongs, as the Church tells us, to the substance of the Catholic way of life. In the physical heart of Christ is not only a symbol of God's love for a sinful mankind. It is all that St. Ignatius meant in his crowning meditation of the Exercises, the Contemplation for Attaining Divine Love. The infallible way to grow in love *for* God is to reflect gratefully on the great love *of* God in our regard.

Theological Retreat is a major contribution to the spiritual literature of our day. It is a safe and sure guide for all who, with the Church, "recognize the tremendous value of the Spiritual Exercises in our times" as in the times of St. Ignatius.

CONTENTS

Dedication xiii
Prefatory Note ix
Contents xi
Key to Abbreviations xvii
Introduction xix

Chapter 1: Life's journey, a pilgrimage to eternal Love 1
  Reason of our being and purpose of our action. 1
  A. God our Savior, destination of the journey of salvation. 1
  B. Fellow-Pilgrims. 4
  C. Itinerary of the journey to salvation. 5
  D. Aggiornamento of the Principle and Foundation - accent
     on its social aspect. 8
  E. Christ the exemplar for the aggriornamento of the
     Principle and Foundation. 9

Chapter 2: Prayer and Method. 15
  A. Method and mystery. 16
  B. Psychological, spiritual and doctrinal advantages of
     the method proposed. 21

Chapter 3: Sin, sins, my sins, our sin. 29
  A. Sin. 29
  B. The Triple Sin: Satan - Adam - the damned. 32
    1. The sin of the Angels. 33
    2. The Sin of Adam. 34
    3. Mortal sin of the damned. 36
    4. Colloquy of Mercy. 37
  C. My personal sins. 39
  D. Our Sin. 43
  Appendix: Prayer for the grace to combat our dominant faults
    by the Particular Examination of Conscience, frequent
    confession, General Confession. 49

Chapter 4: Hell. 59
  A. A truth revealed for our salvation. 59
  B. Meditation and Contemplation on Hell. 61

Chapter 5: The Call of the eternal King, Jesus, for the
  establishment of His Kingdom and to the contemplation of
  His reign. 69
  A. The plan of the Kingdom. ....
  B. Contemplation of the Eternal King, of His temporal
     call and of His reign which will endure forever. 71
  C. The Universal Call of the Eternal King. 72
  D. Three possible Responses to This Universal Call
     of the Eternal King. 74

Chapter 6: The Incarnation of the Son of God. 81
  A. Composition of place: in time, in space. Two preludes. 81
  B. What is desired and petitioned for. 82
  C. Seeing and understanding what the Divine Persons,
     the Angels, the human persons involved are, what
     they are saying, what they are doing. 83
  D. Colloquies with Mary and with the Divine Persons. 86

Chapter 7: Bethlehem - the stable of a God become poor. 93
  A. The mystery and vocation of the Church poor. 93
  B. The scandal and mystery of the stable. 96

Chapter 8: The Confrontation: The call of Lucifer and the
  call of Jesus. The discernment of spirits. 105
  The title. 105
  First prelude: The history. 106
  Second prelude: The place. 106
  Third prelude: Petition for the grace desired................107
  First Part: The Standard of Satan. 108
    First point: Lucifer. 108
    Second point: The universal diabolic mission. 109
    Third point: Speech and strategy of Lucifer,
       enemy chieftain. 110
  Second Part: The sovereign and true Captain Christ
     our Lord. 111
    First point: Presentation of Christ.........................112
    Second point: Choice of Apostles and the Mission of Christ. 112
    Third point: Christ's discourse to His servants and friends. 113
  Colloquies with Our Lady, the Son, the Father and the
     Spirit of the Father and the Son. 116

Chapter 9: Human attitudes and the choice of what is better. 125
   Title and purpose. 125
   First prelude: The "background" of the three groups,
       attitudes and Pairs. 126
   Second prelude: Personal composition of place. 127
   Third prelude: Petition for grace to make an election. 128
   The petition for the contrary of what we desire. The key
       to passing from the second to the third Pair. 130
   Conclusion: Colloquy: asking for what I desire 132

Chapter 10: Three kinds of Humility, of humble love. 137
   First kind: Absolute refusal to commit a mortal sin. 137
   Second kind: Absolute refusal to commit a deliberate venial sin. 138
   Third kind: Preferential choice of the folly of the Cross. 139
   Implicit and explicit social applications of the second
       and third kinds of humble love. 142
   Importance of the Triple Colloquy for obtaining the third
       kind of humility. 143
   Colloquies for acquiring the third kind of humility. 144

*Chapter 11: The ecclesial, salvific and theocentric decision of
   the election.* 149
   A. Choice is to be rational, "ecclesiasticized", divinized. 149
   B. Subject matter of the election. 153
   C. Times and ways of election. 155
   Colloquies for obtaining the grace of a good election. 159
   Confirmation of election by and in the effusion of the
       sacramental grace of the confirming Spirit. 161
   Appendix: Method of amendment and reform of individual
       and social life in the state of life chosen. The ministry
       of almsgiving. 164

Chapter 12: The Sacrificial Supper of the New Convenant. 175
   The grace sought: sorrow and shame. 175
   See, understand, look at the Persons who are at the Supper,
       their words, actions and gestures. 176
   At the sight of what our Lord suffers, shedding of tears. 178
   The Almighty Divinity hides Itself in non-violence. 180
   Response made to the hidden, non-violent God. 180
   Colloquy with Mary, Christ, the Father, the Holy Spirit,
       the Trinity. 182

*Chapter 13: Perseverance in prayer in time of desolation and in
   union with Christ in agony.* 189

A. To wish for and ask for sorrow, anguish, tears in view
of what Christ has suffered for me. 189
B. The agony of prayer, struggle against Satan.................................. 190
C. The holy hour of persevering prayer. 191
D. In time of darkness and desolation, anticipate the light
of consolation. 193
E. Colloquy: acceptance and offering of my future
consoling desolation. 194

Chapter 14: Union with the death of the Crucified Lord. 199
"Father, forgive them for they know not what they do!" 199
"Amen I say to thee, this day thou shalt be with me in
paradise." 200
"Woman behold thy son!" 201
"I thirst." 203
"My God, My God, why hast Thou forsaken Me?" 204
"Now it is finished." 205
"Father into Thy hands I commend My spirit." 205

Chapter 15: The piercing of Christ's side, and the burial of the
Heart of the Lamb before the eyes of Mary His Mother. 211
A. The piercing of the Heart of the Lamb of God. 211
B. The Burial of the Heart of the Lamb. 214
C. The desolation and sorrow of the Virgin Co-Redemptrix
alone before the tomb wherein lay the Redeemer's corpse. 215

Chapter 16: The empty tomb, the triumph and glory of the
Risen Christ. 225
Composition of place: Our Lady's home. 225
Petition for grace: Joy in Christ and His Mother................................ 226
A. Descent into Hell of the glorified soul of Christ,
liberator of the souls of the just.. 227
B. The glorious Resurrection of Jesus, visible sign of the
invisible triumph of the Cross. 230
C. The apparition of the living Jesus in body and soul,
first to His Blessed Mother. 233
D. The risen Christ, consoler of Mary, and the Apostles. 236

Chapter 17: The gift of the Spirit of Truth to the Spouse of
Christ, the Hierarchical, Roman Church. Norms of
orthodoxy. 251
A. Firm adhesion to the Magisterium of the Church, Spouse
of Christ, our Mother, ruled and governed by the
Holy Spirit for the salvation of souls. 253

B. Negative consequences of this contemplation on the
    Church: no public or systematic controversy with
    the hierarchy. 257
C. Positive consequences: praising and speaking prudently. 258
D. Both negative and positive consequences: Benevolent
    dialogue, and if necessary, fraternal and ecclesial correction. 261
E. Colloquy for obtaining the grace to judge and think with
    the Church, the Church in pilgrimage to the heavenly Church. 265

Chapter 18: Contemplating, in human actions and beyond,
    Divine Love. 279
A. Introduction: Genesis and place of the Contemplation to
    Attain Love of God. 279
B. Two preliminary remarks, two preludes. 282
C. Grades of Contemplation. 286
    1. First point: The gifts and the gift of God. 286
    2. Second point: The presence of the Giver in His gifts. 288
    3. Third point: The Giver acting in His gifts. 290
    4. Fourth point: The infinite transcendance of the
       Giver in relation to His gifts. ...., ... 293
D. The response of true love. 295
Conclusion: Consecration to the Eucharistic Heart of Jesus,
    Lamb of God. 299

Bibliography 309

Indices:
    I   Analytical Index...313
    II Index of Names of Authors...315
    III Index of Biblical References 319
    IV Index of the Spiritual Exercises 327
    V   Index of Quotations from St. Thomas 331
    VI Index of Vatican II Documents...333

KEY TO ABBREVIATIONS

Ex.: Spiritual Exercises. Usually followed by a number determined by the Monumenta Historica S.J. (MHSJ), in its 1919 volume presenting the Exercises.

A,V,P 1, P 2: different official and initial texts of the Exercises. A = Autograph; V = Vulgate; P 1 and P 2 = First and second editions of the Versio Prima, according to designations in the Monumenta Historica S.J.

Other symbols:

AA: Apostolicum Actuositatem, Vatican II Decree on the Apostolate of the Laity.

AAS: Acta Apostolicae Sedis, Rome 1909 ff.

AG: Ad Gentes, Vatican II Decree on the Church's Missionary Activity.

AHSJ: Archivum Historicum Societatis Jesu, Review, Rome, 1932 ff.

BAC: Biblioteca de Autores Cristianos, Collection published by the Pontifical University of Salamanca after 1942.

CD: Christus Dominus, Vatican II Decree on the Bishops' Pastoral office in the Church.

CFW: Christ for the World by B. de Mayerie, S.J., Franciscan Herald Press, Chicago, 1974.

CPM: Le Christ pour le Monde, B. de Margerie, S.J., Paris, 1971.

DACL: Dictionnaire d'Archeologie chretienne et de Liturgie. Paris, 1924 ff.

DB: Denziger-Bannwart, Enchiridion Symbolorum, Freiburg.

DBS: Dictionnaire de la Bible, Supplément, Paris, 1928 ff.

DC: Documentation Catholique, Paris, 1903 ff.

DH: Dignitatis Humanae, Vatican II Declaration on Religious Freedom.

DS: Denziger-Schönmetzer, *Enchiridion Symbolorum,* Freiburg, 1963.

DSAM: Dictionnaire de Spiritualité Ascétique et Mystique, Paris 1923 ff.

DTC: Dictionnaire de Theologie Catholique, Paris, 1903 ff.

DV: Dei Verbum, Vatican II Dogmatic Constitution on Divine Revelation.

GE: Gravissimum Educationis, Vatican II Declaration on Christian Education.

GS: Gaudium et Spes, Vatican II Pastoral Constitution on the Church in the Modern World.

LG: Lumen Gentium, Vatican II Dogmatic Constitution on the Church.

MHSJ: Monumenta Historica S.J., Rome (Madrid), 1969.

NA: Nostra Aetate, Vatican II Declaration on the Relationship of the Church to Non-Catholic Religions.

NRT: Nouvelle Revue Théologique, Louvain, 1879 ff.

OT: Optatam Totius, Vatican II Decree on Priestly Formation.

PC: Perfectae caritatis, Vatican II Decree on the Appropriate renewal of the Religious Life.

PG or *MG: Patrologia graeca* (J.P. Migne), Paris, 1857–1865.

PL or *ML: Patrologia latina* (J.P. Migne), Paris, 1878–1890.

PO: Presbyterorum Ordinis, Vatican II Decree on the Ministry and Life of Priests.

RAM: Revue d'Ascêtique et de Mystique, Toulouse, 1925 ff.

SC: Sacrosanctum Concilium, Vatican II Constitution on the Sacred Liturgy.

SC: Sources chretiennes, Paris, 1942 ff.

SCG: Summa Contra Gentiles, St. Thomas Aquinas.

ST: Summa Teologica, St. Thomas Aquinas.

UR: Unitatis redintegratio, Vatican II Decree on Ecumenism.

INTRODUCTION

The work we offer the reader is complex both in its origin and in its objectives. It is not intended to be a systematic commentary on the whole of the book of Spiritual Exercises by Saint Ignatius, nor a new theology of the Exercises, nor an ordinary retreat in the sense of one which would purely and simply follow the Ignatian pattern of an eight day retreat. We thought that in the present religious crisis many priests, men and women religious, and lay people might wish to deepen their experience of the mysteries of Christianity in the framework of the Exercises with which they are already familiar. In this work we offer them a retreat more concerned than other works devoted to the same Exercises with explicating them in the light of Catholic teaching.

Saint Ignatius, a great man of the Church, wished to serve the faith and the charity of the Church in a very special way by the diffusion of his Exercises and so desired to obtain the official approbation of the Apostolic See. The retreatant who makes an Ignatian retreat is often moved by the same desire. He wants to share even more deeply in the mystery of the Church, as well as in her love for the world. The Exercises are first and foremost a doctrinal work, directed to personal and collective salvation.

Pius XII rightly emphasized: "It is the objective of the Spiritual Exercises to put in relief the essential truths of the Catholic faith, which as firm columns sustain the edifice of Christian life. In their constant appeal to the fundamental consists the tremendous value of the Spiritual Exercises particularly in our times."[1]

How could anyone express this better? The spiritual life which the retreat is to nourish, is a life of faith, hope and charity. One can love only what one knows. The Exercises make us know and love Christ and the mysteries about his person he came to reveal.

A retreat, like theology, includes a reflection, in the bosom of faith and charity, on revealed truths. There is a difference however for most often the writing of theologians are quite technical, a quality which the retreat, though still theologically reflective, avoids. In this sense, it may be said that every retreat is reflectively theological or it is not a retreat. In bringing us whole-heartedly to love God every real retreat moves us to love him with all our mind.

We were encouraged to move in the direction of a more specifically theo-logical retreat by the rediscovery, in our times, that Saint Ignatius himself was endowed with a theological charism. Nadal, so well-beloved by the author of the Exercises, had already emphasized such theological concerns. He tells us: "Ignatius read books, consulted theologians as soon as he decided to pub-lish the Exercises. He did so in order that they confirm for him what he had received more from divine inspiration than from books."[2]

Born in the context of the theological tradition of the medieval Church, the Exercises constitute a precise way of reading the New Testament in the Church and are a chosen instrument of the everliving Tradition which is the Church herself. It is by the Spiritual Exercises of Saint Ignatius, among oth-ers, that the Church "perpetuates in her teachings, her life and cult and hands down to each generation all she is, all she believes"[3] as we learn from Vatican II.

The Spiritual Exercises were the result, the fruit of a charism to which Ignatius freely corresponded under the influence of the Spirit of Truth. The title given his work by Father Hugo Rahner, S.J., "Ignatius the Theolo-gian,"[4] aptly expresses the truth which Nadal and other regular disciples and casual acquaintances had perceived: "A doctor of theology, in admira-tion of our father, professed he had never seen anyone who spoke more mas-terfully and majestically of theology."[5]

What he himself says of theologians may well be applied to himself as a theologian. "It is characteristic of the positive doctors, such as St. Augustine, St. Jerome, St. Gregory, and others, to rouse the affections so that we are moved to love and serve God our Lord in all things" (Ex. 363).[6] He af-filiated himself with the great school of monastic and affective theology so magnificently illustrated by Saint Bernard.[7] Of Ignatius as of Bernard it can be said that his watchword is not, "I believe that I may understand"—al-though he did not exclude intelligence—but "I believe that I may experience" and even "I believe that I may serve and love."[8]

We intend to put ourselves at the service of the charism of Ignatius the theologian as it stands out in the Exercises, his greatest, most fundamental, universal work, one which occupied so much of his later life. Of no other work would he have ever written what he wrote unhesitatingly to one of his correspondents on November 15, 1536: "The Exercises are certainly all that I can conceive, know and understand best in this life not only for the per-sonal progress of a man but also for the fruits, the help and the benefit he can derive for so many others."[9]

Our book will follow the same genre of "monastic theology" and, perhaps, this objective is what differentiates it from those works by Fathers Coathalem and Przywara which are so useful. Since the Exercises are the result of this theology, rather than restrict ourselves to reflecting on their content, we shall analyze their theme and with their help study the mysteries of Christianity. We want to help the reader make a formal retreat which will enable him to experience their supernatural and divinely theocentric efficacy. We shall culminate our reflection in colloquies, in prayers addressed to Mary, Our Lady and Sovereign, and to each one of the Three Divine Persons.

To attain this objective we shall have to refrain from commenting on every exercise and restrict ourselves to those which seem more important for an eight day retreat, made annually.. So no one should look for a detailed commentary on the discernment of spirits, for instance, or on the notes provided Directors of the Exercises. Yet, we do think our work will assist and encourage such directors as well as directors of open retreats (Ex. 19) and also the retreatants.[10] It will also be helpful, we hope, for those making directed retreats which are becoming more common today in every country. (Ex. 17).

And so here we have a commentary, even, in certain cases, a study of the principal meditations and contemplations which make up the structure of the Exercises. However, this study will not be made of all the exercises and this explains our title of a "Theological Retreat made with some (not all) of the Ignatian Spiritual Exercises."

We have explained our objective precisely, so now let us pass on to our method. Briefly expressed it is as follows: we shall comment on the Exercises (utilizing and comparing their different official and non-official versions) in the light of the *Summa Theologica* of Saint Thomas Aquinas, of the teaching of Vatican II and in the Sacred Heart of Jesus.

First of all, we shall make use of the version officially approved by the Holy See in 1548, that is, the Latin Vulgate and the "First Version" in its second printing, as well as the text called the "Autograph," written in Spanish by Saint Ignatius, of which a non-manuscript copy has come down to us. We think that by this method which we determined to adopt, there will be given the reader a profound renewal of his knowledge and practice of numerous points—often secondary—of the Exercises. We were inspired largely if not entirely by the works of Father Bernard-Maitre. He has shown that from July 31, 1548 on, the date of the Brief of Approbation of the Exercises, "Saint Ignatius, up to his death, July 31, 1556, that is, during eight years, unfailingly referred to this Latin Vulgate in his Directories which were written in Spanish as the adequate expression of his thinking at that time."[11] Father Bernard-Maitre tells us: "Its (the Vulgate) classical Latin imparts to us clearly the authentic and definitive thinking of its author and clears up for us the unavoidable obscurities of the archaic Castillian of the autograph text, under the control of Ignatius himself and his closest collaborators."[12]

It may be objected that the Vulgate translation is the work of a Latinist who retouched Saint Ignatius original text. That is perfectly true, yet without repeating the observation just made, and as an implicit reply to such a difficulty, we have additional testimony from another author. "Everything leads us to believe that Saint Ignatius himself collaborated personally in making these retouches which today might seem to us as clearly modifying the text of the Spanish Autograph. Some very considerable modifications of the foundation of the Exercises are a clear instance of this.[13]

The reader himself will be able to judge the import of numerous fresh nuances introduced by a methodological comparison of the Vulgate, of the First Version and of the Autograph. We shall even say that therein much light is shed on numerous nuances of the Autograph. Above all, we think that the integral truth of the Exercises, the full thinking of their author appears in the synthesis of these diverse texts which, often, are not mutually exclusive, but rather complement each other. Even at the risk of burdening our text, we have not hesitated to translate frequently the three versions mentioned above of the little Ignatian book by juxtaposing and unifying them.

So we have, without depreciating in any way the Autograph, and its many uses, by-passed it in reconciling the successive historical currents which have dominated the knowledge and diffusion of the Exercises. Up to the generalate of Father Roothaan and his "Literal Version" in Latin of the Spanish Autograph, that is, up to around 1840–1850, the Vulgate was practically the sole known and utilized text of the Exercises. Roothaan so completely reversed the trend that from then on the Vulgate was almost no longer read and no longer constituted the basis for retreats. All now revolved around the Autograph and the numerous translations in all languages. Despite the precautions taken by Father Beeckx,[14] the Vulgate became more and more discredited. Here is an eloquent proof of this. Except for a questionable and controversial American translation, there does not exist, so far as I know, any translation of the Vulgate in any language. All extant translations are based exclusively on the text of the Autograph, even though Saint Ignatius discontinued using it after 1548!

Our commentary, limited as it may be, will thus mark the return to an authentic knowledge of the Ignatian Exercises, in conformity with their spirit. This will be done by taking into account their integral letter which was deliberately and freely presented by the author to be judged by the Church. That what we say will really happen, the future alone will tell!

Next our "Theological Retreat" was written under the light of the *Summa* of Saint Thomas. This may seem incongruous, not to say absurd, to some! The objection will be raised: How can we pretend to analyze the meaning of a text which is situated in the context of monastic theology in the light of an author who was a master of speculative and scientific theology? How can this be done especially since Thomas was more concerned with the correctness, clarity and strict explanation of the subject, than with its warmth and beauty of style?[15] And besides, is he not one who is quite alien to the mentality of a number of our contemporaries?

Such difficulties are not hard to answer. We think, in commenting on the Exercises in the light of Saint Thomas, we are doing what in part Ignatius did and what is consonant with the logical implications of his express and multiple recommendations, as well as with the actual thinking of the Church and with the present needs of retreatants. Saint Ignatius himself, treating of the subject matter to be taught in the Society's universities for the course in theology when he was composing the Constitutions, apart from the Old and New Testament, recommended but one author and that was Thomas and his scholastic doctrine, *"doctrina scolastica divi Thomae."*[16]

This is the theology Ignatius learned in Paris, and there is every reason to believe[17] he wanted to check in the *Summa* the points he had already treated in the Exercises before the definitive composition and publication of the Exercises. Did he not go so far as to recommend very highly the reading of the Second Part, on moral theology, of the *Summa* in which a modern specialist on the Angelic Doctor, Grabmann,[18] sees the masterpiece of medieval theology?

Furthermore is it not the same Spirit, the soul of the universal Church, which offered the Church, its mystical body, both the Summa and the Exercises of Saint Ignatius as precious gifts, complementary and in a way supreme in the category of general assistance to the Church (Jn 14:16,17)? Did not the Magisterium of the Church, aided by this Spirit, recognize the exceptional charism of Saint Thomas and of Saint Ignatius of Loyola in proclaiming them respectively common doctor[19] and patron of all spiritual exercises,[20] and in presenting us, through the words of Pius XI, Saint Thomas as a doctor of asceticism and of mystical theology[21] and Saint Ignatius as the shining beacon for guiding souls on the paths of perfection with the Exercises as the surest road map?[22]

Does not Vatican II encourage future priests, students of theology, to understand as much as possible the mysteries of salvation, study them more in depth and perceive their coherence by means of speculative theology with Saint Thomas as their "master"? We also note with Paul VI that there is "in the Angelic Doctor such power of mind, such sincere love of truth, such wisdom of analysis, of presentation and synthesis of the highest truths; that his doctrine is the most efficacious instrument for establishing faith on a firm basis, and also for perceiving efficaciously and surely the fruits of a sound progress."[23]

Let us emphasize this last statement in particular. The knowledge and appreciation of the writings of Saint Thomas Aquinas is inseparably a factor of security and of progress in theological teaching but also of "emulation in seeking out truth."[24] Vatican II did not restrict itself to such statements but actually cited the works of the Angelic Doctor twenty three times.[25]

It would be difficult, then, to choose a better guide for a profound and renewed understanding of the Ignatian Exercises, under the aspect of their doctrinal presuppositions, than Saint Thomas Aquinas. Does not Saint Ignatius himself, suggest this in the text of the Exercises by what he says in the same passage we cited before? "On the other hand, it is more characteristic of the scholastic doctors, such as St. Thomas, St. Bonaventure,[26] the Master of the Sentences, and others, to define and state clearly, according to the needs of our times, the doctrines that are necessary for eternal salvation, and that help to refute and expose more efficaciously all errors and fallacies" (Ex. 363). [27]

Besides, we have been encouraged in this method by the following observations by a celebrated historian of the Exercises. "I do not know of any commentary on the Exercises in the light of Saint Thomas. Certain authors have studied particular points from this view. But there is no general treatment. Of course Saint Ignatius' orientation is quite different from that of Saint Thomas. He does not intend to explain and analyze theology. His purpose is to put the soul in touch with God, to make it see His will. With him the important thing is spiritual experience, states and attitudes of the soul. All that always presupposes as a basis, a theory, a doctrine. For instance, the gifts of the Holy Spirit, such as Saint Thomas conceived them, are as it were the crown of the Exercises. Without them, one cannot obtain their full benefit." [28]

This may disturb some readers. But let them be reassured. The Thomistic illumination we are trying to shed on the Exercises is discreet, limited and even inadequate. We think that, far from feeling disturbed, they will be helped.

Thirdly, this work is also written in the light of the teaching of Vatican II in accordance with the express wishes of Paul VI. The Vicar of Christ requested that a "re-elaboration of the Exercises" be made in expressing the doctrinal and spiritual riches which gush from the Ignatian book in terms of the theology of Vatican II.[29] He added that "in the original efficacy of the Exercises is found the respomse to all modern needs." [30]

Of course, there is no question of transforming the Exercises into a handbook of conciliar theology. They remain, after the Council as before, a guide which conducts to the fulness of the spiritual life. But it is evident that the theological context and the doctrine of the Church have evolved since Saint Ignatius' time. It is in the light of this evolution that we are to understand and give the Exercises as Saint Ignatius himself would have done.[31] Here is but one instance of this evolution. Catholic ecclesiology is singularly richer today. More clearly perhaps than in the sixteenth century, the Church is seen as the instrument of salvation of Christians, as the co-redemptive Church.[32] We have often developed this important concept.

Finally, this "theological retreat" has been composed under the brilliant light shining out of the Heart of Jesus. As the International Congress of Loyola, held in 1966, has explained: "The synthesis of the paschal mystery as lived in the Exercises, is identical with devotion to the Sacred Heart of Jesus."[33] Were Ignatius living today, he would give the Exercises in the Heart of the Redeemer. Not only his concept of fidelity to the teachings of the magisterium of the Church, but also his passionate love for the Person of Jesus, God-Man—(Cf. Ex. 53, 104)—would incline him to enter spontaneously upon this way even more than ever before. We shall see later that the devotion to the Heart of Christ was not completely unknown to him and that, at any rate, he practiced the devotion to the glorified wounds of Jesus which is at its origin, and pleaded insistently with Jesus: *"Intra vulnera tua, absconde me."* ("Hide me in Thy wounds.")

The devotion to the Heart of our Lord is "a priceless gift"[34] of the Spirit to the Spouse of Christ. It is a gift which evokes a whole hearted, more ardent response by her members[35] to the repeated call of the Eternal King to love and serve His Divine Majesty in all things with a pure love (Ex. 95, 333, 370). This gift could not be rejected without causing sorrow to Christ's Spirit, (cf. Eph 4:30) nor without blocking the pathway to evangelical perfection.[36]

This illumining of the Exercises, especially in colloquies, by the theme of the Heart of Jesus will appear again and again in the course of our work. As we have already made clear, our book is not only a commentary on the Exercises, it is also a theological retreat which speaks about God, for God and even to God. We think many of our readers wish to be helped in their personal prayer rather than receive impersonal instructions concerning God. We think that such a method is also in perfect harmony with the objective as expressed in the Exercises: "The colloquy is made by speaking exactly as one friend speaks to another, or as a servant speaks to a master, now asking him for a favor, now blaming himself for some misdeed, now making known his affairs to him, and seeking advice in them" (Ex. 54).

It is, of course, true that such a colloquuy is eminently personal and that in this sense no one can take the place of another in converse with God. However, we can be helped by another to do so and that is precisely what Ignatius offers us in the texts of the Exercises treating of self-oblation addressed directly to God. (Ex. 97,234).

So, our commentary on the Exercises will be presented, if we are correct, as something new in relation to many others which are praiseworthy and which we have drawn on at times. However none of them[37] has systematically taken into account the Vulgate and the "First Version," the *Summa* and the doctrine of Vatican II. Is there any modern commentary which presents us not only with impersonal reflections but also with personal colloquies?

Besides these methodological innovations, we think we have renewed or deepened many important points: the meaning of a famous composition of place (Ex. 47), the Three Pairs, the theology of election, and its different times and ways, the meaning of the first contemplation of the Fourth Week, today's understanding of "the rules for thinking with the church," and the "Contemplation to Obtain Divine Love."

But it is also true that "every true commentary is a new work." No matter how imperfect and limited our reading of Ignatius' book may be, is not research on the old here and elsewhere the necessary condition for the discovery of the new? At any rate, it will be up to the reader to judge and to say if and to what extent our objective has been attained in accordance with St. Ignatius' line: "The Spiritual Exercises are the best means I can think of in this life both to help a man to benefit himself and to bring help, profit, and advantage to many others."[38]

The Author

Dayton, Ohio, October 7, 1972, the Feast of Our Lady of the Rosary.

NOTES ON THE INTRODUCTION

1. Pius XII, "Discourse at close of Spiritual Exercises", Vatican, December 8, 1945; *Discorsi e Radiomessaggi*, VII, p. 298.

2. Nadal, quoted by Leturia, S.J., *Estudios Ignacianos*, Rome 1957, II, p. 51: "Ignatius libros adhibuit totamque rationem theologiae consuluit saltem ubi illa edere constituit Exercitia, at quae exceperat ex divina potius inspiratione quam e libris, libri onmnes, theologia, sacrae omnes litterae confirmarent." It is of interest to observe that this rooting of the Exercises in Catholic tradition did not in any way prevent Protestants from making them long before Ignatius' death, as early as 1542. (*Cf.* Penning de Vries, S.J. MHSJ, 40, 1971, 476; Iparraguirre, *Practica de los Ejercicios, 1522-1546*, Bilbao, Rome, 1946, pp. 37, 137). Nadal wrote: "It is not required that they go to confession or receive Holy Communion. It is enough if they submit to the Spirit of the Lord and of the Church or at least that they seek the truth they have in common with us. One faith, one baptism." MHSJ, Ep, Nad. Bk. IV, p. 695.

3. DV, 8

4. English Translation (1968) of six chapters taken from his "*Ignatius von Loyola als Mensch und Theologie*" 1964.

5. Nadal, "Exhortation of 1561," FN, II, 198; Larranaga, *S. Ignacio de Loyola, Estudios sobre su vida, sus obras, su espiritualidad*, Saragossa, 1956, p. 29.

6. It will help to observe the parallel between this text of the "Rules for thinking with the Church," and their last rule (Ex. 370), with the "Contemplation for obtaining divine love" (Ex. 233).

7. Dom J. Leclercq, *L'amour des lettres et le désir de Dieu*, Paris, 1957, p. 202.

8. Transl. We give the Latin texts here instead of, as in the original, their translation: "*Credo ut intelligam*"; "*Credo ut experiar*"; "*Credo ut serviam et amem.*"

9. A remarkable statement when we recall Saint Ignatius' humility. To understand it, let

uś recall that he surely must have seen in the Exercises a very great gift of God bestowed on men through him. Once this statement is applied to theologians it is hard to estimate the tremendous influence of the Exercises on theological thinking in the Church in the course of the last four centuries. It suffices but to pose such questions for which there is no possible answer. For instance, What would Catholic theology or the Church herself today be without the Exercises? It can and must be said, without exaggeration, that this booklet has had a decisive influence, as few others, on the history and the life of the Church.

10. *Cf.* C. Espinosa, S.J., *Los Ejercicios de S. Ignacio a la luz del Vaticano II, Congreso internacional de Ejercicios, Loyola,* 1966, Madrid, BAC, 1968, Conclusions 105–9, pp. 656, 57. Introductory Observation 18 could be applied to these open Exercises. (*Cf. ibid.* pp. 637,638, conclusions 100–4.)

11. H. Bernard-Maitre, S.J., *Pour une traduction francaise des Exercices de saint Ignace,* RAM 35(1959) 444. In a particular instance, Saint Ignatius refused to correct the Latin text of the Vulgatè of the Exercises in the light of the Spanish text "on account of the great credit he wanted given to the Holy See and to the things approved by it." (memorial of Camara, April 4, 1555, FN, I, pp. 710, 711; MHSJ, vol. 66, Rome, 1943).

12. H. Bernard-Maitre, *art. cit.* (preceding note) p. 447. Saint Ignatius' mother-tongue was not Spanish but Basque. He learned Spanish when he was about fifteen years old.

13. H. Bernard-Maitre. *Le texte des Exercices spirituels de saint Ignace,* RAM, 33, 1957; 228,229. It is certain that Saint Ignatius at least examined, approved and accepted as his own the Latin translations (V,P2) which he submitted to the examination and approval of the Apostolic See.

14. The same author notes: "The successor of Father Roothaan to the Generalate of the Society, Reverend Father Beeckx, through the French Assistant, as early as 1855 required of Father Jennesseaux that, in his French translation of the notes of the literal version by Roothaan, he should tone down or even suppress sixty five passages where the superiority of the Spanish Autograph over the Latin Vulgate was asserted." (*Le P. J. Ph. Roothaan et la Vulgate latine des Exercices de saint Ignace,* RAM 37, 1961, 209.)

15. Cf. G. Bavaud, *Introduction aux "Huit Homelies Mariales" de Saint Amêdêe de Lausanne,* SC 72, Paris, 1960, p. 16.

16. Saint Ignatius of Loyola, *The Constitutions of the Society of Jesus,* IV, 14, 1 (#464) p. 219 transl. George E. Ganss S.J., 1970.

17. *Cf.* our Chapter XVIII, #20.

18. *Cf.* Martin Grabmann, *Thomas Aquinas, His Personality and Thought* (N.Y., 1928), p. 150: "The moral speculations of Thomas form a gigantic achievement that is also lauded by non-Catholics." On p. 152 he gives us from M. Baumgartner the following appreciation: "No where, as much as in the area of ethics, is Saint Thomas' power of synthesis so clearly resplendent." So it is not surprising that it is precisely Saint Thomas' moral theology that Saint Ignatius, in July of 1556, a few days before his death specifically recommended to a Jesuit student, Stephen Barcelo, in a letter which also treated the importance of study of the Fathers and the Scriptures (Ep. Vol. XII, pp. 186,187). Doubtless this program was like the one he followed personally in Paris.

19. This is how Pius XI (*Studiorum Ducem,* AAS, 15 (1923) 314) characterized Saint Thomas. "Common or universal Doctor, whose teaching the Church has made her own." No Pope, to my knowledge, has ever said anything like this about any other Doctor of the Church.

20. Pius XI, Apostolica Constitutio *Summorum Pontificum,* of July 25, 1922, (AAS, 14, 1922,422). The same year, in his letter *Meditantibus Nobis* (*ibid.* 632), Pius XI, quoting Louis de Blois and Saint Alphonsus Liguori, spoke of "the treasure of the Exercises" given by God to his Church."

21. Pius XI. *Studiorum Ducem* (AAS, 15, 1923, 319,320). The Pope specially praised the ascetical and mystical doctrine of Saint Thomas particularly in regard to the states of life and the gifts of the Holy Spirit. "On these points, it is the Angelic Doctor who must be consulted first.'"

22. Pius XI. *Mens Nostra,* an encyclical wholly devoted to spiritual exercises (AAS, 21, 1929, 689–706): "(Saint Ignatius is) the principal teacher of spiritual exercises." "The Spiritual Exercises is an admirable book, a very sound and at the same time universal code of norms for directing souls on the road of salvation and perfection, an inexhaustible source of very solid piety" (ibid. p. 703). The Pope gave special praise to the "excellence of the spiritual teaching" of the Exercises. It is easy to understand that many have dreamed of having Saint Ignatius declared a Doctor of the Church. In a sense, however, is he not already declared one implicitly by this encyclical of Pius XI?

23. OT, #16, note 36. In quoting Paul VI's discourse, the Council has made its own the text quoted, an extract from an allocution at the Gregorian University on March 12, 1964. We underline the significance of the text: "The teaching of Saint Thomas is not only an instrument of progress but even more *the instrument that is the most efficacious for a sound progress.*" Here is the thinking of Vatican II on theological development. The reasons for this assertion (quite astonishing for more than one reader, doubtless) have been even better presented in another discourse of Paul VI, also quoted by Vatican II (OT, #16, no, 36, toward the end.) and then, it seems accepted as its own in a general manner by the Council: *"The philosophy of Saint Thomas* possesses a permanent capability for guiding the human spirit toward the knowledge of the true, the truth of being which is its first object. It *thereby transcends the particular historical situation* of the thinker who has worked it out and illustrated it as the *natural metaphysics of human intelligence.* Reflecting the essence of really existing things in their certain and immutable truth, it is neither *medieval* nor does it pertain to any particular nation. Rather it *transcends time and space* and is no less valid for every man of today." (Allocution to the Sixth International Thomistic Congress, September 10, 1965). Likewise Saint Thomas' *theology* transcends time and space. So then it is not only medieval but can become the best and most effective instrument for deepening our theological knowledge of the meaning of the Spiritual Exercises of Saint Ignatius.

24. Pius XII. Allocution of June 24, 1939, also quoted in OT 16, note 36. (N.B. Text used in translation Abbott's Documents, note 52)

25. Twelve times in the dogmatic Constitution *Lumen Gentium* alone. Among the doctors of the Church who are not Popes, only Saint Augustine has been quoted more often by the last Council.

26. We should like to see published a Bonaventurian commentary on the Exercise; under certain aspects, it seems evident that Saint Ignatius is even closer to Saint Bonaventure than to the Angelic Doctor. For the seraphic Doctor moves more to love.

27. Here we lollow the text of the Vulgate which presents many notable differences from the Autograph. The Vulgate speaks of *dogmas* while subordinating their more precise definitions to the need of refuting errors.

28. Letter of Ignacio Iparraguirre, S.J. to the author, June 6, 1965.

29. Discourse of Paul VI to the Italian Federation of the Spiritual Exercises, December

29, 1965 and letter of Paul VI to Cardinal Cushing of Boston, June 25, 1966.

30. Paul VI, general audience, June 26, 1968.

31. Conclusions 6 and 7 of International Congress of Loyola, 1966 (*op. cit.* 37).

32. CFW, Ch. XI.

33. Conclusion 61 (*op. cit.* p. 421). Cf J. Calveras, S.J.: *Los elementos de la devoción al Corazón de Jesús. Su contenido y practica en los Ejercicios de S. Ignacio* (Barcelona, 1955).

34. Pius XII: *Haurietis Aquas,* AAS, 48 (1956) 310. More precisely, Pius XII presents the devotion to the Sacred Heart as a priceless gift of the Incarnate Word, as Mediator of grace, to the Church, in these latter, so difficult days.

35. Ibid., p. 346.

36. Ibid., p. 346; B. de Margerie, *The Heart of the Lamb of God,* Rome, Gregorianum, 1972, #45, pp. 34ff.

37. We think, for instance, of the books, in other respects, excellent by Coathalem, *Commentaire du Livre des Exercices,* Paris, 1965 and of Cusson, S.J. *Pédagogie de l'expérience spirituelle personnelle,* Paris, 1968, pp. 427–36; Bovon, *Revue de Philosophie et de Theologie,* 1972, p. 76.

38. Letter to Manuel Miona, November 16, 1536.

1

LIFE'S JOURNEY
A PILGRIMAGE TO ETERNAL LOVE

The Reason for our Existence.

"Man is created to praise, reverence, and serve God our Lord, and by this means to save his soul" (Ex. 23).[1] A concise statement, a basic conviction which constitutes the principle and foundation in Christ Jesus (cf. 1 Cor 3:11), of the construction of the spiritual edifice of our life and of our perfection.

Let us deepen our knowledge of this fundamental principle by an allegory, by reasoning and by raising up our minds to help us perceive in the light of revelation the destination, the companions and the itinerary of our journey of salvation. So we take up this principle considered under two aspects.

A. God, Savior, destination of the journey of salvation.

1. *Allegory.* Our life is our most important journey.

One who travels by train or plane must have above all a definite destination, his last stop. Of course, every other consideration is secondary to this destination, for instance, speed, comfort, scenery. In travelling we are ready to forego such advantages should they hinder us from reaching where we wish to go. What would we say about someone who, not having found a comfortable seat on a train or plane, takes one which provides greater comfort but goes in the opposite direction? Yet what would be abnormal at a railroad station or at an airport frequently happens on life's journey!

The Supreme Author of all mankind has established in advance, for each one, his or her destination. They are destined to arrive at the vision, the possession and never ending love of Eternal Love. This destination has been assigned to all, and for reaching it there is given a destined time of which God alone knows the duration. Each one must at any cost direct himself to this end, even if the conditions of travel are not what one would prefer.

To act otherwise would mean going in the opposite direction, losing God, plunging headlong into the abyss of eternal damnation.

2. *Doctrinal Reflection.*

God does not need our reverence nor the honor we give him. His glory is infinite. No creature can add to it. We are the ones who need to reverence and praise him. When our spirit is submissive to him, we reach our perfection, we develop ourselves and grow in sharing more and more in the infinite Being. Our body is inferior to our soul, and is vivified by it. Likewise our soul is vivified by praising and reverencing its Creator.[2]

God does not create us in order to have a perfection He would not have otherwise, but only to communicate to us a share of his bounty.[3] Though he has no need of our existence, he manifests to us a love of sovereign gratuity in imparting it to us. Although "many of our contemporaries are entirely unaware of, or even expressly reject, the intimate and vital rapport uniting man to God," we rejoice in acknowledging that "the most sublime aspect of human dignity is found in man's vocation to communicate with God. It is by virtue of his very origin that man is invited to converse with God. He does not exist save because God created him for love and does not conserve him save for love. Man does not fully live according to truth unless he acknowledges freely this love and abandons himself to his Creator,"[4] by acknowledging him as the prime author of the universe, by accepting him as the sole supreme objective of his actions.[5]

The last end is the sacred and inviolable rule for every man and of all human action. Man and all his actions are to manifest the infinite perfection of God, for the glory of the Creator.[6] All human actions through their particular and actual ends should pursue the universal end which God has designed, the recapitulation of all things in Christ Jesus his Son. (cf. Eph 1:10).

To serve God is to carry out his holy and sanctifying will, a will for our happiness and our salvation in Christ Jesus. Through his multiple particular and actual wills concerning each one, God brings about ceaselessly his great and supreme, eternal and universal will, the reunion and bringing together of all beings under Christ, chief and head of creation. "For in him were all things created in heaven and on earth, visible and invisible whether thrones, or dominations, or principalities or powers; all things were created by him and in him. And he is before all, and by him all things consist. And he is the head of the body, the church, who is the beginning, the first-born from the dead; that in all things he may hold the primacy; because in him, it has well pleased the Father, that all fulness should dwell; and through him to reconcile all things unto himself, making peace through the blood of his cross, both as to the things that are on earth, and the things that are in heaven." (Col 1:16–20).

So then, the service of God for each one is a contribution to recapitulating the universe in Jesus Christ. The multiple actions of each human person, otherwise threatened by desperation, find thereby a unity which effectively confers on them a meaning, and a unity at the heart of creation.

Man is saved by this recapitulative service to the divine will, that is, he cooperates with grace which saves him by rescuing him from the loss of God and enabling him to enter into the possesion of him. "The contemplation of God is promised us as the end of all our actions and as the eternal achievement of our joys."[7] Man's beatitude does not consist first and foremost in the contemplation of divine effects, of the created world, of other human persons, but in the intuition of the divine Truth itself,[8] one with infinite Love.

3. Invocation

Each and every one of our actions should express praise, reverence and service to the Father, to the Son and to the Holy Spirit. To praise God is, then, to exalt and glorify his innermost life, his eternal processions of knowledge and love; the generation of his Son, who is the Word in which he expresses the knowledge he has of himself and of the universe, and to exalt and glorify, the "spiration" or eternal "breathing" of love, by which the Father and the Son love each other in a reciprocal love of their common lovableness, as this love produces the Kiss of eternal love which unites them, the Holy Spirit.

Father, I adore you in the depths of my soul where neither the world nor the flesh nor the devil can penetrate. It is there that you pronounce the sole Word in which you express fully yourself and in which you know me and create me. In me, Your Word glorifies you. He loves you, and me in you. From this love pours forth your Spirit.

Father, I praise you through your Son in your Spirit when I offer you the Eucharistic Sacrifice, for the Blood of your Son gives you infinite glory.

As the saintly Curé d'Ars said: "All good works together do not equal the Sacrifice of the Mass, for they are works of men while Holy Mass is the work of God. Martydom is as nothing in comparison. It is the sacrifice man makes to God of his life, while the Mass is the sacrifice God makes for man of his Body and Blood."

When I offer or celebrate Mass, I realize my reason for being: to praise, reverence, serve the divine goodness. Life organized around the Mass—there is God's design. It is from the Mass that flows all possibility of sanctification for me, of me, of glorification for God.[9]

Man has been created to save himself by and in the Eucharist. In the Eucharist and not apart from it, salvation is found. In the Eucharistic Heart of Jesus, and by him, I escape my emptiness, my misery, my sin. I find my fulness and richness in his Blood. Cleansed by him, dwelling in the infinite love of the well-beloved Son, I can praise, reverence and serve the salvific love of the Father for the world.

B. *Fellow-pilgrims.*

1. *Allegory.*

In travelling we shun everything, no matter how comfortable it may be, which instead of bringing us to our destination, brings us somewhere else or at least causes unnecessary delays. If, then, any person, any thing, any happening is shown to be an obstacle on the path which should lead to God, it must be avoided and run away from.

On the other hand, once we know where we are going and have checked our route, we are concerned about those who are travelling along with us. They are not strangers but our brothers, destined to become, thanks to us, members of the sole mystical Body of Christ, the Church, if they do not belong to her already.

On our earthly journeys, a very good driver, a more alert telegrapher, a more careful workman, a more concerned traffic policeman can prevent a mishap or an accident and thus give a happy ending to our trip.[10] So, for so many souls now enjoying the vision of the living God, their meeting with an apostle who helped them find the right road, to start out again, to continue on with the journey was decisive.

2. *Doctrinal reflection.*

"The other things on the face of the earth are created for man to help him in attaining the end for which he is created" (Ex. 23).

Among "the other things" there are first of all other men, other created spirits, that is, angels, the world of persons. God has created us and creates us continually not only for his glory and for our individual salvation, but also for helping others be saved.[11]

Faced with the temptations to consider others as objects and as things, or even as idols, the sole light of reason makes us perceive already they have the nobility and worth of ends, though not ultimate ones. They are intermediate ends which are to conduct us to the last end, without ever being able to replace it. We should never want others to rest in us without passing beyond us to God who is present in us.

To love others is to wish them well. To love others purely, is to wish them the Supreme Good, God. Is not the only true benevolence to want to give God to men? And how can we love God with a pure love unless we wish them to have the same pure love for God, loved above and beyond all else because of his sole, infinite bounty? That God be all in all, it is necessary that we be willing to displease at times some persons (*cf.* Gal 1:10). Jesus himself, object of the Father's pleasure, did not seek what pleased himself (Lk 3:22; Rom 15: 1-3), but always sought what pleased the Father (*cf.* Jn 8:29), who willed the salvation of all whom he gives to his Son (*cf.* Jn 6:39,40).

The Christian as such, in so far as baptized in the Blood of Jesus, can make his own the reflection which Blessed Claude La Colombiere applied to the Jesuit:

"Wherever you meet a Jesuit, no matter with whom, he is as one sent by God to talk about the salvation of those with whom he comes in contact. If he does not do this, if he does not seize the opportunity to speak of this, he betrays his ministry and renders himself unworthy of the name he bears. I have, therefore, resolved to be attentive to this in every encounter and to think about the way to make conversation turn on things that are edifying. To do this in such a way that no one goes away without having more knowledge of God than before and more desirous of salvation, if possible."[12]

Are not all baptized and confirmed Christians sent out on a salvific mission by Christ himself, who impels them to this by the sacramental graces of baptism and confirmation?[13]

3. Invocation.

Oh Paraclete, Spirit of the Father and of the Son, you seek constantly the glory of the Son and through his glory that of the Father (cf. Jn 16:14,15; 17:1). You are their eternal and consubstantial communion, their reciprocal love. Make me aware of your action in men, to praise your perfections as seen in their virtues.

Make me aware that to speak without just cause of the faults of others is quite simply to reveal my own, to prefer to seek the non-being of their lack rather than your presence and power in them (Ex 40;39). It, is, then, a manifestation of my blindness, before your action. Are you not, as the soul of the mystical Body of Christ, ever occupied in imprinting on its members the dispositions and inclinations of the Head?[14]

How could I, Spirit of Truth and Love, be faithful to the mission you confide to me in regard to others? How can I carry out this mission you have assigned me by the constant renewal of the sacramental graces of my baptism and confirmation, unless I acknowledge above all that you have been invisibly sent to them by the Father and the Son?

Oh Holy Spirit, light and fire of the love between the Father and the Son, fruit of the eternal generosity with which they love each other in me, grant me to love others in you, by you, with you, for you, Spirit, you who speak through the prophets, speak to each one through me in order to work out his own salvation in fear, trembling and thanksgiving.

C. Itinerary of the journey to salvation

1. Doctrinal reflection.

The last end of all our actions is salvation and all others are intermediate ends to help us attain this ultimate finality. Therefore it will be well to map out precisely the ethical path to salvation. Saint Ignatius does this in these terms: "Hence, man is to make use of them in as far as they help him in the attainment of his end, and he must rid himself of them in as far as they prove a hindrance to him.

"Therefore, we must make ourselves indifferent to all created things, as far as we are allowed free choice and are not under any prohibition. Consequently, as far as we are concerned, we should not prefer health to sickness, riches to poverty, honor to dishonor, a long life to a short life. The same holds true for all other things.

"Our one desire and choice should be what is more conducive to the end for which we are created" (Ex. 23).

Saint Ignatius has admirably expressed here the dialectic of salvific prudence, which chooses the suitable means for the attainment of the end. Once faith has known the last end, it is important to determine what means will bring us to it. Some will have to be adopted, others avoided, others are indifferent but objects of salvific decisions.

Christ Jesus is the model and the principle of this salvific choice, in and by his Spirit. In saving us, God did not choose illness but the weakness of a possible and mortal body. Not the wretchedness of indigence but the poverty of toil and begging; now being honored, now being held in contempt; a temporal life, not long but short, to give us a share in his glorious eternity, for our salvation, that is, to rescue us from the disgrace and the pains of eternal death.

Christ's poverty is my riches; his ignominy merits my glory. From his weakness comes my strength; his short life contains my eternity; my life is in his death. Thus, in Christ, my poverty becomes my neighbor's riches, my dishonor his glory, my weakness his strength, my death his life.

God's design is that there be, in the lives of each of us, for his greater glory, an admixture of health and sickness, of abundance and privation, of good reputation and humiliation, of life and of death.[15] Every human life is short compared to eternity, and lengthy compared to the desire to hasten to attain it. Honors bestowed by men are but dishonor compared to the infinite glory that comes from God, human abundance but indigence compared to the riches of divine mercy, mortal health infirmity compared to the might of the Risen One.

What need have I of honors, health, life? Am I not a sharer by grace of the wisdom, of the eternity, even of the bounty of a God who loves me, dwells with all his infinite perfections in me?

If, according to the expression of Saint John of the Cross, "the entire being of creatures compared to the infinite being of God is but pure nothingness,"[16] the most contradictory options between them take on equally a "tint of nothingness" (Caussade), and it becomes supernaturally easy to make no distinction between health and illness, wealth and poverty, honor and contempt, life and death. Living faith in the wisdom of God, ardent hope help free will to detach itself to such a point from all that, in it, might hinder salvation that it comes to desire and choose solely what leads to it.

Without such detachment the created wills of the sons and daughters of Adam and Eve spontaneously prefer, even when that thwarts the divine plan, health to sickness, wealth to poverty, honor to contempt, life to death. The "Meditation on the Principle and Foundation" is intended to make us rediscover, in the bosom of prayer; the balance of indifference, and above all, the choice of the better in view of salvation. "Seek therefore first the kingdom of God, and his justice, and all these things shall be added unto you" (Matt 6:33). "All these things," that is health, wealth, honor, life. "Seek first salvation," in the full meaning of the word, the salvation of soul and body, the glorious resurrection, and in it you will find health, wealth, glory and life without end. Of all this, the Eucharist is the pledge.

3. *Invocation*

Immaculate Virgin, Mother of our Savior, I honor in you, not only the splendor of salvation worked by your Son but also the model and cause of my salvation.

Virgin pre-redeemed that you would be saved by being our co-redemptrix, save me by aiding me to save others.

So that with you, by you, in you, I may praise, reverence and serve my Savior who is also yours. So that the intercession of your Immaculate Heart obtain for me love of my neighbor in God, in such a way that I do not confuse such charity with complicity with faults of another which would be disloyalty, but on the contrary may efficaciously wish for others the pursuit of their Supreme Good out of pure love.

Now that so many of our contemporaries distort their personality by incessant reading of novels[17] thereby stirring up their passions to the detriment of their free will and the inspirations of grace, you, Queen of All Saints, give us in the lives and writings of your Saints, romances of divine love, an admirable means for praising God, a sign of the power your grace has over human feelings, a manifestation of your victory over disordered passions.

Obtain for us, then, through reading and meditating on their writings the strength to detach ourselves from all that hinders our salvation and to desire and choose solely what brings us more toward our last end, toward the humble, loving, endless possession of your Father, of your Son, and of your Spirit,[18] known, loved, glorified to the highest possible degree.[19] Grant us ever to act for the greater glory, temporal and eternal, in us and about us, of the sole God who is Father, Son and Holy Spirit.

In order that we reach our eternal glory grant us to persevere and grow constantly in the sanctifying grace received in baptism, eventually recovered by contrition and in the sacrament of penance, so that we may become capable of attaining as fully as possible the absolutely last end of all human existence, by rendering to our Creator as much as possible, in the bosom of intuitive vision, for his greater glory, an accidental glory, the very reason for our creation.

By your obedience, you became for yourself and for the whole human race the cause of salvation.[20] Help us perceive that the continual increase of grace and charity is the sole end of our present life in comparison with which all else is but a means. Your Son himself has made himself, in and by the Eucharist, a means and a mediator of the realization of our salvation.

Jesus, my Savior, only Son of the Father and of Mary; giver of the Spirit of Truth, you recapitulate in yourself the itinerary of salvation.

You wish by your Spirit to praise your Father through Christians, by means of all the baptized. You wish to continue through all of them being the Father's Psalmist.[21] So you offer in sacrifice even today praise to the one who sacrificed you.[22]

You ever adore the Father of mercies with deepest respect in all the tabernacles throughout the world. You serve him constantly through the true worship[23] of so many Christians, diligently constructing with them the earthly city. Through your Spirit, you inspire us ever to desire and choose what leads us most surely to the vision of the Father.

Lord Jesus, you are my principle and my foundation, my end. You have created me and you create me that I may save myself by performing good works, deserving eternal life. "For we are his workmanship, created in Christ Jesus in good works, which God has prepared that we should walk in them" (Eph 2:10), to the praise of the glory of his grace (Eph 1:6).[24] You save me by working in me and by me these salvific works "for it is God who works in you, inspiring both the will and the deed." The very consent of my free will is ransomed by the inspiration of your grace. We can say with you: "The Father who abides in me, he does the work" (Jn 14,10).

You have created me and create me to praise you and to honor me on the last day by saving me. For you wish that my salvation be a remuneration crowning in me the gifts of your gratuitous love.[25] The most excellent work you expect from me is that I contribute to the construction of your Church in love (Eph 4:16).

Come, Eucharistic Heart of Jesus, achieve in me and through me, the construction of your Church. Come in me to praise, reverence, and serve the infinite love of the Father, of your Father, of him whom you have made my Father.

D. Aggiornamento of the Principle and Foundation—Accent on Its Social Aspect.

We have been and are created to *praise* God in a very special way in as much as he is present and acting in men, his images, so as to become his perfect likeness. We must praise God in men, acknowledging in their virtues reflections and participations in his perfections.

We are created to *reverence* God in men. There is no reverence of God without reverence for the least of men. There is no reverence of God without reverence for the free will of men, whom we wish not to dominate but rather to help. There is no reverence for God without reverence for the unique, irreplaceable, original call of each human free will. Reverence for man, however, is poles apart from human respect. Reverence for man must manifest the reverence God himself has for his creature.

We are created to *serve* God, serve him in men and through them. The service of God is carried out in the service of the human community. "If any man desires to be first, he shall be the last of all, and the minister of all" (Mk 9:34), on the model of the Son, who, being Lord, "is not come to be ministered unto, but to minister" (Mk 10:45).

This is how we will save our souls. There is no salvation, no happiness possible without this praise, reverence and service for men wholly related to the praise, reverence and service of God, Creator and Lord, their origin and last end.

So as a result we are ready to sacrifice health, wealth, honor and temporal life itself for the salvation of our neighbor, the very reason for our existence.[26]

E. Christ the Exemplar for the aggiornamento of the Principle and Foundation.

Jesus is not only the eternal Son of God, the uncreated Word, but also man and as such a creature. He is the image, the model we are to imitate, the first-born of a multitude of brothers created in his image. He himself has realized, in his temporal and historical existence, in a perfect manner, the vocation of every man, the purpose for which he has created his own humanity. "Behold the Man!" (Jn 19:5). He is *the* Man so much so that no one has been and will ever be so human as he is.

Jesus praised the Father in long nightly prayers: "And rising very early, going out, he went into a desert place: and there he prayed" (Mk 1:35). His major decisions, such as the choice of apostles and the institution of the Eucharist, are made in a context of prayer. "And it came to pass in those days, that he went out into a mountain to pray, and he passed the whole night in the prayer of God. And when day was come, he called unto him his disciples, and he chose twelve of them (Lk 6: 12,13; 22: 19). Before his disciples Jesus proclaims the perfections of his Father." At that time Jesus answered and said: I confess to thee, O Father, Lord of heaven and earth, because thou has hid these things from the wise and prudent, and hast revealed them to little ones. Yes, Father, for so has it seemed good in thy sight" (Mt 11:25,26).

Jesus *reverences* his Father. He prays to him on bended knees (Lk 22:41). His appreciation of his Father's majesty is such that he does not tolerate, despite his forgiveness of so many faults, the profanation of the temple by buyers and sellers and money-changers (Jn 2: 14-16).

Jesus *serves* his Father. He came not to be served, but to serve. (Mk 10:45): "But as the Father has taught me, these things I speak . . . for I do always the things that please him" (Jn 8:26–29). It is thus that the Savior of the world (Jn 4:42), merits to be "saved" by his Father in the mystery of the Resurrection. "Now is my soul troubled. Father save me from this hour" (Jn 12:27; *cf* Ps. 6:3–6; Heb 5:7), where the Son has been saved from death.

The Lord made use of "the things on the face of the earth" to achieve his purpose, to return to the Father: lilies of the field and lambs provided him with parables and he did not disdain to drink our wines. But he also abstained from them at the hour of his death. For forty days and forty nights he fasted in the desert. He removed from his path all that hindered his return to his Father. He was poor, bereft of riches so that he could say that he had no where to lay his head (Lk 9:58). Now he refused, now he accepted honors due royalty (Jn 6:15): (Mk 11:6ff); now he protested, now he kept silence before insults (Jn 18:23; 19:9; Mt 26:63), had his own home (Mt 13:1) and lived in poverty in his brief life of thirty three years indifferent to all created things, without having need, as we have, of making himself indifferent: not wishing for honor more than dishonor, a long life rather than a short one, but desiring and choosing solely to do the Father's will.

Paul fulfilled "those things that are wanting of the sufferings of Christ, in his flesh, for his body, which is the Church" (Col 1:24). It is for us to fulfil in our flesh what "was wanting" of his praise, reverence and saving service of the Father, of his "indifference" as to creatures that the construction, the edification of the Church be achieved.

NOTES ON CHAPTER ONE

1. The translation of the Spiritual Exercises used is that of Louis J. Puhl, S.J. 1951.

2. ST, II. II. 81. 7 c.

3. ST, I. 44. 4 c.

4. GS, 19.1.

5. ST, I.II. 102. 3 c.

6. Pius XII, Encyclical *Musicae Sacrae Disciplina*, AAS 48 (1956) 10. Saint Ignatius does not use the expresion "last end" in his Exercises. He speaks only of "end." But he is acquainted with the term as is seen in the Constitutions X, 2 (813), where he alludes to

our "final and supernatural end." Vatican II mentions it explicitly as a classical expression of Catholic theology, in a text very close to the "Principle and Foundation." (GS 13).

7. Saint Augustine, *de Trinitate*, I, 8, ML 42, 831; ST, II,II, 180.4.

8. *Ibid.* There is to be observed in this text the fruitful distinction of classical theology between primary (essential) beatitude—that which comes to the creature from the possession of God—and secondary (accidental) that which comes of the possession of other creatures. In the midst of the greatest trials, the human person can never be deprived by anyone else of his primary beatitude.

9. SC, 10.

10. We are inspired here by a speech made by Pius XII to railroad workers, DC,55 (1958) #1273.

11. Saint Ignatius, Letter of May 7, 1547 (Cf. Letters of St. Ignatius of Loyola, William J. Young, S.J., 1959, p. 122) where Ignatius writes to the Fathers and Scholastics at Coimbra: "in attaining the end for which God created you; that is, His own honor and glory, your own salvation, and the help of your neighbor."

12. Blessed Claude La Colombière, Retreat, Second Week, Meditation: *Docete omnes gentes.*

13. LG, 34, AA, 3.

14. LG, 7; Pius XII, *Mystici Corporis,* says something similar (DS 3808).

15. It is proper to remark here that if, in the course of the Exercises, Saint Ignatius proposes to the retreatant that he desire poverty and humiliations, he never suggests he desire illness or a short life rather than health or a long life. Would he, then, be inclined to think that poverty and humiliations are normal means of sanctification while illness and a short life would be extraordinary means? However, Saint Ignatius, in his Constitutions (III. 1. 17; #272) requires the ill Jesuit to acknowledge clearly that illness is a gift of his Creator and Lord not less than health. God's might stands out in contrast to my illness, as his glory in my shame, his eternity in my death, his riches in my poverty. By grace I participate in all these perfections of the divine nature, at the very moment I am suffering poverty, dishonor, illness and death.

16. Saint John of the Cross, *Ascent of Carmel,* Bk. I, Ch. IV.

17. Pius XII has ably treated this in one of his addresses to young married people.

18. *Cf.* Rom 5:5; 8:15. The Spirit which has been given us is ours.

19. *Cf.* J. de Guibert, S.J., *Leçons de Théologie spirituelle,* Toulouse, 1943, Bk. I, 8th lesson, pp. 130, 131 (*cf.* pp. 216, 217); DS, 3002, 3005, 3024; RJ, 158, 236, Irenaeus; ST. I, I. 44.4; 65.2; SCG, III. 25; #5; Z. Alszeghy, M. Flick S.J., *Gregorianum* 36, 1955, 361–86). We mention a bit further on that the reason for our creation is the accidental glory we are to give to God. That does not mean that such accidental glory is the absolutely ultimate reason for our creation. To say that would be to subordinate the essential intrinsic glory of God to his extrinsic and accidental glory, the Creator to the creature, since this accidental glory is willed by God as a manifestation of his goodness (*cf.* ST, I. 44.4), which is the absolutely ultimate end of the work (*finis operis*) and of the worker (*finis operantis*). (*Cf.* ST, II.II. 141.6.1.)

20. Mary "*obediens et sibi et universo generi humano causa facta est salutis,*" says Saint Irenaeus. *Adv.Haer.* III.22.4; MG, 7,959 A: LG, 56 quotes this text.

21. SC,100: "And the laity, too, are encouraged to recite the divine office, either with

the priests, or among themselves, or even individually." Vatican II has thus wished that
the new "Liturgy of the Hours" be the prayer of all the people of God. This principle
has been beautifully developed in "*Instructio generalis—Liturgiae Horarum*" (General instruction—of the Liturgy of the Hours, #27) for families whose prayer it is desired that
the new Office be. This Instruction has been promulgated by the Congregation of divine
Worship, April 11, 1971. The Apostolic Constitution *Laudis Canticum,* published by Paul
VI, November 1, 1970, #8 stresses that the new Office was proposed for all Christians.
A wonderful return to the liturgical tradition of the first centuries: the whole Christian
community assembled every day for morning and evening prayer, realizing thus the full
meaning of mankind and of the Church, that is the praise of God. Just as Paul VI says
again (*ibid.*) let us recognize the voice of Christ which echoes in our own voices by celebrating the divine Office.

22. *Cf.* Saint Augustine, *Confessions,* X.34.53: "*Sacrifico laudem sacrificatori meo.*"
The praise of God is a sacrifice, an immolation of the inclinations of the old man by the
new. It is what he suggests: "*Sacrificium tibi famulatum cogitationis et linguae meae, et
da quod offeram tibi*" (*Confessions,* XI,2.3).

23. *Cf.* GS,43.

24. In the Pauline text it appears clearly that my salvation assumes the collaboration,
dominated and instigated by grace, between my will to save myself—by praising and serving God—and the divine will for my salvation. If my salvation is a function of my persevering, generous, trusting will to praise, reverence and serve God, such a will is already
a grace, a gift of salvific grace, for the desire to possess God supernaturally in the beatific vision is beyond every power and possibility of human nature left to its own resources. As Saint Ignatius tells us, without over emphasizing it, later on (Ex. 366–69) in
the *Rules for thinking with the Church* "No one can be saved unless predestined." It
is well to clarify the "principle and foundation," which enforces the human obligation of
salvation, by these rules in which Saint Ignatius not only stresses the danger of minimizing the forces of free will, but also inversely that of minimizing the action of grace
and of the predestining God. Thus the affirmation of faith—God created me that I save
myself—is completed by that of hope—I firmly trust that God predestines me to works I
should perform for working out my salvation. If it "is possible to speak of faith and of
grace in so much as one can do so with divine help, for a greater praise of the divine
majesty" as Saint Ignatius emphasizes (Ex. 369), should I not do so, for the salvation of
my own soul and that of others whom God wills to save too? Is it not under the influence and under the action of grace, in the bosom of faith, that my free will will carry
out the works which will save it? (*Cf.* Jas 2:22, "Was not Abraham our father justified
by works, offering up Isaac his son upon the altar? Seest thou, that faith did co-operate
with his works; and by works faith was made perfect?") In such works, joined with
prayer for final perseverance, included in the second part of the angelical salutation, have
I not an eloquent sign of the efficacious will which God has to save me in Christ and
through myself?

25. Saint Augustine's formula is well-known: "*Coronando merita nostra, coronas dona
tua*" (*Cf.* CFW, 422-434).

26. Cf. note 9, ST, II.II.26.5. We must prefer the salvation of our neighbor to our own
corporeal life, but not to that of our soul. (*Cf.* 1 Jn 3:16.)

N.B. Suggested reading for the "Principle and Foundation."

Saint Robert Bellarmine: *De Gemitu Columbae,* Bk. II, Ch. 8.

Blessed Claude La Columbière, Sermon 46 on the unique matter of salvation (for the last days of carnival).

Bourdaloue. Oeuvres Complètes, Paris, 1864, Bk, V, pp. 447–503: thoughts on salvation. The author explains very clearly the necessity, the value, the desire, the possibility, the narrow way of salvation, concern over and prudence in relation to salvation, final and general end, by contrasting it with all particular and proximate ends.

2

PRAYER AND METHOD

Saint Ignatius presents us with numerous methods of prayer in his Exercises. Does he not thereby answer the concern of modern men and women of our day? Very many desire to learn how to pray. Is not one of the most serious problems of Christian life, if not the most important, that of prayer and of perseverance in prayer? How can we pray well? How could we pray so as to give greater glory to God, in a prayer which would be most beneficial for our own salvation and that of others? How can we set aside a period for prolonged prayer daily?

We do not intend here to make a minute analysis or comparison of the various methods of prayer proposed by the author of the Exercises to the retreatant: meditation, contemplation,[1] application of the senses, general and particular examination of conscience,[2] rythmic prayer. The entire rich ensemble of such methods of prayer has already been studied.[3] It holds an important place in the Ignatian Exercises (Ex. 45–54, 101–109, 121–126, 24–31, 32–43, 258–60).

This variety, often misunderstood, lets us understand that one of the purposes of the retreat is to help the retreatant to better discover that one of the various methods of prayer which is most suitable for him personally and which the Holy Spirit prepares for him. How best am I to converse with my Creator and Lord? If I do not find out this secret, how would my practical choices, my elections, be adequate?

Rather my intention is to sketch an explanation of a method attempting to synthesize various aspects of diverse Ignation methods while at the same time calling on intuitions derived from other sources. I think the method I am attempting to explain is particularly suited to help contemporaries concentrate on prayer, something which is certainly more difficult in the present milieu than in the sixteenth century.[4] And how would that be possible unless we apply a theology of prayer?

Those who have no need of learning how to pray, since the Holy Spirit

15

has already opened up to them their personal way, may well by-pass this chapter unless they find in it a deepening or complementing of what they already know.

After having outlined, in the framework of a concrete prayer on the mystery of the Assumption of Mary, the method we recommend, we shall attempt to show its advantages under diverse plans. We shall show, for instance, how it satisfies the basic facts of Biblical revelation.

A. Method and mystery

It would be ideal were our prayer a prolonged and unique act of love toward God. Were we not created in view of this unique, this never-ending act of beatific love, at once our paradise and our salvation? After death, we will no longer know this multiplicity of acts of intelligence and of will which characterize our discursive knowledge and free will here below.

Precisely the acceptance of the divine will as to the present condition of our human nature includes our desire to dispose ourselves for the perfectly simple intuition of the Kingdom of God by a prayer which does not ignore the steps, the very discursive character, the unavoidable multiplicity in this world. In short, it is well to put into play under the action of grace, a method serviceable for prayer.

1. In the first place, without some proximate and remote *preparation* it is not possible to persevere in prayer. In the light of one's personal needs the subject and the fruit to be gained is to be determined beforehand. "This is to ask for what I desire" (Ex. 104): tears, humility, knowledge of Christ. So, as a rule there is not prayer unless it be preceded by spiritual reading, the *"lectio divina"* of the ancients, for "meditation without reading leads one astray."[5] Saint Ignatius, it is true, does not mention it in the Exercises which, however, he did not intend to be exhaustive nor to explain how one is to prepare for prayer outside of the retreat!

On the other hand, he does treat of immediate preparation[6], "In the preparatory prayer I will beg of God our Lord that all my intentions, actions, and operations may be directed purely to the praise and service of his divine majesty" (Ex. 46). In other words, it is in the very bosom of prayer and a propos of it that the supreme rule inculcated by the "Principle and Foundation" primarily and always applies.[7]

Saint Alfonsus Rodriguez would begin his prayer thus:

"After he dressed (this person)[8] commends himself to God and asks him to let him converse with his divine majesty in prayer, even though his faults make him unworthy of being in the presence of so good a God. At the same time he makes acts of contrition arousing within himself feelings of great sorrow for having offended God. Most humbly he asks for the grace that all acts of his memory, intellect and will serve to honor and glorify him. Finally, he offers himself wholeheartedly to him.

"Then, he makes three profound bows as one now permitted to enter into converse with God and, lifting up his heart to him he begins his prayer."[9]

In this way the Saint adapted to his own case Saint Ignatius'recommendations: "I will stand for the space of an *Our Father,* a step or two before the place where I am to meditate or contemplate, and with my mind raised on high, consider that God our Lord beholds me, etc.[10] Then I will make an act of reverence or humiliation" (Ex. 75).[11]

These saints knew by experience that perseverance in prayer, the finding of God therein, approaching and reaching him (Ex. 20) are linked in fact with the actual awareness of the unworthiness of one who prays to receive such gifts, on account of past sins. They know that "God resists the proud, while to the humble he grants his grace;" and so they "humble themselves under the powerful hand of God" not without "being exalted in the time of visitation" (Prv 3:34; I Pt 5:6). Do they not thus suggest that our failure in prayer, our difficulty in persevering in it, in part, are due to our pride?

2. Likewise, at the beginning of our contemplation of the mystery of the Assumption into glory of the humble Virgin Mary, we can humble ourselves before her, acknowledging our unworthiness to lift up the eyes of our soul toward her splendor and ask her above all to obtain for us the fruit we wish to obtain through this prayer. We beg her to intercede for us that we obtain the grace of the beatific vision and the glorification of our bodies by an intense and daily effort of prayer, especially toward her who is the Mother of God and our mother.

How are we going to obtain this fruit? Here, we think, it is quite permissible to expand, develop and systematize certain insights Saint Ignatius has given us in the Exercises in the light of later developments by the magisterium of the Church, and particularly of the method advocated by Saint Peter-Julian Eymard (1811–1868).

Shortly before his death, the founder of the Fathers of the Blessed Sacrament outlined his method of prayer based on the four ends of the Holy Sacrifice of the Mass.[12] Prayer would consist especially in acts of adoration, thanksgiving, contrition, and petition determined by the particular subject, the fruit of grace sought. Those acts would be concentrated around the particular truth under consideration. In this way private and personal prayer would be patterned on Christ's public prayer and that of the Church in the Eucharistic Sacrifice offered for those foud ends, in perfect harmony with the doctrine professed by the Church, especially later on in the encyclical *Mediator Dei,* issued in 1947 by Pope Pius XII.[13]

The magisterium of the Church merely crystallized and summarized the entire tradition which has always seen, in the acts corresponding to those four ends, the basic orientations of the spiritual life of Christians on the model of Christ.[14]

The same tradition, and particularly Saint Thomas Aquinas,[15] saw in these acts manifestations of the virtue of religion, an acquired and infused virtue, which is to serve the theological virtues of faith, hope and charity. Their acts cannot but constitute the supreme acts of Christian prayer. Did not Saint Paul write: "I desire, therefore, first of all, that supplications, prayers, intercessions, and thanksgivings be made for all men" (1 Tm 2:1): "And now remain: faith, hope and charity, these three: but the greatest of these is charity" (1 Cor 13:13)?

This is what Saint Ignatius and his favorite follower Nadal had to a large extent already perceived, even though they did not set it in a Eucharistic context, explicitly. However, before returning to these Ignatian insights, it is well to apply what we have abstractly explained to a concrete prayer. Each one will be able to do so following the order most suitable for him under the motion of the Holy Spirit.

4. When we contemplate Mary's Assumption, we adore first of all the mysterious design of God who willed, for the benefit of all mankind, to raise up from among the dead, in a privileged and anticipatory manner in respect to the common resurrection, the *Immaculate Virgin*. Our *act of adoration* explicitly acknowledges the sovereign right of God, Creator and Redeemer, exercised and manifested therein. When we adore this mysterious design of God, we also adore the Father's will to resurrect us from among the dead on the last day (Jn 6:38–40). We render him glory[16] along with his Son.

Now comes our *act of thanksgiving.* I thank my Redeemer for having resurrected his mother out of love for me. I thank him for having shown me in this way the power of his promise concerning my future resurrection. I thank him also beforehand, like Saint Paul,[17] for the future benefit of my corporal resurrection.

Then I make an *act of contrition* by which I ponder what I have deserved: not a glorious resurrection, but a shameful reanimation of my body in hell. Such an act may full well combine the motives of imperfect contrition and those of perfect contrition. The first prepares the terrain for the second, as servile fear for filial fear (Ex. 370). Imperfect contrition[18] as servile fear is a gift of God who wishes thus to help us stop committing sin or avoid falling back into it again.

Finally, there comes the *act of petition* or supplication by which I pray God to give me the grace of a glorious resurrection through perseverance in prayer. He who prays is saved; he who does not, is lost. This fourth act would be perfected by "obsecration," a term, used by Nadal,[19] taken from Saint Thomas Aquinas[20] By obsecration the soul, as the Psalmist,[21] calls on God, adducing titles and merits to be heard efficaciously. Thus I shall request of the Risen Christ, by virtue of the infinite power manifested in his glorious Resurrection and in his active role in the Assumption of his mother and in consideration of the infinite merits of his sorrowful Passion, that he bestow on me the favor of a glorious resurrection so that I be forever a heavenly companion of his mother. In other words, obsecreation presupposes consideration of a divine perfection, or of a mystery of Jesus or of Mary, brought to God's attention as a motive for granting such and such a favor.

These four acts, all directly addressed to God are to be joined with the acts of the three theological virtue: faith, hope and charity. These acts are also explicit and by them we can emphasize the "formal motives" of these virtues, namely, the divine perfections of veracity, fidelity and loveableness on account of which the Christian believes, hopes and loves all God has revealed, promised and commanded.

By *faith,* I believe the divinely revealed truths of the Assumption of Mary and of my own bodily and future resurrection. God the Revealer, who can neither deceive or be deceived, has revealed this to me out of his love.

By *hope,* I desire confidently to see with the eyes of the flesh the glorified bodies of Jesus and Mary and with the eyes of the soul to behold their souls and, above all, the Divine Person of the only Son of God. For God is infinitely and lovingly faithful to his promises. I have confidence, then, that I shall receive from him yet more perseverance in prayer and in hope.

By *charity,* I love the divine will to resurrect me gloriously and to resurrect gloriously all other men. And I offer myself wholly to this will which is a salvific will for me and for others.

We think that these seven acts, by actualizing the three theological virtues and the dispositions corresponding to the four ends of the Sacrifice of the Mass and which make up the acts of the virtue of religion, structure mental prayer. Is it not an elevation, a raising up of the mind to God in the course of which we speak to him through acts of adoration, thanksgiving, contrition and petition, of faith, hope and charity; all determined by the particular fruit sought, all centered around the particular truth which is the subject of conversation?

Each one of these seven acts, then, can be offered to each of the three divine persons and—with the necessary changes and modifications[22]—to the Blessed Virgin Mary, mother of the Son, daughter of the Father and sanctuary of the Holy Spirit. In this way we can integrate these seven distinct acts in the rhythm and supernatural harmony of the triple colloquuy provided for by Saint Ignatius, though he did not invent it for it was already in vogue before his time (Ex. 63, 147, 157, 168). We know even that Saint Ignatius not only counselled his retreatant to address himself successively to Mary, to Jesus, to the Father, but also that he himself would ask of the Son and of the Father to grant him the Spirit so to be able to discern the divine will[23] and that he would thus also enter into colloquy with the Holy Spirit[24] (cf. Ex. 109).

5. We want our readers to understand clearly our intent and so we must be faithful to the basic objective of this work which is to present a retreat rather than an abstract discussion. So we shall revert to a more personal

tone, a style of prayer addressed directly to the Creator rather than one of explanatory reflection. In this way we resume where we left off.

Holy Virgin, though I be unworthy to contemplate your splendor, I beg you to obtain for me the grace I seek through this prayer, that is, to attain the beatific vision and the glorification of my body by my efforts at ardent daily prayer, prayer that above all is addressed to you.

Lord Jesus, I *adore* your mysterious design to resurrect your mother from among the dead, before the other elect, for them and for me. To you be the glory of this sign of your love for me. Thus I acknowledge your sovereign dominion as Creator and Redeemer over Mary and over me.

I *thank you,* my Savior, for having in this way shown the power of your promise of my own future resurrection, for it is out of love for me that you have raised your mother from among the dead. Have you not willed that her risen heart beat in unison with the intercession of her immortal and glorified soul on my behalf?

I *am sorry* I have offended you by my sins, not only because thereby I have lost eternal life, merited unending shame, but even and especially because you are infinite bounty. With the help of your grace and relying on the merits of your mother, I am resolved to offend you no more, to detest my past sins and glorify you in your mother.

Lord Jesus Christ, you have told us: "Ask, and it shall be given you, seek and you shall find, knock, and it shall be opened to you" (Mt 7,7). In the name of your infinite might, manifested in your Resurrection, in the name of the infinite merits of your Passion, give me, my Lord, the grace and the glory of your Resurrection, and of life eternal in your company and in that of your mother. And so that I might obtain this, grant me the favor of perseverance in prayer.

Lord Jesus, Revealer, *I believe* all the truths you have revealed and taught us by the Church, especially the mystery of the Assumption of your Mother because you are infallible Truth and can neither deceive nor be deceived.

I hope, Lord, with a firm confidence, that you will grant me by your merits and those of your mother, you who are infinitely faithful in your promises and who place your almighty power at the service of their accomplishment, your grace in this world, the grace of perseverance in prayer, of invoking your mother and, as recompense, the joy of seeing you face to face.

Jesus, my Brother and my Friend, *I love* above all your eternal will, infinitely loveable and loving, to raise me up, with all mankind, glorious from among the dead. I offer myself wholly to your salvific will for the resurrection of all.

6. We may summarize what we have said in the words of Saint Peter-Julian Eymard: "Love adores, give thanks, sorrows for its faults, gives itself wholly to the greatest glory of Jesus." Or as Saint Paul tells us: "Charity. . .bears all things, believes all things, hopes all things, endures all things" (1 Cor 13:7). In the light of Saint Paul, love "informs"[25] adoration,

thanksgiving, contrition, petition, faith, hope. Charity, in absorbing all multiple and diverse acts, unifies them in itself and centers them all, in one way
or another, on the very love that the Divine Persons have among themselves
and for angelic and human persons.[26] And so, the method is "one of love"
and placed at the service of the mystery which is love, under the action of
grace.

B. Psychological, spiritual and doctrinal advantages of the method proxsed

1. Our method, on the *psychological* level, at first sight seems complex,
too involved with distinctions and series, artificial, even over-loaded. (It proposes twenty eight distinct acts to the one praying!). Such objections are not
hard to answer when we recall with Saint Ignatius that the soul will rest
quietly in feelings or acts in which it finds savor without trying to pass on
should grace not be given so to do (Ex. 2).

If, by following this directive we do not misuse the method suggested, we
realize that there is actually question of a diversity and multiplicity of acts,
in succession, of course, but also of acts all of which are of intrinsic value
since they directly link the soul to God. Their variety is not burdensome, for,
on the contrary, they permit the Christian joyously to prolong his prayer. We
say joyously, for in any situation or desolation, it will always be possible to
speak to God in prayer. Is not the secret of success the very perseverance we
have in loving, adoring, thanking, begging pardon, supplicating, believing
and hoping? There is nothing artificial or mechanical about it, but rather a
placing in the service of grace of all our psychic dynamisms, even obedience to the precept of Jesus on prayer, a precept that is also coupled with
a promise "Ask, and it shall be given you: seek, and you shall find; knock
and it shall be opened to you. For every one that asks receives; and he
that seeks, finds; and to him that knocks, it shall be opened" (Mt 7:7,8).

Furthermore—we have already said so but we must insist—this multiplicity
is a unified one: the seven acts mentioned, formulated in respect to four persons successively, all spring from charity which informs them and all have as
their finality its increase through obtaining the fruit of grace chosen.

Especially, to the extent that the Christian expresses to God in diverse ways
the object of his petition, he receives illumination and inspiration from the
Holy Spirit, sees more clearly and savors more deeply the divine will on the
matter under consideration. Besides, the simple framework of the four ends
of the Eucharistic Sacrifice and of the three theological virtues facilitates the
task of memory, and so fosters attention and concentration so difficult today.
We pass on from one act to another even in dryness and desolation; it is
easier not to remain in uncertainty. Of course, this method does not dispense from preparation, from previous spiritual reading, nor from having an
open book before our eyes, as Saint Theresa used to do for help in case of
need.

We think, then, that by offering a concrete possibility of multiplying, each time it is useful and not harmful, distinct and successive acts of the intelligence and loving free will (*cf.* Ex. 3) of the human person in regard to the divine Persons and to Mary, such a method constitutes an exceptional support for helping the Christian persevere in prayer. There is no need to say that Mary is inserted here, due to her Divine Maternity. Also we add that this method at the same time respects, and even in some way divinizes, the discursive character of the Christian's intelligence and free will, without prejudice to the immediacy of his relations with God and Mary, Who would ever think an hour of prayer superfluous or excessive for placing these twenty eight acts?

2. On the level of the *spirituality* of the Exercises, and of the methods they propose, we note that the seven distinct acts treated above are all, though some of them under other terms, mentioned by Saint Ignatius in his Spiritual Exercises.

Is not the act of adoration[27] the principal fruit of the "Principle and Foundation" (Ex. 23), repeated at the beginning of every prayer, as we have already pointed out?

Acts of thanksgiving, of petition and of contrition do they not make up the General Examination of Conscience (Ex. 43)? Is not obsecration at least implied in the meditation on personal sins (compare Ex. 59, 61)? The acts of faith, hope and charity correspond quite exactly to the triple grace asked for in all contemplations starting with the Incarnation (Ex. 104): "To ask for what I desire. Here it will be to ask for an intimate knowledge of our Lord, who has become man for me, that I may love him more and follow him more closely." We know Christ by faith and in it we follow him in hope and love him in charity. These acts, increasing[28] the theological virtues, are identical with the consolation described by Saint Ignatius: "I call consolation every increase of faith, hope and love" (Ex. 316).

We also observe, somewhat generally, that this method by exercising the mind, the will and the memory in acts of faith, hope and charity brings about the exercise of the three powers (Ex. 45–54)[29] in contemplation (Ex. 101) and even in the application of the spiritual senses (Ex. 121–125). For— and Saint Thomas Aquinas had seen this clearly[30]—faith exercises the sight and hearing of the soul, hope the sense of smell and taste, charity the sense of touch.[31]

The method proposed here, then, corresponds well to the intention manifested by Saint Ignatius in explaining the first method of prayer. "This manner of prayer is . . . meant to supply a *way* of proceeding and *some practices* by which the soul may prepare itself and profit so that its prayer may be acceptable to God" (Ex. 238). However, there is probably a difference in that our method is not only preparatory for prayer but is a method of prayer properly so called, while Saint Ignatius did not see in "the first method of prayer" a "method of prayer": "This manner of prayer is not

meant so much to provide a form and method of prayer properly so called"
but "a way to which the soul may prepare itself" (Ex. 238).

The method proposed here concentrating the mind and the will by successive and diverse acts regarding the same object—in this case, the Assumption
of Mary in its relation to my spiritual destiny—prepares, obviously, the terrain
for applying spiritual senses. Especially, if we follow the advice given by Saint
Ignatius in a letter of June 13, 1533, [32] one of the first letters of "Inigo poor
in goodness," by directing the various acts mentioned to the Divine Persons. This we do in so much as they present in us, in the innermost depths
of our soul, and in as much as they are present to us with their infinite
love. [33]

We note, too, that the suggested method answers Saint Ignatius' concern
by inserting and framing the exercises and the increase of moral virtues,
acquired and infused, in the direct relationship with the living God realized
through the theological virtues. For, habitually, the fruit intended, the grace
requested, will be related precisely to these "theological, cardinal and moral
virtues", attacked by "the enemy of human nature" and of "our eternal
salvation," to employ Saint Ignatius' expression (Ex. 327).

Finally, the choice of the subject in the context of which we have presented our method, that is, the Assumption contemplated for obtaining
perseverance in prayer, is not made without calling on the second method
of prayer and its "contemplation of the meaning of each word of a prayer
. . . of the 'Hail Holy Queen' and of the Creed" (Ex. 249, 253). Does
not the "Hail Holy Queen" assume that Mary has gloriously left exile "in
this valley of tears" while we are still "mourning and weeping," and is no
longer" a prisoner in a corruptible body among brute beasts" as we are
(Ex. 47)?..

What prevents us, then, from thinking that the method we propose is
as it were a synthesis of different methods found in the Ignation Exercises? [34] Corresponding perfectly to the data of revelation, it puts these methods into practice.

3. *On the doctrinal* level, the solution indicated has the singular advantage of shaping private prayer on the model of the public and official prayer
of Christ and of the Church in the Eucharistic Sacrifice, prayer of the whole
Christ, Head and Body. The ends of Christ, priest and victim come to
fashion the personal prayer of the Christian.

Private prayer thereby becomes at once the imitation and the prolonging
of that of Jesus, the great prayer. This method helps us to talk to Christ
of God, of Christ to God, according to the definition of prayer the French
Oratorian Nulleau has handed down to us from the seventeenth century
in the light of Jn 17:1. It makes of mental prayer a prolonging, an unfolding of the eucharistic act of thanksgiving which Pius XII sees as an im-
mersion in the adoration, the actual thanksgiving and supplication of Christ
really present in the body of the communicant. [35] Does not this method place

daily prayer more intensely under the radiance of the sacramental grace of the Eucharist? Does it not do so while disposing us toward an ever more fruitful participation in the Bread and in the Chalice of eternal Life?[36]

Does it not contribute, too, to making of prayer a sacrifice integrated into the grand and triumphant sacrifice of the whole Christ? Is not the prayer of adoring love, acknowledgement, reparation, supplication, faith and hope the intimate sacrifice (signified by the consecrated bread and wine) through which the soul offers itself to God as to the principle of its creation and as to its beatifying end?[37] Is it not to him above all that we must bind ourselves again and again by this exercise of the virtue of religion which ordains us to God?

Daily prolonged prayer thus becomes the great daily bond which unites us to God, our indefectible principle, who makes us constantly direct to him, as our last end, our choices and our decisions. If God pardons us our negligence, our sins, we regain him in some way by the exercise of faith.

Prayer conceived thus constitutes an unfolding of the Eucharistic Sacrifice by which we offer ourselves as victims to the Father with the Son and in the Holy Spirit.[39] Thereby we exercise to the highest degree the virtue of religion by positing acts which re-unite us directly with God, and by ordaining to our last end all the acts which mediately[40] link us to it. Prayer becomes a return to God. It brings about the concrete application of the "Principle and Foundation"

The method proposed here, in the service of the contemplation of the mystery, brings the Christian to respond to the counsels of Saint Augustine:

"Pray in hope, pray faithfully and lovingly, pray earnestly and patiently. In faith, hope and charity, by a constant desire, we pray always. Far from us be abundance of words, but not abundance of prayer."[41]

NOTES ON CHAPTER TWO

1. A. Brou, S.J. rightly observes: "The term contemplation is not used in the technical sense, that is, a privileged looking on God Himself, seen still through the veils of faith, God being the formal object of this prayer and this looking being a kind of simple intuition without multiple acts. It is still a discursive prayer, but one having for its subject episodes of the Gospel such as will easily be able to hold the attention, readily be prolonged and in which the eyes of the soul will find delight. This prayer will be intellectual or affective according to cases, and more strictly contemplative if God so wills. The sacred humanity of Jesus is not banned, as the Quietists wished, from the highest prayer. The use of the term contemplation for designating a prayer having as its object the person, the acts, the words of the God-Man is in no way abnormal" (A. Brou, *Saint Ignace Maître d'Oraison*, Paris, 1925, pp. 159,160).

2. In this category is the "First Method of Prayer" (Ex. 238–48) which is itself at the source of the "Contemplation to Attain Love of God," as we shall try to show later.

3. Brou, *op. cit.*; M. Giuliani, S.J. *Prière et Action,* Paris, 1966.

4. It was already difficult at this period (Ex. 12, 13). However, Saint Ignatius had to struggle against a trend that is very rare today, namely that of prolonged prayer to the detriment of apostolic action. Our contemporaries, accustomed as they are to the frenzied pace of TV, have more difficulty in concentrating on prolonged prayer.

5. Guigues II, the Carthusian, in his "*Scala Claustralium*" brought out some points which are still true: "Reading without meditation is arid; meditation without reading leads one astray; meditation without reading is tepid; meditation without prayer is barren. Prayer with devout contemplation is nourishing; but to arrive at contemplation without prayers, is a rare and miraculous case" (Ch. XII, 13; ML 184).

6. It would be fitting to quote another passage from the Exercises here (Ex. 73,74) directing the reflections to be made after retiring and on awakening. These Ignatian directions "to help one to go through the exercises better" show the advantage of morning prayer in relation to prayer during the day or in the evening (if the latter is not prepared the day before but the day itself); the latter benefits by a period of a very positive "psychological incubation" of images, thoughts and desires evoked since the preparation, all this favored by sleep.

7. For the preparatory prayer of the Exercises is always the same. (*Cf.* Ex. 55,62,65, 91,110 etc.)

8. The reference is to the Saint himself.

9. Saint Alphonus Rodriguez, S.J., *Vie admirable,* Paris, 1890, p. 81. This work contains a collection of the Saint's "manifestations of conscience" to his superiors.

10. The Latin translation of the Vulgate reads: "*Considerem Dominum meum Jesum ut praesentem, spectantem.*"—words, in this instance, more moving than the Ignatian expressions of the Spanish autograph.

11. Here we have modified Father Courel's translation. (Father Puhl follows suite.) They both use "humility" instead of "humiliation". This has been done to keep a priceless nuance of the Spanish Autograph which has the term "humiliation," hinting that, for the sons of Adam, reverence implies an act of voluntary humiliation, which undoubtedly casts new light on the first sentence of the "Principle and Foundation" (Ex. 23).

12. Cf. Saint Pierre-Julien Eymard, *La Divine Eucharistie, Premiere serie, La Presence Réelle,* Tourcoing, 1887, 10th ed., pp. 21-31).

13. Pius XII, *Mediator Dei,* AAS, 39 (1947) 549,550. The third end is presented (in regard to the Sacrifice of Christ, it cannot be otherwise, since Jesus as sinless had no personal sin to expiate!) not as contrition but as expiation. We imitate Jesus' expiation by our contrition.

14. This tradition is rooted in the Old Testament which presents us with distinct sacrifices, holocausts (to which corresponds the purpose of adoration), of thanksgiving, of expiation for sin and of petition or votive sacrifices: (Lv 1–7). Christ abolished, recapitulated and fulfilled all these sacrifices in his sole sacrifice on the Cross. (*cf.* St, I.II. 102.3) where the objective of thanksgiving in the peace-giving sacrifice is underlined (*ad* 8).

15. ST, I.II. 102.3.8.

16. This is how Pius XII (*Mediator Dei*) presents adoration, the first end of the sacrifice.

17. Phil 4:6; "Be nothing solicitous: but in every thing, by prayer and supplication, with thanksgiving, let your petitions be made known to God." Saint Paul suggests therefore that in the very exercise of prayer of petition it is proper to thank God beforehand for the gift, not yet received, which we are asking of him.

18. Cf. DS, 1676-1678 (Council of Trent).

19. M. Nicolau, S.J., J. Nadal, sus obras y doctrinas espirituales, Madrid, 1949, analytic index (Obsecracion), esp. pp. 211-217.

20. ST, II.II. 83.17 citing as an example Dn 9:17,18, based on the Vulgate, of 1 Tm 2:1; rendering the Greek by "obsecration."

21. Passin, particularly Ps 143.1.

22. There is clearly no question of rendering worship (latria) to Mary, a pure creature. Her Queenship and sovereignty over creation, acquired by her consent to be God's Mother, and her acceptance of the sacrifice of her Son, can and must be acknowledged. (Cf. Pius XII, Ad Coeli Reginam, DS, 3913-3916.) Likewise, the close and indissoluble association of Mary with the work of redemption and with the sacrifice of Jesus justifies and demands reparation paid to her Immaculate Heart (Pius XII, Haurietis Aquas, DS, 3926) since we have contracted toward our heavenly mother a debt of "love, of gratitude and of reparation" (ibid). The transformation suggested here is therefore well founded in the Mariology of the Church.

23. He did so on Monday February 11, 1544. Cf. Diario espiritual, Obras completas de San Ignacio de Loyola, Madrid, BAC, 1963, p. 321.

24. Ibid.

25. ST, II.II.23.8. Charity is the form of virtues because it orders them all to the last end. Cf. G. Gilleman, S.J. Le primat de la charité en théologie morale, Bruxelles-Paris, second edition 1954.

26. It is the object of the devotion to the Sacred Heart, such as presented by Pius XII, (Haurietis Aquas, AAS, 48, 1956, 327,346,350; DS, 3924).

27. Saint Ignatius only mentions adoration in the Exercises when he quotes Gospel texts (Ex. 267,274,301), but he does not seem to have integrated it, at this time at least, into his personal vocabulary.

28. Cf. ST, I.II.52.2.3.

29. Cf. also Ex. 238, where the Saint suggests a form of prayer based on the three powers of the soul.

30. S. Thomae Aquinatis super Epist, ad Phill. Lectura, Lectio II, #52 In Phil 2:4, Marietti, Turin, 1953, vol. II, p. 100 Cf. Saint Bonaventure, Itinerarium, 4,3.

31. Cf. Hans Urs von Balthasar, La gloire de la Croix, Paris, 1965, vol I, pp. 309-322; Hugo Rahner, S.J., Ignatius the Theologian, N.Y., 1968, pp. 181-213. He analyzes the therapeutic value of "the application of the senses" proposed in the Ignatian Exercises. He thinks this exercise restores unity between, on the one hand, the superior psyche and reason, and on the other, the imagination, sensitivity and affectivity. That is why this exercises is decisive for assuring the integration of the human person and his overcoming of disordered affections (cf. Ex. 1), as well as the ordering of life, which are the aim of the Exercises (Ex. 21). These pages originated in a conference given by Father Rahner May 3, 1957 during a gathering of priests and therapists.

32. Letter of Saint Ignatius to Agnes Pascual; the Saint speaks to her of her son, Juan

and writes: "May it please God our Lord to give him the grace to know himself perfectly, and may he sense his Divine Majesty in his soul (*dentre en su anima*) so that, as a prisoner of his love and of his grace, he be perfectly free from all creatures of the world." (MHSJ, i, Mon. Ignatiana, Epist. I. p. 92).

33. *Cf.* Pius XII, *Haurietis Aquas,* AAS, 48 (1956) 327; DS 3924.

34. *N.B.*: colloquuy of the meditation of the three powers, contemplation, general examination, application of senses, various methods of prayer. We also call attention to the fact that the "seven acts", exercised in relation to each Divine Person and (*mutatis mutandis*) to Mary bring out the significance of the number seven which, according to Father Fessard, has great import in the structure of the Spiritual Exercises.

35. *Cf.* Pius XII, *Mediator Dei* AAS, 39 (1947) 568.

36. We suggest for the four ends of prayer Father K. J. Healy, *New Catholic Encyclopedia,* 11 (1967) 671: art. "Prayer."

37. ST, I.II. 85.2.

38. ST, II.II.81.1.

39. Pius XII, *Mediator Dei,* AAS, 39 (1947) 557; LG, 34; SC, 48.

40. ST, II.II. 81.1.1.

41. Saint Augustine, *Epist.* 130.16,29: "*Ora in spe, ora fideliter et amanter, ora instanter et patienter. In ipsa ergo fide, spe et caritate, continuato disiderio, semper oramus. Absit ab oratione multa locutio, sed non desit multa precatio*" (*Ibid.* 9,18; 10.20); ML, 33,506, 501,502.

3

SIN
SINS, MY SINS, OUR SIN

We have seen in a previous chapter, that we have been created to praise, reverence and serve the Father, the Son and their Spirit, and so attain in the highest degree sanctifying grace here below and heavenly glory after death. That is the reason of our existence, of our actions, every moment. That is what we must obtain at any cost.

Face to face with this ideal, there stands before our eyes the sad reality: the blasphemy of those who should praise, or the simple negligence, open rebellion or hidden disobedience of God's free creatures. Briefly, in a word: I have sinned. I have often resisted or turned my back on my last end, on my reason of existence, I have preferred creatures over the Creator.

Saint Ignatius' Exercises present us with a meditation on our personal sins framed within the consideration of their conditions—the sin of the angels, "originating" sin of Adam—and the consideration of their source, "originated sin." We shall observe this order, not without reflecting first on sin in general.

A. Sin

Living in a world where the denial of sin is as frequent as that of God, we must most clearly set before the eyes of our spirit the nature and malice of sin.

To sin grievously is to turn away from the last end, God, infinite Good, toward whom each one of our acts should tend, and to turn toward the creature, to reject the Creator to turn, culpably, toward a created good, erected, at least implicitly, into the last end.[1]

Serious sin is, then, not only a transgression against the divine law but also though not always directly, nor always openly, a contempt of the love of personal amity between God and man,[2] and consequently an offense truly unspeakable against God. It is even ungrateful rejection of the love God offers us in Christ.[3]

For a sin to be grave, it is not necessary that the sinner directly turn away from God, make an act of express hatred of him. It is sufficient that he freely pursue the enjoyment of a forbidden created good, an enjoyment which he knows implies aversion from God.[4]

The sinner desires in so disorderly a way a created good that he prefers to break away from God rather than not enjoy this creature.

Thus, to sin gravely, is in the last analysis, to put his last end in a creature, to judge that a created good, be it a person, act or thing, exhausts all the reasons for existing and acting and so ought to become the center of existence without any reference to the Creator and Lord of all created beings and of all human actions.

There is, then, the transforming of a means, even if this means has the dignity of an intermediate end, into an ultimate end. The contempt of God inherent in grave sin always implies thereby a certain idolatry.

Grievous sin is called mortal because it deprives the soul of spiritual life. Just as the body is living by its union with the soul, the principle of life, the will of man is living when it is joined by right intention to the ultimate end, its object, and when it adheres by love to God and to the neighbor. Then it is moved to act rightly by an inner principle; this spontaneous action is a sign of life. When the intention of the last end and adherence to God and to the neighbor by love is eliminated, the soul is, as it were, dead and no longer moves spontaneously to do good but either ceases acting or does so with loss of its autonomy, out of fear. All sins, consequently, which contradict the intention of the last end and of love are mortal.[5] They deprive man of the divine life of sanctifying grace. They cause spiritual death. Mortal sin is always at once spiritual suicide and an offense against God.

While venial sin is a simple spiritual illness which does not take away the habitual orientation of the soul toward its last end, yet none the less endangers it. This orientation is not present and active now when there is venial sin. It is, therefore, a voluntary disorder in its ordinary relationship with God, yet without turning away from the last end. The one who commits venial sin is not a spiritual corpse, he is, however, sick at soul.[6]

This does not mean that there is not a certain infinite seriousness in venial sin. An act in itself of a finite creature, it is infinitely serious in this sense that it offends an infinite Goodness, even without causing its loss.[7] So it is also, under this aspect, an infinite evil.

Mortal sin, venial sin, these categories, which some of our contemporaries lightly ridicule, strongly express basic facts of the Christian conscience in its negative relationship with the God who polarizes it, with the mystery of sanctifying grace, of interior justification. To lose or to preserve, though precariously, the grace of trinitarian indwelling, is not a vain distinction. To be ill and yet still alive is not quite the same as being dead. To tend still, although only habitually and potentially, toward the last end, is not at all to have lost and rejected it.

So long as the history of human sin goes on, these categories will, un-fortunately, retain their unfailing actuality and the Church will ever have to present, in its catechesis,[8] to the faithful and to the world a distinction which is also liberating, since it calls to mind that numerous sins, even if they do offend God, do not constitute a tearing away from him.

We must admit this quite readily, of course. But other difficulties remain which obscure our understanding of sin, most unintelligible to the world. We are tempted to see in sin a fault of the ego against the super-ego, not against God. If, however, we do recognize that sin offends God, we ask ourselves what wrong can it cause an infinite Being for we know that nothing can be taken away from him. Finally, what 's the relation of sin to the supernatural order to which our humanity has been freely raised?

For many who are familiar with Freudian theory, sin would be a simple fault of the ego, in connivance with the "id" against the superego, a fault against oneself sanctioned by the self-punishment of remorse, chastisement of self by self. So there would be no sin but rather complexes of culpability, or neuroses of guilt. The so-called sinner would be but an executioner of himself ever condemned to condemn himself in the course of an impossible effort of self-justification.

Christian revelation, without denying pathological deviations, shows that sin is a fault against the absolute Other, against God[9]. By the very fact, man who cannot pardon himself, can receive pardon from God, and the inevitable aware-ness of sin is no longer a generation of interior poisonings of neuroses.

This divine pardon means that sin had actually offended the absolute Other. It is true that God finds his infinite happiness in himself, rather, that he is happy in himself, and that creatures cannot destroy this happiness. If divine beatitude is indestructible, nevertheless, sin can destroy something in the creature, something that God wanted, by a real will, conditional, not purely and simply, by a will that traditional theology calls antecedent and not consequent. Maritain[10] magnificently says: "If I sin, something that God has willed and desired shall eternally not happen, and this out of my own first initiative. I am thus an annihilating cause of a privation in regard to God, a privation as to the term and the effect willed, in no way as to the good of God himself.

Every change is on the part of the term. The immanent act, absolutely immutable and absolutely necessary by which God loves himself constitutes freely something as loved and willed. If he had not willed that thing, there would be nothing changed in him. Sin does not only deprive the universe of a good thing; it deprives God himself of a good thing which was con-ditionally willed, but actually willed by him.

"If we sought a comparison, no matter how imperfect, it would be neces-sary to think of a saint in transforming union. His peace is imperishable.

Some one kills his friends. There is reason for his heart to break. Yet his peace remains unruffled.

"Moral fault in no way reaches to the Uncreated in himself. He is absolutely invulnerable. Yet in the things, in the effects he wills and loves, God is the most vulnerable of beings. No need of poisoned arrows, of cannon and machine guns, it is enough to wound him by an invisible movement of the heart of a free agent, deprive his antecedent will of something here below which from all eternity he willed and which will never be."

Now then this divine will of which we treat here is not only that of the Author of nature, but also a salvific will which freely elevates man to the supernatural order. In the real, concrete supernatural order in which we live, sin puts on a malice infinitely graver than that of contempt of the last end. Now that human nature cannot, even by suicide, suppress itself, since souls are ever immortal and all bodies will rise from the dead—whether they wish to or not. Serious sin wholly suppresses the supernatural life of the human person, the supernatural being, while wounding without destroying its natural being. It is therefore a real supernatural suicide, with this difference, in a sense, from natural suicide which suppresses life but not natural being, whether of the soul or of the body.

Briefly, serious and mortal sin is more than an infinitely ungrateful injustice of a creature toward its Creator. It is also ingratitude of the servant, adopted as a son, toward his adoptive father. It is even, and this is the viewpoint of which Saint Ignatius is particularly aware (Ex. 53), the rebellion of the servant become a son against the Brother and the Creator who has redeemed him in and by his infinitely precious Blood, snatching him from his worst enemies, "it is the ungrateful rejection of the love God offers us in Christ," to repeat what was quoted earlier from Paul VI. "And this is the judgment: because the light is come into the world, and men loved darkness rather than the light: for their works were evil . . . For everyone that does evil hates the light" (Jn 3, 19-20).

Sin is then a triple offense against the creative, divinizing, redemptive love of the Father, Son and Holy Spirit for the created world. It is contempt for and hatred of this triple love. It is not fully unveiled save in the light of the Blood of the Lamb.

B. The Triple Sin of Satan, of Adam and of Every Damned Soul.

In a first prelude of the First Exercise (Ex. 47), there is what is called a "composition of place" by which our attention is called to the material place, in a situation on earth. Our souls are "imprisoned" in these "corruptible bodies". The Ignatian expression brings to mind the Old and New Testaments: "For the thoughts of mortal men are fearful, and our counsels uncertain. For the corruptible body is a load upon the soul, and the earthly habitation presses down the mind that muses upon many things" (Wis 9:14;15)?

The body, as mortal and corruptible, provides the devil with the opportunity to enslave through fear of death, throughout their whole lives, those who have become slaves of sin (Heb 2,14-15; Jn 8,34), and whom Christ comes to set free (Heb 2:15). The body, a good creature of a good God, has become by sin, chain and prison in which the sinful soul groans, prisoner of the devil through fear of death.

Christ, risen, who promises us the resurrection, and gives us the pledge of it in his Eucharistic Body, delivers us thus from the fear of bodily and spiritual death.

But, while awaiting the resurrection of the flesh, composite man, synthesis of immaterial and immortal soul on the one hand, of material and mortal body on the other, remains exiled, far from the angels who are pure spirits and whose company he is destined to enjoy,[11] "among brute beasts," among irrational animals without immortal and immaterial souls, among these animals which live without any consciousness of it, without any interior life, without liberty. We live isolated one from another, without perceiving the consciousness that others have of themselves, nor of their interior life.

We live exiled not only from the angels but also from the spectacle of the splendour of souls in the state of grace. Our disordered affections keep us away from the paradise of the unitive way (Ex. 10) and we must therefore devote ourselves to the exercise of the purgative way. Cherubim armed with a sword of fire have been posted by God before the garden of paradise, the Immaculate Heart of Mary! The way toward deep intimacy with this Heart will not be open to us so long as we remain attached to venial sin. The gleaming sword of guardian angels keeps watch over the path (Mary's) which leads us to the Tree of Life, to the Eucharistic Christ and perfect union of pure love with him.

In the "Second Prelude" we ask for "Shame and confusion because I see how many have been lost on account of a single mortal sin, and how many times I have deserved eternal damnation because of the many grievous sins that I have committed" (Ex. 48).

Shame and confusion, this grace is all the more priceless since I have the tendency to pride myself on my ignoble acts, even on my sins. The sinful act, to disguise itself, not only denies its sinfulness, but also justifies and exalts itself.

1. *The sin of the angels.*

Saint Ignatius does not say: "The sin of Satan and the demons" as he might have done. His expression reminds us that demons are not essentially evil, but were created, not only good, by the good God, but even in a state, not of consummated glory and beatitude, but of grace and initial beatitude.[12] They were not evil; they became evil. Their supernatural elevation, their destiny, the beatific vision, was beyond all the forces of their angelic nature.

That is why they received at once grace as a principle of their inner activity which was to bring them to glory.[13] We must recognize that, for every created spirit, and especially for an angelic spirit, to have to receive from Another the greatest act of its existential pathway, the very act which enables it to reach its end, constitutes a reminder of its radical dependence on the Creator.

In what does the sin of the angels consist? In that, contrary to the obligation to acknowledge this radical dependance, they "fell into pride" (Ex. 50), wishing to attain their final beatitude, that is, the vision of God beheld face to face, by their 'own natural power, and not by grace. Therefore, they wished to put their ultimate beatitude not in God, but in themselves, which is God's privilege. There are so many different ways of saying the same thing[14] which Saint Ignatius expresses by these simple words: "They did not want to make use of the freedom God gave them to reverence and obey their Creator and Lord, and so falling into pride, were changed from grace to hatred of God, and cast out of heaven into hell" (Ex. 50).

The sin of Satan and of the demons is the symbol of my sins of pride. All my sins, in some way or other, are sins of pride.[15] At the root of this pride is the proposal to be myself wholly, to attain my beatitude exclusively by my own powers, without any help from God. I propose to become a god without God, against God. It is refusing supernatural elevation.

All our rebellions against the divine will are also, and always, refusals and rejections of the gifts from the infinite liberality of God. There is greater joy in giving then in receiving, Jesus said (Acts 20:35). That is so, when there is question of men. But we can give them or God nothing save what we have first received from him. We must acknowledge and accept our inability to be self-sufficient. We have a radical need for the gifts of God to be wholly ourselves.

The fallen angels did not become fallen except by refusing but once the free gift of supernatural elevation! And I, how many times have I implicitly or explicitly refused it, and by refusing to help myself by actual grace and the sacraments to attain my supreme end, the vision of a transcendent God who is in me? Not created, but re-created in grace by baptism, have I not rejected the dynamism of my baptismal grace? Have I not thus fallen from the vestibule of heaven (grace) into that of hell (mortal sin)?

2. The sin of Adam.

Saint Ignatius considers here the "sin at the origins," the "originating sin," the personal fault of Adam as it affects the human nature of all his descendants and deprives them of sanctifying grace and original justice, by being transmitted to them by generation, constituting all of them thereby in a state of "originated—original sin" at the moment of their creation. Such is the "corruption" which was the consequence for the human race of the sin of Adam (Ex. 51).

Let us briefly recall the Church's doctrine on this subject. It was recently formulated by Paul VI[16] in his "Credo of the People of God."

"We believe that in Adam all have sinned, which means that the original offense committed by him caused human nature, common to all men, to fall to a state in which it bears the consequences of that offense, and which is not the state in which it was at first in our first parents, established as they were in holiness and justice, and in which man knew neither evil nor death. It is human nature so fallen, stripped of the grace that clothed it, injured in its own natural powers, and subjected to the dominion of death, that is transmitted to all men, and it is in this sense that every man is born in sin."

This text harmoniously links the "originated" original sin, as it exists in men who come into this world, to the "originating" original sin, the sin of origins, the sin of Adam. Saint Ignatius emphasizes in the "second point" of the meditation, the consequences of the latter for Adam and Eve themselves: "cast out of Paradise, they have lost original justice, and for the rest of their life, lived without it in many labors and much penance" (Ex. 51).

Why? Was it not to make us understand that, having sinned more often than Adam and Eve we should, as they, make our whole life one of penance and thus contribute to the salvation of those whom our sins have endangered? It is understandable, then, why the Greek Church invokes Adam's and Eve's intercession, in a liturgical feast,[17] for all their descendants. We who are, because of them, cast out of paradise and oblige to live our earthly life without original justice, subject to suffering and death, can ask, through their intercession, of the new Eve and the new Adam to obtain for us from the Father the gift of the Spirit in whose might it will be easy for us, accepting our human condition of existence, to mortify our flesh and its disordered passions.

However, an even more profound thought is suggested here by Saint Ignatius when he shows the result "of Adam's and Eve's sin"[18] for their descendants: "the great corruption which came upon the human race that caused many to be lost in hell" (Ex. 51).

This is illuminated by a delicately expressed statement of Saint Catherine of Siena, to whom Saint Ignatius had such great devotion: "By my sins I am indirectly but actually culpable for the sins of the whole world. Your people is in death, darkness envelopes Your spouse, chiefly because of my sins and not of those of other creatures."[19]

It is perfectly all right for a penitent Christian to think that, by his own unfaithfulness to grace, he has deprived men of all times, Adam included, of graces which would have preserved them efficaciously from the sins into which they fell. In this sense, of which Saint Augustine does not seem to have thought, his famous formula: *"Omnis homo Adam: omnis homo Christus*[20] (Every man Adam; every man Christ) takes on a new meaning. The doctrine of original sin presupposes a universal solidarity of iniquity, the reverse of the

communion of saints. In this light there is no objection to Dostoievski when
he acknowledges he is culpable for every thing towards everyone.[21] We have
shown this at length elsewhere.[22]

Each one of us, then, can consider himself another Adam, responsible for
the universal corruption of the human race and for the fact that all peoples
are marching "toward hell," to use Ignatian expressions already quoted.
Other texts of the Exercises, we shall see later on, incline us to think that
the awareness by the Christian of his universally co-redemptive vocation is
in part linked with the recognition of the universal extent of his culpability.
A single human act has reactions on every wave of universal history. I have
the terrible and magnificent power of reaching to the extremities of time and
space. By the fine point of my free spirit, I dominate the history in which I
am engaged.[23]

3. *The mortal sin of the damned.*

Here, important and significant corrections of the Spanish Autograph of
Saint Ignatius, made by the Latin versions, approved by the Church officially,
and which Ignatius himself preferred to use and always wanted to defend,[24]
oblige us to depart from the customary translations.

Saint Ignatius wishes to have us meditate on the monstrous gravity and
the eternal punishments of every mortal sin, which deserves hell—a truth of
faith—in the context of the simple hypothesis of the self-condemnation of
numerous men, all separated from God forever by a single mortal sin, or
by fewer mortal sins than mine. In other words, he invites the retreatant to
help himself, by a historical hypothesis, to set before his eyes an absolutely
certain truth of the Catholic Faith and so become more vividly aware of the
mercy which up to now he has received from Christ.

The majority, or rather, by moral unanimity, all the translators of the
Exercises have preferred to transmit to the public the original thinking of
Saint Ignatius.[25] On the other hand, we think that his final thought, the only
one that is identical with that of the Church, is the one most worthy of
being considered and one that does not mislead the retreatant. Does not any
author have the right to correct himself and to have his correction taken
seriously as the final expression of his thinking? That is why we give the
Paris and Rome final text of Ignatius, corrected in conformity with the
thinking of the Church. The Church does not wish to have us meditate on
myths by converting simple hypotheses into realities.

"Third Point: In like manner, we are to do the same in regard to any
particular mortal sin—which we shall call the third sin to distinguish it from
the two preceding sins. We shall consider that by such a sin, even though
committed once, many others *perhaps* have been cast into hell. We shall also
consider that countless men, because of sins much less numerous and less
serious than mine, are *perhaps* suffering eternal pains. Hence, I recall to
memory and ponder how much is the gravity and malice of my sin against

the Creator and Lord of all things" (Ex. 52, Vulgate).

The stress, then, in placed, in the context of a hypothesis relative to the multiplicity of the damned, on the truth of faith: mortal sin deserves hell. I would deserve hell if I sinned grievously; if I have already sinned grievously, I deserve it without any doubt more than many others.

What is of special concern to the author of the Exercises here is leading the retreatant better to perceive the infinite malice of sin." He who has sinned and acted against the infinite goodness, has been justly condemned eternally." Ignatius' corrections were intended to prevent a truth of faith presented thus (Ex. 52) from being obscured behind a theological hypothesis which is not certain.

More profoundly still, we may ask why Saint Ignatius mentions at least three times in this meditation, the theme of contrast between on one side those who are in hell–the demons–and those who would be in hell–men condemned–for having committed a single mortal sin, and on the other side I who am not there although I deserve to be there, condemned for-ever for my so numerous sins.

Some have seen here only the intention to contrast the "severity of God in regard to some others with His indulgence toward me." Such an in-interpretation is not the only one possible. For it does not seem precisely to express Ignatius' thinking during the "First Week." We should not only consider two modes of conduct in God but also two manners of perver-sity in creatures: some sinned but once (perhaps, more grievously and that is without doubt the case of the angels), but I, I have sinned again and again. By so doing I have offended not only the divine goodness, but the divine mercy which is that goodness returning to the sinner after each of his faults, and thus arousing his confusion-sought for and asked for by him. [26]

The fallen angels had sinned only against infinite goodness. They there-fore are justly condemned forever by that infinite goodness. Numerous others, so numerous that Saint Ignatius says (hypothetically) almost countless (Ex. 52, Vulgate), have been justly condemned forever for lesser sins than mine by this divine mercy. Adam and Eve have been spared by God, at the price of a long life of penitence. Yet this divine mercy up to now, not only has preserved me from long penance, but even from the eternal and just con-demnation I had deserved.

4. Colloquy of Mercy

There remains for me, then, to ask Christ crucified: "How it is that though he is the Creator, he has stopped to become man, and to pass from eter-nal life to death here in time, that thus he might die for our sins" (Ex. 53)?

The answer could only be this: "Not your sins but my love[27] for you obliged me to become a man in order to expiate those sins."

What have I done, what am I doing, what will I do for Christ? I who might have been a fallen angel, or a man set in final impenitence, justly condemned forever, yet am I the object of an incomprehensible predilection and indulgence?

When I look at myself[28]in the light of the two Adams, I see myself as a prisoner, imprisoned in the prison of my corruptible body, far from the glorious liberty of the holy angels. I see myself in exile, cast out of the consummated Kingdom, in a vale of tears. I am a man baptized but fallen, deprived of original justice, not the immortal, impassible man, the perfectly integral man I should be. I live not only among brute beasts but among savage men who, in great numbers, do not walk but run toward hell. As Adam, I wished to eat the fruit of the tree of the knowledge of good and evil,[29] that is, to plan out my future by human means, cut off from trust in the Providence which directs them.

But Adam and Eve, saved by the grace of Christ who inspired them to a life of penitence, intercede for me, that I not be numbered among the damned. Are not their salvation, their intercession, signs[30] of Christ's salvific will in my regard?

What have I done for you, Christ crucified? Alas, it would be better to ask what have I done against you and what have I not done for you!

Against you, I have in my way shared in "the mystery of iniquity"[31] the constant activity of the devil, the "prince of this world," within the human race, intended for the annihilation of grace and, along with it, even of human nature, whether by pride or by sensuality, present in some way or other in all my sins. Indeed I am neither a pure spirit nor a body without a soul, and all my sins engage the totality of my psycho-somatic nature, and even, in some way, are causes of all other sins, including those of devils and others who are damned.

What have I not done for you, Jesus crucified, my Creator and my Savior? Re-created in your grace, another Adam, I have not wished to help my weak liberty by the grace you offer it constantly for ever greater growth in your love, to save others. I have not imitated either the long penance of Adam and Eve and of all the saints, nor their numerous labors for your glory. Must I not do penance for my very impenitence?

What *am I doing for* you, Jesus crucified? But again it is what you are doing for me,[32] for without you I can do nothing, not even persevere in faith in you, in your Church! Without you, apart from you, I cannot offer any satisfaction acceptable to your Father, and to you for my sins. In comparison with the infinite gravity of my offense,[33] and of the infinite value of your satisfaction, mine remains ever finite, insufficient.[34]

What *will I do for* you, Jesus crucified? You have accepted that the immortal soul you had taken on for love of me be, as it were, imprisoned in your mortal and passible body, because of my sins. You lived a life of exile, far from the glory which was rightfully yours. For love of me, you renounced the preternatural privilege to which you had a title. For love of you, I will accept my condition of exile far from Paradise, the human and earthly condition of a prisoner deprived of original liberty and justice. It is in this condition and not as an angel or as an innocent Adam that I must carry out my humanizing and divinizing mission. So that I may not run toward hell by depressing thoughts of self-love, should I not run toward heaven by frequently lifting up my heart in what used to be called "ejaculatory prayers"?

Lord Jesus, give me through apostolic penitence, not only to make reparation in you, with you, for my ungrateful rebellions–part of the rebellion of Satan, ratifications of those of Adam–but also to work with you for the salvation of all those whom I have caused to be lost! Clothe me in garments of skins (Gen 3:21),[35] that is, of your Passion. Grant me the favor of contemplating it in the poor, of stripping myself as you did for their enrichment. May my life be the sacrifice of a co-redemptive[36] penitent, offered at Mass in union with your victorious death expiatory of my sins, for vocations to the Christian apostolate, to the religious life, to the priestly ministry.

O Blood of Jesus crucified, you thirsted to be drunken, offered, adored: grant me to provide you with chalices for your greater glory. Give me above all the confusion of knowing my unworthiness and my ingratitude. I have abused your numerous gifts and favors by offending you so much.[37] I am not worthy to look upon your wounds, nor to offer your death to your Father.

Father,[38] your Son Jesus has loved and loves me for love of you. You have given me to him. He loves you in me. You have delivered up your only Son for me.

What have I done for you, for him, for your Spirit? What am I doing, what shall I do in your Spirit through your Son, for you? You did not spare the culpable demon, or the sinner Adam, or your innocent Son. How will you spare me if I do not repent? If I do not offer you, as a member of your Son, those long and painful labors (Ex. 51)[39] destined to save so many peoples who are going to hell and act against your infinite goodness?

C. My Personal Sins

The fruit sought in this meditation is the grace of an intense sorrow and contrition for my sins (Ex. 4,44,55,87), of so crushed and broken a heart that tears might spontaneously flow from my eyes. A sorrow so great and so loving that it might obtain the immediate pardon of my crimes, even before their intended and resolved[40] confession, and even the remission of the temporal punishment due to my sins.[41]

The first point is an examination of conscience which prepares at least remotely for a general confession (Ex. 56,44), more beneficial and more meritorious[42] during the retreat, "because of the greater sorrow experienced for all the sins and perversities of whole life." To facilitate this examination of conscience and the general confession, the retreatant will be able to utilize either the general examination provided for by Saint Ignatius (Ex. 34–42), or the first method of prayer on the Ten Commandments of God, the capital sins, the powers of the soul and the senses of the body (Ex. 238–48).

After this "record of my sins" rather material, but already of importance for obtaining the grace of a perfect contrition, comes, in the second point, the suggestion that each one weigh the gravity of his sins and detest them as loathesome and malign, which they would be even if they were not violations of God's positive law, but only of the natural law.[43]

When this record has been checked and then evaluated, the retreatant is invited to humble himself in his own eyes, by a series of comparisons. 1) What am I compared with all men? 2) What are all men compared with the angels?[44] 3) What is all creation in comparison with God? Then I alone, what can I be? (Ex. 55). If all creation is pure nothing in comparison with God, what can I be, I an infinitesimal part of this physical universe, an individual bound to so many others?

Saint Ignatius provides us with a reply that is quite radical. He envisages successively the body and the soul which compose my person. He then invites me to consider the corruption and ugliness of the former, and my soul as an abscess whence have issued the sins I want to deplore, and the infectious poison of their malice.

Let us cite the text of the Vulgate which is much more impressive than that of the Autograph which we mentioned here. "What can I be, I a little man? I shall, then, ponder the corruption of *my whole person,* the depravity *of my soul* and the filth of my body, and will regard myself as a wound and an abscess, whence issues the poison of so many sins, and the pestilence of so many vices" (Ex. 58, Vulgate).

If my whole person is corruption, it is not entirely so.[45] My intellect, still capable of attaining truth and being, is corrupted culpably by so many errors and by so much ignorance; my will ever capable of acting virtuously, is perverted by so many evil inclinations and habits! And the poison of my sins and of my vices has not only corrupted my person, I have caused it to overflow into the hearts and souls of my brothers and sisters.

I thought I was someone, a personage. It was enough for me to re-examine myself under the light of Christ crucified, to see again the consequences of my sins and to weigh them in their intrinsic malice as well as to compare myself with the universe and with God to find out that I am a "less-than-nothing," a "good-for-nothing," a being morally and physically corrupt and a corrupter of others. A public poison!

Saint Ignatius was so convinced of his own corruption that he admitted it spontaneously, as the following anecdote testifies. "Leonor Zapila, told how Ignatius entered her house one day to beg for alms. She said to him in a tone of reproach: 'I am sure you are something of a scamp, since you go about the world in that garb. You would do better to go home again, instead of wandering around the countryside like a good-for-nothing and a great sinner.' The Saint answered her humbly, thanking her for her admonition and admitting that she had spoken well, for he was indeed a good-for-nothing and a great sinner! Her heart was touched, and she felt such respect ˙for Father Ignatius that she gave him alms. And from that hour she regarded him as a saint."[46]

After this third point of self-humiliation, the author of the Exercises invites me to consider, by contrast, in a fourth point: "Who God is against whom I have sinned." Here, too, the Vulgate text is more suggestive. Saint Ignatius asks me to "bring together and compare the perfections attributed as proper to God with my contrary vices and faults: the *supreme* power, wisdom, goodness and justice of God with my *extreme* weakness, ignorance, malice and iniquity" (Ex. 59, Vulgate).[47]

Have I not offended the almighty love of the Father by my wilful baseness, the infinitely wise and just love of the Son by my guilty ignorance, the goodness and mercy of the Holy Spirit by my perverse resistance? Had I not received from the Father, from the Son and from the Holy Spirit all the grace wanted for not sinning?

Since He is goodness itself and wishes my good, God hates my sin as infinitely as he loves me. I would not love myself if I did not detest my sins.[48]

Faced with the infinite power of God who has made himself weak and powerless for me in the crib and on the cross, all my strength is but an abyss of impotent weakness, linked, in fact, with the "will to power of the sinner"[49] which must acknowledge its defeat.

Faced with the wisdom of Christ crucified, I have nothing of my own save my ignorance and my errors, while the truths I have attained and known are God's gifts.

Faced with the goodness of the Holy Spirit, I have nothing of my own save the malice and perversity of my own will,[50] by which I have profaned and prostituted the natural and supernatural dignity of my soul and of my body, gifts of God Creator and Author of Grace.

This amounts to saying that I cannot know adequately and exhaustively all my extreme weakness, my ignorance, my iniquity, and my perversity. For that, I would have to know adequately and infinitely the infinite wisdom, the power, the justice, and the goodness of God which is impossible for a creature. If the highest knowledge I can have of these divine perfections is that they surpass all knowing,[51] the highest knowledge I can obtain of my human imperfections is that they also surpass all knowing.

We can, therefore, say with Saint Ignatius: "May he at least grant all of us his infinite mercy that we may experience his love more each day and abhor all our imperfections and wretchedness without exception, that we might attain to participation in the eternal light of his wisdom, which is inseparable from his infinite goodness and perfection, before which any defects of ours, even slight ones, become perfectly clear to us and are something we cannot tolerate. Then, by crushing them, we weaken and diminish them by the grace of the same God our Lord."[52]

Will we not make our own the prayer which John Pascual often heard Ignatius recite at Barcelona: "Oh my God, you are infinitely good, for you tolerate a man as evil and wicked as I!"[53]

Such a prayer already places us at the threshold of "the cry of wonder accompanied by surging emotion" which constitutes the fifth point (Ex. 60). "As I pass in review all creatures,"[54] I will say to them: "How is it that you have permitted me to live, and sustained me in life! You, angels, though you are the swords of God's justice, why have you tolerated me, guarded me, and prayed for me! You saints,[55] why have you interceded for me and asked favors for me! And the heavens, sun, moon, stars, and the elements: fruits, birds, fishes, and other animals—why have they all been at my service![56] How is it that the earth did not open to swallow me up, and create new hells in which I should be tormented forever!"[57]

Let us take up this cry of wonderment. "Guardian angels of my brothers and sisters, how could you have borne with my lack of justice and charity toward your protégés and even furnished me with possibilities to make amends to them? Saints, how could you have interceded for me, with the abcess of my sins and the stench of my vices before you, that I be not excommunicated and banished by the Church? Was not that what I deserved?"

Since the angels and the saints belong to the Church, their intercession manifests again her love for me, her mercy for me. O prodigious mercy of the Church for me!

"Holy and sanctifying Church, Church of sinners, though you hate my sin, not only have you not rejected me, but you immolate yourself for me each day countless times at each Mass! You offer yourself constantly as a victim in expiation for my sins and in petition for my conversion! Ceaselessly you make yourself the slave of my salvation, co-redemptive Church, giver of life eternal!

In your mercy toward me, as in your pity for the whole universe, I see shining out the infinite love of the Heart of the Lamb of God for me, and, inseparable, the mercy of the Father and the Holy Spirit.

Creatures answer me: "We have let you live, conserved, sustained, protected, prayed for you, interceded for you. We have refused to swallow you up and to become for you the torturers of the public prosecution by your eternal Creator because he has loved you to the point of willing to become man and die for your sins. The universe, which should have been an instrument of the wrath of the Lamb against you, has become a sign of his will to pardon you."

I have now but to finish my meditation by the colloquies with the Lamb of God, the Spirit of the Lamb and the God and Father of the Lamb (Rv 12: Ex. 61), for giving thanks to each "that up to this very moment he has granted me life." My life would not appear to me from now on more than an unmerited survival, the unexpected magnificent occasion for amending it with his grace, by living all my existence in the numerous labors and sufferings of apostolic penitence.

"O patience of God, I owe you all that I have. Without you I would have been plunged long ago into the abyss, in the depths of perdition. You have spared me and you close your eyes on the innumerable offenses I commit each day. Oh! that I may never disdain you, for you have clearly shown how terrible God's wrath will be against one who will not make use of the time of mercy. Oh! patience of God, how you have confounded my own impatience at the least sign of contradiction or of malevolence! Be ever praised, adored and imitated as much as you can be by a creature as unfortunate and wretched as I."[58]

D. Our Sin.

If the meditation on the triple sin had as its purpose to obtain shame and confusion because of our sins and the next exercise was intended to arouse perfect contrition, the third exercise of the first week (Ex. 62), is a repetition of the two previous ones polarized on the horror, the hatred, the detestation of sin, of my personal sins. The second was intended to make us grasp their perversity so that we shed tears over them. Now the question is of detesting them down to their roots, to prevent my falling into them again.

After I have paused at the points in which I will have felt the most consolation or desolation—in the two preceding exercises—I will make the three colloquies with Our Lady, the Son and the Father (Ex. 62-63), and it will not be amiss to add a fourth with the Holy Spirit of the Father, the Son and Mary.

Each colloquy asks for a triple grace. We shall therefore, consider each of the three graces requested; as well as the manner in which the request is made.

The first grace sought is that "of a deep knowledge of my sins,"[59] accompanied by "a feeling of abhorrence for them." Such an interior knowledge will make us perceive in sin not only an extinguishing of the divine light, an aversion from God, light of the soul, but also a calling out to the darkness of the devil, a conversion to the prince of darkness. Not only to the created world in general but also to its prince, Satan. As a result of such a conversion, the intellect is dimmed or inclines to sin. If perchance I—partially converted to Satan by my sin—a sinner, have acquired an earthly wisdom, it is as a sword in the hand of a raging fool.[60]

The second grace to ask for is "to understand and abhor the disorder of my actions, to amend them and properly order them according to God". (Ex. 63, Vulg.). The Spanish Autograph speaks of "operations," already mentioned in the preparatory prayer (Ex. 46). Analysis of Ignatian vocabulary shows that *"intentions, action, operations"* correspond to *desire*, to *election* of the "Foundation" and its *external execution*, respectively. The

second grace looks to a purity of intention ever greater by way of its mani-
festion in execution. Does not operation, in departing from the election,
reveal an impurity in the intention? The rectification of intentions is hardly
possible without that of external actions. This second grace asked for corresponds in a negative way to the grace positively asked for in the preparatory prayer," that all my intentions, actions and operations be directed purely to the praise and service of His divine Majesty" (Ex. 46, Autog).[61]

It may be said that in a wider sense, less immediately contributing to the
precise acceptance of the term "operation," in the Ignatian vocabulary, but
identical to the profound aim of the author of the Exercises in this triple
colloquy, the second grace requested is that of constant struggle against the
concupiscences of the flesh in the sense of the Biblical and patristic tradition. That is, against the consequences of original sin.

In fact, "to direct his operations," the grace requested here insistently corresponds to the very aim of the Exercises as they are defined by their author: "their purpose is the conquest of self and the regulation of one's life
in such a way that no decision is made under the influence of any inordinate attachment" (Ex. 21). To overcome oneself and to direct one's life
are practically synonymous expressions. They are also explained by the saint
elsewhere. "To overcome oneself, that is, to make our sensual nature obey
reason, and to bring all of our lower faculties into greater subjection to the
higher" (Ex. 87); "For every one must keep in mind that in all that concerns
the spiritual life his progress will be in proportion to his surrender of self-
love and of his own will and interests" (Ex. 189).

The second and third graces asked for by the retreatant, disciple of Saint
Ignatius, are those of fighting against the flesh and the world, instruments
of the devil, in the Pauline meaning of the three terms.

"In Saint Paul, of the two enemies of man which make up the world
and the flesh, it is especially the flesh which has the predominant role.
The opposite is true of Saint John. With him one may say the flesh takes
on a color too pallid for a real enemy."[62]

Father Bouyer whom we have just quoted, explains very exactly[63] the
Pauline sense of the term "flesh."

"The material, instrumental element of our composite being, instead of
serving our 'ego', itself fundamentally in accord with the inspirations of the
'pneuma theou', shows itself dominated by an external power. That power,
thanks to its intermediary, acts not only on us but in us, introducing its
enmity against God into the very sources of our actions. The mentality of
the flesh, Saint Paul tells us, the design that it has gotten into its head
and its dispositions for carrying it out, 'to phronema tes sarkos,' is death
(Rom 8:6-8). There is, in fact, a positive design the flesh seems to bear
inscribed on itself (pronoia, Rom 13:14), there is a desire of the flesh (epi
tumia, Rom 5:16,17); it has its wills (thelemata Ephe. 2:3) and finally its
works are carried out by men (Gal 5:19). Paul goes so far as to use the

paradoxical expression *"nous tes sarkos"* (Col 2:18); "the mentality of the flesh."

It is clear that the Christian use of the term "flesh" for every moral disorder in us whether in consequence of original sin or of actual sins is due to Saint Paul[64](Gal 5; 1 Cor 2-3; Rom 7; Col 3; Eph 4). It is certainly in this Pauline and general sense that Saint Ignatius speaks in the Exercises of carnal love (Ex. 97), when he seems to identify "inordinate attachments" with "the flesh" (Ex. 157) and presents the divine vocation as without any admixture of flesh or inordinate attachment, and the election without any yielding to flesh and blood (Ex. 172-173).

Beyond Paul and Ignatius, Saint Thomas Aquinas, profiting by the Augustianian tradition, had identified the *"disordered* turning to created good" with "concupiscence" and with the material element of original sin, formally constituted by the privation of original justice and by the voluntary aversion of man in regard to God. "From this voluntary aversion the disorder in all the other faculties of the soul has resulted."[65]

Then, somewhat further on,[66] the Angelic Doctor explains the necessity of distinguishing different disorders, should one wish to explain the genesis of venial sin in us. There are disordered movements of sensuality which come from inadequate subjection of sensuality to reason—it is these Saint Ignatius has in mind when he says that our sensual nature should obey reason (Ex. 87)—and there are disordered movements which exist in reason itself and come from the fact that reason, in the exercise of its act, is not perfectly submissive to its end—and it is these Saint Ignatius has in mind when he states: "every one must keep in mind that in all that concerns the spiritual life his progress will be in proportion to his surrender of self-love and of his own will and interests" (Ex. 189).

The second grace asked for is, then, that I may know and detest the double disorder of my interior operations which is reflected inevitably in the exterior: the insubordination of the senses, of sensitivity and of the passions to reason and will which are superior to them and the insubordination of reason and will to the divine wisdom and will which are absolutely superior. Under this last aspect, the second grace is connected with the first. It includes it some way.

However, the second grace corresponds to the consciousness of every just man—according to Paul, Augustine, Thomas Aquinas[67]—, of the fact, that, spiritually restored by the grace of Christ, he is not wholly so on account of concupiscence (Rom 7: 19-23). Augustine and Thomas Aquinas have understood what Saint Paul meant when he wrote: "For I do not do the good that I wish, but the evil that I do not wish, that I perform . . . For I am delighted with the law of God according to the inner man, but I see another law in my members, warring against the law of my mind and making me prisoner to the law of sin that is in my members" (Rom 7: 19-23). They understood the sorrowful experience. that Paul described in these words, of every just man—even after his justification—who comes up against interior concupiscences, and their "disorder."

The Council of Trent solemnly recognized that "concupiscence remains in the baptized. As it is left in them in view of a struggle, it cannot harm those who do not consent to it and who resist it courageously by the grace of Jesus Christ." And the Council stressed that such resistance merits for the Christian athlete the eternal crown (2 Tim 2:5).[68]

In our journey toward final justice, the original sin of our first parents, though pardoned, expiated, washed away, influences us still—or tries to do so—through concupiscence, "the negative existential of rebellion against our supernatural vocation." At the same time, as an agent of "destruction of our human development," it exerts its influence, to use an expression of Karl Rahner.[69] We are, though justified, in the world and in the humanity of original sin. The decision of our salvation was made in the context of concupiscence.[70]

It is known that Luther saw in concupiscence a sin. The Council of Trent while recognizing that Saint Paul sometimes called it thus (Rom 6:12ff), declared forcefully and under pain of anathema, that the Catholic Church has never understood that concupiscence is called a sin because it is the result of personal sin but rather conduces to it.[71]

Vatican II has equally alluded to concupiscence in these words: "Examining his heart, man finds that he has inclinations toward evil too. . . . Therefore man is split within himself. As a result, all of human life, whether individual or collective, shows itself to be a dramatic struggle between good and evil, between light and darkness. Indeed, man finds that by himself, he is incapable of battling the assaults of evil successfully, so that everyone feels as though he is bound by chains."[72]

The second grace asked for, then, relates to the consequences in us of original sin, even though we are justified by baptism. These consequences are an inordinate inclination to the created world, an inclination which readily leads to venial sin.

Such an inclination, however, is not that of an isolated individual without any relation to others. On the contrary, it exists simultaneously, although in various ways, in everyone who is justified. It is rooted in a certain socialization (in reality very anti-social) of concupiscence just as every man is a social animal. That is why Saint Ignatius invites his retreatant to ask for a third grace: "A knowledge of the world, that filled with horror, I may put away from me all that is worldly and vain" (Ex. 62). The text of the Vulgate introduces a nuance for in it there is asked the grace to know and abhor "the depravity of the world."

There is obviously here question of one of the Biblical meanings of the term "world" (kosmos). There is no question here, for the author of the Exercises, of world in the sense of the whole creation or of mankind (Jn 3:16). Rather there is involved what, in this mankind, has fallen under the control of Satan, the prince of this world (Jn 14:30), to the point of serving his designs.

According to the Gospel of Saint John, the world knew not the light although it was present in it and was its author. It cannot receive the Spirit of truth. The peace that Christ gives is not as that of the world. The world hates Christ and his disciples, for they are not of the world nor is Christ. Christ convicts the world of sin. The joy of the world as its peace is contrary to that which Christ gives. Christ has overcome the world. Christ does not pray for the world. He says so explicitly. The world knew not God (Jn 1:10; 14: 17,27; 15: 18,19; 17: 14-16; 16: 8,20,39; 17: 9, 25.).

An even darker picture of the world is given in the first epistle. "Do not love the world, or the things that are in the world. If anyone loves the world, the love of the Father is not in him; because all that is in the world is the lust of the flesh, and the lust of the eyes, and the pride of life; which is not from the Father, but from the world. And the world with its lust is passing away, but he who does the will of God abides forever"; "And the whole world is in the power of the evil one"; "All that is born of God overcomes the world. And this is the victory that overcomes the world, our faith." (1 Jn 2:15-17; 5:19; 5:4).[73]

All this, but especially the texts of the Johannine epistle, is background for the third grace asked for by Saint Ignatius. Just as what the world symbolizes in Saint Paul—and which will equally be included in the Johannine sense of the word—: a general organization of the forces of evil, superimposed and more or less identified with the organization of the universe, which the term *kosmos* formally expresses.[74]

One might say without fear of contradiction that the world is the organization of concupiscence, if not on its ontological level—disorder cannot be organized!—at least on its psychological level.

However, the specific note of the third Ignatian request for grace, consists undoubtedly in the link established between wowliness and vanity "that I may put away from me all that is worldly and vain" (Ex. 63). The intramundane organization of disorder seems essentially, in Ignatius' eyes, vain. First of all, because it refuses to recognize the bond which orders our immediate finalities to our ultimate finality. All that is not done under the influence of charity, out of love of God, is in some way vain and will remain eternally sterile. Next, this organization is also vain because it will crumble like a house of cards before the divine plan, at the hour and on the day of Christ. "The world with its concupiscence passes, but he who does the will of God lasts forever," as Saint John tells us.

Briefly, we might sum up the point of the triple demand for grace presented here by Saint Ignatius with the help of these words of Father Bouyer who certainly was not thinking about the Exercises: "The world and the flesh are as instruments which the powers of darkness play, instruments which are shown in sin."[75] This triple colloquy of struggle against sin, the world and the flesh is intended to snatch the Christian and mankind from the designs of Satan, prince of the world.

Before expressing it in our own terms, it is well to bring out also certain structural factors.

It is quite remarkable to see Mary designated by the expression our Lady, parallel to the expression frequently used by Saint Ignatius in the Exercises a propos of either God or of Christ: "Our Lord." He never calls Mary "our mother." He prefers, as a Christian might, to treat her as "our Lady."

He calls on her to intervene with Him who is inseparably "her son" and "her Lord." Ignatius exalts Mary's royalty only to exalt even more that of Jesus Christ, Lord of his mother. So the absolute primacy of Christ in the economy of salvation stands out clearly.

On the other hand, it is as mediator with the Father that the Son, as incarnate, is asked to intercede in the second colloquy: "that he may obtain these graces from the Father for me" (Ex. 63).

The Christ of Ignatius is at the same time he who is adored as Creator—and Advocate—the Mediator whose intercession with the Father is solicited. "The dialogue between Christ Mediator and Christ Creator is one of the essential characteristics of Ignatian mysticism," writes Rahner.[76] He is he who is prayed to and he who prays for those who pray to him. He is God made human prayer.

We have considered the graces asked for and certain modalities of requesting them. There remains but to ask for them.

Colloquuy with Mary Immaculate.

Holy Virgin, our Lady, we venerate the splendor of your Immaculate Conception. You are so full of the grace of your Son and Lord for all mankind that in you there has never been found stain or place for sin, or inclination to sin. Nothing carnal in your immaculate flesh, nothing vain or worldly in your heart. No disorder in your perfect mastery, oh queen, of your heart and of your body. Everything in you is ordered to your soul, perfectly subordinated to God. You are the Immaculate Conception, that is, the maximum of created perfection realized in a pure creature.[77] Handmaid and mother of your son and Lord, obtain for us the grace to abhor the disorder of our operations and to order them to the glory of your Son. May the splendor of the immaculate order of your heart reign in ours, so stained by actual sins. Reveal to us, in the mirror of your heart, the abyss of our disorder.

Lord Jesus, Son of Mary, eternal Son of the Father, crucified to expiate my sins, risen to put order into my operations, you have overcome the world. You triumph over it ceaselessly. You will ever conquer it. Mediator of my salvation and of my personal social and ecclesial integration, make known to me all my disorders which pervade my fears and my desires, my memories and expectations, my joys and sorrows, my loves and hates, obtaining for me from the Father the gift of the Holy Spirit that I may know and hate myself[78] in him for love of you. Thus you will grant me and will obtain for me the grace of truly loving myself, without which I can neither love my neighbor nor you. Grant me to flee from and hate the corrupt and corrupting world which is in me and in others, the old Adam. Crucify him in me in the power of your Spirit. New Adam, grant that in your splendor I may know, discern and measure the enormity of my faults, the chaos of my inner disorder so as to preserve and increase the life of grace. Grant me this holy hatred of myself which will keep burning in me the fire of your charity.[79]

Father of mercies, God of all consolation, grant me, in the name of the merits of your Son Jesus, to share your and his hatred of my sins, of the disorder of my operations, of the vain world which is in my heart. Grant me to hate the tendency toward the earthly establishment, toward fixing my abode in this world, rather grant me to consider myself perpetually as a pilgrim on the way to eternity, ever ready to come to you, my Father and my fatherland! Grant me, then, this hope of eternal life which uproots me from this present life!

Spirit of the Father and of the Son, purify me, you who are the Holy Spirit. Grant me your gift of wisdom, for ordering in me my loves and for subjecting all my passions to you, who are eternal love of the Father and of the Son. Grant me the abundance of your gifts of knowledge, understanding and power for knowing, detesting and eliminating the multitude of my venial sins, deliberate or semi-deliberate, the perversity of my operations, the corruption of my heart and of my spirit. Grant me to know this almost infinite malice which is in me and which I do not see since I do not enter seriously into my heart. Grant me, despite the efforts of the devil,[80] to do so.

Come into me, Spirit of compunction,[81] to remind me of my crimes, the future pains they have deserved, the oases of the long sacramental stages of my pilgrimage, the thirst for the inexhaustible source from which I must here below drink lest I grow faint on the way. Eternal breath of the Father and of the Son, make me breathe toward them. Sprinkle my desert heart and melt it by the tears of a contrite heart.[82] I am disorder, vanity, worldliness. Make of my chaos a cosmos, an order resplendent with your holiness.

Prayer for obtaining the grace of struggling against a dominant fault by the particular examination, frequent confession and a general confession.

Lord, triune and one, infinite holiness, you know my dominant fault and vice, its relation to my temperament. You know that it compromises the main quality you have given me and which you have perfected by a special attraction of grace.

Better than I, you see how this fault and dominant vice renders me vulnerable to the assaults of Satan. "The conduct of our enemy may also be compared to the tactics of a leader intent upon seizing and plundering a position he desires. A commander and leader of an army will encamp, explore the fortifications and defenses of the stronghold, and attack at the weakest point. In the same way, the enemy of our human nature investigates from every side all our virtues, theological, cardinal and moral. Where he finds the defenses of eternal salvation weakest and most deficient, there he attacks and tries to take us by storm" (Ex. 327).

My dominant fault often takes on the appearances of a virtue. (Cf. 2 Cor 11:14.) If I do not know what it is, I cannot fight against it. If I do not fight against it, I have no true interior life.

Reveal to me, making me examine my tendencies and daily preoccupations, the causes of my sorrows and joys, the ordinary origin of my sins, the complaints of others about me, the temptations I most often undergo, the sacrifices which your grace often asks of me.

Lord, show me the main obstacle to my sanctification, the one which prevents me from benefiting from the graces I receive and also from the external difficulties which would be of profit to my soul if I knew better how to have recourse to you when the occasion arises.

So long as I do not know it, so long as I will not overcome it, my virtues which I received from you, are they not rather natural good inclinations than true and solid virtues? Are they rooted in me?

Grant me the grace better to perceive this dominant defect and vice by means of a general examination (Ex. 32–43), of a good general confession (Ex. 49), and of fighting against it—to the point of overcoming it ever better and better—by the particular examination (Ex. 24–31).

Take this struggle under the aegis of your sacramental grace by frequent confession of my venial sins. Would this not be incomparably helpful for me to make progress in self-knowledge and in humility, to resist spiritual torpor, to purify my conscience, strengthen my will, provide me with the opportunity for spiritual direction and increase of grace within me (DS 3813)?

Lord Jesus, my Redeemer, I beg you, as a very great favor, to sacramentalize my struggle against my dominant defect and vice by the frequent reception of the sacramental grace of penance.

Will I not thus come gradually to be myself in the best sense of the word, myself supernaturally without my faults? Should I not, instead of submitting to my temperament, transform it by retaining what is good in it, in order that my character be, in my temperament, the imprint of the virtues acquired and infused, and above all of the theological ones?

Will I not then be inclined to relate everything not to me, but to God?

(Cf. R. Garrigou-Lagrange, *Les Trois Ages de la Vie Intérieure*. Paris, 1938, vol. I, Part II, Ch. V, pp. 428–37).

NOTES ON CHAPTER THREE

Preliminary observation

We know that the subjects proposed by Saint Ignatius for our prayer in this first week: venial and mortal sin, original sin, hell etc. pose quite a few problems for modern man. Although we will clarify certain concepts, we shall avoid turning this theological retreat into an apologetic one—if that be possible!—and shall assume that our reader-retreatant has already the Catholic faith which he desires to deepen in prayer, without feeling the need to defend it against all possible and imaginable objections. Somewhat like Saint Ignatius assumed that, after the first week, problems of chastity have been regulated, though not those of poverty.

1. ST, I.II. 71,6. There can be seen in this definition the material and formal aspects of sin (the first consisting in turning to a created good, the second, in turning away from the supreme Good). A little further on, (*ad* 5m), Saint Thomas profoundly observes that for the philosopher sin is an act contrary to reason, while for the theologian it is an offense against God. He states precisely that the theological definition is more profound since the eternal law rules us in many things which surpass human reason.

2. Precisely because the turning to a created good is sometimes, even often, clearer than the turning away from God, yet always present in a serious sin; *cf.* I. McGuiness, *New Catholic Encylcopedia,* 13 (1967) 242 col 2 (art.*"sin"*); Pius XII, AAS, 36 (1944) 73.

3. Paul VI. *Indulgentiarum Dominus*: AAS, 59 (1967) 7: *Menti autem Christianorum omnium temporum clare apparebat peccatum, non solum transgressionem legis divinae, sed insuper, etsi non semper et aperte, esse contemptum vel neglectum personalis amicitiae inter Deum et hominem, et veram ac numquam satis aestimabilem Dei offensam, immo ingratam rejectionem amoris Dei in Christo nobis oblati, cum Christus discipulos suos amicos vocaverit, non servos."* The document cites: Wis. 7:14; Is 17:10; 44:21; Jer 33:8; Ez 20:27. The Exercises give the same meaning (Ex. 52).

4. *Cf.* note 2. The text of Pius XII quoted there says: "When man says yes to the forbidden fruit, he says no to God who forbids it."

5. SCG, III. 139 last line; *cf.* Ex. 35. The distinction between mortal and venial sin was a practical and decisive problem in the life and apostolate of Saint Ignatius: *cf.* Ch. VII of his autobiography. Did he not on account of it have to make his theological studies in Paris for more than four years? In fact, the Dominican inquisitors of Salamanca, while declaring his teaching free from error, forbade him to define "this is a mortal sin, or a venial sin" before he had studied for four years. He concluded that the door was closed for helping souls in Salamanca so he decided to go and study in Paris. It is curious to note, besides, that Saint Ignatius does not define precisely the difference between mortal and venial sin in the Exercises.

6. ST, I.II. 72.5. The distinction has a Biblical basis (Eph 5:5; Gal 5:19–21; certain sins exclude from the Kingdom: Jas 3:2; 1 Jn 1:8; Ecc 7:21).

7. It is true, however, that venial sin, on losing supplementary degrees of sanctifying grace and hence of celestial glory, in a sense, loses God. Saint Ignatius rightly observes in a letter to Saint Francis Borgia, at the end of 1545 (Epist. I, 339–342), that "No sin can be said to be slight in as much as its object is the infinite and supreme Good." Nevertheless it is well to note here with Saint Thomas (ST, I.II. 72.5.1), that the infinite difference between venial and mortal sin, results not from the turning to a created good, which exists in both cases, but in turning away from God.

8. *cf.* "*Dutch Catechism*" or "*Introduction à la Foi Catholique,*" Paris, 1968 p. 573; also DS. 1680,1707. Luther rejected the confession of venial sins, extolled by Pius XII (DS, 3818). The "supplement" to the *Dutch Catechism* has also stated more presisely the concept of the gravity of mortal sin which was left somewhat vague in the text cited above.

9. *Cf.* J. M. Le Blond, S.J., *L'influence salutaire de la réparation sur la vie psychique de l'homme, Cor Jesus,* Rome, 1959, vol. II, p. 346.

10. J. Maritain, *Neuf leçons sur les premiers principes de la philosophie morale,* Téqui, Paris, 1951, pp. 174–176.

11. *Cf.* Ex. 47. Saint Ignatius does not say, (neither in the Vulgate nor in the Autograph) "irrational animals" which is usually found in translations, but "*bruta animalia*" which has the same meaning in medieval Latin. *Cf.* on this simile the analyses by Fessard, S.J., *La dialectique des Exercices Spirituels,* Paris, 1966, vol. II, pp. 52–61; W. J. Ong, *Theological Studies,* 15 (1954) 34–51, in an article: "St. Ignatius' Prison-cage and the Existentialist Situation." Despite Fessard's contrary opinion (*op. cit.* p. 54), we think that in Ignatius' eyes, "*bruta animalia*" designates sinners without implying any contempt of his neighbor on the part of the author of the Exercises (*ibid.*). Such an interpretation seems to us the most probable in the light of the contemplation on the Incarnation which shows men on the earth as blaspheming, fighting and killing each other, and *all* nations in great blindness descending into hell (Ex. 106–108 Vulg). Above all, it seems to us that Saint Ignatius was thinking about the necessary co-existence here below with tempting devils. Why? The rules for discernment of spirits of the first week lead us to a solution: "However, if one begins to be afraid and to lose courage in temptations, no wild animal on earth can be more fierce than the enemy of our human nature. He will carry out his perverse intentions with consummate malice" (Ex. 325). The devil, then, is compared to a wild beast, the fiercest of all. Now, the meditation on the two standards shows us how this devil "summons innumerable demons, and scatters them, some to one city and some to another, throughout the whole world, so that no province, no place, no state of life, no individual is overlooked" (Ex. 141). Our earth is populated by "innumerable demons" and this corresponds perfectly with the biblical fact: "the spiritual forces of wickedness on high" (Eph 6:12), in the air (Eph 2:2), between the earth and the abode of God "the devil and with him his angels were cast down to earch" (Rv 12:9). So we understood, if we recall, too, that devils appear in Scripture under the likeness of serpents, lions, dragons, frogs (1 Pt 5:5; Rv 12:3; 15:13,14), that Saint Ignatius could intend to mean these demons among which the human composite is exiled, in this valley of "misery" (V) under the simile of irrational animals. Have not the devils, by the corruption of their rebellion and by their fall, fallen below irrational animals? The Christian, who, as a consequence of original sin is condemned to associate here below with demons, can then apply to himself what Plato says: "Like a man fallen among wild beasts in whose rages he refuses to take part" (*Republic* Bk. VI, 496, d.). And as sinners often are the willing tools of the diabolical temptations of others, the simile applies perfectly to them.

12. *Cf.* Ex. 50: "*angeli creati primum in statu gratiae, quod necesse erat ad beatitudinis consummationem*" (Vulg.); ST, I.62.3; Saint Augustine, "*De Civitate Dei*", XII. 9, ML, 41, 357 quoted by Saint Thomas: "*simul in eis condens naturam et largiens gratiam.*"

13. ST, I, 62.3.3.

14. ST, I, 63.3; *cf.* J. Maritain, "Le péché de l'Ange: essai de réinterpretation des positions thomistes," *Revue Thomiste,* 56, (1956) 197–239; Philippe de la Trinité, OCD, "Du péché de Satan et de la destinée de l'esprit d'après saint Thomas d'Aquin," *Et. Carm.* 27 (1948) 44–85.

15. Eccl. 10, 15; ST, I.II.84.3; 77.4.

16. Paul VI. "Credo of the People of God," *Doc. Cath.* 65 (1968) 1254. Prior to this Paul VI had stated precisely in regard to evolution, in his allocution of July 11, 1966: "The theory of evolution will not seem acceptable to you when it does not consider as decisive for the destiny of mankind the disobedience of Adam, the universal first parent" (AAS 58 (1966) 654; *cf.* DS, 3897; GS, 13 and 22.). The magisterium of the Church continues expressing itself in a monogenistic language (just as does the Ignatian meditation on the triple sin), but without closing its eyes to the questions brought up by scientific findings. (E. Dhanis, S.J., *Supplément au Nouveau Catechisme,* p. 22). It would, then, be not at all impossible to explain the second point of the Ignatian meditation on the triple sin in the context of a polygenistic theology, but it is not necessary to do so, on the one hand because polygenism is not proven, and on the other because the Church continues to profess monogenism, for serious reasons. Furthermore, dogmatic-moral monogenism (Adam the sinner recapitulating mankind) is compatible with a biological polygenism: human generation is specified not by its origin, but by its term (*cf.* Philippe de la Trinité, OCD, *Doctor Communis* 21 (1968), 357).

17. "The common holding in the Church has always been that Adam received from God forgiveness of his fault and never again fell into the state of sin: Irenaeus, *Adversus Haereses* III.23; Jerome, *in Ps. 98;* Aug. *Epist. 164.*3: ML 33,711; *cf.* Wis 10:1; the Greek Church publicly venerates Adam and Eve and celebrates their feast on December 19; E. Palis, *Dictionnaire de la Bible* (Vigouroux), vol. I (1895) 177 art. "Adam." There was question there even of an important point for Irenaeus and other fathers who wished to underline thus, against the Gnostics, that the God of the New Testament is the same as the good Creator of the world.

18. The expression is in the singular and seems to assume that in the eyes of Ignatius original sin was committed jointly by a morally one act, although physically and ontologically a double act of our first parents. Father Dhanis observes: "Scholastic theologians have quite generally understood that Adam alone lost original justice for himself and for all his descendants" (*op. cit.* pp. 19,20). Many recent theologians, however accept the position which Saint Ignatius seems to have taken already (*ibid*). Father De Letter, S.J., however, has shown that Saint Thomas Aquinas' position (and apparently that of Paul VI in the Credo which does not mention Eve: *cf.* text cited in note 16), is not the result of an outdated view of the passive role of the woman in generation, but of a more profound view of the universal causality of Adam as the head and source of human nature (I.II.81.5); *Irish Theological Quarterly,* 29 (1957) 342, 343: the transmission of original sin. Saint Ignatius' expression can be reconciled with this view.

19. Saint Catherine of Siena, *Dialogue,* ch. 13, vol. I, p. 52, ed. Hurtaud, 1913.

20. Here is the exact text of the African Doctor: "*Omnis autem homo Adam, sicut in his qui crediderunt, omnis homo Christus, quia sunt membra Christi*" (*In Ps. 70,* sermo 2 #1: ML 36, 891). His thought becomes clearer in the light of this other text: "In the history of two men, one of whom sold us to sin and the other ransomed us from sin, one of whom ruined us in himself by doing his own will and not that of his Creator and the other saved us in himself, by doing not his own will but that of him who sent him: in the history of these two' men Christian faith consists" (*Liber de Peccato originali,* 24,28: ML, 44, 598).

21. "Take on your shoulders the sins of men. In fact, my friend, as soon as you answer sincerely for everyone and everything, you will see right away that it is often so, that you are to blame for everyone and for everything." Words spoken by the Staretz Zosime, in *The Brothers Karamazov.* For Dostoievski such is the means of salvation: "There is

only one means of salvation. Take on your shoulders the sins of men" (*ibid.*). Nicholas Berdiaieff expresses this in the same way in "*Un Nouveau Moyen Age*", Paris 1927, p. 186: "Bolshevism is my sin, my fault."

22. B. de Margerie, S.J., *Christ for the World,* esp. pp. 292-293. This concept is distinct from that of the "sin of the world."

23. Cf. SCG III, 61; II, 55; 79; GS 10; 76§3.

24. *cf. The letter of Saint Ignatius to Saint Francis Borgia, of January 5,* 1555, MI, Epp. VIII, 253; *Exercitia Spiritualia,* MHSJ, vol 100, Rome, 1969, pp. 137-139.

25. Cf. G. Fessard, S.J., *La dialectique des Exercices spirituels,* Paris, 1966, vol. II, pp. 99-103. The author in bringing this point to our attention seems to minimize the importance of the evolution of the Ignatian expression treated here. *Cf.* Ch. IV, note 31.

26. W. De Broucker, S.J., "La première semaine des Exercices," *Christus.* 6 (1956) 29. We have modified the author's thought in citing him, utilizing restrictions expressed by the words in parentheses. Instead of opposing, as he seems to do, his new insight to the ancient interpretation, we have preferred to complete that old interpretation by the new one.

27. *Cf.* Philippe de la Trinité, OCD, *What is Redemption,* New York, 1961, pp. 72-73: "in the strict sense of the term, the cause of Christ's death is not sin. His own, non-existent, or ours. The cause of his death is his love, on the occasion of our sins, love of his Father and for us. *Cf.* Saint Thomas Aquinas, *In Jo.* 14, lectio 8 (Marietti) nn. 1947-1976. . .Sin could not cause directly, it could only occasion the Savior's death. Yet it can rightly be said and preached that Christ died because of our sins: only an indirect causality of an occasion" (*ibid.* pp. 57,58, n. 16).

28. Ex. 53: "I shall reflect upon myself"; "*considerando meipsum*" (Aut, P2); GS, 22.

29. Gn 2:17; 3,4 Would it not be a way of eating of the fatal fruit of the tree of knowledge of good and evil, to read exclusively modern philosophers without bothering to discern them in the light of "the philosophical patrimony ever valid" (*innixi patrimonio philosophico perenniter valido*)? This perennial philosophy truly can refute the errors uncovered in their very roots, according to the directives of Vatican II (OT, 15). Such an exclusive reading would take away even the possibility of such discernment, and of· such recourse to the "ever valid patrimony." The Holy Spirit, on the other hand, inclines us, by the Church, to nourish ourselves along with her on the doctrine of Saint Thomas Aquinas (DS, 3139, 3140, 3665).

30. Saint Irenaeus seems to suggest this, *Adversus Haereses,* III.23.

31. *Cf.* 2, Thes 2:7: we have been inspired here by M. J. Scheeben, *The Mysteries of Christianity,* St. Louis, 1958, ch. XI, #49.

32. Saint John of the Cross, "Prayer of the enamoured soul," *Maxims.*

33. *Cf.* text quoted in note 7.

34. None of our satisfactions would suffice of itself or apart from that of Christ; *cf.* Pius XI, *Miserentissimus Redemptor,* AAS, 20 (1928) 170. But in Him, our satisfactions become really satisfying: "But no creative power of men was sufficient for expiating crimes unless the Son of God took on human nature" (*cf.* ST, III.1.2.2).

35. *Cf.* Gn 3:7; Fessard, *Dialectique,* II, p. 97; E. Haulotte, S.J., *Symbolique du vêtement selon la Bible,* Paris, 1966, p. 188: "Vesting. . .afirms the dignity of fallen man and the possibility he still has of re-vesting himself in the glory of God which he has, from his origins, compromised." The text here, (Gn 3:21) should be clarified and understood (*sensus plenior*) in the light of the Pauline concept of "putting on Christ," (Rom 13:14; Col 3:10; Eph 4:24); *cf.* on this subject Haulotte (*op. cit.* pp. 210-20). This is why we say

"Clothe me in your passion." We cannot put on the new man Jesus, unless we take off the old man, crucifying him.

36. Saint Ignatius, by the` word *"trabajos"* (Ex. 51. labors, Autog.; c. 93,95), has in mind at the same time the difficult tasks undertaken for the glory of God and also the sufferings, which result from them. On emphasizing that Adam and Eve lived their whole lives without the original justice they had lost (Ex. 51, "for the rest of their lives, they lived without it in many labors and great penances"), the translation does not bring out the ambivalence of the Spanish term.), he evokes Gn 3:16-20; 5:5. His twofold allusion to Adam and Eve's penitence (Ex. 51), shows that he too had received the patristic tradition about Adam's salvation salvation doubtless by way of Ludolph the Carthusian. *Cf*. Fessard, *Dialectique*, vol. III, p. 97.

38. We are attempting to express here what Ignatius recommends in Ex. 54, 61: "I will conclude with a colloquy, extolling the mercy of God our Lord, pouring out my thoughts to him, and giving thanks to him that up to this very moment he has granted me life. I will resolve with his grace to amend for the future. Close with an Our Father." The final sentence indicates that God our Lord does not mean Christ but the Father despite the contary opinion of Fessard, *Dialectique*, vol. II, p. 28, n. 1.

39. *cf*. Jn 14:12-14: in Biblical language (Sermon on the Mount) as well as in patristic and Ignatian, the labors of a long life of penitence comprise prayer, fasting, almsgiving, which re-establishes a Christlike contact of men with God, with his body and with the material world, the neighbor (*cf*. Ex. 210-17; 337-44).

40. DS, 1677; SCG, IV.72 at end, where the Common Doctor states precisely that grace is more abundantly received when there is sacramental absolution. It may be concluded— and this is not without importance—that the penitent who makes the Exercises of the first week is already washed in the Blood of Christ, already receives sacramental graces of penance in the course of these meditations, the fruit of which is thus "sacramentalized."

41. *Cf*. ST, III.86.4.2.3; Supplement, 5.2. Perfect contrition preserves us from purgatory.

42. This word "meritorious," as well as the words "merit," "to merit," which the Council of Trent definitively introduced into the language of Catholic theology, is often found under the pen of the author of the Exercises: 14, 15, 20 b, 33,34,40,44. Vatican II has retained it and used it often (*v.g*. LG, 41,48,49).

43. The enigmatic formula of Saint Ignatius, "and see the loathesomeness and malice which every mortal sin I have committed has in itself, even though it were not forbidden" (Ex. 57), is explained in the light of ST, I.II.71.6.4. Saint Ignatius means "even if it were not forbidden by a *positive* law," and was still forbidden by the natural law. (It is well, although sometimes the opposite is said, to emphasize that Vatican II expressly had recourse to the concept of the natural law in GS 89.) *Cf*. on this point, L. Teixidor, "El punto segundo del segundo exercicio," *Manresa* 11 (1935) 317-26.

44. *cf*. Dn 7:10, "thousands of thousands ministered to him, and ten thousand times a hundred thousand stood before him"; it is reasonable to suppose that immaterial substances are almost incomparably more numerous than material substances, and a fortiori than man!; Fessard, *Dialectique*, vol. II, p. 113: "For Ignatius, the angels are at least as numerous as the men of all times, since each individual has a guardian angel. Perhaps they form in his eyes a countless multitude corresponding to the divine ideas."

45. As in an inverse sense, the elect sees God in the bosom of the Beatific Vision, "*totum sed non totaliter*" (ST, I.12.7.3.); So, differing from Lutheranism, the Church has never accepted the idea of a total corruption of human nature by original sin. *Cf*. ST, I.II.85.1; GS, 15,17.

46. Hugo Rahner, *Saint Ignatius Loyola: Letters to Women* (Eng. transl. Herder and Herder, 1960), p. 176; cf. ST, II.II.161.3.2.6, on humility.

47. The expression "bring together" a propos of divine perfections" recalls ST, 1.13. 4.3.

48. *Cf.* ST, II.II.25.7: "*ea quae sunt multipliciter et divisim in aliis, in ipso sunt simpliciter et unita.*"

49. An expression of Fessard, *Dialectique,* II, p. 120.

50. "*Nemo habet de suo nisi peccatum et mendacium.*" Augustine, *ad Jn.* 1,33: ML 35, 1414; DS 392. As the note indicates, this sentence, "*crux theologorum,*" should be clarified in the light of the Church's condemnation of various Jansenist propositions (DS.2307, 2311,2439ff.).

51. *Cf.* ST, I.12.12; 13.8.2; commentaries on the Divine Names by Denys, Bk VII, ch. 4, Marietti, Rome, 1950, #727-733; pp. 274,275 ("*hoc ipsum est Deum cognoscere quod nos scimus nos ignorare de Deo quid sit.*")

52. Letter to Theresa Rejadella, October 1947, Rahner, p. 342. *op. cit.*

53. *Ibid.*

54. We have made the passage in which Saint Ignatius uses the third person into a direct address.

55. We are inspired here by the "prayer from the Kingdom" (Ex. 98).

56. *Cf.* Vulgate 60: "*debitae vindictae loco,*" This phrase is not found in the Autog. nor in P2, (nor in Puhl). It is a wholly Biblical concept (*cf.* Wis 5:17–22; 11:17; 16:24; 19:6: 1 Thes 4:7).

57. Here again the Vulgate is more exact than the Autograph. It reads "a thousand" while the Autograph has "new" hells.

58. Clorivierè, *Notes Intiones,* t. 2, p. 38.

59. Vulg. 63 (instead of "sins" as in Autograph and P2, as in Puhl).

60. Laynez, J., S.J., Institutio scholaris christiani, *Disputationes Tridentinae,* Oeniponti, Rauch 1886, vol. II, p. 448.

61. Inspired by Fessard, *Dialectique,* vol II, pp. 50-52.

62. L. Bouyer, "Les deux économies du gouvernement divin: Satan et le Christ," *Initiation Théologique,* collective work published by Cerf, Paris, 1952, vol. II, 523.

63. *Ibid.* p. 507.

64. L. Teixidor, El desorden de mis operaciones, *Manresa* 4 (1928) 99.

65. ST, I.II.82.3.

66. ST, I.II.89.3.

67. Saint Augustine, *Sermo 151:* ML, 38, 814; *Sermo 154;* ML, 38, 837; Saint Thomas Aquinas, *Commentary on the Epistle to the Colossians,* ch. 3, lectio 1. On Col 3:5; "Therefore mortify your members which are on earth." *cf.* Teixidor, *art. cit.* 63.

68. DS, 1515.

69. *Cf.* Leo Scheffczyk, *Sacramentum Mundi,* art. "Concupiscence," vol. I. p. 404, N.Y., 1968.

70. *Ibid.*

71. DS, 1515.

72. GS, 13,2. To be noted is the parallelism with Ex. 74. "As though he is bound by chains" (GS); "loaded with chains" (Ex.).

73. L. Bouyer, *op. cit.*, note 57, pp. 523–25, has assembled these texts. We have modified their translation following the Jerusalem Bible.

74. L. Bouyer, *op.cit.* pp. 507–8; *cf.* J. Bonsirven, *Les enseignements de Jésus-Christ,* Paris, 1945, p. 94, note 3: the Joannine and Pauline "world" is close to the actual "*eon*," "this century," which designates the ensemble of earthly goods in as much as they turn us away from the Kingdom of God, the present kingdom of Satan as opposed to the future Kingdom of God. *Cf.* on this subject B. de Margerie, S.J., CFW, p. 172.

75. *Cf.* L. Bouyer, *op. cit.* pp. 507–8.

76. Hugo Rahner, S.J., *Ignatius the Theologian,* N.Y., 1968, pp. 121,122.

77. *Cf.* E. Piacentini, O.F.M. Conv., "Maternita divina e spiruale nel pensiero mariologico del P. Kolbe," *Marian Library Studies* 2 (1970) 41–44; G. Croisignani, *Divus Thomas* (Pl.) 57 (1954) 409–21. These texts explain the theological import of the words of Mary at Lourdes: "I am the Immaculate Conception." We note on this subject that Saint Ignatius was personally favorable to the Immaculate Conception but wanted to avoid controversies with the Dominicans. *Cf.* MHSJ, vol. 73, Rome 1951, p. 499.

78. *Cf.* P2.: "*Meipsum odio habens, corrigar et me ordinem.*" The various manuscripts of the Autograph do not carry the text in the same way. Some read: "hate myself." while another (followed by Father Courel in his translation) omits the pronoun which comes after the participle "*aborreciendome.*" It is however, the first recension which seems the most probable and understandable in the context. It responds perfectly to Luke 14:26. The Vulgate has preferred to soften it.

79. Saint Catherine of Siena, *Letter 30.*

80. *Cf.* L. Lallemant, S.J., *Doctrine spirituelle,* III, ch. I, art 3, #4, Paris, 1959, p. 141.

81. *Cf.* Zec 12:10, "And I will pour out upon the house of David, and upon the inhabitants of Jerusalem, the spirit of grace, and of prayers, and they shall look upon me, whom they have pierced; and shall mourn for him as one mourneth for an only son." Acts 2:37, "They were pierced to the heart." The theme of compunction is most prominent in patristic spirituality to which corresponds the first week of the Exercises. We were inspired here by Saint Fulgentius (*Epist. 4, to Proba,* ML, 65, 339–44); Isidore of Seville, *Sententiae* II,12 (ML, 83,613); Saint Gregory the Great, *Dial.* III,34 (ML, 77.300); *Moralia* XXIII, 22.41 (ML 76,276); *cf.* Puyol, *Doctrine du Livre De Imitatione Christi,* Paris, 1898, p. 489.

82. *cf.* DS. 392; J. Calveras, S.J. analyses the very interesting role of tears in the Exercises (*Manresa* 8, 1932, 15-18).

4

HELL

Hell is a difficult subject so it is well to recall some data of theology before entering into dialogue with Christ crucified, as Saint Ignatius counsels, on the subject of hell.

A. A Truth Revealed for Our Salvation.

We are writing for believers so we have no need of refuting current objections against hell, nor do we intend to start our discussion from the data of moral conscience for demonstrating rationally the necessity of an eternal punishment of an immortal and rebellious soul, which nonetheless is a profound approach, poles apart from sentimental denials of hell.

We prefer to start with the teachings of Jesus Christ, our Savior, and so intend to establish the importance of hell in the economy of Christian revelation. This we shall do briefly.

Jesus speaks to us about hell sixteen times in the Gospels. He calls it the fire of gehenna (Mt 5:22;cf. Lv 18:21); he speaks of going into hell's unquenchable fire, where the worm dies not, and the fire is not extinguished (Mk 9:42-49); he gives his friends the formal commandment to fear his and their God who can condemn to hell (Lk 12:4,5).

Jesus, meek and humble of heart (Mt 11:29), Jesus who will not extinguish the smoking flax (Mt 12:20), calls the Scribes and Pharisees, sons of hell and asks them how they will flee from the judgment of hell (Mt 23:15,33).

Jesus tells us what the punishments of hell are. He says there will be weeping and wailing and gnashing of teeth; he speaks at the same time of darkness and torments in the flames of hell (Lk13:28; Mt 25:30; Lk 16:24; Mt 5:22). The torments are not the same for all. They will be more tolerable for the land of Sodom than for Jewish unbelievers (Mt 10:15). The punishment will be eternal; "eternal fire, eternal punishment, unquenchable fire" (Mt 18:8; 25:41; Mk 9:42-49). It were better not to be born than suffer

59

this punishment (Mk 14:21); a punishment in keeping with an eternal and impardonable sin against the Holy Spirit.[1]

Christ's remarks on hell are not only in the synoptics but also in the Gospel of Saint John. There Christ warns us: "They that have done evil, shall (come forth) into the resurrection of judgment" (Jn 5:29). Jesus presents hell as a chastisement not only for the soul but also for the body.

There are few points on which the Revealer and Redeemer has insisted so much. Could he show us a greater love than by these many warnings intended to help us work out, in fear and trembling, out eternal salvation (Phil-2:12)? He who has seen and knows, cannot help but tell what he has seen and what he knows about the peril we run. The revelation about hell, confirming and making clearer the light of natural reason, is, together with that of the Eucharist (Jn 6:53) to which it is linked, a sign, in a supreme sense, of the salvific love of Christ Jesus for sinful mankind, for each one of us.

It is a revelation the purpose of which is our preservation.

Catholic theologians in explaining this salvific revelation distinguish two aspects of the punishment meted out to the damned: the "pain of sense" inflicted on the damned by creatures, and the "pain of loss," the loss of God. The first responds to the "material" element of every sin, that is, the inordinate turning to the created world that it implies; while the second responds to the "formal" element, namely the turning away from uncreated good, God.

Maritain, philsopher, theologian, mystic, has described in somber splendor the drama of the pain of loss.

"The will of the damned is rent. Supernatural beatitude is the unique term by which and in which its natural ordering to God can be satisfied. It has become for the soul a good called for by its whole being, a *bonum debitum*, ontologically due, not morally, we may be sure. It is a good, the absence of which is a deprivation, the worst of all deprivations.

"Yet, at the same time it detests God by a free act in which the will is fixed and prefers over true beatitude the false beatitude it has, in its pride, chosen. There is the soul's last end, willed above all else, even at the cost of all kinds of sufferings and privations: to be a god by its own powers. It cannot revoke this choice, for that one choice involves the last end and has been made in full spiritual light, in such wise that all subsequent acts of willing will be carried out only by virtue of that act. A rending, therefore, without repentance.

"Thus eternal justice must be designated, if we look for human comparisons, less as the mysterious wrath than as the mysterious patience of God who permits his mercy to be finally rejected so that a creature forever and by its own free choice be its own god."[2]

The damned wants to be a god without God and against God while never ceasing to desire to see him.

For each human person, hell just as mortal sin and pride is a real possiblity. For me also it would be even the sole possibility had I been left to the weakness of my own powers alone.

This is what Saint Theresa of Avila, Doctor of the Church, understood and described[3] for us, in her *Autobiography*, in her "vision of hell".

"All of a sudden I found myself wholly transported to hell. The Lord wanted to show me the place the demons had prepared for me there and which I had deserved for my sins.

"I felt fire in my soul, the nature of which I am powerless to describe, while my body underwent unbearable torments . . . I saw this torment was to last forever without interruption. My soul was depressed, in anguish, inflicted with excruciating pain, a pain so desperate and deeply imbedded that I could not express what it was. If I say they constantly tear your soul apart it is an understatement. Here the soul itself is the one that rends itself. I felt myself burning and cutting myself into pieces. What is most frightful, I repeat, is this inner fire and this despair of the soul."

So the Saint experienced the interior rending (mentioned by Maritain) in her soul, and, at the same time extreme physical torments: a momentary anticipation of the two fold eternal pain of loss and of the senses in which, without preventive grace, she would have fallen.

In contrast to the saints, most men, believers and even fervent ones, are more sensitive to corporal than to spiritual evils. We are more afraid of corporal pain than of spiritual. The pain that deprives us of the greatest good (the disorder of the soul, loss of virtue or of the enjoyment of the divine vision, supreme happiness of man) affects us less than external and corporal injuries. Do we not think spontaneously that the sins of men remain unpunished here below because we do not perceive that God, granting them external goods refused to the just, abandons them, as a punishment, to new[4] sins?

These remarks by Saint Thomas Aquinas help us grasp better what Saint Ignatius' reasons are for requiring the retreatant to meditate on the pains of sense, or, if preferred, of the senses.

As the solemn affirmations of Vatican II show in its dogmatic Constitution on the Church[5], such a meditation is not less beneficial today now that the revealed truth of an eternal hell, seems so dangerously denied by so many Christians.

B. *Meditation and contemplation*[6] *on Hell*

This meditation, after the preparatory prayer "as usual" (Ex. 65), is made up of two preludes, five points and a colloquy (or dialogue).[7]

The first prelude is a "composition of place".[8] Here we are "to see in imagination the length, breadth and depth of hell" (Ex. 55). Hell is vast, many men, almost countless, are burning there perhaps (Ex. 53, Vulg.) for sins less numerous and less serious than mine, not to say because of mine.[9] This length, breadth and depth of the hatred of hell corresponds inversely to the length, breadth, height and depth of Christ's love which surpasses all understanding and which the damned have criminally despised and rejected (Eph 3:18,19). It is by taking refuge and dwelling in the Heart of Jesus, our Redeemer, that we meditate and contemplate the mystery of the eternal[10] hatred of the damned for God and for us.

In a second prelude, I ask "for what I desire. Here it will be to beg for a deep sense of the pain which the lost suffer, that if through my faults I forget the love of the eternal Lord, at least the fear of these punishments will keep me from falling into sin" Ex. 65)[11]; In sin, whether it be mortal or venial, which can indirectly lead to hell, by weakening the will before temptations to serious faults.

"Lord, grant me this habitual fear—were it not habitual how could it be actual, spring up at the moment of temptation?—an habitual fear of hell capable of preventing me from falling into "eternal sin" (Mt 12:32), into the unforgiveable sin of final impenitence, the sanction for temporary but prolonged impenitences against the Holy Spirit. Did you not give me the gifts of your Spirit and was not one of them the gift of fear?[12] fear to prevent me from sinning against him? How would I not cultivate through "servile" fear, the filial fear of offending you, and of becoming, in my own eyes, the last end of my own actions and of endeavoring to reduce others to being just means ordained to my actions?[13] Grant me, Lord, by fearing to be separated from you and punished by you, to remain in your love and to remember thus your eternal love for me.[14]

Do not imperfections, especially deliberate venial sins, bring about forgetfulness of the love of predilection of your Heart toward me? Have they not already produced it in me? Has not such forgetfulness already resulted in the cooling of my love for you? You have saved so many saints through this meditation and this contemplation of eternal hell; will you not grant me the same grace?"

After the two preludes come the five points of the meditation, contemplation proposed by Saint Ignatius. They consist in seeing, hearing, smelling, tasting become souls encased, as it were, in bodies of fire (Ex. 66–70), wailing, howling, blaspheming in the remorse and filth of a corrupt conscience (Ibid.).

Must it not be feared that the poisonous abcess of my sinful personality (Ex. 58) become an eternal filthy sewer in hell?

Have I not, at least remotely and indirectly, deserved by the evil use of my eyes, ears, sense of smell, taste and touch, the endless burning of these senses? Has not my soul deserved to be forever incarcerated in a body, not only corruptible but definitely corrupted by it (Ex. 47), as in a prison of fire? Have I not deserved to weep forever by my lack of tears,[15] my impenitence?

The damned have confirmed themselves in mental blasphemy, in vocal blasphemy after their resurrection, against Christ and against all his saints,[16] in blasphemy which will go on forever. Their will is fixed in detestation of the divine goodness,[17] and this is sin in its very essence.[18]

Also the flames envelop and burn their souls filled with hate (Ex. 70). The fire of hell owes its origin to, and is fed by, the patient and ever loving anger of God. It tortures directly the spirits which it will burn endlessly, without ever destroying or enlightening its victims, but plunging them into darkness.[19]

To see with the eyes, not only of the imagination but much more with those of faith, the vast fires of hell; to hear with faith the word of Christ about hell; to feel and taste the sadness, the remorse, the despair of the damned; conversely to taste the immense mercy which has spared me up to now and which makes me meditate on hell in order to make me hope to escape it forever; to touch and to love the devouring fire of divine love present in the depths of my soul for its purification, for detaching it and fixing it in that love.[20]

Here then I begin the colloquy (Ex. 71) of my soul with Christ, its Lord. "I recall to memory that of those who are in hell, some came there because they did not believe in the coming of Christ; others, though they believed, because they did not keep the Commandments."[21]

Those who have been condemned were finally damned, either for not having subjected their intellect to the authority of God, the revealer, or for not having subjected their wills and their bodies to the authority of God, orderer and supreme end of the universe. In both cases, they have been condemned because they have refused to submit to and to serve their Creator (Ex. 23), and all this, indirectly through my fault.[22]

I must believe, fear, flee from and announce hell. If I feared hell would I not speak of it and would I not help thereby others, at the same time as myself, not to fall into it?

"Lord Jesus, deign through me, to continue speaking of hell, of its fire and its tears, to my contemporaries, as you spoke of it to yours. Through my lips, I beg you, present salvation against the background of the threat of hell. Is not hell fearfully possible for each one? Should not the Christian apostle help his brothers descend alive by meditation and contemplation into the shadows of hell, so they might avoid sin which would bring them there after death? And if you have spoken of hell at least as much as about baptism and the Eucharist, why should I be silent on this subject?

The mouth speaks out of the abundance of the heart. If I sincerely desire to save myself from eternal hell, will I not speak of it? If I keep silent, is my desire sincere, profound, entire? Ought I not then ask others what they know, believe, fear about hell, its nature, its duration?

"Jesus, my Savior, I thank you for not having let me fall into hell neither before your coming; nor during your lifetime, nor after your resurrection, in the time of the Church.[23] My survival, outside of hell, is a permanent and extraordinary sign of your mercy and of your predilection for me.

"Plunge me deeper and deeper into the flames of your divine Heart's love that I may thus never forget this eternal love and, consequently, avoid hell. Grant me, Lord, the holy fear of forgetting your love. Do not permit me to be separated from you: *"ne permittas me separari a te"*. [24] Would not hell be the wilful and despairing, contemptuous forgetfulness for all eternity of your eternal love for me?

"Lord Jesus, I believe that you have manifested your friendship (*cf.* Lk-12:4) by revealing to me the existence of hell and its possibility for me and above all in dying to snatch me away from it and to safeguard me from it, as you have done up to now.

"I hope, by the merits of your precious, redeeming Blood, for the efficacious grace of repentance and conversion by which you will safeguard me for the future. [25]

"I love above all your will to save me. As a token of my gratitude to you, I will explain to others the hell of the past—which we have escaped—, the hell of the present—that of the devils and the damned—, the hell of the future—that which threatens us and which we hope to avoid. I will announce to all, believers and unbelievers, following your example (Mk 16:16), the mystery of your justice manifested in hell. Your justice and your anger are really one with your patience and your love, in the infinite simplicity of the Divinity.

"Your cross obstructs and closes the long and broad way which leads to the lake of fire and sulphur. You draw all to you. You open up constantly the narrow gate of salvation to men, ever numerous, who cast themselves into hell and to eternal hate. This narrow gate is your transpierced Heart.

"You have ever had for me, purulent and poisonous abcess, such great pity and mercy! I do not refuse to be punished. Chastise me, my Savior, either by sorrow or confusion, or by the loss of all I love, or, if you so wish, by all evils at once. But do not punish my sins through other sins, my slight faults through grave ones. I only fear from your justice this kind of punishment, all others seem to me to come from your mercy." [26]

"Immaculate Virgin, Mother of Jesus, conscious of having been preserved from sin and hell by the mercy of your Son and Redeemer, preserve me, your son, from hell, [27] helping me announce its mystery and that of the judgment of your Son, the judgment of the living and the dead. Pray for us, now and at the hour of our death. Obtain for us the grace of continual and final repentance."

"Holy Spirit, Spirit of love, you will the eternal salvation of all men. Make us understand that the most bitter regret of the damned is not to have loved. [28] Hell is the work of human and angelic hate rather than of divine love. [29] If after all you condemn obstinate sinners who reject your love, it is still out of love. You have chosen among possible worlds, ours, You have only permitted evil since it was useful for saving the elect. For many of Your elect and of your saints, eternal hell has been the powerful and definitively efficacious stimulus of their salvation and of their holiness. It is ever an occasioñ of grateful joy and of love. [30]

"If, after sin, heaven can no longer be entered without doing violence to oneself, after Jesus Christ, that is, basically, always, it is no longer possible to go down to hell without doing violence to God." [31]

NOTES ON CHAPTER FOUR

1. Cf. Bartmann, *Précis de théologie dogmatique,* vol. II, #213, pp. 518,519.

2. J. Maritain, *Neuf leçons sur les premiers principes de la philosophie morale,* Paris, 1951, pp. 189,190.

3. Saint Theresa of Avila, *La vida de la Madre Teresa de Jesus* (Biblioteca Romanica) 306,307.

4. SCG, III.141. Saint Ignatius himself was one of the saints whose virtue had rendered him relatively insensitive to the pain of sense since he had become so sensitive to the pain of loss. Actually he confides to us in his spiritual diary (March 7, 1544) these thoughts: "If God should put me in hell. . .I distinguished two things: one, the suffering I would undergo there; the second, how his name is blasphemed there. As to the first pain I could not feel the pain I would suffer there, and so it seemed and it appeared to be more upsetting to me to hear his most Holy Name blasphemed" (*Obras completas,* S. Ignacio de Loyola, BAC, Madrid, 1963).

5. GS, 48.

6. It is of interest to note, apropos of Ex. 65, that the Autograph and P2 entitle the fifth exercise of the first week: "Meditation on the subject of hell" while the Vulgate entitles it "Contemplation." Some see in this exercise an "application of the senses." They might invoke in this sense Ex. 122, where the meditation and contemplation are seen associated, in this category, precisely of an application of the senses. Cf. for the opposing view, H. Coothalen, S.J., *Commentaire du livre des Exercices,* Paris, 1965, p. 135.

7. Ex. 65. The term "colloquy" may be translated by dialogue, since both words imply reciprocity in verbal exchange. The word we address to God always consists in a response to the word God addresses to us by His Revelation and by His Church. If that be not admitted, the Ignatian concept of colloquy is unintelligible.

8. Cf. T. Barreira, "La composicion de lugar. Explicacion de la misma segun la doctrina de Santo Tomas," *Manresa,* 11 (1936) 158–68.

9. cf. our Ch. III, notes 21 and 22.

10. We give here the word "eternal" a sense found in the expression "eternal life," used in regard to the elect, and which signifies an endless duration, although one with a beginning.

11. Ex. 65; cf. Ex. 370. The Church at the Council of Trent (DS, 1526,1558), solemnly condemned the theses according to which the fear of hell is a sin. She sees in servile fear, on the contrary, a directing by divine pedagogy toward the filial fear of God, a fear solely of offending Him. We note also that the comparison between Ex. 65 and Ex. 70 confirms there is not question here first of all of the love of the Lord for us but rather of the love we should have for Him.

12. ST, II.II.19.4 and 6.

13. *Cf.* ST, I.II.84.1 and 2.

14. If the Christian does not exercise himself in love of God, he comes little by little to forget the love which God has for him, since one forgets gradually what one no longer thinks of, what one no longer loves.

15. Ex. 69 evokes in an evangelical way the eternal tears of hell (*cf.* Lk 13:28). This text signifies that if we do not wish to weep here below for our sins—the grace asked for by Ex. 55—we risk weeping for them forever.

16. *cf.* Ex. 67.

17. *cf.* ST, II.II.13.1.3.4.

18. ST, Suppl; 98.5: II.II.34.2.

19. *Cf.* the thoughts of Passaglia quoted by A. Michel, DTC, V. 2 (1924) 2224, art. "Feu de l'Enfer." Saint Thomas Aquinas (SCG, IV.90) shows how man, including his soul, is punished in hell by being subjected to inferior creatures with which he is closely associated, particularly fire; Scheeben has profoundly developed this point of view in the *Mysteries of Christianity*, VIII, ch. 25, #97.

20. *Cf.* our ch. II where we showed that the application of the senses is an exercise of the theological virtues (notes 30 and 31).

21. We observe, on this subject, an important explanatory statement made by the theological commission of Vatican II relative to the existence *de facto* of human persons condemned to hell. The commission judged it useless to emphasize it since the Gospel texts quoted (LG, 48) are in the future tense. C. Pozo, S.J. pointing out this fact, observes that these verbs are not in the conditional: *Teologia del más alla,* Madrid, BAC, 1968, pp. 198,199. In like manner, it may be said that the point of the colloquy proposed by Saint Ignatius is twofold: a) I can be lost within the Church despite my faith, if I do not obey the commandments of Christ and the Church; b) it is not only before the Christian era and during the earthly life of Christ that souls have been lost but also in the time of the Church.

22. *Cf.* ch. III, notes 21 and 22.

23. *Cf.* Ex. 71; our note 21.

24. invocation taken from the *Anima Christi,* so dear to Saint Ignatius and so often recommended in the Exercises.

25. We note the time element in Saint Ignatius' presentation of hell. It is future (Ex. 65: will keep me from falling); present (Ex. 66–70), past (Ex. 71: what I have escaped from up to now).

26. Thoughts inspired by Blessed Claude la Colombière, S.J., Sermon sur le péché véniel, premier point, *Oeuvres Complètes,* Grenoble, 1901, vol. IV, p. 37.

27. Mary, ransomed by Jesus (*cf.* Pius XII, *Fulgens Corona,* DS, 3909) invited the witnesses of Fatima, after their vision of hell, to repeat after each decade of the Rosary "Oh my Jesus. . .preserve us from the fire of hell and bring all souls to Heaven!" Paul VI evidently alluded to this private revelation in his exhortation *Signum Magnum,* wholly based on the public revelation of the New Testament: "Thus through love and though the design of appeasing God for the offenses against his holiness and his justice, and animated at the same time by his infinite mercy, we should bear the sufferings of the spirit and of the body in expiation of our sins and of those of our neighbor and for avoiding the two-

fold pain of loss and of the senses, that is, the loss of God, sovereign good, and eternal firs.'' The Document is of May 13, 1967, the fiftieth anniversary of an apparition of Mary at Fatima. *Cf.* AAS, 59 (1967) 473.

28. Formula of Saint Peter-Julian Eymard, who added: "Oh! I understand hell, after so great a love!''

29. Inversely, the immediate end of hell is the glorification of divine justice, and its mediate end that of other divine perfections, including the divine goodness.

30. *Cf.* Richard, DTC, V.1 (1924) 117; Saint Thomas Aquinas sees in the eternal hell of the damned an indirectly medicinal pain, intended also to promote the eternal salvation of the elect: *Supplement*, 99,1.3;94. 3; ST, I.II.87.3.2.; SCG, III, 144. He makes use of the image of the perpetual exile inflicted on the criminal for the benefit of others.

We observe that God's mercy is shown even in hell, for God does not punish the damned more but less then they deserve (ST, I.21.4.1): *"citra condignum"*.

31. *Cf.* Mgr. Charles Gay, *De la vie et vertus chrétiennes,* vol. II, Paris, 1888, p. 286. We note here with M. Richard that it "is highly probable, as many theologians think, that God does not send the sinner to hell for an isolated mortal sin, especially one due to weakness, but only does so with inveterate sinners. Besides he grants all men extraordinary graces for helping them avoid mortal sin though we cannot explain just what these helps are. So it is true to say that hell is only for the punishment of an obstinate contempt of divine love (DTC, vol. 1924, col. 116, art. "Enfer; *cf.* Lacordaire, 72nd conference of N.D., 1851: "De la sanction du gouvernment divin"). K. Rahner rightly observes: "We must maintain side by side and unhesitatingly the truth of the almighty salvific will of God, the redemption of all by Christ, and the duty of all men to hope for salvation, as well as the truth of the real possibility of eternal perdition. . .The emphasis placed on the possibility of hell should be equalled by the constant encouragment to confidently rely on the infinite mercy of God" (*Sacramentum Mundi,* ed. Eng. vol. 3, 1969, p. 8, New York).

This is what Father Garrigou-Lagrange calls "the invincible and laborious hope": invincible because it never gives in to despair; laborious, because it hopes without presumption, doing penance.

5

THE CALL OF THE ETERNAL KING
JESUS, FOR THE ESTABLISHMENT
OF HIS KINGDOM AND
TO THE CONTEMPLATION OF HIS REIGN[1]

After the exercises of the first week, corresponding to the purgative way, Saint Ignatius lays the foundation, the meditation[2] and basic contemplation, which opens up and orients the exercises of the illuminative way, the second week of the Exercises (cf. Ex. 10). The retreatant is invited to construct on the mystery of Jesus establishing his Kingdom and his reign the edifice of his acquired cardinal and moral virtues (cf. Ex. 327), in view of freely exercising, under the inspiration of the Holy Spirit, the theological virtues (ibid.), in the unitive way of the third and fourth weeks. Through Christ the way, and the light, to Christ the life; through the man Jesus to the Eternal Word, to the Father and to their Spirit.

We shall describe here, first, the basic aim of the contemplation on the eternal king, next we will engage in a contemplation of this call, this eternal king, his reign which will never end.

A. The Plan of the Kingdom

Hugo Rahner has admirably summed up in a single sentence the plan of the perfect "ordering of life" and so the aim of the Exercises, in the light of the contemplation on the Kingdom and the meditation on the two standards:

"Man is created to be able, in reverent service of the Holy Trinity, by likeness to Jesus crucified, to wage successfully, in the Church militant, the good fight against Satan and so to enter into the glory of the Father".[3]

Further, the same has also summarized his thought on the core and intent of the Exercises: "service of the Church, under the standard of the cross, for the glory of the Father."[4]

Christ's combat is not over. His Church is still militant. He continues through her to combat Satan. The Christian is a combatant. His heart is a battlefield between Christ and Satan. Christ calls me to the unveiling of love by a liberating combat against myself.[5]

The contemplation of the combatant which the Basque Captain proposes to us after losing an earthly battle in the service of a temporal king, is a factor and an event in the construction by Jesus of his eternal, spiritual and transcendental Kingdom of which the unique and universal Church is the dawn.

His Kingdom is eternal. This is the fundamental difference between it and the happiness and kingdoms of this world.

His Kingdom is interior and spiritual. It does not consist essentially in external signs (fasting, prayers, works of zeal or of mercy) but in charity. To establish the Kingdom of Christ in our hearts we must banish that of the flesh and of the world. To reform our memory, intellect and will we must fashion them on the same model as the memory, intellect and will of Jesus Christ. Only the Spirit of Christ can establish in us the thoughts and feelings He has given to Christ. The Spirit acts in the same manner in the Head and in the members (cf. Rom 8:9-11). Jesus, by his Spirit, governs us in a manner at once gentle and contrary to self-love. His voice is without sound of words. He demands nothing by force. We can shirk, deceiving ourselves that he is not speaking. For hearing the soft whisper of his voice, for carrying out what he asks, without resistance, recollection in contemplation and courage of action are necessary.

His Kingdom is transcendental. For the Church transcends all the carnal kingdoms of the face of the earth. This transcendance shines out in the means employed for its establishment: the weakness, the folly, the ignominy of the cross which has a hidden force and charm. If we contemplate Jesus Christ in poverty, humiliation and suffering, he will take over our hearts, and will drive out of them every inclination and feeling not in conformity with his.[6]

This eternal and transcendant, interior and spiritual Kingdom does not fail to be also visibly inserted in space and time, visible and knowable. It is the organ and the sacrament of salvation,[7] the Church of this world, militant and in pilgrimage toward her eschatological consummation, toward her leader and spouse, under the inspiration of the Holy Spirit.

The contemplation of the Kingdom is then a contemplation of the mystery of Christ unfolding himself and prolonging himself in the Church. It invites the retreatant to an ecclesial option for Christ, but not any kind of option, but one that is for Christ as head of the Church, as king of the Kingdom of the Church. It is an option for him wholly immersed in the option of the Church, dependent on her, to the point of being an option that is Christocentric by, with and through the Church. Is not the Church constantly produced by Christ as a response to his call which is ever renewed? Might she not be designated a call ever heard?[8] Is not the ecclesial horizon the setting for the personal combat against carnal and worldly love? Has not the Christian been invited to sacrifice himself so that the mystical Body of Jesus shine out in greatest glory?[9]

Since the Church is the "beginning" Kingdom[10], the word of the call of the temporal king corresponds profoundly to the ecclesial structure of the contemplation. Though already an anticipation of the heavenly Jerusalem which in her has descended to the earth, the Church is also, like the earthly Jerusalem of the Old Testament, the Kingdom of God of which this ancient covenant borrowed the concept from the consideration of earthly kingdoms. The allegory directs us to the visibility of the Church, to her institutional nature, to the only human king "to whom all Christian leaders and all their men" owe respect and obedience," precisely because he alone has been "chosen by the hand of God our Lord" [11] to command (all) to do what is necessary for their own eternal salvation, that is, the vicar of Christ on earth, the Sovereign Pontiff. [12] Is not the Pope, in a sense, a very temporal king, very temporary, of the earthly kingdom of the Church? Popes come and go; the papacy goes on, but will finally disappear, just as will all the other sacramental structures [13] of the Church, as soon as the Son of Man, Jesus Christ our Lord, will offer the established Kingdom to His Father (1 Cor 15:24-28).

The Church of the New Testament is at once a reign, that is the exercise of an actual dominion of Christ, and his Kingdom, that is, the people over whom this dominion is exercised, the People of God made man. Just as the Church of the Old covenant, ancient Israel too, the Israel of God, the Church of Christ is to come, is eschatological.

If the Sovereign Pontiff is at one and the same time the visible instrument of the eternal reign of Christ and the temporal king of his Kingdom inserted into time and space, the allegory is in a perfect pre-established harmony with the special service of the papacy for the greatest glory of Christ, to whom quite a few years later, Saint Ignatius will consecrate his future society.

However, the contemplation of the Kingdom has, of course, a significance much more universal far beyond the particular instance of the Society of Jesus. It projects us onto a universally Christly and ecclesial horizon. It tells us— and we borrow the terms from Father de Grandmaison—"All men must become Christians and all Christians must become saints," [14] by obedience to the visible Church which presupposes abnegation of carnal and worldly self-love.

B. Contemplation of the Eternal King, of His Temporal Call [15] and of His Reign Which Will Endure Forever.

In the course of the first prelude, we see the place: we see in imagination the synagogues, villages, and towns where Jesus preached. [16]

Christ continues today his preaching by and in the universal Church. Always, everywhere, Christ speaks, preaches His Church and Himself. [17] The eternal Word is never silent. The Church speaks constantly in the name of Jesus. In my life, Christ "goes about preaching." The eyes of faith show him to me.

In the second prelude I ask for "the grace I desire. Here it will be to ask of our Lord the grace not to be deaf to his call, but prompt and diligent to accomplish his holy will" [18] (Ex. 91; Vulg. and P2).

"Lord Jesus, I have so often been deaf to your call, deaf to your word, to your voice which is like the voice of many waters (Rv 1:15) since it has made its own and brought together so many of its diverse echoes in the bosom of the Church. I have been dead to what you told me through your Church (Lk 10:16; Jn 14:24); deaf to your call to announce your gospel which you wish to see quoted and proclaimed; deaf to your call to abnegation and the interior life (Mt 16:24) without which no apostolate is possible. If i lived constantly in your Heart, hearkening to the only Word of the Father which you are and in which all is said by him, would I not myself become your word and your message, eternal Word, a living call of your saving love? Is it not your most holy will to make me dwell in you by the announcing of your Word crucifying for the one who pronounces as well as for the one who hears it? "He who hears my word, has life everlasting" (Jn 5:24).

Are you not ever ready to listen to the Father's voice and to transmit his commandments? The Father who has sent you, has himself commanded you what you are to say and make heard (Jn 12:49,50; 8:26). You are, face to face with your Father, the model of the obedience I owe to your call. I must contemn the voices of the flesh, of the world and of the devil so that I may be able to hear your voice speaking through your Church, in the Holy Spirit. For having listened to the world and the devil, I have become deaf to your words. Restore to me the spiritual hearing of faith (*cf.* Ex. 123).

Your most holy will wills my sanctification, wills that I participate, by the very fact of listening to your Church, in the eternal construction of that Church. Your call comes to me, first of all, through allegories of human calls, since they are really such. You call and invite me to the perfecting of your creation,[19] in view of the perfecting of your Church. Should I not first of all perfect myself?

d. The Universal Call of the Eternal King

Saint Ignatius sets each human person in the presence of all mankind on the one hand, of Christ, eternal and universal king, on the other. Christ the Lord makes a personal appeal on behalf of his reign over all other members of the human family. The Christ who is shown to us is at the same time the prophet who preaches and announces his own reign (Ex. 91,95), the priest who merits it by his sacrifice on behalf of his subjects, the eternal king who establishes as definitively his that reign announced and merited (Ex. 95 at the end).[20]

Prophet, priest and king, Christ Jesus, Son of Man, recapitulates and brings together in his Church all the men to whom he addresses his call, for as many as wish to hearken to him, to participiate in his sacrifice, to immolate themselves as victims with him, to the glory of the Father.

Each one of them is personally called to "conquer the whole world" with and under Jesus as well as for him. Each one of them is called to participate in his triple office of prophet, priest-victim, and king, for the construction and establishment of his prophetic, priestly and royal body, the Church of which all members are prophets, priests and kings.[21]

"For from him (the head) the whole body . . . derives its increase to the building up of itself in love" (Eph 4:15,16). "You, however, are a chosen race, a royal priesthood, that you may proclaim the perfections of him who has called you out of darkness into his marvellous light" (1 Pt 2:9).

Just as each human person is in solidarity responsible for all the sins of the world and for the "sin of the world,"[22] so is not each one called to exercise his salvific and co-redemptive influence to the outermost reaches of time and space? Every man is called to weave the one robe, the one prophetic, priestly and royal garment of Jesus which we call universal history.[23]

If each one ought to help each other to become aware of his universal vocation and of the irreducibly particular modalities of this vocation, if the *essential* apostolic mission to which the Lord calls me is the same for me and for anyone else (to conquer the whole world for him by offering myself with him as a victim on my daily cross), it is perfected by the labors and sufferings of my *accidental and particular* mission in the precise field of activities and passivities which his Providence assigns me. By the eucharistic sacrifice, and in it, the Christian inserts and integrates his efforts and the fruits of his accidental and particular apostolate in the universal and essential mission of Christ and of the Church.

The universally co-redeeming sacrifice: such is the meaning of the call of the eternal king, desirous of establishing his eternal Kingdom, to offer it to his Father in the Spirit (1 Cor 15:24–28).

Let us hear now the call the glorious Christ addresses today to each human person and wants to address through his Church.

"It is my will to conquer the whole world and all my enemies (Is there not in each man a hostile zone, an unfaithful zone to evangelize?) and thus to enter into the glory of my Father. Therefore, whoever wishes to join me in this enterprise must be willing to suffer with me, to labor with me, that by following me in suffering, he may follow me in glory. While eating my Flesh and drinking my Blood, he who will come with me must be contented with a nourishment, with a drink, and a garment like mine, in poverty of spirit. I will be his nourishment, his drink, his garment. He must suffer with me by day, watch with me by night, that he may share in my victory and my joy, is so much as he will have been my companion in labors and in sufferings. Such is my most just will."[24]

Before your call, Lord, each one of us asks like Thomas: "Lord, we do not know where you are going, and how can we know the way? You tell us: in the glory of my Father. Where is your Father's glory?" (*cf.* Jn 14:5). "Rabbi, where do you dwell?" (Jn 1:38). To which you answered:" Do you not believe that I am in the Father and the Father in me? (Jn 14:10). Do you not believe that I am in the Spirit and that the Holy Spirit is in me, that Spirit whom the world cannot receive, but whom you know because he dwells with you, and is in you. (*cf.* Jn 14:17). To follow me, to come with me, that means to enter into the intimacy of my relationships with the Father and the Spirit, to contemplate the Father, the Son and their Spirit. He who wishes to come with me to the bosom of my Father, to enter into his glory(into the glory which as Son I give to my Father and which I receive from him in the spiration of the Spirit, who is ours) must labor, suffer and die with me.

"But, as Word, as only Son, I dwell in you with my Father and our Spirit. We come to you constantly, and we take up our dwelling in you (*cf.* Jn 14:23). It is there that you are to follow me, unite yourself to me by the exercise of my presence, believe in me, desire to see me face to face, to love me above all else, renouncing every disordered exercises of intellect, memory and will. Follow me, come to me in yourself in the bosom of my Father. Enter into the glory hidden in you, that I may continue through you to enter into the glory of my Father, in the Spirit who is the glory of my Father as he is mine. Enter into my most holy will, distinct from and transcending every creature, unknowable by merely natural means, without grace, in many circumstances. Is it not one with my divine uncreated being, in the absolute simplicity of my eternal essence?

"Briefly, in abnegation, contemplation and apostolic action, exercise your royal priesthood of baptized, your prophetic mission of confirmed, conquer and save the world for me and for my Father, so that you may enter with me into the Father's glory, which is the Spirit, the eternal bond of love between the Father and me."[25]

e. Three Possible Responses to This Universal Call of the Eternal King

In the allegory of the temporal king, and only there, Saint Ignatius considers a refusal to respond. After the call of the eternal king, he shows us the difference between an acceptance which is at once rational and total, without mystical transport, and another type of acceptance, one which is stamped by desires which go beyond pure and simple acceptance (Ex. 94, 96–98).

We know that many men have presented, distinctly and successively, each of these three replies to the eternal king. There are not so many who live ever on the level of acceptance stamped by the Ignatian "*magis*," by the desire of a   spiritual "plus" value. And there are few indeed who live ordinarily on the level of total acceptance. Saint Ignatius himself thought that no one knows nor can know at what point he is resisting grace.[26] We can think, then, that, even without sining gravely, we very often live on the level of the first response, sometimes on that of the second, rarely on that of the third.

Often I do not accept, I have not accepted the call of the eternal king to universal sacrificial co-redemption. I have refused the request, oh King, eternal and divine, so liberal and so human (Ex. 94). I have refused to obey[27] your requests which were also demands as well, so I am worthy to be contemned, blamed by all men and regarded by them as a perverse, cowardly and lazy subject, soldier and knight.[28]

So many times, I have refused to cooperate with your universal salvific will, Lord, eternal king of all men. I have refused to save and so love my brothers. I am, therefore, worthy of their contempt and do not deserve to be loved by them.

Whatever be the trials of the task, what are they in comparison with the torments of hell which I have deserved so many times (*cf.* Ex. 50,66–71)? Light and momentary labors which will produce a store of glory, will rescue others from hell and will obtain for them eternal beatitude in heaven.[29]

Lord, you call even your enemies. Is it not astonishing that I am one of those called?[30] Am I not still in the power of your enemies—the world and the flesh which are mine. Is not my salvation impossible if I do not join with you against them? Would not a refusal be an affirmation of my captivity? Not to answer your call—would it not be also to renounce the glory you promise, that is, eternal salvation?[31]

Do not my past refusals show that, far from having judgment and reason,[32] far from using the judgment you had given me for my salvation and for your glory, I am worthless and a fool (Ex. 96;167), and that I should consider myself such, and worthy to be treated as such by others and, therefore, very unworthy of being considered, without giving any warrant for it, a fool for your glory?

I am worthy to be contemned by the whole world which I have poisoned and corrupted. Yet you persist in asking me to help you conquer it! Once deaf to your call, I am truly deserving of all today in your service. While you ever remain the same generous king, since you share in the combats of your subjects and recompense them magnificently, and while you ever remain the same humane king, since you might have been content giving orders but prefer also to invite, the better to manifest your respect for the liberty of your subjects which you constantly advance.

Lord Jesus, offer then, through me, my whole person for the co-redemptive sufferings and labors provided for me by your Father (Ex. 96).

Yet I want to love you even more, to distinguish myself in your service, eternal king and universal Lord, I wish to go against what is sensual in me, to fight against my carnal and worldly love, to make you consequently an offering of the highest price and of the highest importance and to say to you:

Supreme king and Lord of the universe, despite my very great unworthiness, yet sustained by your grace and your power, I offer myself entirely to you, and submit to your will all that is mine. I attest before your infinite goodness under the eyes of the glorious Virgin, your Mother, and all the saints of your heavenly court my intention, my desire, my firm resolve to learn how (and provided that this be for your greatest service and highest praise) to follow you as closely as I can in bearing all wrongs and adversities with a true spirit of poverty, spiritual as well as material, if it please your holy majesty to choose me and to admit me to such a state of life.[33]

Lord Jesus, you are the sign of God par excellence, the singular sign of your Father's bounty. Make of me *a* singular sign of your love for men. A singular sign of your poverty and of your redemptive Passion. Grant me the favor of not calculating risks, of not being passively led by others but rather of becoming one who sets the pace for men, unconcerned about blows and wounds. Grant me, by abnegation itself, to develop my true personality, placing all my past and all that is best in it at the service of your Church of today, for your coming into the world, to build with you not only the Church in this world, but also that of heaven, the Kingdom of pure love which will never pass away, where your mother, your saints reign with you forever.

I remember, Jesus, Son of Mary, that you wished to come here below only in manifold dependence on your mother.

Mary, your glorious mother, has been indissolubly associated by the Father in the proclamation, preparation, realization and the consequences of your coming.

Mary is for you, new Adam, a living and faithful Eve in all your labors, in all your mysteries, especially the most sorrowful.[34] So I firmly believe you will achieve only through her what you have begun through her. You will only triumph with her and only with her and by her will you reign.

You, eternal king, king of truth and love, you have laid down a condition for your universal and full reign, a condition that is indispensable and unfailing: the reign of your most holy mother.

You have put in my heart, Lord, as in that of John, of Saint Ignatius, of Margaret Mary, of Louis-Marie Grignon de Montfort, fondness toward your Mother.

You have given me to her as her child and her slave[35] of love. It is through her that you wish that I conquer and save the world for you.

Your reign, oh my queen and my Mother, will be—for the greater glory of your king, Jesus—the great thought of my life.

Come, then, Mary, hasten to reign! Reign in all hearts for subjecting them wholly to the universal Lord, your son Jesus!

Queen of the universe and queen of my heart, I surrender and give myself to you not only to be your slave but also to be the apostle of your reign.

You have suffered for me at the foot of the cross, and so have engendered me for divine life. I want to follow you in poverty and in trials in order to reign with you, and to make you reign with your son in all hearts, for the glory of the Father.

Father, I offer you my desires to overcome carnal and worldly love, to distinguish myself in your service, to imitate your Son by accepting to suffer contempt and poverty with him. I do not offer you these desires as they are in themselves but such as they are in your Son Jesus, their source of merit. They are in him better than they are in me, his member. he will present them to you as I could never do.

Spirit of the Father and of the Son confirm me in the thoughts which you have given to Jesus and to Mary by the sacramental graces of confirmation glorify in one and by one, Jesus humble and poor. Is he not the King and the Kingdom?

N. B. On the ecclesiology of Saint Ignatius cf. H. Rahner, S.J., "Esprit et Eglise: un chapitre de théologie ignatienne," *Christus,* no. 18, (1957, pp. 163-184; *cf.* the word "Iglesia" in the analytic index of *Obras completas de S. Ignacio,* BAC, 1963. For a study in depth of the contemplation on the Kingdom proposed her, G. Cusson, S.J., *Pédagogie de l'expérience spirituelle personnelle,* Paris, 1968, ch. V. pp. 202-255. The entire chapter is devoted to this contemplation and emphasizes its ecclesial nature.

NOTES ON CHAPTER FIVE

1. Saint Ignatius entitled this exercise now as "the call of an earthly king" to "help us contemplate the life of the eternal King" (Ex. 91, Autog., P2, and Puhl), now as "a contemplation of the Kingdom of Jesus Christ starting out from the allegory of the earthly king summoning his subjects to war"(Vulg.). However, we think that the call of the temporal king is already that of the eternal King. So we have tried to combine, in the title of this chapter, the advantages of both Ignatian titles. The first emphasizes the person of Jesus, while the second stresses his work, the Church.

2. We say "meditation" because the call of the earthly king, as such, and if we abstract from the call of the eternal King, which it presents, cannot be an object of contemplation, but rather of meditation. *Cf.* ch. II, note 1.

3. Hugo Rahner, S.J., *Saint Ignace de Loyola et la genèse des Exercices,* Toulouse, 1948, p. 15; *cf.* p. 82: "A reform of life," ("*ordinatio vitae*"), in likeness to God, abasing himself to the Incarnation and the death on the cross, in a combat against Satan, in the Church, to the total destruction of the kingdom founded by the enemy chieftain."

4. H. Rahner, *op. cit.,* p. 135.

5. Formula of Father Joseph Thomas, S.J.

6. *Cf.* Clorivière, Exercices de 30 jours, 1924, hors commerce, pp. 97–109; The Church, according to Vatican II, is an eternal (GS, 39) interior and spiritual (LG 8 and 5), transcendant (LG, 13). Kingdom. Ps 144 illustrates the eternity of the Kingdom of Jahweh: "Thy kingdom is a kingdom of all ages; and thy dominion endureth throughout all generations."

7. LG, 48; *cf.* LG, 8, which likens the Church to the *organ* of salvation, the holy humanity of the redeemer.

8. The word "ekklesia" means "convocation," "call."

9. *Cf*. B. de Margerie, S.J., *Christ for the World,* Chicago, 1974, 287; the entire Ch. XI.

10. LG, 3,5: "The Church . . . receives the mission to proclaim and to establish among all peoples the Kingdom of Christ and of God. She becomes on earth the initial budding forth of that kingdom." The Ignatian meditation already knows of the eschatological orientation of the Kingdom of Christ which is the Church. The present dominion of Christ is oriented toward a future fullness.

11. Ex. 92, Autog. The mention and the simile of the divine hand is no longer in the Vulg. nor in P2.

12.R. Orlandis in the course of a series of articles in the review *Cristianidad* in 1950, sees in the allegory an echo of the crusade against the Turks inspired by a bull of Leo X March 6, 1518. On the concept of Christ's Vicar and his importance *cf*. B. de Margerie, *op. cit.* ch. XIII.

13. *Ibid.* at the end.

14. Formula quoted by Cardinal J. Daniélou, S.J., during a retreat.

15. The call of the eternal King can be said to be *temporal* in so far as it pertains to the temporal being of man, and obliges him to make an option in the course of history.

16. Ex. 91, lines 12,13, (Vulg.) adds to the text of the Autograph: "*et sic de locis aliis.*" We have tried to render this nuance in our presentation of the first prelude.

17. We say: "Christ preaches His Church," because the Church is the Kingdom, his Kingdom which He preaches (*cf*. LG, 3,5). We add: "and Himself," because, in preaching the Kingdom, it is also himself that Jesus proclaims: "In Christ's word, in his works, and in his presence this Kingdom reveals itself to men. . .The Kingdom is clearly visible in the very person of Chirst" (LG, 5).
We might add that Christ continues in the towns and villages of the entire world to proclaim his Eucharist, his oblation to his Father and to men, to the Father in sacrifice, to men in communion, his adorable and adoring Real Presence of human and divine love. It is by and in the Eucharist, in eucharistic communion that Christ submits to himself all rebels helping them to overcome their rebellion.

18. Formula of P2, which is quite different from that of the Autograph as well as from the Vulgate.

19. We are inspired here by a thought of Father A. de Soras, S.J. More recently in the same sense it has been observed that Saint Ignatius by the allegory of the temporal king wanted to arouse a latent generosity active in every human heart, considering such a generosity as an "evanglical preparation," so as to put this "messianism" more or less implicitly at the service of the true Messiah, thereby transforming it (Cong. of Loyola, 1966, concl. 26; *cf. Los ejercicios de San Ignacio a la luz del Vaticano II,* Madrid, 1968, pp. 205–6).

20. Texts of Vatican II, passim; *cf*. B. de Margerie, *op. cit.* ch. X.

21. *Ibid.* ch. XVI, pp. 485-494; XV, 461 ff.

22. *Cf*. Ch. III of this work; by "sin of the world" may be understood collective sins, especially those described by Saint Paul in Rom 1-3.

23. *Cf*. B. de Margerie, *op. cit.,* Chs. XI and XIV, pp. 447, note 69.

24. In a free translation we combine with other notions, the two calls, that of the temporal and that of the eternal king, found in Ex. 93 and 95. We think this is consonant with the more profound intention Saint Ignatius had (although the temporal king in so far as he is identified with the Roman Pontiff, did not personally lead his troops against the Turks!). Besides, we emphasize at the end a specific datum of the Vulgate: "the most just will," implying the idea, so traditional, that God's will is in no way arbitrary, but is infinitely wise. Finally, we insert various allusions to the New Testament: Mt 20:23; "Of my cup you shall drink"; cf. Jn 18:11, "Shall I not drink the cup that the Father has given me?"; Eph 4:22–24 etc.

25. Saint Gregory of Nyssa (*Hom. 15 in Cant.*, MG, 44, 1116 C–1117 B) thinks that the Holy Spirit is the glory the Word possessed before his Incarnation (*cf.* Jn 17:1,5). Our trinitarian interpretation of the call of the eternal king seems to us eminently consonant with Ignatian mysticism.

26. A thought expressed in a letter.

27. *Cf.* Ex. 94, Vulg., "*Si quis non obediret.*"

28. We have combined the texts of the Vulgate and the Autograph.

29. *cf.* G. Nonell, S.J. *Los Ejercicios espirituales de N.P.S. Ignacio,* Manresa, San José, 1896, Bk. II, ch. VIII.

30. *Retraites du P. Olivaint,* pp. 49,50 (retreat of 1861).

31. *Ibid.* pp. 175–77 (retreat of 1864).

32. Ex. 96; *cf.* 87, 234.

33. *Cf.* note 21; we have proceeded here in the same manner, emphasizing points proper to the Vulgate ("Virgin").

34. *cf.* LG, 55–59.

35. *Cf.* Saint Louis-Marie Grignon de Montfort, *Traité de la vraie devotion,* #1; and "Le livre d'or du manuel complet de la vraie dévotion," Paris, 1938, pp. 755–59.

6

THE INCARNATION
OF THE SON OF GOD

Saint Ignatius seems to have viewed this exercise as at one and the same time a meditation and as a contemplation.[1] It is made up of three preludes, three points and a colloquy (Ex. 101). It intends, by placing the Christian who meditates and contemplates the "humanation"[2] of the Son of God, in contact with the world of God and the God of the world, to sharpen yearning for the salvation of men. This exercise may and should be considered as a complement to the meditation and contemplation on hell,[3] but even more directed toward action in view of the salvation of others.

A. Composition of place; in time and in space. The first two preludes.

The first prelude is historical, the second geographical.

The historical setting presents the mystery at the crossroads of eternity and of time. "The three Divine Persons look down upon the whole expanse or circuit of all the earth, filled with human beings. Since they see that all are going down to hell, They decree in their eternity that the Second Person should become man to save the human race. So when the fullness of time had come, they send[4] the Angel Gabriel to our Lady" (Ex. 102).[5] They wish to help men who are going down to hell to ascend to heaven. The Incarnation changes the sense of history. It is not the Father, nor the Spirit, but the Word of the Father (with him spirator of the Spirit), who becomes man.[6] To save mankind, eternal Life becomes temporal death (Ex. 53). Thus the Word glorifies the Father and the Spirit. God's glory is the ultimate reason for the salvation of the world.[7]

Because the Son is the eternal mediator between the Father and the Spirit, he becomes, in time, man and priest, the one mediator between the Trinity and mankind.[8]

Among so many places on "the surface of the earth,"[9] Saint Ignatius, in the second prelude, calls our attention to the only one to which "the Immense, the Infinite" is going to descend and become part of the finite and the measurable: the house and the chamber of the blessed Virgin Mary, our Lady,[10] in the town of Nazareth. "So many different peoples" (Ex. 103), for whom was wrought the humanation of the eternal Son of God, seem gathered in Nazareth, where Mary represents them all[11] and recapitulates in herself their yearning for salvation. The destiny of the universe and of mankind of all ages is in some way confined in this oratory[12] in Nazareth, where the Immaculate Virgin prays for the salvation of her sinful brethren. Her Immaculate Heart becomes already the refuge of sinners and of peoples so numerous and so diverse who are rushing toward hell. Mary is the true world capable of containing in her virginal and maternal Heart the countless human generations. Above all the eternal Trinity dwells in this immaculate Heart full of grace, from the very first instant of her existence.

B. What is desired and petitioned for.

The third prelude presents "the request for what I desire"[13] (Ex. 104): an intimate knowledge of our Lord, who has become man for me, that I may love him more ardently and so follow him more closely" (Ex. 104).[14]

To know, follow, love: we have already seen that consolation, the increase of the theological virtues (Ex. 316) are inscribed implicitly in these words.[15] We want to love Christ more ardently, in a twofold sense relative and absolute: more ardently than others love him, more than we have loved him up to now. Do others have, as much as I, reasons for ardently loving Jesus the Christ? Have they experienced to the same degree as I the delights and favors of his love? And how, having known the infinite lovableness of Jesus, and his infinite love for me, how would I not grow constantly in his love? Did he not become man in order to become my food in the Eucharist, to remain in me that I might remain in him?

We do not want only to know Christ intimately, love him more ardently, follow him more closely: we also ask for the grace to make him known, followed and loved by the greatest possible number of men for whom he has become man.[16]

For them as for me, the *intimate* knowledge of your divine Person, become flesh of my flesh and bone of my bone, Lord Jesus, is brought about in Eucharistic Communion, when I eat your Flesh, drink your Blood, receive your Soul, in my very self. Is not this intimate knowledge above all a knowledge of your love for me, in me? Of your love, in me for others? In communicating, by that very act, am I not eating and drinking your salvific love for others, your will to rescue others from the eternal fire of hate and from hell in order to consume them in the eternally benign fire of your Spirit?

To know you intimately, in your humanation of love, is it not to know your infinite might which can so easily sanctify me, your infinite mercy never thwarted by my innumerable infidelities, your infinite wisdom which knows me infinitely better than I know myself?

If I truly knew your infinite love for me, this love which surpasses all knowing, would I not imitate, to save them, your meekness and your kindness to men, would I not follow you more readily in your suffering and apostolic labors, would I not love you more than all?

C. Seeing and Understanding Who the Divine Persons, the Angels, the Human Persons Involved Are, What They Are Saying, what They Are Doing.

a. Saint Ignatius invites us to contemplate the human persons in their variety and diversity, which, however, does not hinder the unity of their orientation or rather of their disorientation. Whites and blacks, fortunate or unfortunate, the sick and the well, the new born and the dying, men individually and socially live and in a great blindness as to the divine Persons who see them unceasingly, so rapidly, in so great numbers, descend into hell because of their contempt for their last end (Ex. 106). Men do not see, do not contemplate the creating and redeeming look turned on them. It is the disregard of the eternal and infinite Look which is wilful and guilty blindness. For is not the "royal throne," visible everywhere, "the (one) throne of the majesty" of the three Divine Persons, the universal Church, prolongation and manifestation of the eternal king, Jesus Christ?[17]

Blind, leaders of the blind, so many men push each other and rush into eternal hell (Ex. 108, Vulg.), since they are unmindful of the love of the Redeemer who loves them and has ever loved them. Most men, perhaps, not to say probably, live willingly in the state of serious sin.[18] The revelation of eternal hell, joined to that of the eternal mercy of God infinitely offended by the malice in some way infinite of a single mortal sin, is and must be the great stimulus for my apostolic zeal, its constant spur. If I love men, how would I not speak to them of the shipwreck to which they are exposed, of the eternal prison and fire which they must avoid at all costs? How would I not relay to them the words of Jesus which show us his longing to rescue mankind from hell? To speak of hell, far from being an act of severity, is an act of mercy and one of the greatest proofs of fraternal charity,[19] not only on the part of a priest, but also of parents and teachers.

To keep silent about the eternal consequences of mortal sin, in reference to the salvation of men and to God's glory, would be a crime.[20] Can I conceal from a youth that he is very seriously obligated, when there are no religious classes, to provide for himself his religious instruction by reading—if he is capable of profiting from it—and that the rejection of religious culture constitutes a grave sin of contempt for the revealer and Savior of mankind?

b. It is pitiful to listen to what most men say, even believers, when the question of hell and salvation comes up. I hear my brothers "swear and blaspheme" (Ex. 107 and 67), transforming thus the earth into an antechamber of hell where already can be heard "the howling, the cries and blasphemies against Christ our Lord and against all his saints," and especially against his mother, queen of all saints, without forgetting so many impure conversations which lead to blasphemy. The import of many a proposal may readily be summed up thus: "Let us work for our own damnation and that of mankind!" (This is what is described in Revelation 13:1–5; 16:9,11,21.)

Counter to this, the Divine Persons say: "let us work for the salvation and redemption of mankind" (Ex. 107, P2).[21] Men blaspheme—God blesses. Men want to be damned—God wants to save them. Jesus alone, with his Father and their Spirit, is the Savior of the world. If I want to cooperate with the redemption and the salvation of mankind, ought I not transform myself into Jesus by the Eucharist? Ought I not thus become an echo of this Word which the Father speaks eternally, and in which he says everything and everyone?

To become an echo of the Word eternal and incarnate, I must speak of Jesus Christ. The more men want to keep silent about his name, his Person, his acts and words, to their own perdition, the more must I proclaim them loud and clear for their salvation and my own.

Blessed John Colombini tells us: "Everywhere there are more and more people 'going about doing good', there is greater scientific knowledge than ever before, yet if there was charity there would be many more saints. However I no longer see that true charity which Christ enkindles in souls.

"The first remedy for this evil is to speak in season and out of season of Christ and of his love. The louder you speak, the more deeply will you yourself feel. The heart is impressed by what the tongue expresses. He who is steeped in the world, has his love already cooled and is beginning to think as the world thinks. He who speaks of Christ acquires the feeling of Christ.

"My dearly beloved, know that there is no worse pretense than that of hiding the Lord's benefits and his gifts, for the sweetest speech about Jesus Christ is the food of the soul. So, then, even when everyone would bid you keep silent about this blessed name, scorn them all, for whoever will confess Christ's name before creatures will be confessed by him before his Father."[22]

So long as Christians respond to the "grace of discourse,"[23] to the charism of the word, when it is granted them, the Father, the Son and the Holy Spirit continue, through them, to tell the world of our day: "Let us work for the salvation and redemption of mankind."

Have they not begun to work for it through the conversation held by the Virgin Mary and the Archangel Gabriel? "Upon arriving, the angel said to her: 'Rejoice, O highly favored daughter (Hail full of grace). The Lord is with you. Your son will rule over the house of Jacob forever and his reign will be without end" (Lk 1:28–33). "For nothing is impossible with God." The Virgin, then, consents, in the name of mankind, to the spiritual marriage of each human being with the Son of God,[24] saying: "I am the servant (the handmaid) of the Lord, let it be done to me as you say" (Lk 1:37,38).

Today, in the Church, the conversation between Mary, the Mother of God, and the Archangel Gabriel continues uninterruptedly: countless human beings pass on the angel's message when they recite the Rosary as individuals or in groups, in public or in private or at home.

Does not the recitation of the Rosary mean that the Father, the Son and the Spirit, to whose glory Mary is ever hailed, continue, through her, to "work for the salvation and redemption of mankind"? To recite the Rosary while contemplating its mysteries, to recite it every day, everywhere, without human respect, is that a "fruit,"[25] and not a minor one, of the conversation between Mary and the angel, messenger of the Trinity, and especially of the "eternally redemptive conversation" between the Divine Persons?[26] Rather than listening to the insulting conversations of men,[27] a dialogue of blasphemy, why not choose to listen through the Rosary to the co-redemptive dialogue of the Immaculate and the Trinity, to the "dialogue of salvation"[28] between the Father and the Son, in the Holy Spirit?

"Let us work for the salvation and redemption of mankind!" Is not the Bible as a whole this exhortation by the Father, the Son and their one and common Spirit? Is it not the word of salvation, the message of salvation, the message we must pass on (Acts 13:26)?

Divine and angelic beings, just as Mary, do not restrict themselves to being and to speaking, they act.

c. However, their actions are quite different from those of human persons. Human beings "wound, kill and rush into hell"[29](Ex. 108, Vulg), as Satan, "who brought death from the beginning" (Jn 8:10), whose desires they thereby fulfill (Jn 8:44).

Evidently, this does not apply to all human persons, but is predicated precisely of those whom the "first version," (Pl, P2) apocalyptically calls "inhabitants on the face of the earth"[30] (cf. Rv 13:8,12,14; 6:10; 8:13; 11:10; 17:2,8; 3:10) and who adore the murderous dragon; precisely, there is question, too, of what all human beings would do if they had not mercifully been preserved by the Lamb-Shepherd, who sacrifices himself instead of slaying, and thus merits to reign with the Father on the sole throne of the Divine Majesty (Ex. 106; Rv 5:6; 7:11; 22:1).

It is in this context that the most Holy Trinity carries out its work (Ex. 108,V), and the eternal decree (Ex. 102) of the most holy Incarnation (Ex. 108; A,P2.). If it is true that the Second Person alone became incarnate, his singular Incarnation is nonetheless the work of the three Divine Persons, the term of their one and eternal decree and design.[31] The Father, who does not become man, gives his only Son; the Holy Spirit, who, too, is not incarnated, comes upon Mary, and as a result of this sending of the Spirit[32] the Incarnation is accomplished. By accomplishing the "most holy Incarnation" or humanation of the only Son, the creative Trinity achieves a new creation, the raison d'être of the first. It achieves its greatest work of all, its masterpiece. In response to the unleashing of sin, the Trinity lets loose a new flood, the flood of the Blood of the Lamb, and the universal Church outrides and floats over this deluge like a new ark of salvation, on this ocean of graces, to save men, until the end of human history. The Father continues offering sinners his greatest gift, his only and well-beloved Son. And both offer their enemies the bond and tie of their mutual love, the one Spirit in whom they love each other. The Incarnation of the Son is paschal and inseparable from the sending of the Spirit.

God is so mightily active in human history that he has become part of it through Jesus Christ forever. Nothing will ever be able to dislodge him from it, not even the sin of millions upon millions of men banded together against their Savior. The gates of hell will not prevail.

"Lord Jesus, from the very first moment of your humanation, You are 'a-man-for-me' and for others. Being ever since at your Father's side, you are ordered to me, whom you know and love in[33] your Father. You are humanly and divinely wholly for me, out of love for your Father.[34]

"From this very first moment, all mankind is present to your Heart, known by your human intellect, loved by your human, created, voluntary and sensory love, and not only with a love that is but eternal, uncreated.[35]

"You have received this gift from your Father, without previous merit, out of pure liberality. On seeing yourself so preferred and so gratuitously loved, a fire of love is enkindled in your Heart for all men, as a fire of zeal for the glory of your Father. From your very first instant, you offer yourself to your Father for my salvation and decide to die for me (Heb 10:5ff.).

"If I should not acknowledge this, could I say that I know you intimately, Son of God for me made, of old, a passible and mortal man?"

By accomplishing the "most Holy Incarnation" in Mary's womb, the Holy and Blessed Trinity also accomplished the supreme and unique act,[36] the human and divinized act which so wondrously unifies the entire pre-paschal and post-paschal life of the Incarnate Word: the act of the beatific vision. The Son of God who makes himself part of human history is the great human seer of the eternal majesty of the Trinity, the perfect adorer who humbles himself before the incomprehensible, infinite love which he is himself.[37] It is by humbling himself humanly, by rendering thanks as a man, to his Father, under the inspiration of the Holy Spirit, that Jesus inspires by his human will his mother "to humble herself, and offer thanks to the Divine Majesty" (Ex. 108).

From this very first moment, the colloquy of Jesus with his Father merits[38] for each one of us the grace of entering into conversation with his mother, with himself, with his Father and with their Spirit.

d. Colloquies with Mary and with the Divine Persons.

"The exercise should be closed with a colloquy. I will think over what I ought to say to the three Divine Persons, or to the eternal Word Incarnate, or to his mother, our Lady. According to the light that I have received, I will beg for grace to follow and imitate more closely our Lord, who has just become man for me" (Ex, 109).[39]

Let us speak first to the holy Archangel Gabriel and to the angels who play so important a role in the mystery of the redemptive Incarnation.[40]

"As you, Gabriel and all the guardian angels of each human person of the past, present and future, I, too, am called to announce to men their redemption and to obtain their consent to their twofold state of being a rescued and co-redemptive creature. To consent to being rescued and to rescue others, herein lies all that I have been sent to obtain. That I may carry out this mission, O pure spirits who know how to speak to men, obtain for me the ability to change my carnal and worldly language into a spiritual one, one that is concerned with the salvation of those to whom I speak (Ex. 38–41). Enlighten them, guide them, protect and govern them: make of me an instrument of your action."

Then, turning to Mary: "Immaculate Virgin, my queen, our mother, you are truly the Blessed Virgin Mary (Ex. 102,V)" Yes, blessed Mary! Blessed because you have believed; blessed because you have fully consented to God's will; blessed because Jesus Christ brings to you with himself all that he is and all that he loves: his Heart, his cross, his twofold zeal for his Father's glory and the salvation of men; blessed because you have spoken little and loved much, seldom appeared and merited greatly, thought little of yourself and suffered much."[41]

"Mother of Christ, you have been the temple where a God has paid first homage to God, where has been seen for the first time this grand and marvellous spectacle: a God submissive and obedient, a God poor, a God emptied, in order to enrich and liberate men, his brothers.[42]

"Handmaid and Mother of the Lord, how should I not thank you for having consented in my name, so much more perfectly than I could ever have done, consented to my spiritual marriage as rescued and co-redeemer? By consenting to it in my name, you have merited for me, in dependence on your Son and Savior, the grace to consent to it and to ratify your consent, on my part.

"Pray for us, poor sinners, now and at the hour of our death. Pray that, enlightened by your sweet presence, my death may not be a descent into hell, nor even into purgatory, but an ascent to heaven, a passage to the vision of your maternal love for all your children in your only Son.

"Make of me the instrument for the consolations of your maternal and merciful heart for the dying."[43]

Next we turn to the Divine Persons. "Spirit of the Father and of the Son, Holy Spirit, you who have worked and still work this Incarnation of the Son (from whom you proceed eternally), for the sake of my salvation work in me the external incarnation of the inner faith you give me in regard to your principle and your unction. Everything is possible for you. Grant me the grace to speak fluently, joyously, ardently of your love, infinite "incarnator," for men. Inspirer of Holy Scripture, make rise up in my memory, in my heart and on my lips the words of love and of fire you have spoken through Paul and John. You are the Spirit speaking through the prophets for the glory of the Father and of the Son: speak through me, of him who is the Word, the *Verbum.*"

"Lord Jesus, you have come into this world to unite men among themselves, which is their salvation,[44] and to unite them thus to your Father, by rescuing them from damnation by their mutual divisions.

"Son of God, well-beloved Son of love, you have made yourself a human and feeling heart out of love for me, so hard of heart, so cold, so unfeeling, for me who, perhaps, was rapidly going down to hell, and bringing others down there with me by my infidelities.

"You are the light of the world and the Son of him who is light. You have assumed human eyes to give me the enlightened eyes of the heart (*cf.* Eph 1:18). You gave them to me and to so many others who were so wilfully blinded!

"Your human Heart loves me with a feeling love, alone adorable among so many other sensible loves. Your sensible love for me, present in the Eucharist, expresses the saving, divine, uncreated love which you have for me and compared to which all sensible loves of humans for me seem to evanesce.

"May your Eucharistic Heart teach me to desire, even more than the reciprocity of the sensible and supernaturalized love of others, the universality of this sensible love toward each one, a love of even the most abandoned.

"Men are on the road to hell because they hate themselves out of hatred for your love (cf Jn 15:23,24). You have become incarnate to make yourself a human heart, doctor, corporeal and spiritual,[45] food and remedy of our hearts, wounded by selfishness and injustice, in your Eucharist.

"Eucharistic Heart of Jesus, make of me an instrument, an apostle, a teacher of social and world justice and peace. You become man, eternal Word, to humanize me while divinizing me. Humanize me perfectly through Eucharistic Communion in your virtues. Grant me a new and glowing heart in your likeness. May this glowing heart radiate yours to the ends of the earth, in and through the mystery of the communion of the saints.

"God and Father of Jesus, You who have become in him and through him my Father, I thank you for having given me to him and for having given him to me.[46] Through and with your Son, I adore your will to save the world. You are eternally, with your Son and your Spirit, will and decree of salvation for men. You are eternally, with your Son and your Spirit, the worker and author of salvation, by being eternally the incarnator of the *Verbum,* the giver, with him, of your Spirit. Work constantly in us our efficacious decision of cooperation for the salvation of mankind."

"Holy Trinity,[47] we adore you as being the decision and the eternal operation of our salvation, in the Eucharist."[48]

NOTES ON CHAPTER SIX

1. *Cf.* Ex. 101: The very title of the exercise is not the same, in the Vulgate on the one hand (*meditatio*), in the Autograph and P2 (*contemplatio*). It is likely, however, that the word "*contemplatio*" better reflects the characteristic thinking of Saint Ignatius (though we cannot be sure of this). At any rate, if he knowingly admitted these variations, we may see therein an indication that flexibility in vocabulary did not offend him.

2. *Cf.* B. de Margerie, S.J., *CFW, 14-17,* for the meaning of this word used by the fathers of the Church. *Cf.* New English Dictionary: "humanation = incarnation"; 1651 Howell, Venice, 185: The humanation of our Savior; 1659, H. L'Estrange, Alliance Div Off. 179.

3. *Cf.* chapter V, especially note 6, where there is found an analogous flexibility in the use of the terms "meditation" "contemplation"; but there, contrary to what we have seen here in note 1, the text of the Vulgate presented the exercise on hell as a contemplation.

4. The verb is in the imperfect tense in the Vulgate and Autograph texts, while it is in the present in 2.

5. Here the Vulgate brings out two priceless nuances: the first describes the Incarnation, in terms of technical theology, by the expression of "assumption of human *nature*"; the second speaks to us, not only of our Lady, but of the Blessed Virgin Mary.

6. The text of the Exercises, already mentioned, speaks of the "*Second Person*" who, alone, in the decision of the *Three Persons,* becomes incarnate. Thus there is found the suggestion of the idea that, neither the First, nor the Third Person, became incarnate.

7. *Cf.* B. de Margerie, *op. cit.* Ch. I.

8. *Cf.* ST, III.3.8 c; ad 3rd; SCG, IV.42; When we call the Word mediator between the Father and the Spirit, we mean the Son receives divine nature from the Father and gives it wholly to the Spirit, who receives it from the Father through him.

9. Ex. 103: We prefer to avoid the term "immensity" used in his translation by Father Courel. It has philosophical implications not found in the Ignatian text: "*magna capacitas*" does not mean "immensity" but rather "the dwelling place of numerous inhabitants."

10. We bring together here various Ignatian ways of speaking of the Mother of Jesus in Ex. 103, Vulg. and P2.

11. ST, III.30.1: "The Incarnation is, in some way, a spiritual marriage between the Son of God and human nature. This is why, by the Annunciation, the consent of the Virgin was asked for, *loco totius humanae naturae.*" This text has often been quoted by the Popes in their encyclicals, particularly by Pius XII, in "*Mystici Corporis,*" at the end.

12. *Cf.* Ex. 220.

13. Let us note the priceless nuance which distinguishes Ignatius' original thinking (Autograph, P2: "*petere quod volo*" and the final "*gratiae postulationem*"); we have tried to render it in our translation. Clearly, the Vulgate wanted to avoid the appearance of what today we would call voluntarism and to emphasize the role of grace. We might go so far as to say that asking for grace is also an effect of grace.

14. Here also, the nuances of the Vulgate are priceless. As P2, but differing from the Autograph, the Vulgate introduces the notion of an *ardent* love. I also retain the translation of P2: "The Lord assumed humanity," which suggests better perhaps (than the term "humanation") the social connotations of the Incarnation. *Cf.* the texts referred to in note 2.

15. *Cf.* Chapter II, note 28.

16. Thought from Saint Anthony-Mary Claret, in his *Autobiography*, #8-17; 205-13.

17. *Cf.* P2: *"considerare tres Personas divinas in solio regali seu in throno suae divinae majestatis."* (Ex. 106). It is quite possible, not to say probable, that Saint Ignatius was thinking, (at least at the time of the final Roman edition of the Exercises), of the book of Revelation and its presentation of the throne of God and of the Lamb (22:1; 4:2,10; 5:11), on which are seated all who triumphed (3:21).

In another context, Vatican I presented us with the miracle of the Church as a perpetual motive for belief and an irrefutable testimony of her divine mission (DS, 301). The universal Church is the throne of a God who reigns here below despite his enemies, who are powerless to prevent him from accomplishing his designs of saving love even and especially in our visible world. The three divine Persons are present everywhere and streams of love flow abundantly from their cosmic throne. Each human person is called to become their human throne and also seat himself with them on their ecclesial throne (Rv 3:21).

18. This is what is at least implied in Matthew 7:13,14: "Enter through the narrow gate. The gate that leads to damnation is wide, the road is clear, and many choose to travel it. But how narrow is the gate that leads to life, how rough the road, and how few there are who find it." This seems to be Saint Ignatius' opinion if we compare Ex. 48,51,52,71,102, 106,108. Not only before but also after the historical event of the redemptive Incarnation, human crowds precipitate themselves, plunge into *eternal* hell (Ex. 65).

19. *Cf.* Saint Anthony-Mary Claret, *op. cit.* #14.

20. *Ibid.* #17.

21. A more complete text than that of the Autograph (*"hagamos redempcion del genero humano"*) or of the Vulgate (*"divinae vero Personae in Caelo de redimendo humano genere colloquentes"*). Let us note the difference between the concepts of salvation and redemption: the latter implies the liberating ransoming (*cf.* de Margerie, *op. cit.*, p. 303, no. 4), while salvation signifies the acquistion of all good things and the disappearance of all evils.

22. Quoted by L. Ponnelle, *Saint Philippe de Neri*, Paris, 1928, pp. 157,158, It is obvious that the saint made use of many biblical texts: "The mouth speaks whatever fills the mind" (Mt 12:34); "Those others belong to the world; that is why theirs is the language of the world and why the world listens to them" (1 Jn 4:5; Mt 10:32,33).

23. *Cf.* I Cor 12:8-10: "To one the spirit gives wisdom in discourse. . .prophecy is given to one; ST, II.II.177; de Margerie, *op. cit.* pp. 160-166 (the problem of "religious language").

24. *Cf.* note 11 of this chapter.

25. *Cf.* Ex. 106, 107, 108 (V. P2) clarified by Lk 1:42, "And blest is the fruit of your womb!"

26. Ex. 107, Vulg.: *"divinae Personae de redimendo genere humano colloquentes."*

27. Ex. 107, Vulg. *"Homines in terris. . .sibique invicum convitiantes."* The concept is wanting in the Autograph and in P2.

28. The subject of the first encyclical by Paul VI: *Ecclesiam Suam*, in 1964; *cf.* de Margerie, *op. cit.*, Ch. III.

29. We translate *"ruant"* of Ex. 108, Vulg. as "go headlong down to hell."

30. Perhaps the allusion is intentional; W. J. Harrington, O.P., in *The Apocalypse of Saint John*, London, 1969, p. 37, emphasizes that the term "inhabitants of the earth" cor-

responds in Revelation to the "world" of the Fourth Gospel and of the Joannine Epistles, that is, to the unbelieving world.

31. ST, III.3.4: Saint Thomas distinguishes the act of assumption and its term following Saint Augustine. *Cf.* G. Lafont, O.S.B., *Peut-on connaître Dieu en Jésus-Christ,* Paris, p. 140. *Cf.* also SCG, 4,39.

32.-*Cf.* AG, 4; H. N. Manteau-Bonamy, O.P., *La Vierge Marie et le Saint Esprit,* Paris, 1971, pp. 15,16.

33. *Cf.* Jn 1:18; 17:23; 14:30.

34. *Cf.* H. de Lubac, S.J., *La Foi chrétienne,* Paris, 1969, Ch. III; "Trinité economique," pp. 97–103: "When Luther wrote 'Christ has two natures; how does that concern me?' "— not without saying the opposite elsewhere—Father Rousselot answered him: 'In this very fact consists the substantial reparation of mankind. This central fact of the history of being, directly, personally, profoundly concerns every living intelligence. From the moment that this touches the base of being, this touches me fundamentally.' " There is question here of the conditions of the possibility of Christ's redemptive action; *cf.* on this subject de Margerie, *op. cit.,* Ch. IX: The Christ of Trent.

35. *Cf.* Pius XII, *Mystici Corporis,* AAS, 35(1943) 230; DS, 3812.

36. *Cf.* B. de Margerie, *op. cit.* p. 421.

37. *Cf.* Diepen, O.S.B., *La Théologie de l'Emmanuel,* Bruges, 1960, p. 212: "The human act by which Christ addresses himself to the Father is performed by the Son alone, who is the sole, indivisible subject of every operation *ad extra.* Finally, this act is addressed to the Father directly and principally, but not exclusively." *Cf.* texts of Saint Thomas quoted in note 31.

38. Due to the infused knowledge possessed from the first instant by Jesus; *cf.* ST, III. 9.1=3; and not due to beatific knowledge.

39. This is the only passage of the Spiritual Exercises in which Saint Ignatius explicitly speaks of a colloquy with each of the three Divine Persons. It is, however, also the only text in which he shows us the action of these three Persons, which already constitutes an implied invitation to a colloquy with each one.

40. The Gospel of Saint Luke is particularly clear in this regard (22:43) and still clearer that of Saint Matthew.

41. L. de Grandmaison, S.J., Retraite biblique, *Ecrits spirituels,* vol. III, p. 134, Paris, 1953.

42. *Cf.* Bossuet, Sermon pour l'Annonciation, 1661, Premier point, *Oeuvres complètes,* Paris 1885, vol. VI, p. 339.

43. Notably on inducing them to gain the plenary indulgence granted *in articulo mortis* in order to be, in so far as it depended on them, preserved from purgatory.

44. UR, 2; GS, 45.2; de Margerie, *op. cit.* pp. 14-17.

45. Saint Ignatius of Antioch, Ad Eph, 7,2; SC,5.

46. Jn 17:24; 3:16

47. Saint Ignatius of Loyola (*St. Ignatius own Story as told to Camara,* ch. III, #28) relates that at Manresa he prayed daily not only to the three divine Persons as individuals, but also added a fourth prayer to the Trinity.

48. The decisions and actions of God are identical with his essence which is infinitely simple.

7

BETHLEHEM
THE CRIB OF A GOD
BECOME POOR

The "stumbling block of the crib" (*cf.* 1 Cor 1:23), places us face to face with the mystery of a poor God. The infinitely rich is presented to us in the swaddling clothes of poverty (Lk 2:7).

This paradox ever, but especially today, demands our attention. We are by vocation, the Church of the poor. The better to contemplate with Saint Ignatius, the mystery of the crib, let us recall first of all some points on the mystery of the poverty of the Church, through which shines and must shine that of the infant Savior.

A. Mystery and Vocation of the Church Poor.

The Church, which proclaims Christ's poverty, which inculcates his message on behalf of the poor, *appears* rich to many of our contemporaries or even, on the contrary, uninterested in the spiritual good of the rich people, to many others.

We do not intend to apologize here for the Church, but rather to recall to ourselves, as faithful who come into contact with Christ's poverty by way of his Church, the inherent tensions in the mystery of her sharing in the poverty of her Savior.

In comparison with the divine treasures of grace, with the immeasurable riches of Christ (*cf.* Eph 3:8), the Church, his spouse, *is* poor, since she receives them entirely from him, without being able in any way to contribute anything to the acquisition of the treasures of Redemption.[1] In as much as she is the body, the prolongation, the manifestation, the sacrament of Christ Savior and mediator, the Church *is* fully endowed with the riches of Christ which it is her mission to distribute to the world.[2]

In comparison with the nations of the world, the Church *appears* often, though not always, relatively poor and bereft of the goods of this world, incapable, without the assistance of these societies and nations, to come to the help of her poor and theirs, fully and with universal efficiency. All her institutions do not stop her from remaining the mendicant Church which seems never to stop desiring and asking for the goods of this world. Better: they incite her to do so.

Briefly, in her, inextricably, there *appears* wealth and poverty associated and united on the spiritual as well as on the material level. We might say that the spiritual poverty of the Church, in as much as she is and wishes to be detached from the goods of this world—"Get purses for yourselves that do not wear out, a never-failing treasure with the Lord which no thief comes near nor any moth destroys. Wherever your treasure lies, there your heart will be" (Lk 12:33-34).—is a constituent element of her riches in God's eyes.

Although the diverse forms of avarice hinder a number of her members from sharing in the poverty of the pre-paschal Christ (and the same holds true of local churches; contrast, for instance, the church of Laodicea with that of Smyrna: Rev 3:17; 2:9), nonetheless the universal Church is still the faithful[3] spouse of the poor Christ, the poor Church of the poor, which communicates to the rich as well as to the poor the riches of the poverty of Christ the Savior.

"You are well acquainted with the favor shown you by our Lord Jesus Christ: how for your sake he made himself poor though he was rich, so that you might become rich by his poverty" (2 Cor 8:9).

The poverty of Christ and of the Church is a mystery which surpasses human reason. Earthly goods are valuable, so why deprive ourselves of them? We may say of them what may be said of sexuality in marriage. God, the Creator, who is at their origin, does not deny these values, but saves them by becoming a poor and chaste Redeemer. Original sin had deprived men of harmonious and spontaneous submission of the body and of the passions to the free will of the immortal soul, a state which characterized original justice and which our first parents were to pass on to all mankind. Man's rebellion against God's will brought in its train the rebellion of the lower passions and of the body against the soul. In expiation thereof, and to give man the example of mastery of himself and of the world, it behooved the Son of God to live here on earth the life of a poor and celibate man. This, not out of contempt for the goods of this world, or of human sexuality, of which as the only Son of God, He is, with the Father and their Spirit, the Creator, but on the contrary, to give man more abundantly the power to subject himself to his Creator in the use of these goods and values. Christ could well have been rich, but that was not appropriate for his redemptive mission. He came to save men who were more impulsively inclined to pleasure, to riches, and to their disordered use than to suffering and poverty or than to the ordered use of the goods of this world.[4]

Indeed, the Christ whom the Gospels present us and, after them, the Church,[5] to which they have been entrusted and under the control of which they have been written, this Christ is at once a poor man who shares largely the lot of life of the poor, having nowhere to lay his head, and the model of owners, the Lord who has in no way renounced the exercise of his right of ownership (Lk 9:,51-58; Jn 12:6; 13: 28,29). He is apparently the owner of a house (*cf.* Mt 13:1)— of a purse common to himself and to his apostles (Jn 12:6; 13:29) and he has alms distributed to the poor, while at the same time he accepts to be "helped" by the goods of wealthy disciples (Lk 8:3). It suffices to say that the poverty of which Jesus is the model and counsellor (Mt 19:21) does not mean, in its complexity, contempt of created goods, but awareness of the dangers wealth brings in its train to salvation. "It is easier for a camel to pass through the eye of a needle than for a rich man to enter the kingdom of heaven." Salvation, impossible for men, is possible for God, since God alone can detach men from riches and the desire to be rich.[6] That is why the Christ of the Gospels is a poor owner, the almighty Savior of the rich whom he renders poor of heart and of spirit through the sacrifice and example of the crib and of the cross.

In his Church, the privileged will be, not the rich, but the poor. The salvation of the rich depends on the poor, and on the acceptance, by them, of the alms the rich offer them (*cf.* Rom 15:31; II Cor 8-9). It is then, not so much the rich who do a favor to the poor by offering them alms, but rather the poor who become benefactors of the rich by accepting such alms.[7] Thus the humble exercise, in poverty of spirit and heart, of the right of ownership becomes a means of salvation for most Christians, while Christ, to facilitate the supernaturalization of this exercise, invites a minority to renounce even the exercise of the right of ownership. The evangelical counsel of perfect poverty is ordered to the eternal salvation of those who are divinely called to be owners and to be married.

If the problem of the proper attitude, for a Christian, in the face of the goods of this world, has therefore never been simple, it is more than ever complex in our era of material development, as Vatican II has perceived. On the one hand, the Council has stressed that many men, distressed by misery, do not consider the dramatic situation resulting from the interior division of man (a consequence of original sin).[8] For liberty is weakened when man falls into a condition of extreme need.[9] Extreme poverty, then, is not a good, not an evangelical value, but an evil counter to the divine plan.[10] This does not mean that we deny that God can make it a part of his plan, but it still is an obstacle to the development of the human personality, and one against which God wants us to fight, particularly by stressing the right of the poor in case of extreme necessity.[11]

On the other hand, and precisely that their struggle be fully conformed to the divine plan, Vatican II has wished to associate the desire of personal and collective development with the spirit of poverty, "glory and sign of the Church of Christ.[12] It is this spirit, at the service of charity, which impels some to deprive themselves of superfluities and even of what, at first sight, seems necessary,[13] to rescue others from indigence and misery for advancing their full development. This presumes not only a more abundant productivity, but also a better distribution of the goods of this world. This is actually impossible without the austerity of personal privations which enrich others, without detachment in regard to temptations of personal enrichment.

More profoundly, the Council has wished anew to proclaim the poor blessed, above and beyond all especially united to Christ suffering for the salvation of the world,[14] a beatitude to which the rich themselves are called to share, if they want to be saved. Poverty of spirit constitutes their true wealth before God. Should they not prefer, out of love for Christ and for their brothers, to choose a level of life materially inferior, yet one which does not block the way to heaven and leads them there, rather than a higher standard of living which casts them into hell?

So it pertains, not only to religious institutes,[15] but to the whole People of God, body of Christ, to the whole Church, to give a collective testimony of love of the poor and of poverty of spirit on their behalf. This testimony will constitute par excellence the riches of the Church in the eyes of mankind and of the Trinity, supreme source and ultimate end of all earthly goods. Leon Bloy has said: "Fortunately for the poor there are poor people." It is above all from those who will willingly be poor, at the same in spirit, of heart, and in fact, that the salvation, even temporal, of other poor is to be expected. The Church is the society of the poor disciples of the Christ who wants to enrich mankind with his poverty.[16]

It is in the context of the hunger and misery of an important sector of mankind that the Church invites us to come and contemplate the immeasurable spiritual riches and the temporal poverty of the infant Savior born in a stable.

B. The Scandal and Mystery of the Crib

In the first prelude, which is historical, Saint Ignatius invites us to recall what happened: "Here it will be that our Lady, being about nine months with child, set out from Nazareth, as may be piously believed, seated on an ass, and accompanied by Saint Joseph and a maid, leading an ox. They are going to Bethlehem to pay tribute that Caesar imposed on those lands" (Ex. 111).

Today we are quite surprised to see the allusion to a maid whom the Gospel does not mention. It seems Saint Ignatius wanted to signify that Mary and Joseph were not poor in the sense of being reduced to beggary, but rather were so spiritually, having a sufficiency of material resources, which was to make them more sensitive to the inhospitality of Bethlehem and of the stable. It is quite in keeping with what we mentioned before, about Christ as owner. Mary and Joseph, to face up to their responsibility for the life of the God-Man, were to be owners and so obliged to pay tribute to Caesar. By registering, they seemed to anticipate by their action the decisive statement of Jesus: "Render to Caesar what is Caesar's and to God what is God's" (Mt 22:21). Through them, it is Jesus himself who renders to Caesar to render to his Father, supreme source of all that Caesar can possess (Jn 19:11) of money or of power.

The second prelude, geographical, has us see the way from Nazareth to Bethlehem and the journey made by Mary bearing Jesus and accompanied by Joseph, and then the stable where the Creator of the universe is born and laid in a manger. This, as if to signify a poverty as a rule moderate, but at times extreme, a poverty appropriate for the historical journey of the eternal Creator (Ex. 112).

In the third prelude (Ex. 113), we ask for the grace of an inner knowledge of the immeasurable human and divine riches of the Lord, become a poor man for love of me, in order that I might love him more ardently in his poor members and follow him in his poverty.[17] Consequently, we ask for the grace to know Christ in his poor of today and to put ourselves at his service in them.

The first point (Ex. 114) has us consider the persons: the divine Person of the Incarnate Word in whom dwell the Father and the Holy Spirit, then Mary, Mother of the Word made Flesh, and Saint Joseph, his chaste father, the spouse of the Mother of God.[18]

Saint Ignatius adds here several lines which are among the most touching of his Exercises. "I will make myself a poor little unworthy slave, and as though present, look upon them, contemplate them, and serve them in their needs with all possible homage and reverence" (Ex. 114).

Before this infant who is infinite wisdom, power, goodness, how would I not have the highest possible respect and how would I not adore these tiny hands which rule the world? Before his infinite richness, how could I not realize my poverty, my misery to the point of "making myself a poor little one" and the slave of infants and of the poor, the slave of their evangelization? Does not Jesus reveal himself to us through them, does he not want to become our liberator inspiring us to put ourselves at their service?

"Infant Jesus, my Lord and my God, I thank you for having become poor to expiate my avarice. Today, too, you are cold in so many hearts and in so many bodies. I adore your right to be warmed by the fire of our loving poverty. In offering it to you for the evangelization and for the salvation of your poor, I renew my resolve to associate myself with your poverty and to enrich myself with it.

"You have come into this world thanks to this very special form of poverty which was the virginity of your parents (Lk 2:41,43). We are all born spiritually of the poverty according to the flesh of their chaste marriage. All of us together are its fruit, in the "fruit" which you alone are.

"We, indeed, recall the words of Saint Jerome: "Joseph was a virgin through Mary so that a virgin Son be born of a virgin marriage."[19] You are born of this marriage and of the mutual virginal love of Mary and

Joseph in this sense that they have been the condition, divinely willed and protected, of your coming into this world, for our salvation. And it is also in this sense that we can all say, we your disciples, that we are spiritually born of the mutual love, virginal and sacrificial, of Mary and Joseph.[20]

"You could have come into the world through richness of the flesh, in the midst of wealth. It has pleased you to make yourself a part of the great human family through the poverty of virginity, not in the bosom of need and misery, but in the stable of a poverty momentarily needy as a consequence of the inhospitality of the hearts you came to save. Your poverty and your celibacy are not the condemnation, but the salvation of marriage and ownership, restored by purity of heart and poverty of spirit."

Today, Jesus, Mary and Joseph, in the wealth of divine glorification, wish to introduce in their holy family countless poor and chast men and women. Will I know how to contemplate them and serve them in their present needs, in the needs of the Church of which they are the head, the mother and the privileged protector?

To be able to do so, I must "look at, observe and contemplate what they say" following the paradoxical expression found in the second point of the Ignatian Exercises (Ex 115, Autograph and P2). That is listen with the ears of faith, to the words of Jesus, Mary and Joseph. The words of the infant Jesus? The eternal Word, the only Word the Father pronounces in an eternal silence and which can only be heard in silence,[21] has become an "infans," a "non-word." The eternal Word has become temporal silence. He does not even want, for the moment, to know the richness (apparent and real[22]) of human language. He prefers, as later during his passion, to be silent in a silence which begins and already anticipates his expiation of our inane words. His silence of humility and of poverty speaks to us more eloquently than any and every word.

"Eternal Word become human silence, I adore your silence, which surpasses all our praise and which mutes all our words. Silently, I listen to you and I see you, light in our darkness, silent Word which does not pass.

"If you do not speak, you weep, and you bring together in your inarticulate groaning, the groanings of all creation in labor, all our inner groanings, while we await the redemption of our bodies (cf. Rom 8:22,23).

"Heaven and earth will pass; the riches of so much of our speech and the laxity of so much of our silence will pass. Your words and your silences and your tears will not pass.[23] They recapitulate and save the sufferings and weeping of so many innocent infants, the silent tears of so many adult victims of our injustices. Perhaps, before your tears, Mary and Joseph have nothing to tell us other than their own silence of love, of adoration, of compassion, of thanks-giving and of supplication, naught but the silence of their tears."

Let us, therefore, look at and consider, not only what they are, what they do not say that we may weep in silence over it, but also, in the third point, "to see and consider what they are doing, for example, making the journey and laboring[24] that our Lord might be born in extreme poverty, and that after many labors, after hunger, thirst, heat and cold, after insults and outrages, he might die on the cross, and all this for me" (Ex. 116).[25]

What they *do,* is therefore, what they *suffer:* first, Mary and Joseph, by accepting the tribulations of their journey; next, Jesus in transforming his whole life in a painful journey to his Father for me. All his life, in his passible and mortal Body, becomes a passion, his supreme act on my behalf. Is not all his passion the action of his Father and of his Spirit in him? Is not Jesus supremely active in offering to his Father this passion for me? Granting me his Spirit?[26]

The extreme poverty of Jesus Christ, in the mind of Saint Ignatius, is, then, a suffering, a humiliating poverty. Jesus is poor for he was born in indigence, worked hard, endured hunger and thirst, heat and cold, insults and outrages. So, the poverty of the Lord of the universe is not merely nominal but real, and so sincere. It is a poverty of dependence, since it is a factor of his obedience to his Father's salvific plan. It involves labors, active and passive suffering, charitable and generous, for all other poor men (*cf.* Jo 13:29).

His imitators are to love, embrace and follow Christ the owner of the Universe, and yet Christ poor, at times even indigent and naked, in a twofold contempt, active and passive, of the world, of its riches and of its honors. In accepting this form of poverty which consists in dependance on others in a thousand things, they imitate Jesus acknowledging the sovereign dominion of the Father over all creation, a dominion which is also that of Jesus as Word Creator: a dominion in which poverty itself makes the disciple of Jesus share. "We seem to have nothing, yet everything is ours" (II Cor 6:10); "All these are yours, and you are Christ's, and Christ is God's (I Cor 3:22,23.)"

He who has not renounced everything, all that he has, cannot be a disciple of Jesus (Lk 14:33) nor, then, can he know that all is his in Christ who is given to him (Jn 3:16; Rom 8:32). To be attached to something in particular, is to show that one has renounced possession of the universe and of its Lord, and this attachment to it is the sanction. Private property should not deprive another person of the use of a good if its owner wishes to enjoy, in Christ, universal ownership of all.[27] "Poor, yet we enrich many." (II Cor. 6,10).

"Lord Jesus, in virtue of the merits of your hunger and thirst, of your patience in bearing heat and cold, of your birth in great need and of your perpetual poverty, of your humble acceptance of alms from your disciples and of your generous offerings of alms to other poor, grant me, through the intercessions of Mary and Joseph, your parents, the grace of sharing the triple redemptive desire for privations, sufferings and outrages, for the salvation and evangelization of the poor and of the poorest of the poor, the rich.[28]

"You have told us: 'There is more happiness in giving than receiving" (Acts 20:35). Grant me to give to others by accepting their gifts, in acknowledgement of my need, and grant me to offer joyously: "God loves a cheerful giver" (2 Cor 9:7). Have you not the power to crown me with all sorts of graces; so that having always and in all things all I need, I shall have enough left over for every good work (2 Cor 9:5)?[29]

On receiving a human body from Mary, you have wished to receive from her the capability of being hungry and thirsty, of suffering heat and cold, of being born, and born of her, in extreme indigence. You have wished to receive from Mary and through Mary the capability of being poor, of being the poor owner of the universe. As you turned to her to be and to become poor, so I turn also, under the inspiration of your Spirit, to her who has rendered you poor, you the infinitely rich."

"Virgin full of grace and rich in poverty of spirit, you became the mother and handmaid of your Savior and of our salvation. By consenting to be the Mother of God made man, you proclaimed yourself his handmaid: "I am the servant of the Lord; let it be done to me as you say." (Lk 2:38). Your maternity put you wholly at the service of your child. You became the slave of his saving love for sinful man. You, the immaculate, you put yourself at the service of sinners, as their slave of love, the handmaid of all the poor.

"May your intercession obtain for us to put ourselves at the service of the poor, our masters. Make us your slaves of love,[30] by putting us, in imitation of you, at the service of the Universal Church of which you are the type, the mother, the protectress. Make us slaves of the poor. Enrich our hearts, that our bodies may live in the extreme poverty of your Son, even accepting from time to time his indigence. May the poor, in whom your Son lives, thus escape extreme need. May your virginal hands continue, through ours, to enwrap them in the swaddling clothes of your motherly love, each time they do not find room in the inns of this world. Through them, your Son will ever say to you: "For I was hungry and you gave me food, I was thirsty and you gave me drink. I was naked and you clothed me" (Mt 25:35, 36).

Your Son, in the poor, is ever in need (cf. Ex. 114). We are poor little ones, unworthy slaves of Jesus, unworthy to serve him in the poor.

You have given a Savior in the setting of your virginal marriage to Saint Joseph, who has thus cooperated in our redemption."

"Saint Joseph, I address you as the spouse of Mary, my mother, as the chaste father of the infant Savior, as my protector, my patron, my father in Christ. You are the protector of all mankind, of the whole Church of the poor. You have worked hard to nourish by the fruit of your labors him who is the Bread of eternal life and to prepare for all the poor thereby a remedy and a food of immortality.

"As a token of gratitude for the gift of Christ, and for your intercession, I give myself and consecrate myself to you.[31] Protector of workers, of the dying and of the universal Church, I ask you to obtain for me the grace of proclaiming by my words and deeds, the scandal of the crib and of serving in this way all the poor out of love for Jesus poor.[32]

NOTES ON CHAPTER SEVEN

1. *Cf.* Pius XII, *Mystici Corporis,* AAS, 35 (1943); DS, 3805; CFW, 279.

2. Pius XII, *Mystici Corporis, Passim;* DS, 3806, 3807, 3813; Eph 1:23; CFW, 284.

3. GS, 43,6: "*Ecclesia, ex virtute Spiritus Sanci, fidelis Sponsa Domini sui,;* and CFW, 270-275.

4. *Cf.* CFW, 317-320 (ch. XII); SCG, III, 133; the raison d'être and the purpose of poverty are to liberate man from earthly concerns by enabling him more freely to engage in spiritual and divine matters. It is not good "*secundum se,*" but in function of this result, the Angelic Doctor states. In *De rationibus Fidei,* Ch. 7, he also explains the design the Son of God has had in taking on the nature of man:" to show by his acts and his sufferings that men should regard as nothing temporal things, good or bad, lest, as a consequence of a disordered love for temporal realities they have less attachment for spiritual things. This, as you see, is how Christ acted. He chose parents who were poor though perfect in virtue, so that no one is to boast of the nobility of his birth and of the wealth of his parents. He led a poor life to teach us to condemn riches. He lived without honor to rescue us from disordered love of honors. He bore the fatigue of toil, hunger, thirst, bodily chastisements, in order that on account of the rigors of this life, we might not turn away from the good of virtue in pursuit of pleasures and enjoyments. Finally, he suffered death in order that no one abandon truth out of fear of death, and the kind of suffering he chose, that of the cross is the most demeaning, in order that no one fear to expose himself to an infamous death for the sake of truth. . .And so was to be verified what Saint Peter says in his first epistle: 'because Christ has suffered for you, leaving you an example that you may follow in his steps' (1 Pt 2:21)." This wonderful text clearly sums up the salvific motivation of the various "mysteries" of the prepaschal life of Jesus.

5. The Bull, *Cum inter nonnullos* of John XXII (November 12, 1323; DS, 930, 931) condemns as heretical the opinion according to which Christ and the Apostles had owned nothing either in common or individually. John XXII condemned only those who denied to Christ the right to property, but he admitted that the Savior had renounced the exercise of this right in certain cases. Jesus did not forbid Himself the possibility of buying or selling. The Bull "*Quid quorumdam*" of November 10, 1324 by the same Pontiff concluded with this explicit definition: "He will be considered as a heretic whoever will maintain that Jesus Christ and his apostles had over the things they used only a use of fact. It cannot be induced, actually, that this usage they had was illicit, which would be a blasphemous conclusion." In the Bull "*Quia vir reprobus*" of November 16, 1329, John XII explained the doctrine for the last time: "As a Person of the Holy Trinity, Christ is master of all, although as man he has willed to live poor." *Cf.* G. Mollat, DTC, XIII, 1 (1924), 635,636).

6. *Cf.* Mt 19:23–26.

7. Bossuet, Sermon sur l'éminente dignité des pauvres, 1659. *Oeuvres complètes,* Paris, 1885, vol. VI, pp. 186,187.

8. GS,10: *"miseria oppressit."*

9. GS, 31: *"Libertas saepe debilior fit, ubi homo in extremam incidit egestatem."*

10. SCG, III.133: *"inquantum vero paupertas aufert bonum quod ex divitiis provenit, sc. subventionem aliorum et sustentationem propriam, simpliciter malum est. . .Bonum autem sustentationis propriae adeo necessarium est quod nullo alio bono recompensari potest: nullius enim boni obtentu debet homo sibi sustentationem vitae subtrahere."*

11. GS, 69: "If a person is in extreme necessity, he has the right to take from the riches of others what he himself needs." The Council quotes here the saying of the Fathers: "Feed the man dying of hunger, because, if you have not fed him, you have killed him."

12. GS, 88.

13. GS, 69: "The fathers and doctors of the Church held this view, teaching that men are obliged to come to the relief of the poor and to do so not merely out of their superfluous goods." (*cf.* another part of this text quoted in note 11.) The note 223 on this makes clear what is meant by quoting the norm laid down by John XXIII: "The obligation of every man. . .is to reckon what is superfluous by the measure of the needs of others" (AAS, 54,1962, p. 682).

14. LG, 41 at end.

15. PC, 13.

16. The Church, as Christ and his apostles, enjoys an inalienable right of collective ownership, sign and instrument of her independence in relation to the powers of this world, in view of carrying out her mission (*cf.* DS, 2926, 2927). Religious institutes which profess a collective poverty also enjoy a right to a collective property (cf. n. 29) limited by the right to life of each human being. In fact, Vatican II (GS, 69) calls to our attention (*cf.* note 11), the ancient principle: "In case of extreme necessity all goods are in common, that is, all goods are to be shared" (note 224; ST, II.II.66.7).

17. *Cf.* Ex. 104, V. We have commented on this in Chapter VI and we adapt it here to the particular case of Christ's poverty.

18. *Cf.* Ex. 114, V:*"aspectus personarum ut Virginis Deiparae, et Joseph conjugis."* Joseph mentioned as spouse of Mary is not found in the Autograph, P1 and P2 in Ex. 114. It is found, however, in A and P2 in Ex. 264. Leo XIII, *Quamquam pluries,* 1889, DS, 3260–63, has magnificently shown how Joseph's marriage to Mary rendered him a sharer in the dignity of the divine maternity by endowing him with a paternal authority over all Christians. About the marriage of Joseph and its importance in the economy of salvation, in the eyes of the pa . Bertrand, C.S.C., *Saint Joseph dans les écrits des Pères* Paris-Montr. , the views of Saint Augustine and of Saint Peter Chrysologus are particularly rich.

19. Saint Jerome, *Adv. Helv.* 19, ML, 23,223; *cf.* B. de Margerie, S.J., *Le Coeur de Marie, Coeur de l'Eglise,* Paris, 1967, pp. 25–29.

20. *Cf.* Paul VI, speech of March 19, 1969. *Ephemerides Mariologicae* 19 (1969) 504: Joseph was a man of "a profound interior life" whence came the decision to place immediately his freedom, his ligitimate human vocation, his conjugal happiness at the disposal of the divine designs. He did so by accepting the condition, the responsibility and the burden of a family, and by renouncing, through an incomparable chaste love, a *natural* conjugal

love which constitutes it and nourishes it to offer thus, by a total sacrifice, his whole existence to the imponderable exigences of the wondrous advent of the Messiah. (Taken from *l'Osservatore Romano* March 20-21, 1969; translation from Italian.)

21. *Cf.* Saint John of the Cross, Maxime 147, *Oeuvres complètes,* Bibliothèque Europeenne, Paris, 1967, p. 1318.

22. Human language has a real value and richness as it expresses the action and being of man, image and word of God, in his social relations. Its value is merely apparent each time it is reduced to but "nonsensical idle talk" (Heidegger). Saint James describes this in his epistle (1:19-22; 2:16; 3. 2-12).

23. Due to their fruits in this world and in eternal life, though they may have already passed historically. *Cf.* Mt 24:35, "Heaven and earth will pass, but my words will not pass."

24. The text of Ex. 116 V introduces a subtle consideration which is found neither in the Autograph nor in P2: "*ex expectatione. . .itineris, laborum et causarum, ob quas summus omnium Dominus. . .*" It is the entire complex and hierarchical ensemble of the finalities of the mystery of the Redemptive humanation of the Son of God which is in cause and at stake.

25. Let us observe here also the priceless distinctive traits of the Vulgate: a conscious contrast of the birth of Jesus in a "supreme indigence" with his life of 'perpetual poverty" (*summa egestate, perpetua paupertate*). The term "poverty" does not necessarily imply indigence or beggary as does the term "egestas." It seems that the translator of the Vulgate, with Saint Ignatius' approval, has intended to mark the difference between the miserable circumstance of the birth and the less extraordinary poverty, less "extrem," of the whole of Christ's life. The Vulgate differs quite clearly here from P2 and from the Autograph. The whole content of Ex. 116 is crowned in P2 by the verb "*perferat,*" which replaces the expression "*mei causa*" of the Vulgate and "*por mi*" of the Autograph in a much more "active" sense, indicating at the same time some passivity. Let us, finally, observe that this paragraph (Ex. 116) may be perfectly understood in the light of Saint Thomas' text quoted in note 4.

26. Of course, Saint Ignatius does not deny that the supreme action of Jesus in the mystery of his birth as in all others, is his human and divinized act of "seeing" the Father. Nor does he deny that thus the supreme and immanent act of the man Jesus is a "rejoicing" (*cf.* Jn 6:46 CFW, 230-233). Finally, he does not deny that the supreme and transitive act of Jesus as God is the creation of the world, his supreme and immanent act as God being the production of the Holy Spirit with the Father.

27. In Christ, in whom we possess all, we retain what we possess only to the extent that, following God's will, we accept to give it to him. A Christian paradox: he loses all if he refuses to give a share he ought to give, and on the contrary, he retains the possession in God of what he gives! And that above all!

28. "You deep saying: 'I am so rich and secure that I want for nothing.' Little do you realize how wretched you are, how pitiable and poor, how blind and naked" (Rv 3:17)! The expression "triple redemptive concupiscence" is inspired by the commentary on the Exercises by I. Bellecius S.J. of Poland (1704-1757), whose work was published in Spanish (Madrid 1945). The original is in excellent Latin.

29. cf. PC 13; "Communities (religious) should willingly contribute something from their own resources to the support of the poor." Precisely in this same number the Council upholds the right of religious institutes to own property yet in the likeness of Christ the poor owner. (*cf.* note 16.)

30. *Cf.* Saint Louis-Marie Grignon de Montfort, *Traité de la Vraie Dévotion a la Vierge Marie*, #120–25 and 202–12.

31. *Cf.* the prayer of consecration to the Holy Family recommended by the Holy See in 1890: AAS 23 (1890) 318–20; *cf.* DSAM, art. "Famille, Sainte."

32. It may be asked here whether the maid imagined by medieval piety and by Saint Ignatius as present in the stable with Mary and Joseph is not intended to present us a model somewhat more accessible (as less sublime) than that of Mary, of the concept of service to Jesus poor which the author of the Exercises wants to stress. In fact Ex. 114, which mentions the servant girl, invites us to make ourselves poor little unworthy slaves of Jesus, Mary and Joseph. Such an expression, which involves not only Jesus but also Mary and Joseph (as is seen not only in the Autograph but also in the Vulgate and P2 as well as in Puhl) contains explicitly the concept of consecration to the Holy Family extolled by Pope Leo XIII (*cf.* note 31) and from which we have deduced the liceity of consecration to Saint Joseph, for the glory of Jesus and Mary "serving them in their needs." Finally, let us observe in Ex. 114, a curious paradox of the Autograph: in presenting Mary as our Lady "*Nuestra Senora*" Saint Ignatius seems to forget that Mary presented herself as Handmaid, *ancilla Domini,* to the archangel Gabriel (Lk 1:38), and to reserve the role of servant to the one he calls "*ancilla*" and whom he say is Mary's servant.

But perhaps the author of the Exercises wanted to suggest by presenting Mary to us as our Lady and without any insistence on the handmaid of the Lord, the grandeur of the objective consecration of the Virgin by the Divine Maternity (LG, 53), which can not be reduced to any kind of service of the Lord, not even an exceptional one, since it makes the Virgin Mary enter into the order of the hypostatic union.

8

THE CONFRONTATION
THE CALL OF LUCIFER
AND THE CALL OF JESUS
DISCERNMENT OF SPIRITS

We now come to the exercise which is without doubt the most famous and which constitutes, along with the "Contemplation on the eternal King and His Kingdom," the backbone[1] of the Second Week: the Meditation on "Two Standards." Nowhere does Saint Ignatius call it a contemplation but always and everywhere he calls it a meditation. However, here as in the exercise on the King and his Kingdom, the call of Jesus is set against the background of another call, there preparatory, here contrasting. The objective aimed at is the obtaining of the grace for discernment of spirits, a manifestation of the Spirit in view of the common good (*cf.* 1 Cor 12: 10,7). We shall try, especially, here, to comment step by step on the Ignatian text.

The Title.

The Autograph entitles the exercise: "A Meditation on the Two Standards, one, that of Christ, our supreme leader, and Lord, the other, that of Lucifer, deadly enemy of our human nature" (Ex. 136).

It is important to note here that the term "standard" does not mean only a flag, but also a group, We would say today: program and party. In contrast with Christ, Lucifer is briefly described as "the deadly enemy of our human nature." He is the one who wishes and has ever wished to destroy it corporally and spiritually (*cf.* Jn. 8:44,40); the one who is the archfoe of men (V); the one who wishes the death, in time and eternity, of each human being. There is, in the world, a created intelligence (followed by many others!) which wishes, with an immortal perseverance, my ruin and my eternal damnation. I do not live in a universe that is neutral as far as I am concerned. I have powerful foes. They do not, however, evade the all-mightiness of my sovereign Lord.

Two leaders, two armies dispute over the freedom and happiness of my soul, one to save it, the other to kill it.

First prelude: the history

This prelude develops what was virtually contained in the title: "Christ calls and wants all beneath his standard; and Lucifer, on the other hand, wants all under his" (Ex. 137). Each, the Vulgate makes clear, wants to "enlist" them under his standard.

Jesus, the Christ, has established his Church as the "induction center," the gathering place (into one flock, *"grex"*) of all his disciples and intends that the Church be the permanent and indefectible sign,[2] among men and nations, of his saving love. It is in this sole and universal Church and through her that the Lord wants to gather all under the triumphant standard of his cross, through the Eucharist.

The call of Jesus is not only personal, it not only concerns individuals one by one, but it is also a social, collective call; Jesus wants to gather[3] into the Church those whom he is constantly calling. To save, for him, is to rescue from dispersion, it is to unify.

Thus, the Church herself becomes the standard of Christ, the sign which extends and displays his triumphant might. It is due to her that he is recognizable by all generations, in her that he can be touched, seen, heard, loved and eaten.

Inversely, Lucifer wants to gather men in visible counter-churches, organizations the common bond of which is hostility to the visible and holy Church.

However, Saint Ignatius does not invite us to fight against these counter-churches, or against their members, but against Lucifer.

Second Prelude: the place

The author of the Exercises invites us "to see a great plain, comprising the whole region about Jerusalem, where the sovereign commander-in-chief of all the good is Christ our Lord; and another plain about the region of Babylon, where the chief of the enemy is Lucifer" (Ex. 138).

Jerusalem, Babylon: Augustinian and Biblical symbols.

In fact,[4] it seems that the grand, Biblical current has reached, on this point, Saint Ignatius by way of medieval Augustinianism. On reading the lives of the Saints, the convalescent young knight noticed this passage from the *City of God* which sheds a bright light on his meditation on the "Two Standards": Christ is the king of Jerusalem, the devil, the king of Babylon. Two loves have become two cities, love of self, growing into contempt of God, has built the city of the devil; love of God, growing into contempt of self, has built the City of God.[5]

The Church is the new Jerusalem, where Christ[6] the leader of the "good" reigns. In the combat against Babylon, she readies herself for her spouse (*cf.* Rv. 21:1 ff).

It may very well be that Saint Ignatius had in mind here the second eschatological combat described in Revelation: "(Satan) will go forth to seduce the nations in all four corners of the earth, and muster for war troops numerous as the sands of the sea . . . *They invaded the whole country and surrounded the beloved city where God's people were encamped;* but fire came down from heaven and devoured them" (Rev 20:7–9).

It is important to note that only here in the Exercises (Ex. 136, 137, 138) is Satan called Lucifer, the Morning Star. Everywhere else, except when he speaks of devils, which is not often, (Ex. 141, 281), Saint Ignatius speaks rather of the "enemy of human nature," or quite simply, of the "enemy." Why is the title "lucifer" used here? We think there are two reasons. On the one hand, to remind us, in the context of a meditation on the wiles of the enemy, that "It is a mark of the evil spirit to assume the appearance of an angel of light" (Ex. 332,4; *cf.* 2 Cor 11:18). He wants to seduce, to deceive. On the other hand, Saint Ignatius wants to suggest that the devil is already vanquished: "How have you fallen from the heavens, O morning star, son of the dawn! How are you cut down to the ground, you who moved down the nations!" (Is 14:12; *cf.* Lk 10; 18; Rv 8:10; 9:1; 12:9), and so, in a sense, is no longer to be feared. The believer, reader of Scripture, knows that Babylon has been conquered by Jerusalem, Satan dethroned by Christ. Still, will Satan be definitely dethroned in his own soul? So then, the use of this unusual title for the devil prepares the retreatant for a more ardent desire of the peculiar fruit of this meditation: "Knowledge of the deceits of the rebel chief and help to guard myself against them," awareness and defense against the ruses of him who presents himself as the morning star, Lucifer, but who actually is the prince of the world of darkness (Eph 6:12).

Third Prelude: petition for the grace desired.[7]

That is to say: "In addition to a knowledge of the deceits of the rebel chief, and help to guard against them, to ask for knowledge of the true life exemplified in the sovereign and true commander, and the grace to imitate him" (Ex. 139).

It is the very request of *discernment of spirits,* "a fine sense of the divine and the demoniacal in the happenings of history as in the trials of the interior life," a "perfect competence in all that concerns Jerusalem and Babylon."[8] The grace sought is inseparably one of light and of power, of light for the intellect, of power for the will. Often deceived by the devil, I ask the favor of being undeceived in regard to him. Ignorant of the true life, I want to become a disciple of Christ who teaches it. The wiles of the devil, mortal enemy of mankind, would lead me to death; the grace and teaching of Jesus bring me to life.

The true life is eternal life, begun here below,[9] through acts of the theological virtues.[10] "What is seen is transitory; what is unseen lasts forever."

(II Cor 4:18). Satan, "the god of this present age" (II Cor 4:4) wants to draw me into an idolatry of temporal life,[11] to convert me to a disordered conversion toward created and changing good. This is one of his principal ruses.

Compared to the true captain, Jesus, Satan is a bandit chief,[12] whose shares are, quite contrary to what he intends and in spite of him, means of action in the service of the victorious Christ. Christ makes use even of his foes to carry out his hidden designs of grace and glory. The temptations of the devil occasion meritorious acts. I have nothing to fear from them. Yet my freedom is still fragile, my intelligence of the demoniacal wiles very limited. The global triumph of Christ on Calvary does not necessarily mean his future victory in me and over me. Even if I am (and I cannot be absolutely sure[13]) among the "good" of whom Christ is the leader (Ex. 138), I am also a "wound," an "abscess," a wound imperfectly healed, capable, alas, of going over to the enemy, to the camp of the "wicked," of those who, by mortal sin, are mortal enemies, as is Lucifer, of the human nature assumed by the Son of God and of the "camp of the saints, of the well-beloved city."

First Part: the Standard of Satan: First Point: Lucifer

"Imagine you see the chief of all the enemy in the vast plain about Babylon, seated on a great throne of fire and smoke, his appearance inspiring horror and terror" (Ex. 140).

Lucifer is seated on a throne of fire, immersed in the flames of his eternal condemnation which he would like to share by spreading erroneous doctrines (the smoke of this fire). The fire which accompanies the fixity of his prodigious natural intelligence, fixed in the wilful and culpable rejection of supernatural mysteries, keeps spewing forth the smoke of an "earthly, animal, diabolical wisdom which does not descend from above" but ascends from below. "Wisdom like this does not come from above. It is earthbound, a kind of of animal, even devilish, cunning" (Jas 3:15). Brilliant doctrines, but confused, obscure, filled with contradictions, and above all with error: liberalism,[14] idealism, Hegelianism, Marxism; the anguish of atheistic existentialism, hedonism,[15] all alike reject in one way or another, the economy of salvation established by the humble mediator Jesus. All these doctrines alike constitute the background which obsesses most of our contemporaries, the "drama of atheistic humanism;" the conflict waged is above all concentrated against the ethic of Christ and of his Church.[16]

From his lofty "throne of fire and smoke," on the "plain of Babylon the great, the immense and mighty city, resort of demons" (Rv 18: 2,10), Lucifer teaches: "For she has made all nations drink the poisoned wine," heady with errors and his "lies" (Rv 18:3; Jn 8,44). He hides and disguises his "horrible and terrifying appearance," the ugliness of his apostasy and of his rebellion as well as the eternal sanction of despair meted out to it, a chastisement the retreatant is invited to "imagine" and to see with eyes of faith.

Second Point: The universal diabolic mission (cf. Rv 12:4,7,9; 16: 13-16).

Here Saint Ignatius considers "how the chief of all the enemy summons innumerable demons,[17] and scatters them, some to one city and some to another, throughout the entire world, so that no province, no place, no state of life, no individual is overlooked" (Ex. 141). Why this summons? To "harm" (V), by the diffusion of perverse doctrines,[18] as we mentioned before.

The author mentions only demons sent out by Lucifer. He does not speak of men. It may be conjectured the reason for his silence is to bring out: "our battle is not against human forces, but against the principalities and powers, the rulers of this world of darkness, the evil spirits in regions above," (Eph 6:12),[19] precisely for the salvation (always possible) of those led astray, rather than the denial of the possibility or of the fact of men enlisting permanently and organically in the service of furthering Lucifer's perverse objectives (Ex. 332).

The parallel with the second point of the second part of the meditation (Ex. 145) where Christ sends out men, forbids the conclusion that Satan does not do so. In fact, Saint Ignatius does not speak of angels sent out by Christ and yet does not thereby deny the fact. Likewise, he does not deny that false prophets are sent out by Satan. As Saint Paul tells us: "Such men are false apostles. They practice deceit in their disguise as apostles of Christ. And little wonder! For even Satan disguises himself as an angel of light. It comes as no surprise that his ministers disguise themselves as ministers of the justice of God. But their end will correspond to their deeds" (2 Cor 11: 13-15).

"False prophets" are not necessarily conscious of being "ministers of Satan" yet still not being less so. They do not speak in the name[20] of Satan though Satan can foment their illusion of being true prophets. In fact "false prophets"[21] believe even that they speak in the name of Jesus Christ, when they favor (as did those of the Old Testament) the various forms of temporal messianism, of worldliness. In one way or other, they preach "another Jesus,[22'] a different gospel" from the ones Saint Paul and the Church announce (II Cor 11:4). Briefly, the devil has his theologians. Even when he does not inspire them, they concur in his designs.

Am I sure I have never in my life been "a minister of Satan disguised as a minister of justice," a false prophet, speaking without credentials, without or contrary to divine inspiration, the will of the eternal? Am I sure I have never placed my intellect, my memory, my will, my words, my deeds at the service of the universal diabolical mission, of the innumerable demons dispatched by the chief of the enemies of human nature? Or, then, have I, for lack of discernment of spirits, not taken for "divine ministers of justice" and of holiness "deceitful spirits and things taught by devils" (I Tim 4:1)? Or, too, have I not collaborated with them? Cooperated in spreading their doctrines?

Third point: Address and strategy of Lucifer, enemy chieftain.

Saint Ignatius wants us to "consider the address" Lucifer makes to these innumerable demons whom he summons and "how he goads them on to lay snares for men, to seek to chain them" (Ex. 142). What are these snares and chains? Lucifer's address to his troops will tell us:

"First they are to tempt them to covet riches (as Satan himself is accustomed to do in most cases) that they may the more easily attain the empty honors of this world, and then come to overweening pride.

"The first step, then, will be riches, the second honor, the third pride. From these three steps the evil one leads to all other vices" (Ex. 142), the author of the Exercises sorrowfully adds. The snares of riches and honor lead to the chain of pride, which renders man a prisoner of Satan.

Satan is not looking for willing adherence on our part to his program. He wants to take our free will by surprise through his wiles in order to enslave us. By the *"moral vices"* of avarice and ambitious vanity, Lucifer wants to bring us to the other *"horizontal vices"* and especially to *"vertical vices"*, theological vices of unbelief, despair and hatred of the divine Redeemer of men redeemed, to plunge us into eternal hell and its flames to which he willed to condemn himself. Out of avaricious and vain pride,[23] Lucifer wants to set us on the road, by murder and blasphemy (Ex. 106–108), and to ever unbelieving, hateful pride. From social pride to pure pride, from worldly pride to infernal pride.

Let us note the significance of what Saint Ignatius has to say, as it were in parenthesis, in presenting the demonical exhortation a propos of the concupiscence of riches" (as Satan himself is accustomed to do in most cases)." It seems highly probable[24] that there is in this a clear allusion, direct or indirect, to a text of Saint Thomas Aquinas[25] which explains the words of the Apostle: "The love of money is the root of all evils" (I Tm 6:10). This text is but an expression of a common saying current in the profane literature of the period.

The Angelic Doctor explains: Just as the root nourishes the whole tree, so man by riches acquires the concrete possibility of committing any sin whatsoever, since money helps acquire any good whatsoever.[26]

It is understandable that Lucifer tempts man by avarice rather than by lust. Man, being corporeal, is spontaneously inclined to the pleasures of the flesh, so such a temptation would be from the start superfluous, while avarice, despite certain appearances, is a sin of the spirit. The avaricious man in his mind anticipates future pleasures which he presently does not know. "On account of its object, avarice holds an intermediate place between spiritual sins, such as pride, and purely carnal vices, seeking bodily pleasure related to an object that is also corporeal.[27] Lucifer, a pure spirit, therefore tempts man at the first by a sin of the spirit, a sin which, however, is within the confines of the flesh. Saint Ignatius, besides, has slightly modified the Angelic Doctor's thought on which he drew. Saint Thomas judged that avarice was ordinarily, but not always, the root of other sins. Saint Ignatius speaks of the first object of diabolical temptations inducing man to sin.[28]

The riches envisioned by the avaricious may be, too, something material, also effective or intellectual: "all that the heart possesses, and which possesses the heart, all that makes nature overflow and drown out grace may be called riches."

Riches, honors, pride: these three steps of the fall into eternal damnation and hell can also be considered as three aspects taken on by every sin committed by a human being, who is ever a cosmic, social and metaphysical animal. There is in every grave sin a disorderly conversion to a created good of the universe, of society and of one's own person, in contempt of the author of this triple good, God. A love of self growing into an inordinate desire for money and honors, into a contempt of the Creator. And venial sin, tends toward this horizon and at least indirectly disposes to it.

Has it not happened to me, not only to listen to Lucifer's address, but also to become its mouthpiece? Have I not been his minister, drawn others to the desire of riches, flattered them, set Satan's snares, chained men to their pride instead of setting them free?[29]

And when grace was given to me to close my ears to Lucifer's call, to reject the selfish desire for money and honors, have I not let myself be overcome by succumbing to pride in my victory?[30]

Second Part: The sovereign and true Captain Christ our Lord.

After he has had us consider the person of Lucifer, his address and his program, the author of the Exercises introduces us to the second part of the meditation in these words: "In a similar way, we are to picture to ourselves the sovereign and the commander, Christ our Lord" (Ex. 143), "the supreme and excellent leader" (Ex. 143, V).

There is suggested in this way the idea that Lucifer is not a supreme chief and was not to be put on the same ontological plane as Christ his Creator who drew him out of nothing and preserves him in being, Christ who is still his Lord even after the rebellion and fall of this morning star. Satan, even while he dispatches countless demons to tempt men, is still an instrument of Christ the Savior. Christ, who tempts no one, wills to permit men to be tempted for their good and for rooting them in virtue. Lucifer's call serves to bring out an appeal by Christ to resist him and thus to merit eternal life. These snares of Satan are never beyond Christ's control. The wicked chieftain, the mortal enemy of human nature never escapes the dominion of the Word become man, the true, the good leader.[31] Perversity, despite itself, is at the service of love.

First Point: the presentation of Christ

While Lucifer, in Babylon, is as it were seated on a throne of fire and smoke, horrible and terrifying to behold, "Christ our Lord, is standing in a lowly place in a great plain about the region of Jerusalem, his appearance beautiful and attractive" (Ex. 144). "Handsome in stature and supremely lovable in appearance" (V).

Jesus, on whom reposes the septiform Spirit, "shall not judge by appearence nor by hearsay shall he decide, but he shall judge the poor with justice, and decide aright for the land's afflicted" (Is 11:2-5). He is the living antithesis of the king of Babylon, symbol of Lucifer (Is 14, 4-21).

In the "great camp" of the heavenly Jerusalem come down upon the earth, the Church, Christ stands today in a lowly place," that is, in the earthly Jerusalem, known as Rome. The Rome of the pagan Caesars was the heir of Babylon. The Rome of the Popes is and will be the continuation of Jerusalem[32] through his vicar on earth. Christ lives on to govern and enlighten his Church, the "great camp of the saints" which constitutes the one, universal Church.

In contrast to Satan so horrible, Jesus is "beautiful and attractive." The external and especially the inner splendor of his holy humanity is the most perfect reflection among creatures of the infinite and ineffable beauty of his Divinity, before which all created beauties are, as Saint John of the Cross says,[33] nothing but an abyss of ugliness.

Will my soul consent to be a Jerusalem, a vision of peace, a city of repose, a humble and beautiful refuge for the Son of God and for his infinite beauty? Will the depths of my soul, opened up to the infinite, become the "great camp" whence the eternal Word will go forth on ever new conquests and new sacrifices?

Second Point: Choice of Apostles and the Mission of Christ.

Here the retreatant is invited to "consider how the Lord of all the world chooses so many persons, apostles, disciples, etc., and sends them throughout the whole world to spread his sacred doctrine among all men, no matter what their state or condition" (Ex. 145). For this sacred doctrine is "salvific" (Ex. 145, V). It is the "word of salvation,"[34] the Word who saves.

If by "condition" is meant undoubtedly both health and social status,[35] "state" means either the ordinary Christian vocation of observing the commandments, or marriage, or evangelical perfection (cf. Ex. 135, 189). Let us note this: our Lord sends his apostles not only to the laity, to married persons, but also to men and women religious.

The "chosen" disciples are, in a general but very profound sense, all baptized and confirmed Christians. "The lay apostolate, however, is a participation in the saving mission of the Church itself. Through their baptism and confirmation all are commissioned to that apostolate by the Lord himself." [36] Vatican II emphasizes: "Upon all the laity, therefore, rests the noble duty of working to extend the divine plan of salvation ever increasingly to all men of each epoch and in every land." [37] All the laity, each epoch, every land . . . everywhere the laity should spread, sow [38] the doctrine of Christ himself by their works, by the witness of their lives of course, but also by "looking for opportunities to announce Christ by words addressed" [39] to be others.

If the disciples are equivalent to all the baptized, are not the "apostles" chosen by Christ those whom he invites to receive the sacrament of orders (the diaconate, the priesthood, the episcopate)? [40]

And are not all, disciples, apostles, laity and priests, called to the acquisition of a solid, personal knowledge, by reading, study, reflection and prayer, of this doctrine of Christ, sacred and salvific, which they should spread? How could they present it acceptably if they did not know it profoundly?

Christ's doctrine is his revelation, [41] the message received from the Father to be transmitted to mankind. "My doctrine is not mine but of him who has sent me" (Jn 7:16).

The disciple, the apostle is not sent to announce or preach his own opinions, but Christ's doctrine and that of his Church (cf. Gal 1:8,9).

In this visible mission, envoys of Jesus the Lord, are invisibly assisted by angels, [42] and by the intercession of the saints. Men's guardian angels pray for the success of apostolic efforts made on behalf of their proteges. The human and earthly word of the apostles is mightely re-echoed by heavenly voices. Through the numerous men chosen by Christ, the angelic legion at the service of the only Son announces his gospel to his brothers (cf. Mt 26:53; 28:5). The human-divine word is borne on the wings of angels.

Third Point: Christ's discourse to His servants and friends.

The author of the Exercises presents us the program of Jesus, a complement to the call of the Kingdom, no longer addressed to all men (Ex. 95) and to each one among them, but only to his "servants and friends," [43] to men in the state of grace and friendship with the Son of Man which is furthermore everyman's vocation.

"I recommend to you to seek to help all (Jn 15:15), first by attracting them to the highest spiritual poverty, and should it please the Divine Majesty, and should he deign to choose them for it, even to actual poverty. Secondly, you should lead them to a desire for insults and contempt, for from these springs humility.

"Hence, there will be three steps: the first, poverty as opposed to riches; the second, insults or contempt as opposed to the honor of this world; the third, humility as opposed to pride. From these three steps, you are[44] to lead men to all other virtues."[45]

"Seek to help all": the offer of help becomes the great visible means of the "will to conquer" of the eternal king (Ex. 95). "Attract them to the highest spiritual poverty": if they become, thanks to your word, aware of not having anything of their own, anything coming from themselves, except, in the last analysis, their faults, sins and vices,[46] their covetousness, vain mundane honor and pride, they will be inclined no longer to desire to accumulate riches, but rather to regard themselves as administrators who are to render an account to the supreme owner, God the Creator and preserver of the universe.

This "supreme poverty of spirit" is not satisfied with refusing to make absolute the desire for earthly goods, by limiting the desire for them in accordance with the divine will, with a conditional desire.[47] It goes beyond that and includes the surrender of one's own judgment, of all self-will, of every desire inspired by them, ever ready to renounce social esteem for the glory of God. Therefore, it divorces itself from all aspirations of having, of making a show, in order to be. It is detachment vis-a-vis every inordinate affection and even from every creature whatsoever. "My God and my all!"

Attract all men, all whom the Divine Providence of the Father will have cross your path, not only to this supreme inner deprivation possible thanks to the gift of the Holy Spirit,[48] but also to effective, actual poverty, a poverty of renuntiation of property, or of the liberty in the use of goods. Do not say only: "How blessed are the poor in spirit: the reign of God is theirs" (Mt, 5:3), but also: "If you seek perfection, go, sell your possesions and give to the poor. You will then have treasure in heaven. Afterward come back and follow me."[49] The treasure in heaven, is it not Jesus Himself?

In the second place, attract all men to desire insults, humiliations, in contrast with worldly honor. A paradox, is it not? It is precisely poverty, and especially humiliations men have a horror of. To that, too, we have a mission of attracting them!

Vatican II speaks the same language: "Just as Christ carried out the work of redemption in poverty and under oppression, so the Church is called to follow the same path in communicating to man the fruits of salvation."[50]

Neither Vatican II nor Saint Ignatius could say anything different, for the Gospels know but this: "Blessed are you when they insult you and persecute you and utter every kind of slander against you because of me. Be glad and rejoice, for your reward is great in heaven" (Mt 5:11,12).

A program like this shocks me of all times. But perhaps it shocks even

more our contemporaries. Do we not live in an era which exalts development and personality? How can we reconcile these economic, social, personal
aspirations with the counsels of the Gospels and of the saints?[51]

As a matter of fact the conflict is artificial. If one considers the whole of
the New Testament as well as the lives and writings of the saints, it vanishes
in a tranquil tension constantly sustained by the exercises of complementary
and related virtues, unified and summed up by charity.

Personal love of each one for spiritual poverty, the oft renewed desire for
insults should not be seperated from the struggle against insults and misery
unjustly inflicted on Christ today in others. Otherwise, this love and this desire would not be genuine.

Furthermore, the thirst for spiritual and actual poverty, the desire to be
humiliated and contradicted for the glory of God are indispensable for the
true and complete development of a personality ever threatened with being
stifled by the concupiscence issuing from original sin, by the consequences
of personal sins, even by acquired vices, not to mention temptations by the
devil. This thirst and this desire re-establish the balance of personality and
thus condition its development. Without them, there is no access to humble
love which alone can enter into possession of the immutable, eternal Good in
the exercise of charity.

All men, even the poorest, are in some way rich. There is need to renounce
some riches of "self" to enter fully into the supernatural order. In the same
way, "none of you can be my disciple if he does not renounce all his possessions" (Lk 14:33).[52] There is need to renounce the selfish possession not only
of money but also of ideas, human relations, and even of suffering.[53]

Why are we so attached to money, to knowing, even to suffering itself unless it be to gain recognition of our worth from others? Likewise, inordinate
attachment to consolations, (Ex.323,324) is also contrary to the humility which
puts its trust in God and to supreme spiritual poverty. It may equally have
horizontal connotations, be allied to a seeking of the glory which comes from
men (Jn 12:42) and not that which comes from God. There may be preferred
the reputation of being a man of prayer rather than that of self-denial without which no prayer is wholly aggreeable to God.[54]

So there appears for what reasons we help and succour most others when
we lead them, under the action of grace, to supreme spiritual poverty and to
the desire of insults, conditions of a perfect humility.[55]

So let us sum up the meaning of the tactic of Jesus Christ and of his program in contrast to Lucifer:

—that God be truly the supreme value in my own eyes, I deny my innate tendancy to regard myself as being a supreme value. I remain without
value, in my own eyes: supreme spiritual poverty;

—to attain this degree of inner deprivation, I desire to be also without
value, nothing, in the eyes of others: desire for insults;

—to be without worth in the eyes of others, I adopt the degree of actual and effective poverty compatible with my state of life or with that to which God calls me: men, in general despise poverty.

Of course, I know that the being I have from God, as well as my vocation in the divine plan, are values, and charity toward others obliges me to desire for them the good of holding them in esteem. But my innate tendency, the result of original sin, to erect myself into an absolute and to desire to be adored by others brings about that the old man in me is not satisfied with a limited esteem, one referred to the supreme good, an esteem opening my eyes to my limits and faults. In the eyes of my self-love, there is question of a contempt, a contempt for which the desire of insults for the glory of Christ comes as a remedy of truth, within the bosom of the totality of the divine plan.

Spiritual and actual poverty, the desire for humiliations, ready me so that, without vain fear of men, I can love them to the extent of proclaiming the mystery of their own salvific cross included within the cross of Christ. "Perfect love casts out all fear" (1 Jn 4:18).

Father Rouquette therefore was able to synthetize the meaning of the Exercises and particularly the "Two Standards" in this luminous passage:[56]

"The precise purpose of the Exercises is to raise up true Apostles . . . A difficult task: the apostle has no need of a superficial enthusiam which will soon die out. He will radiate Christ to the extent that he is to identify himself with Him, the Christ bearing scars. *To raise up an apostle is, therefore, to induce a men to choose freely, with full consciousness, by a definitive option, the cross, the poverty and the humility of Christ as supreme values.*"

Not only does Christ call all men to supreme spiritual poverty, to the acceptance of contempt and desire for it, to the humility of the daily cross, but he calls each man—and so all—to call each and every other person—and so all. In fact it is by inviting others to spread around them the desire of imitating and following Christ's poverty and humility that they will be invited themselves to share in it most efficaciously.

The apostles and disciples of Jesus, invited to present his salvific doctrine of spiritual poverty and of joyous desire for humiliation, are thus called to liberate the liberated, still partically captives, by the exercise of liberality. No one is helped and no one liberated save by becoming a slave (Mk 10: 44,45). Saved, I should, out of gratitude, be a savior.

It is not enough, however, to *consider* (Ex. 141,142,144,145,146). It is necessary, too, to *"ask for what I desire"* (Ex. 139). That is why the author of the Exercises invites us to ask Mary, then Jesus, and finally the Father what the meditation has suggested we desire. It is the triple colloquy ending with the "Hail Mary", the *Anima Christi"* and the "Our Father" (Ex. 147). The simple fact of the supernatural request makes more penetrating and more profound the desire I already had.

Colloquies with Our Lady, the Son, the Father and the Spirit of the Father and of the Son.

"Immaculate Virgin, obtain for me from your Son and Lord the grace to be received under his standard, in supreme spiritual poverty and not less in actual poverty, if his Divine Majesty is to be served thereby and is willing to choose and receive me,[57] then, suffering humiliations and wrongs,[58] in order to imitate him moreover thus, provided I may suffer them without sin on the part of any other or without displeasing his Divine Majesty.

"You have perfectly triumphed over Satan, without ever having been his slave. New Eve, you have never let yourself be deceived by Lucifer, but the God of peace has through you crushed under your heel the infernal serpent (Rom 16:20; Gn 3:15). Now the Devil has come down to us furious with rage and knowing that his days are numbered. He wars against the rest of your children (Rev 12:12, 17).

"God has reared an irreconcilable enmity between your children and the tools of Satan, the infernal legions of his satelites (Gn 3:15). You have such power to overthrow and crush the head of the proud and impious rebel who fears you more than all angels and men. Your humility lays low his pride more than the divine might manifested by that humility.

"You ever unveil the serpent's malice, as well as his machinations. Ever will you dispel his diabolical counsels. To the end of time, you will protect your loyal servitors from his snares.

"They will be little and poor in the world's esteem, debased in the eyes of all, but rich in God's grace which your Immaculate Heart will impart to them in abundance.[59]

"Out of love for Jesus, you have been poor, spiritually and actually, you have suffered, you the Mother of God, the Immaculate, humiliations and wrongs, you have drunk the chalice of your Son. Grant that I may whet my lips on that chalice! Obtain for me the grace to make known to the world your external poverty and your riches and immaculate fulness of interior grace, the sublime dignity of the Divine Maternity to which you have been elevated and the depths of humility with which you have received it, your desire to share in the *kenosis* and in the cross of your Son and the glorious Assumption which came about to recompense your compassion."

"Lord Jesus, poor sweet and humble of Heart, I ask you, as my only mediator with the Father to obtain for me from him the same graces. Since you are my creator, I beg you too, purely and simply, to grant them to me!"

"You build the heavenly Jerusalem on and out of the ruins of Babylon.[60] The temptations of concupiscence[61] for riches and honors are the instrument by which you wish to strengthen and deepen in us this priceless gift: the desire for spiritual poverty and humiliation in your name.

"You call some to the actual poverty of full deprivation only in order to call, through them, all their brothers to the supreme poverty of complete detachment in the midst of the wealth and ordinary use of the goods of this world, in the bosom of a perfect spiritual and sacramental communion.[62] Actual poverty would lose all meaning if it did not pursue the achievement of its purpose: communion among men in the use of earthly goods, impossible without spiritual poverty.

"The Church which you have founded and animate constantly by your Holy Spirit is precisely a mystery of universal communion in charity and poverty of spirit. Of this universal communion you have willed to leave us an efficacious sign: the papacy. Through your vicar on earth, you continue to govern your Church and enlighten the world, directing it toward the perfect development of all human persons.[63]

"Satan, in his hatred of your reign, tries in vain[64] to destroy the indestructable rock on which you have founded your Church. Less in vain, he endeavors to separate a number of Christians from it, oppose a number of men to it.

"Jesus, you are the head of Your Church: today invisible to our bodily eyes, you become visible in your vicar on earth.[65] Give us such spiritual poverty, such surrenderring of our own judgment and will, that Satan may never be able to seperate us from the visible, universal pastor of your Kingdom. Preserve us from the diabolical doctrines of false prophets who would wish to prevent our hierarchical and full communion with him, seperated from whom we would be cut off from you.[66]

"The supreme spiritual poverty to which you invite me is one with pure love of your Person. In loving you for yourself, because of your infinite goodness and lovableness, which surpasses all your gifts, I possess all in you alone (cf. Ex. 370 and 236). Your love for me and for the world impoverished, humiliated, abased itself. You have desired for my salvation to be abject and humiliated. Your Heart, crowned with the thorns of my avarice, my vanity, my pride, has ever told me so. The open wound of your Heart is the standard in and under which I want to combat my pride and that of Lucifer.

"Soul of Christ, sanctify me; from the malice of the devil, defend me; water flowing from the side of Christ, wash me; O Jesus, in the sacred wound of your Heart, hide me. Your wounds are my riches and my glory."

Father, in the name of the merits of your only Son, in the name of his poverty and of his humility, grant me the abundance of the gifts of your Holy Spirit, that I may be able to discern the spirits, the snares of Lucifer and of his troops from the inspirations of your angels."

"Spirit of the Father and of the Son, you came abundantly to me the day of my confirmation to strengthen me against Satan by fortifying me with your gifts. By them, the struggle against Lucifer becomes easy. Grant me to discern the spirits, the movements which are in me,[67] to recognize the deceits of the liar, to shun riches and honors, thanks to your gifts of counsel and strength. Would not the fear of humiliations, of contempt, and of poverty be the main obstacle which might prevent me from being an apostle, and an apostle proud of the cross, of the ignominy of Christ's poverty?[68] By your unction, I have received you, Spirit of strength, to be able to confess before men, in word and deed, Christ, your Anointed par excellence, Christ poor and humiliated, triumphing over Lucifer by his poverty and by his humility. Spirit of Jesus, eternally proceeding from the Word, sent in time by him, glorify through me the only Son and his Father (cf. Jn 16:14; 14:13). Give me the grace to persevere to my last day in the struggle against the powers of darkness[69] disguised as angels of light.

"Spirit of love and of light, term and fruit of the mutual and eternal love of the Father and the Son, work in me these joyous, perfect, and savory acts of affective and effective poverty, of humility and of the desire for humiliations which constitute your fruits[70] and put me on the road to the supremely blessed act of the perpetual vision of your eternal procession."

NOTES ON CHAPTER EIGHT

1. "From the beginning of his conversion and of his vocation, when he had withdrawn into the seclusion of Montserrat (Ignatius) devoted himself chiefly to two exercises, that of the Two Standards and that of the King preparing for war against the infernal enemy and against the world." This is what Father P. O. Manare, one of the first companions of Ignatius tells us (Exhortationes, p. 344, quoted by A. Codina, Los origenes de los Ejercicios espirituales, Barcelona, 1926, p. 14). What Father Rahner writes is quite understandable in view of this: "The Society was born out of the fundamental meditation of the Two Standards" (S. Ignace de Loyola et la genèse des Exercices, Toulouse, 1948, p. 128).

2. This is the teaching of Vatican I (DS, 3012,3013) and of Vatican II. "The Church has never ceased to be a sign of salvation on earth" (GS, 43), a standard set up for the nations (Is 11:12), under which the children of God dispersed are gathered together in unity, until there is one fold and one shepherd (SC, 2) and which offers mankind the gospel of peace (UR, 2 at the end). Such is the concept that is taken up, contained in and made more profound in that of the Church, sacrament of salvation, so dear to Vatican II. The sacrament is more than a simple sign. It communicates and contains the grace it signifies. In this sense, the Church is the standard of the salvation wrought through Christ. It is a standard which gives and contains him.

3. Cf. LG, 9: "It has pleased God, however, to make men holy and save them, not merely as individuals without any mutual bonds, but by making them into a single people . . . an instrument for the redemption of all" (LG, 9 toward end.).

4. Cf. H. Rahner, S.J., op. cit. p. 45.

5. Saint Augustine, De Civitate Dei, ML, 41.436; cf. Enarrationes in Psalmos 61:6 and 64:2; ML, 36,733,734,773.

6. Cf. Rv 20:7-9; LG, 6: The Church is "the holy city, the New Jerusalem, coming down out of heaven from God when the world is made anew, and prepared like a bride adorned for her husband (Rv 21: 1ff).

7. Ex. 139, V.: "ad gratiam petendam; P2: "Petere quod volo."

8. H. Rahner, op. cit., pp. 59,60.

9. See the Gospel of Saint John, passim, but especially 17:3; 3:36; 5:24; 6:40: he who believes in Christ has eternal life. He has it already.

10. *Cf.* Ex. 316: "I call consolation . . . every increase of faith, hope and love", For such an increase, infused, is brought about by acts of these virtues.

11. AA, 7. The Council adds: "Many . . . have fallen into an idolatry of temporal things and have become their slaves rather than their masters."

12. Saint Ignatius never employs the Spanish word "caudillo" about Christ. He reserves that term for Lucifer: Ex. 138,139,140,327 (A).

13. *Cf.* DS, 1534;1563. A moral certitude is possible.

14. Here too we think not only of philosophical and theological liberalism which denies "the moral duty of man and his associations toward the true religion and the one Chruch of Christ" (DH,3) but also of an economic liberalism which is partly a consequence of it and which Vatican II has also condemned (GS, 65) at the same time extolling rights, properly understood, of human freedom.

15. GS, 72,2.

16. It is, for instance, the attitude of Nieztsch: "The only problem of the truth of Christianity—the existence of its God or the historicity of its legend is a very secondary problem so long as the value of Christian morality is not questioned." *Volonté de Puissance,"* trad. Bianquis, vol. I, p. 140; H. de Lubac, *Le Drame de l'humanisme athée,* Paris, 1945.

17. *Cf.* ST; I.63.8 c,1; 2; I, 109, 2, c, ad 3; I, 114,2. Devils are not equal by nature. On the other hand the devil tempts with a proximate end in view, to find out what he does not know, an end ordered to another end, to harm by precipitating into sin. God alone knows the interior state of man, according to which certain men are more inclined to one vice than to another. Consequently, the devil tempts by exploring the interior state of man to find out to which vice he is more inclined (ST, I.114.2.2; *cf.* Ex. 327). So what the Vulgate says, that the devil tempts in order to harm (Ex. 114, V), is exactly in agreement with Saint Thomas' thinking.

18. *Cf.* Ex. 332 on the perverse designs of the devil; I Tm 4:1; "The Spirit distinctly says that in later times some will turn away from the faith and will heed deceitful spirits and things taught by demons." By his perverse doctrines the devil wants to combat the sacred and salvific teaching of Christ, His true doctrine. (Ex. 145,164).

19. *Cf.* H. Schlier, *Principalities and Powers,* New York, 1961, pp. 33–39; and *passim;* and Y.M.J. Congar, O.P. "Here (Eph 6:11,12) we touch on a point often forgotten: the existence and activity against the Church which is the Kingdom of God on earth, of an anti-kingdom, an anti-church, a cabal of spiritual personal forces striving against all that is redemption through the word and the cross of Christ. The real struggle of the Church is waged mainly against the seductions of the spirit. At any cost it is necessary to preserve the chastity of souls, the purity of doctrine for the purity of charity. The Church also demands avoiding being touched by evil spirits, so as to serve God alone . . . Against Lucifer, we who are made of slime and who must none the less be lights of the world, we have need of the angels" (*Vie spirituelle,* 37, 1933, pp. 26-28).

20. *Cf.* ST, I.114.2: "The proper function of the devil is to tempt for, if sometimes man tempts in this way (that is in order to harm) he does so as a minister of the devil." I.114.3: Every sin does not proceed from temptations by the devil, at least directly; Suarez, however, gives a nuance to this opinion of the Angelic Doctor as follows: "The devil can exercise his ability to press a temptation coming from another source. If he does so in every temptation, he will be the moral cause of all sins which come from this, and a proximate cause, although not a necessary, but still a voluntary one" (*De Angelis,* Bk.

VII, Ch. 19, no. 20). A bit further on (no 21), the Doctor "*Eximius*" quotes in support of his opinion I Pt "Your opponent the devil is prowling like a roaring lion looking for someone to devour" (I Pt 5:8).

21. *Cf.* Acts 20:29,30; Mt 7:15; 1 Tm 4:1; II Cor 11:2ff; Gal 1:8; I Jn 4:1; Jer 6:13; 26:7,8; 27:16; 28:1. Father Bonsirven gives us here some useful reflections: "The false prophet does not speak in the name of false gods. He pretends to be inspired by the God of Israel, but proffers oracles such as please his hearers, that is, favor their natural and earthly views. The false prophets foretold by Jesus Christ will pretend to speak in his name, as will the false apostles, against whom Paul rose up, claiming to preach the gospel of Christ . . . They were often dupes of their own illusions" (*Epîtres de Saint Jean*, Paris, 1935, p. 208).

22. In this context, it is useful to note that Vatican II, in the decree on ecumenism (no. 20), while emphasizing the faith common to many occidental Christians who belong to various eclesial communities, in Christ, our Lord and sole Mediator, does not neglect to note "the not slight differences" . . . between their positions and "the doctrine of the Catholic Church, even on the subject of Christ, Incarnate Word, and of the redemptive work." Is not the Christ of Luther and of Calvin, for instance, different from the Christ of Paul and of the Roman Church? Such a statement clearly shows the wish to avoid "the false conciliatory approach," which "harms the purity of Catholic doctrine and obscures its assured genuine meaning" (*ibid.* 11). This does not hinder the Catholic from rejoicing "to see our separated brethren looking to Christ as the source and center of ecclesiastical communion" (*ibid.* 20).

23. *Cf.* ST, I.II.84.3; II.II.162.5. This thought may be expressed thus: A venial sin of pride (venial because of the imperfection of the act), leads to avarice, vanity, and finally the mortal sin of pride and all other sins.

24. *Cf.* L. Teixidor, "*Um pasaje dificil de la meditación de Dos Banderas y una cita implicita en el mismo de Santo Tomas de Aquino*", *Manresa*, III (1927), 298–309, esp. 309.

25. ST, I.II.84.1.3: we quote the Latin text so that the implied quotation from Saint Ignatius becomes clearer: "*in moralibus consideratur quod ut in pluribus est, non autem quod est semper, eo quod voluntas non ex necessitate operatur. Non igitur dicitur avaritia radix omnis mali quin interdum aliquod aliud malum sit radix ejus: sed quia ex ipsa frequentius alia mala oriuntur.*"

26. ST, I.II.84.1, corpus et ad 2m: riches are not desired for themselves but ·as a means for acquiring temporal goods in general, the raison d'être of the sin which always rises from the appetite for created, changing goods. The inordinate turning to the created, temporal, changing good constitutes the material aspect of every sin, while on the contrary aversion in regard to the immutable good, God, constitutes the formal aspect of mortal sin.

27. ST, II.II.118.6 (on avarice).

28. *Cf.* the texts of Suarez alluded to in note 20.

29. In the light of Suarez's texts (cf. note 20), it may be thought the demon is the moral cause of every sin even venial. Consequently the venial sinner who leads others is a collaborator and tool of Satan in his fight to damn souls. Men in the state of mortal sin especially may be said to be even more clearly agents of Satan. Revelation in Chapter 13 shows the "beast" directly as a symbol of the Roman Empire, and indirectly of all powers hostile to the Church, receiving its power from the diabolical dragon. Then it shows the second beast, as symbol of false prophets, leading men to adore the first and, through it,

the dragon.

30. *Cf.* "Réflexions chretiennes" of Blessed Claude La Colombière, "on vainglory": "Our victories are the arms the demon makes use of to conquer us, he takes advantage of the opportunity to inspire us with pride" (*Oeuvres complètes,* Grenoble, 1901, vol. V, p. 203).

31. *Cf.* Ex. 143, V: "*Summus optimusque noster dux et imperator, Christus.*"

32. On the one hand, for Revelation (Ch. 17), Rome is "Babylon the great, mother of harlots and all the world's abominations. I saw that the woman was drunk with the blood of God's holy ones and the blood of those martyred for their faith in Jesus". (*vv.* 5,6). On the other hand, "in the eyes of Ignatius, Rome gradually assumes the place of Jerusalem. The Kingdom of God is still visible today in exactly the same way it was once in the small towns and synagogues of Palestine. The whole world is the Holy Land; Christ is still present. There where he is visible, so to say to the maximum, in the Pope of Rome, is found the norm by which every spiritual motion is to be judged wherever the call for and the decision of the election are not absolutely clear." *Cf.* H. Rahner, S.J., "*Esprit et Eglise,*" *Christus,* V, 1958, 168. Ignatius, on celebrating his first Mass at Rome on Christmas of 1538, almost eighteen months after his ordination to the priesthood, had underlined that, in his existence, and forever, Jerusalem had become the Rome of the Popes, in the service of which his Society would be wholly consecrated. See P. de Leturia, "*La primera misa de S. Ignacio de Loyola y sus relaciones con la fundación de la Compañia.*" *Estudios Ignacianos,* Rome, 1957, vol. I, pp. 223–35.

33. St. John of the Cross, *Ascent of Carmel,* I,IV,4. The saint said there also: "All the riches and glory of creatures, compared with God's sovereign riches, are but absolute poverty and profound misery. The soul which is attached to the possession of them, is sovereignly poor and miserable before God."

34. Acts 13:26; CFW, 129-132; 162-166.

35. Health; Ex. 14: financial circumstances, Ex. 344.

36. LG, 33.

37. *Ibid.*

38. We note that in the Spanish text of the Autograph there is the same word "espargir" in *Ex.* 141,145, applied to the devils and to the doctrine of Xr.

39. AA, 6.

40. Ex. 145, V says that Christ sends "*apostolos, discipulos et ministros alios per orbem.*" This expression takes the place of the "etc." of the Autograph and of P2. Perhaps the translator of the Vulgate was thinking about bishops (*apostolos*), priests (*discipulos*) and baptized (*alios ministros*), at least of those the hierarchy entrusted with special tasks of the apostolate. Some imprecision remains that is not easy to erase. Could religious also be considered as "*ministros*"?

41. *Cf.* DV, #2: Revelation is inseparably real and verbal; Christ is at the same time mediator and the fulness of revelation, the one revealed as well as the revealer. Likewise he is the king and the kingdom. To announce Christ's sacred and salvific doctrine, is at the same time to communicate his complex message and the absolute simplicity of his eternal and composite Person.

42. The evangelizing mission of the angels in the service of the well-beloved Son appears particularly in Lk 1–2 (Annunciation-Nativity) and 24:5–7 (Resurrection).

43. If Jesus no longer calls his "disciples" servants, he does not forbid them to call themselves thus, Paul calls himself "servant of Christ" or of God (Rom 1:1; Ti 1:1).

Slave would be a better and more exact translation.

44. There is to be observed here a strange and actual difference between the Autograph and the Vulgate. The Autograph has: "From these three steps, let them lead men to all other virtues," that is, the servants, and friends sent on an apostolic mission and expedition, while the Vulgate attributes to three stages or degrees (*gradus*) the fact of introducing salvation (ST, II.II. 8.15.2); the same rule holds for desires. All desires must be subor- the virtues into the soul: *ita tres consurgunt perfectionis gradus . . . quae ex diametro divitiis, honori et superbiae opponuntur, ac virtutes omnes statim introducunt.*" It is true that these two versions are not contradictory; for the Vulgate is concerned with the proximate cause, the Autograph with the more remote cause.

45. We have presented Christ's address directly though the author of the Exercises presented it indirectly. Perhaps he did so because there is question of a meditation and not of a contemplation, and so he presented it differently from the call of the eternal king (Ex. 95).

46. *Cf.* Ex. 63; DS, 392: "*Nemo habet de suo nisi mendacium et peccatum*"—a text which should, however, be qualified and understood in the light of DS, 2311, 1927.

47. Prayer is only meritorious and worth being heard if it asks for things necessary for salvation (ST, II.II.83. 15,2-16); the same rule holds for desires. All desires must be subordinated to this divine will.

48. Likewise the Spiritual Exercises are exercises made under the direction of the Holy Spirit "which governs and rules for the salvation of souls" (Ex. 365). And so it is that the spiritual povery extolled by Jesus (Mt 5:3) is granted by the Spirit, with the Spirit, for the glory of the Holy Spirit, at the request of the Son. It is under the Holy Spirit's influence that it is requested.

49. Mt 19,21: The rich young man was attached to his great wealth and so was wanting in spiritual and actual poverty.

50. LG, 8,3.

51. We have also treated this point, but in a different way, in our book *Sacraments and Social Progress,* Franciscan Herald Press, Chicago, 1974, Ch. I.

52. This text is frequently commented on by Saint John of the Cross: "He who does not renounce all things he possesses cannot be my disciple. This is not only to be understood of corporal or temporal things but also of depriving self of spiritual things, including spiritual poverty in which the Son of God places beatitude" ("Living Flame of Love," III, 9). All possession is against hope (*ibid.* III, 6).

53. "O blest is he who suffers without being attached to his suffering and seeks but to die the better to love the one who wounds him!" This is what Saint Paul of the Cross wrote in his poem: "Vive la sainte croix" (*cf.* Gaëtan de saint Nom de Marie, *Doctrine de Saint Paul de la Croix sur l'oraison et la mystique,* Louvain, 1932, pp. 310,311). "To nourish oneself always on the divine will in naked, hidden, abstract suffering, since it is wholly absorbed by holiest and purest love" (*ibid.* p. 249).

54. *Cf.* the thoughts of Saint John of the Cross on spiritual avarice in his "Night," I,3.

55. Despite the social and current use of this word, a use which is above all "horizontal", we take this work here, as doubtless did Saint Ignatius, in its vertical sense, attested to particularly by Saint Thomas Aquinas: "Humility, insofar as it is a special virtue, concerns mainly man's submission to God in view of which man submits himself also to others by abasing himself" (ST, II.II.161.1.5; 2.3.3).

56. R. Rouquette, S.J., *Saint Ignace de Loyola et les origines des jésuites,* Paris, 1944,

p. 26. By the term "supreme values" he intends rather eminent values, values fitted to lead to the supreme value, the beatific vision.

57. If God calls all men to the perfection of charity, He *chose* those He wished to make come there by the voice of the evangelical counsels of poverty, obedience and chastity, vowed to God (*cf.* LG, 43). It is understandable that Saint Ignatius suggests to all who have reached this point in the Exercises the conditional request for the grace of a religious vocation if the norm given by him to the director be recalled: "Let the director see to it that the retreatant know clearly that there is need of the greatest signs from God to know he is called to the precepts rather than to the counsels. For Christ our Lord recommends the counsels for all, while he makes them see the difficulty which possible riches present in the way of the precepts" (*Autograph Directory of St. Ignatius,* MHSJ, vol 76, Rome, 1955, p. 72). Such a clarification does not lessen the respect due from the director to the retreatant's freedom and to the free action of the Holy Spirit in him, a respect insisted on by the author of the Exercises (Ex. 14,15). On the contrary, the instruction recommended reveals the director's respect since ignorance in this matter would lessen that retreatant's freedom.

58. The term "wrongs" translates "*injurias*" of the Autograph (Ex. 147). Etimologically the word "*injurias*" implies a violation of justice, an injustice, a wrong.

59. *Cf.* Saint Louis-Marie Grignon de Montfort, *Traité de la vraie dévotion à la Vierge Marie,* #51–54.

60. *Cf.* Caussade, *Abandon à la divine Providence,* Bk. II, ch. 4, sections 11,12; and also ST, I.114.1: Diabolical temptations come from the malice of demons, but they are instruments at the service of the divine goodness. The entire article explains well the meditation on the "Two Standards." We quote the Latin text: "*Impugnatio ipsa ex demonum malitia procedit . . . Sed ordo impugnationis ipsius est a Deo, qui ordinate novit malis uti, ad bona ea ordinando.*"

61. It is helpful to recall here that riches and honors, instruments of diabolical temptation, are not evil of themselves, but are good. It is as a consequence of inordinate inclinations, which are the effects of original sin in us, that they become dangerous for us.

62. *Cf.* our, *Sacraments and Social Progress,* ch. VI.

63. *Cf.* DS, 3051, on the raison d'être of the institution of the papacy; Paul VI, Encyclical *Populorum Progressio,* (1967) *passim.*

64. Mt 16:18; Lk 22:31,32.

65. Pius XII, *Mystici Corporis,* AAS, 35 (1943) 210,211; CFW, ch. XIII.

66. Pius XII, *Mystici Corporis,* AAS, 35 (1943) 211; *cf.* DS, 872.

67. "The meditation on the Two Standards introduces a demanding reflection on subjective dispositions, intentions, spirits. Actually there is no need to interpret this term only of the tempter situated outside of us but also of the connivance he finds within us, of the interior response his suggestions meet, briefly of the spirit which inspires our acts" J M. Le Blond, S.J., *Christus,* IX (1962) 81,82.

68. cf. ST., III. 72.9.

69. GS, 37: "For a monumental struggle against the powers of darkness pervades the whole history of man. The battle was joined from the very origins of the world and will continue until the last day as the Lord has attested (Mt 24:13; 13:24-30, 36-43). Caught in this conflict, man is obliged to wrestle constantly if he is to cling to what is good."

70. ST, I.II.q.69,70.

9

HUMAN ATTITUDES
AND THE CHOICE OF WHAT IS BETTER

Title and Purpose

Now we address ourselves to the spiritual exercise traditionally known as the "meditation on the three pairs[1] or classes of men." The title of this exercise is not the same in the Autograph, the Vulgate and P2. There we have three pairs, three classes or *differences,* three attitudes. But in all three cases there is question of pairs, classes, differences, or dispositions of men with the aim of "choosing that which is better" (Ex. 149). The object of the exercise, therefore, is to induce the free human will to scrutinize its innermost attitudes so as to help it obtain a perfect indifference requisite for a good election. It is an exercise, therefore, the point of which is not only a clarification of the intellect, (as in the previous meditation of the two standards), but rather a reinforcing of the will, a sounding of the retreatant's generosity, for intensifying it in order to adopt the most adequate means for the realization of our purpose.

The exercise, however, is in every case (A,V,P2) designated as a *meditation.* For in itself it implies, if we distinguish it from the purpose intended, a reflection on the conditions of a perfect supernatural exercise of human liberty. We propose, therefore, to meditate here step by step on the Ignatian text, developing its implications. Our meditation, following the very indications of Saint Ignatius, will now and then transform itself into prayer.

Often, in the manner of giving this meditation, there is emphasis exclusively on the inordinate affections under the form of attachments, not bringing out forcefully their other dimension of fear and repugnance which none the less the text mentions (Ex. 157). We shall have from beginning to end concern for focusing our minds equally on inordinate fear and repugnance "in order 'the better' to embrace what is the better." The expressions: more, better, more highly, these expressions, so frequent in the language of Saint Ignatius of Loyola, indicate the constant spiritual tension, the perpetual dissatisfaction in regard to what has already been attained, the characteristic of pilgrimage toward the absolute which marks Christian life.

First prelude: the "background" of the three groups, attitudes and pairs

"Each of them has acquired ten thousand ducats, but not entirely as they should have, for the love of God.[2] They all wish to save their souls and find peace in God our Lord by ridding themselves of the burden arising from the attachment[3] to the sum acquired, which impedes the attainment of this end" (Ex. 150). This attachment is not only an obstacle to peace of soul, but also constitutes a "hindrance to salvation" (V).

An inordinate attachment (or fear) is, then, at the origin of an actual possession or else an actual non-possession of a good one would have to possess. Let us note it well: there is not a question of a good possessed through dishonesty, or in violation of certain rules, but of an attachment which does not have as its source, form and object the pure love of God, and so is the result of a "diligence" alien to the worship and love of God (P2,V).

Consequently, this inordinate attachment (or fear) constitutes a burden which hinders the soul from flying to God, freely, an obstacle on its pilgrimage to the eternal. The imperfection in how the temporal good was acquired (or not acquired) impedes it from fully possessing, with savor, God who is still its own. Possessed by an attachment or fear, the soul cannot purely and simply possess God who brings about in it a consciousness of this disorder, and so neither can it possess in peace the temporal good acquired.

There is no need for the improperly acquired (or not acquired out of fear) treasure to be only external. For each of the three groups, it may be identified with a culture (in the most diverse fields). Are not the "ducats" I acquired, perhaps, the human culture, even theological and spiritual, as imperfect and fragmentary as it may be, which I have today and which is perhaps not, whether in its positive elements, or in what it does not include, the fruit of intellectual choices most in conformity with the designs of divine wisdom and with the demands of pure love for the Blessed Trinity?

I do not know what I ought to know; and I have spent too much time studying what it would have been more worth while (comparatively) not to know. Has there not been self-love in the motives, the methods and the objectives of my cultural effort? These ducats, are they not (if I have them) my *diplomas* which symbolize them most exactly and which are not necessarily the fruit of pure love of God?

We know, in fact, that today the most appreciated capital is constituted by acquired professional talents.[4]

It might also be said that the "ten thousand ducats" are the character which, on the base of temperament, each one has forged for himself. This character-capital, just as the culture-capital, reveals the itinerary and the ends of freedom in its effort at auto-genesis, generally mixed with imperfections.

So, a single inordinate, and wilfully so, attachment impedes (if it is habitual) the perfection of the soul.[5] It renders it captive. It is only in unconditional surrender before the sollicitations of divine grace that the soul can be freed from the prison in which it was voluntarily immured: the prison of finiteness.

Second prelude: Mental representation of the place.

"Here it will be to behold myself standing in the presence of God our Lord and of all his saints to desire and know what is more pleasing to his divine goodness" (Ex. 151).

Here Saint Ignatius invites me not only to put myself in the presence of God (to recall that all that is created, including the saints, in comparison with God, is nothing, that I in particular have naught but my corruption, my physical and moral ugliness, and am a wound, an abcess whence seeps so many sins).[6] He desires that I put myself in the presence of God and of all his saints, so as to recall that the omnipotent can, and how easily, make of me a saint, as he has been able to do with so many others who had set like obstacles against him. They have become saints only by resolving to become so. The infinite might of God can operate in me, too, even if there be required a moral miracle, such a resolve and render it efficacious. The saints have their eyes fixed on me, benevolently and lovingly. They intercede for me that I posit decisive acts; they ask for me the passionate wish for holiness. "You must be perfect as your heavenly Father is perfect" (Mt 5:48).

More precisely, all the saints intercede with the Father, the Son and the Holy Spirit that I may "desire and know" what can be more highly pleasing to the divine goodness. Let us note the inversion of the expected order. Ignatius does not write: "know and desire" but the contrary. Why? Perhaps to suggest to us that if it is true that only what is known can be desired, only that which is obscurely desired can be known. Too often if one refuses to know a truth, a requisite of grace, it is because one does not desire the sacrifices such knowledge would bring in its train! It is necessary to desire in an indefinite way God's will as yet unknown in order to be able to embrace his known determinations.

There is question of desiring to know not only what is pleasing to God, but also what is most pleasing, "more highly" pleasing to his divine goodness. The devil goads us on to what is less good (when he cannot incline us to what is intrinsically evil) as Saint Ignatius says in the rules for discernment of spirits (Ex. 333). The Holy Spirit, on the contrary, spurs us on to what is better.

What is more pleasing to the divine goodness is always in some way related to the salvation of souls, to their sanctification. Do not the saints desire to be joined by their brothers of the earth in the lasting possession of heavenly holiness, a sharing in divine holiness? In this amazing "composition of place" we are now commenting on, the absence of all explicit mention of "wayfarers", of men still on the way to the eternal, in no way signifies their exclusion, quite the contrary. When I see myself in the presence of God and of all his saints, I contemplate the harmonious union of their salvific wills in regard to wayfaring men and their desire to associate me to it. Here how can I not but quote the beautiful thoughts of Saint John Climachus?

"The most pleasing of all the gifts we could offer God is to consecrate to him our souls by penitence. The whole universe is not comparable to a single soul.

"So we ought not esteem as blessed those who present Jesus Christ with earthly goods, such as gold or silver, but those who will offer him as a gift rational and spiritual lambs. However, it is not enough for them to present souls to God, they must also labor to make them pure so that this holocaust be of the finest." [7]

The divine goodness which we should please *is* salvific love in regard to all men, as we have already stressed a propos of the contemplation on the Incarnation.

Third prelude: Petition for grace to make an election

Here it is "to beg for the grace to choose what is more for the glory of his Divine Majesty and the salvation of my soul" (Ex. 152 P2). [8]

In the supernatural realism of the petition, what I wish, my choice, my election, is considered as a gift of divine grace putting me on the road to my salvation for God's greater glory. If I choose, if I wish, it is because I am chosen, [9] I am willed, my very decisions (in as much as they are assumed and supernaturalized by the author of grace) are willed and decided [10] by the Creator of my being and of my freedom. Therefore I can ask and beg as graces, as so many gifts, gratuitous and unmerited, the very decisions of my freedom. [11]

The apparent silence on the apostolic implications of this request for the grace of election might be surprising. Actually, a parallel text by the author of the Exercises (Ex. 166) shows us that "the service, honor and glory of the Divine Majesty" are essentially realized by "the spiritual welfare of souls" and not "through personal gain and temporal interests." "The salvation of my soul" envisaged here, is not brought about save by my cooperation in the "spiritual welfare of souls," at the cost, though not always, but frequently, of my own gain and temporal interests.

Attitudes of the first, second and third pairs or groups

Ex. 153 "The first class. They would like to rid themselves of the attachment they have to the sum acquired in order to find peace in God our Lord and assure their salvation, but the hour of death comes, and they have not made use of a means."

Ex. 154 "The second class. They want to rid themselves of the attachment, but they wish to do so in such a way that they retain what they have acquired, so that God is to come to what they desire, and they do not decide to give up the sum of money in order to go to God, though this would be the better way for them."

Ex. 155 "The third class. These want to rid themselves of the attachment, but they wish to do so in such a way that they desire neither to retain nor to relinquish the sum acquired. They seek only to will and not will as God our Lord inspires them, and as seems better for the service and praise of the Divine Majesty. Meanwhile, they will strive to conduct themselves as if every attachment to it had been broken. They will make efforts neither to want that, nor anything else, unless the service of God our Lord alone moves them to do so. As a result, the desire to be better able to serve God our Lord will be the cause of their accepting anything or relinquishing it."[12]

We have preferred to present these three points in conjunction: these three pairs with such different attitudes (Ex. 153-155).

The first pair *would like* to overcome the attachment, the two others *will* invited to the banquet of the Kingdom (Lk 14:15-24). The second brings to mind the rich young man (Mt 19:16-26). The third recalls some of the calls mentioned in the Gospel, such as that of Matthew (Mt 9:9).

The first pair *would like* to overcome the attachment, the two others *will* to do so.

The first thinks: "I would like to be a saint." The second: "I want to be a saint, but. . . . " The third: "I want to be a saint, whatever it may cost me!" He adds, with Blessed Claude La Colombière:" I am resolved for everything! I do not intend to consider parents, friends, honor, gain, life."[13]

The first retains his inordinate attachment up to the hour of death, a moment so uncertain as to the dispositions which should accompany it. The second practices what Saint Ignatius calls "seeking last, what they ought to seek first" (Ex. 169) and which assumes that one wishes, not to change one's own self, but to change the dispositions of the unchangeable God.[14] While a propos of the third, Saint Ignatius does not even mention whether or not he keeps the ten thousand ducats (a secondary consideration)[15] but he shows how he detaches himself from them interiorly. He "will make efforts neither to want that, nor anything else, unless the service of God our Lord moves him to so so" for his supreme good and, in a sense, only good, is the infinite good, God himself.

The first is afraid to detach himself. The second fears the loss, but no longer (apparently) the detachment. The third fears neither the loss of the external good, nor the inner detachment. Love, within him, banishes fear. He reduces, simplifies, unifies his desires to the point of having but one: to serve God. For in God he possesses.all, interiorly.

The first rejects, the second, temporizes, the third liberates himself.

Do you not recognize your own personal history in one after the other, in the attitudes of the three pairs? How many rejections, how much temporizing in our lives, in my life? In the face of these rejections and temporizings of our past life, Ignatius proposes a radical remedy in this sense that he gets right at the root of the evil. He suggests we consider that we have now re-nounced everything on the affective level, *"reputat secum quod omnia re-linquit affectu"* (Ex. 155, P2). Then he adds immediately: "They will make efforts neither to want that, nor anything else, unless the service of God our Lord alone moves them to do so. As a result, the desire to be better able to serve God our Lord will be the cause of their accepting anything or re-linquishing it" (Ex. 155).

The radical remedy consists, therefore, essentially in a purification and discernment of our desires. The renunciation of the world and of self pene-trates the area of desire (the not desiring of a particular thing, the desiring of a greater service of God by keeping it or by renouncing it). The desire is no longer directed to the thing as such, but to the service of God and to the thing in as much as it is a means for serving God. The specific reality, whether desired or not, is situated from now on between a desire coming from God (Ex. 184) and this same desire in as much as it goes toward God, that is: goes back to its source. On desiring such and such a thing, I desire only God, who is revealed as being the source and the end, not only of all reality, but also of the desire I have of it. And in God, who con-tains eminently all things, I desire all, I possess all. In the very measure I renounce every particular desire, all my power of desiring becomes universal, if yet polarized by the desire which desires its proper source and proper end, God.

The remedy for the sinful specificity of our desires consists, therefore, in their being universalized and divinized. The meditation on the three classes contains a veritable theology and a therapeutic of human desires.

But how to arrive at this divinization of our desires? If they are an "ob-lique choice," a temporizing by distorting the relationship of means to end, if they wish to put God at their service, how might such a perversion be corrected without an intervention by him whom there is precisely question of desiring for himself above and beyond every particular desire polarized by him? Left to its own strength, the human desire will often remain oblique. Only the grace of the absolute desire can purify it fully and free it from its delusions.

So, this grace is usually obtained only by prayer. This is what the author of the Exercises has seen. And that is why he concludes with a twofold call to prayer.

Petition for the contrary of what we desire. Key to transition from second to third pair.

After having told the retreatant "to make the same three colloquies em-ployed in the preceding contemplation[16] on two standards" (Ex. 156), Saint

Ignatius adds: "It should be noted that when we feel an attachment opposed to actual poverty or a repugnance to it, when we are not indifferent to poverty and riches, it will be very helpful in order to overcome the inordinate attachment, even though corrupt nature rebel against it, to beg our Lord in the colloquies to choose us to serve him in actual poverty. We should insist that we desire it, beg for it, plead for it, provided, of course, that it be for the service and praise of the divine goodness" (Ex. 157).

This text makes explicit what was implied in the triple colloquy of the meditation on the two standards. Indeed, there we requested already "to be received, under his standard, in the highest spiritual poverty, and should the Divine Majesty be pleased thereby, even in actual poverty" (Ex. 147).

The making of this explicit is, moreover, of great pedagogic value. It makes us understand that the precise and conditional petition for what arouses repugnance for a liberty that is imperfectly liberated, is the best means for its perfect liberation. It shows that the prayer of petition is not a magical formula, by which man would endeavor to place his Creator at his service, but on the contrary can and must be an expression and a means of submission of created liberty to uncreated and creative Liberty.

Let us explain the suggestion made here by the author of the Exercises in the light of "Introductory Observation 16," at the very beginning of the little book which has revolutionized the world: "Hence, that the Creator, and Lord may work with greater certainty in his creature, if the soul chance to be inordinately attached or inclined to anything, it is very proper that it rouse itself by the exertion of all its powers to desire the opposite of that to which it is wrongly attached. . . . Let him be insistent in prayer and in his other spiritual exercises in begging God for the reverse, that is, that he neither seek such office or benefice, nor anything else, unless the divine majesty duly regulate his desires, and change his former attachment. As a result, the reason he wants or retains anything will be solely the service, honor, and glory of the divine majesty.

However, whereas the observation quoted above is confined to petitioning God to purify the motives of our will, the note appended to the meditation on the three classes goes much further, for it explicitly petitions God to call us to the contrary of what our carnal impulses would desire (Ex. 157).[17] Nevertheless, by a tipping of the scale found exclusively in the Vulgate, Saint Ignatius does not want to convert this conditional prayer into an anticipation of the final decision, nor consequently to convert the conditional petition of the opposite into a decision for the contrary, for he adds: "However, meanwhile we shall maintain the freedom of our desire, by which it will be permissible to enter upon a more suitable way (or: the most suitable) for the divine service" (Ex. 151, V: this is without parallel in the Autograph and in P2).[18]

The conditional prayer which Saint Ignatius recommends therefore, is accompanied by a conviction: God, and God only, can, in His omnipotence, act on my deepmost affectivity, remove its self-centeredness and order it to his greatest glory. To this profound conviction, the conditional petition joins an act of the will, an express desire: "I neither seek this office or benefice, nor anything else, unless the divine majesty, the supreme grandeur of the divine goodness, [19] duly regulate my desires, and change my former attachment, so that the motives of my desires in regard to anything at all be only for his service, honor and glory and the eternal salvation of all souls, and not for my own personal temporal gain."

And so it is that at one stroke two other related questions are cleared up: the meaning of the *"agere contra"* of the Kingdom (Ex. 97) and the affective meaning and so not the materially but the spiritually actual meaning of the attitude of the third class (Ex. 98,155).

The meaning of former: it is essentially by the prayer of petition, and not by force, that we "go against" the sensual in us and our carnal and worldly love: "for offering ourselves wholly to the eternal Lord who is at the same time ours and that of all things."

The meaning of the latter: (*"todo lo dexa en afecto; omnia relinquit affectu"*) (Ex. 155, A, P2). [20] For the transformation in depth of human *affectivity* reveals best of all the *efficacy* of divine grace, the effect of which is interior before being exterior.

Briefly, on recognizing the extreme spiritual importance of the "conditional petition for the contrary," Ignatius admirably synthetizes the inner, horizontal and vertical dimensions of Christian life: the struggle against self (*"agere contra"*), the concern for the salvation of others ("the spiritual welfare of souls"), and the prayer of petition, precise and definite," an initial, continual and final[21] salvific act of human liberty, an act which often conditions and accompanies its supreme exercise: the act of charity."[22]

And just as there is no one who has no inordinate inclinations, no one who does not suffer the consequence of original sin ("concupiscence which leads to actual sin"),[23] from this there results that, for ali[24] the conditional petition of the contrary is the master key of the passage from imperfection to the perfection of charity, the therapeutic best of all for this being of desires which is man, the means of passing from the inordinate desire of self and of the world to the passionate desire for the possession and vision of God, transcendent, alone absolutely desirable.

Conclusion: Colloquies of desire.

"Virgin Immaculate in your desires, communicate to me a share, even very limited, in the loving splendor of your pure desires, so perfectly without selfishness and pride. Purify, enlighten, inflame all my desires, so troubled, so obscured, so cold, in the light and charity of your Immaculate Heart. Free me from all inordinate attachments to wrongly acquired ducats of my culture, my diplomas, my role in human society. Obtain for me the grace to desire only God's desire for me.''

"Lord Jesus, I beg You, through the intercession of all the saints who have made the Exercises, to make me 'desire and know what is more pleasing to his divine Goodness,'' and which will, in some way, always be fasting, giving alms, and prayer: the inner, horizontal and vertical exercise of pure love of self, of others and of God. Continue in me your fasting, through me your almsgiving, by me your prayer.[25] Replace in me all capricious desires of having with self-sacrificing desires of giving. Overcome in me the ever recurring repugnance I have toward giving, toward giving myself, toward giving you.

"For concentrating my desires in you, teach me to pray (cf. Lk 11:1) and to frequently repeat, slowly, humbly, perseveringly, with faith these 'ejaculatory prayers,'[26] these short invocations without which I would ordinarily fall back into the perverse intentions of the flesh, of the world and of the devils, and thanks to which your holy will will become the light in my darkness, the lamp on my way, the fire of my heart. By them, sanctify me whatever it may cost, at any price.

"Jesus, desirable and desired, you are infinite and eternal desire for my salvation and happiness, as well as of all my brothers. You have desired and you desire with a great desire (cf. Lk 22:15) to come to me to communicate to me the purity of the desires, so perfectly, so fully, unified, of your Heart. Take from me the contradictions and disorders of so many of my desires to immerse me into the absolute simplicity of the sole and incomprehensible desire that you are, in the innermost depths of my soul.''

NOTES ON CHAPTER NINE

1. It is not unlikely that Saint Ignatius chose this concept alluding to the inner division of the human will (old man, new man), nor is it unlikely, too, that he intended to suggest the social context of all our inner attitudes. At any rate, it is expressed in terms used by moralists of the sixteenth century and in their cases of conscience.

2. Here we modify the translation by Father Courel in the light of P2.

3. A literal translation would require the word "affection" (affectu).

4. Cf. GS, 71,3: "The forms of such dominion or ownership remain . . . a source of security not to be underestimated, . . . This is true not only of material goods but also of intangible good, such as professional skills."

5. Saint John of the Cross put special emphasis on this point, of the theological problem relative to moral imperfection. Cf. E. Desreumaux, S.J., Catholicisme, 21, 1342–46 and B. Zomparelli, DSAM, 7 (1970) 1625–1630.

6. *Cf.* Ex. 158.

7. Saint John Climachus, *Letter to a Pastor,* nos. 78,79.

8. The text of P2 supposes that the election itself, made here, is a grace. The Autograph does not suppose it so explicitly, as Father Courel's translation shows ("ask for grace, in order to choose what may contribute more to the glory of his Divine Majesty,"), to which translation we have preferred another, based on P2.

9. *Cf.* Jn 15:16.

10. *Cf.* Phil 2:13, "It is God who, in his good will toward you, begets in you any measure of desire or achievement."

11. *Cf.* ST, I.II.111.2.

12. Let us note here the translation which is a veritable interpretation of the Autograph, given by the Vulgate: *"affectum insincerum volens abjicere . . . prout ad divinum cultum commodius fore, vel ex diverso instinctu vel ex rationis dictamine, animadverterit"* (Ex, 155 V). The translator of the Vulgate seems to have intended to anticipate Ex. 175 and 184, where the election by divine inspiration is described (in Thomistic terms, we might speak of an election made as a result of an operative grace of God, *cf.* ST, I.II.111.2) as contrasted to the deliberated election (cooperating grace, *ibid.*). There is emphasis here that indifference, in relation to the object of inordinate attachment, may be either inspired or deliberated.

13. A thought taken from Blessed La Colombière, Sermon 64 sur l'habitude vicieuse, *Oeuvres complètes,* Grenoble, 1901, vol. IV.

14. Saint Ignatius' famous letter on obedience, contains a parallel sentence in his condemnation of "oblique obedience": "Never try to draw the will of the superior to your own will. This would not be making the divine will the rule of your own, but your own the rule of the divine, and so perverting the order of his wisdom" (March 26, 1553), *Cf. Letter of St. Ignatius of Loyola,* William J. Young, S.J., p. 290, Loyola University Press, Chicago, 1959.

15. Secondary, just as the counsels, relative to the gospel commandment of charity and yet very important since the meditation of the three classes prepares the retreatant for the election by which he will renounce, if it please God, the symbolic ten thousand ducats in favor of poverty not only affective but also actual.

16. Let us note this apparent rupture of the consistency of Ignatian vocabulary, since the author of the two standards called this exercise not a contemplation but a meditation (Ex. 136). But it may be asked whether consistency is not actually kept. In fact, here, at the moment of inviting us to renew the triple colloquy Saint Ignatius speaks of a contemplation! Everything takes place as if he wanted to suggest that on passing from reflection to colloquy, there is also to be a passing from meditation to contemplation.

17. *Cf.* H. Coathalem, S.J., *Commentaire du livre des Exercices,* Paris, 1965, p. 200: "The *notandum* of the three classes (157) does it not serve two functions with the triple colloquy? The perspective is actually the same, but the *notandum* makes it pass on from overall views to individual problems and personal applications."

18. Let us note here a subtle difference of meaning between the Autograph on the one hand, the Vulgate and P2 on the other. For the Autograph "the third pair wants only to wish to keep or not the good acquired in accord with what God our Lord will place in his will *and* in accord with what will seem best to him . . . " The divine inspiration and the rational reflection seem combined to obtain the result. For P2 and the Vulgate, there

is, quite to the contarary, a disjunction and opposition between the two: "*vel ex divino instinctu, vel ex rationis dictamine*". So, does not the insistence, in Ex. 157, on the inspiration of the Holy Spirit prepare the way, in Ex. 155, V, for the greatest insistence of Ex. 157, V, on the retreatant's freedom? Does not Ignatius seem to say: "the petition for the contrary, at the same time that it liberates the retreatant from the inordinate attachment, still obliges him to nothing, since he is ever susceptible to be moved by the Holy Spirit inclining him to retain, for supernatural motives, the object for which he had prior to this an attachment in an inordinate manner"? How can we explain otherwise the strange expression: Meanwhile we will retain the freedom of our desire ("*servabimus tamen interea desiderii nostri libertatem*")?

19. We have expanded here the translation of "*Majestas*" by explaining it by "grandeur." Certain political connotations of our times render difficult the translation of the Ignatian expression.

20. It is known that Father Roothaan had thought there was a typographical error in the Autograph here (which put "*afecto*" instead of "*efecto*"). This interpretation is widely rejected today. Perhaps it may have come from a misunderstanding of the actuality of what is affective!

21. We take the adjective "final" in a wide sense: in the series of the last meritorious acts of freedom, will be found the prayer of petition, which might not be quite the last meritorious act of redeemed freedom.

22. *Cf.* B. de Margerie, S.J., *Reinhold Niebuhr, théologien de la communité mondiale;* Musaeum Lessianum, Section Theologique no. 64, Bruges-Paris, 1969, pp. 329–32.

23. *Cf.* DS, 1515.

24. Doubtless "for all" but not at each moment. It is well to state here that we cannot agree with the evaluation made by the Congress of Loyola on 1966 on the "petition of the contrary," In Its conclusion 49 (*Los Ejercicios de S. Ignacio a la luz del Vaticano II,* Madrid, 1968, p. 319), reducing Ex. 157 to "Introductory Observation 16" which, (and it is to be admitted) does not contain the petition of the contrary. For the Congress, there would be no question in Ex. 157 precisely of the petition of the contrary, but of intensely imploring the divine majesty to order our desires, by changing our first attachments. And then of imploring God to bring us to acceptance of the love of what we fear, if that be pleasing to him. Such a petition would already be very helpful, assuredly, but it would still not have the same meaning, the same force, the same result as the conditionally explicit petition of the contrary, actual and not only affective.

The profound reason, doubtless, why the petition of the contrary is explicitly suggested by Saint Ignatius might be this: it is a way, for the human person, to travel toward this state where it desires no more than the divine will without ever desiring anything in particular in an unconditional manner. Absolute desire of the divine will, and that alone. Here is what the conditional petition of the contrary means and obtains.

One of the best interpreters of Ignatian thought, Nadal, has left us this reflection: "If there comes to you a desire to do something good that your superior does not order you to do, you should incline yourself to desire the opposite in order to make yourself indifferent for willing no more than what is commanded. This manner of acting is more perfect, more soothing to the soul, that is: not to will or desire anything but to be naked, completely open to what will be commanded you to do" (Mon. Ign. I, vol. 12, pp. 662,663). Nadal's favorite expression was: "I incline myself to not inclining myself" (Mon. Nadal, I, p. 292). The conditional petition of the contrary is besides closely related to another Ignatian principle: "Temptations ought to be anticipated by their opposites, for example, if someone is observed to be inclined toward pride, by exercising him in lowly matters thought fit to aid toward humbling him, and similarly of other evil inclinations" (Const. #265).

Is not such a "dialectic" attitude a normal consequence of the general principle laid down by Saint Paul: "The flesh lusts against the spirit and the spirit against the flesh: the two are directly opposed" (Gal 5:17)?

25. Mt 6:1-8; 4:2; Jn 13:29; Col 1:24.

26. *Cf.* E. Vansteenberghe, DSAM, 1 (1936) 1017-25: art. "Aspirations." The article shows clearly the great usefulness of "aspirations" in the purgative, illuminative and unitive ways.

10

THREE KINDS OF HUMILITY
THREE KINDS OF HUMBLE LOVE

The "Meditation on the Three Classes," analyzed in our preceding chapter, was intended to help the retreatant sound out the attitudes of his will, before committing himself to the principal step of the election. A final step remains to be taken beforehand, related to the human heart and tending to open it up to "the true doctrine of Christ our Lord": "to consider attentively the three kinds of humility" to use Ignatian terminology (Ex. 164).

In other words, in Ignatius' eyes, the genuine choice of human freedom, adhering to the divine will, is conditioned by the "*habitus*," acquired beforehand, of participation in the "folly of the cross." The co-redemptive[1] decision is the option of one crucified on his daily cross.

We shall keep to the rythm of Ignatian thinking. After the meditation of the "I," the contemplation of the triple colloquy. Let us recall, only as a preliminary, that the different kinds of humility[2] are those of submission to the divine goodness as well.

First Kind: absolute refusal to commit a mortal sin.

"This is necessary for salvation. It consists in this, that as far as possible I so subject and humble myself as to obey the law of God our Lord in all things, so that not even were I made lord of all creation, or to save my life here on earth, would I consent to violate a commandment, whether divine or human, that binds me under pain of mortal sin" (Ex. 165).

In other words, neither promises of success, nor threats of death, will be able to separate me from the sanctifying grace of Christ the Lord, if I am loyal to the sollicitations of this grace. Saint Ignatius underlines the absolute necessity of such abasement and of such humble obedience for attaining eternal life, and for working out my salvation.

This first kind of humility, therefore, recapitulates the first affirmation of the "principle and foundation": "Man is created to praise, reverence and serve God our Lord and by this means to save his soul "(Ex. 23). Man

137

serves God by obeying the law of God (an expression which goes beyond
that of the divine will).[3]

What does all this mean? Not even to consider or deliberate on[4] violating
a commandment even mediately divine[5] which binds under pain of mortal
sin. Consequently, to be ready for martyrdom or to the sacrifice of life, by
obedience, not only to God, but also to men, the State and the Church.[6]
The grace of the first kind of humility is that of martyrdom.

Thus, for instance, the officer or the soldier who receives the order to carry
on total war, a war of genocide, of the assassination of civilian populations
should refuse even at the risk of his own life.[7]

Or, too, no earthly gain can ever justify the denial of a single truth of the
faith, of a single dogma of the Church.

This is what the martyrs of the French Revolution understood when they
sacrificed their lives in order not to betray the loyalty due to the primacy
of the Roman Pontiff, and so in order to avoid schism.

Briefly, to the death of the soul, I must prefer that of the body, if I
have no other choice.

Such a kind of humility already marks an ardent desire of eternal salvation,
a great love for God.[8] A profound conviction.

Love abases itself, humbles itself, subjects itself. The whole world, lost or
gained is nothing in comparison with God lost or possessed (*cf.* Ex. 58).
"What profit would a man show if he were to gain the whole world and
destroy himself in the process" (Mt 16:26)?

At the same time, each one among us knows that, without the help
of divine grace, he would not sacrifice the whole world to save his soul.

To abase myself and to humble myself as much as possible in order to
obey in everything God's law, I have need of his grace, and must ask for it.
I have need to see, with the eyes of faith, that this law is a law of love, and
everywhere asks for love. Charity sums up, without suppressing them, all
the commandments. "Love is the fulfilment of the law" (Rom 13:10).

Second Kind: absolute refusal to commit a deliberate venial sin.

"This is more perfect than the first. I possess it if my attitude of mind
is such that I neither desire nor am I inclined to have riches rather than
poverty, to seek honor rather than dishonor, to desire a long life rather than
a short life, provided only in either alternative I would promote equally the
service of God our Lord and the salvation of my soul. Besides this indifference, this second kind of humility supposes that not for all creation, nor
to save my life, would I consent to commit a venial sin" (Ex. 166).

This second kind of humility contains the indifference of the "Foundation."
On this occasion, for the first time in the book of Exercises there appears
as equal in different situations the service of God and his praise. The text
even implies that in certain cases the greatest glory of God could include the

possession of riches, honor, a long life.[9]

In fact, Saint Thomas Aquinas points out[10] that the good of the offender himself (who is to be helped to cease offending) as well as that of numerous other persons (compromised by these offenses) requires that in certain cases the offended defend himself against the offense. This is just what Saint Ignatius did at Rome, in 1538, having recourse to ecclesiastical justice.[11]

As a result of the consequences of original sin, and of my innate preferences for honors and riches, it is not always easy and at times very difficult to be morally certain whether such and such a means contribute equally to a more or less greater service of God our Lord.

Hence the necessity of perfecting indifference by the absolutely unconditional refusal to commit venial sin, despite all promises and threats. Such an attitude of the will will facilitate a keener perception, by the intellect, of what constitutes a lesser, an equal or a better service of God.

God's true servant never considers committing a venial sin for keeping or winning the friendship of any person or group whatsoever. He knows that friendship always depends on the Providence of God. What would a friendship won at the cost of fidelity to this Providence be worth, were it possible? How could it have the stability of what is founded in God?

Third Kind: preferential choice of the folly of the Cross.

"This is the most perfect kind of humility. It consists in this. If we suppose the first and second kind attained, then whenever the praise and glory of God would be equally served, I desire and choose poverty with Christ poor, rather than riches, in order to imitate and be in reality more like Christ our Lord; I choose insults with Christ loaded with them, rather than honors; I desire to be accounted as worthless and a fool for Christ, rather than to be esteemed as wise and prudent in this world. So Christ was treated before me" (Ex. 167).

This text poses a problem that has long divided commentators on the Exercises. There is a difference between what Saint Ignatius proposes in the "contemplation on the Kingdom" and what he proposes here. Here he asks us, no longer only to choose poverty and humiliation as the way to a *greater* glory of God (Ex. 98), but also to prefer them "whenever the praise and glory of would be equally served".

These differences in interpretation of a delicate problem were partly due, as Father Cantin has shown,[12] to an insufficient understanding of the Ignatian concept of God's glory. For most modern commentators, the glory of God is the perfection (above all, not to say exclusively, innermost) of the good act in as much as it reflects the excellence in which it participates. If God's glory is *only this,* one does not see well, it must be admitted, why we would choose one or the other of two terms of the option, if we suppose this glory equally attained in both cases. Or, more exactly, we are to have recourse to an analysis of the justification for the choice of Jesus himself, an analysis in every way necessary, as we shall shortly see.

For Saint Ignatius, God's glory is rightly this, but it is also the perfection of the result or of the spiritual fruit produced by the act. The point of view is concrete, apostolic, social. God's glory is the concrete realization of the Kingdom of God on earth. It is not enough that the act be good or excellent in itself and in regard to God. It must also be suitable, evidently with God's grace, to act upon the neighbor with whom we deal.

Briefly, for Saint Ignatius God's glory has a horizontal and not only a vertical aspect. For preaching fruitfully, he had need of his reputation before God and before men, and so it was necessary to remove all suspicion of his doctrine and of his conduct.[13] Ignatius of Loyola identifies equal glory and praise of the Divine Majesty with equal apostolic returns.

We may understand the Ignatian solution thus: even if I could make God known and loved *as much* by being rich and honored as in being poor and contemned, it will be convenient to prefer being poor and contemned, provided nevertheless that I do not thereby wind up making the Lord *less* loved and known by men. Why? Because, we think, in Ignatius' eyes, as well as in those of tradition, from which, perhaps inadvertently, some too logical commentators on the Exercises have departed, the equality in the glory given God is apparent rather than real: or, and this may happen, God wishes to be honored more in the well-ordered enjoyment of riches and of honors, or still, and perhaps more often, he wishes to be glorified more by the acceptance of their absence. It is the cross of Jesus which is the glory of God.[14]

For usually God's omnipotence shines out more clearly in weakness than in the strength of man, his infinite riches in our poverty accepted than in our abundance, and his honor in our acceptance of ignominy than in good repute.

There we find a consequence of the disorder of our tendencies, of our passions and of our affectivity, of the concupiscence which itself results from original sin.[15] The lower faculties, yet not negligible nor to be despised, of our personality are not longer, now, spontaneously and immediately subject to our reason, our free will, just as reason and free will no longer are submissive, without a struggle, to the eternal wisdom and love which is present deep within them.

Whence come the thirst, the avidity of our senses and imagination, in relation to material goods, even superfluous ones, in regard to riches and honors (*cf.* Jn 5:44)? Spontaneously, when the glory of God seems equal, we turn rather to riches and honors, even when they do not serve for the glory of God. They are the object of our innate, perilous and ever recurring preference.

Faced with this carnal, terrestrial, mundane spontaneity, Saint Ignatius, as many other saints, thinks it is indispensable that we implant into our very selves the opposite tendency, not only when the glory of God is found evidently to be greater in our acceptance of poverty and humiliations, but also when this is   doubtful, at first sight. When there is equal apostolic return, equality of perfection in our manner of acting, in the inner structure of our action which divine eyes alone penetrate, we glorify God more by embracing privations and injuries than in the enjoyment of riches and honors. Here, we think, is what Saint Ignatius means, when he suggests that all the plan of divine wisdom is at stake in the example given by Jesus loving us to the folly of the cross. We think that the view (developed by many commentators) according to which the third kind of divine love is justified only by the passionate desire of imitating Jesus and of being with him would have need of being much deepened. For it passes over in silence the reason for the choice made by Jesus. He might have saved us by a single act of innermost love, a fortiori by a happy life, in the midst of riches, surrounded by honors. Catholic theologians know this from the inspired author of the Epistle to the Hebrews: "Jesus . . . instead of the joy which lay before him endured the cross" (Heb 12:2). The passible and often suffering life of the pre-paschal Jesus is not just a run of the mill fact but a factor in the design of an infinite wisdom. It must be scrutinized, plumbed to the depths, under pain of superficiality in the analysis and understanding of the profound meaning of the evangelical expression "to follow Jesus."

It is because he came as Savior and Redeemer of a humanity whose menbers, after the first Adam, were lost by pride and sensuality, by putting at the service of their sins the gifts of God which are material goods and human honors, that it was fitting for the Word of the divine goodness to embrace a poor and humble life, and to desire to be regarded as a fool by fools. It was fitting for him to show preference for a salvation by way of the cross. His very love for us led him to present himself as the model of those who would have to be saved by poverty and humility. Jesus had no need of this for himself, but for us.

Yet it must also be noted, under pain of infidelity to the total choice of the Redeemer and Revealer, that if he wished to merit our salvation by his Cross, and the humble poverty it implied, he also wished to realize it effectively in us by means of his Resurrection.[16] The option of the Creator and Savior joins and binds inseparably his Cross and his Resurrection, his death and his coming back to life, his poverty and his immense riches, his humble desire to be contemned and his will to be glorified, the infirmity of his Passion and the glorious health of his definitive triumph.

In as much as He is the eternal and infinite God, Jesus is life, riches, glory and health; he has only chosen infirmity, poverty, ignominy and death by choosing also to transfigure thereby his humanity by the glorious riches and vivifying health of his divinity.[17]

Briefly, the total choice by Jesus of weakness and of strength, of poverty and of riches, of ignominy and of glory, of death and of life, is found reflected in our lives by the successive alternations of desolations and consolations, of weakness and health, of ignominy and honors, of death and

of life (*cf.* 2 Cor 4:7-12; 12:10), none the less with an accent placed on infirmity, contempt, privations, death, in the likeness of the pre-paschal Christ.
In our pre-paschal lives, before the pasch of our death and resurrection,
we must imitate the crucified rather than the glorified [18] Christ, by the practice
of humble love.

If there is *at times* more glory given God in the sue of riches and in the
midst of honor, by imitating thus the Creator risen from the dead, there
is, *more often,* more opportunities for glorifying him by the desire (not
always fulfilled) of humiliations and privations, in imitation of the crucified
Creator.

Humble love also knows that in choosing out of principle, "as far as we
are allowed free choice" (Ex. 23), a poor and humiliated life, reputed at the
same time to be useless and senseless, it chooses that which brings me more
surely to the definitive glory of a richness which will never pass; while, on
the contrary, the ordinary choice, in case of doubt, of goods and of honors
of this world for glorifying God would open the way to the eternal, proud
and ignominous privation of hell. The choice of the third kind of love wishes,
then, to embrace the whole in the nothing [19] and divides only the better to
totalize.

The glory of God, such as is manifested in the totality of the Christian
mystery which Ignatius glimpses in the Exercises, is the cross of Jesus who
is going to rise, it is the Resurrection of the crucified—with their double
radiation in our lives: infirmity and health, riches and poverty, humiliations
and honors, death and life. When this two fold radiation is (or appears to
be) equally present in two conducts, both excellent, or seems to bear equal
spiritual fruits for the salvation of the neighbor, it is then that it is fitting
to desire rather poverty, humiliations and to be reputed a fool with Christ
and following him, the better to make the same choice as the Father in
relation to, and in favor of, his well-beloved Son, and of all his members. [20]

*Implicit and explicit social applications of the second and third kinds of
humble love.*

No matter what the advantages or the inconveniences resulting for me, I
cannot accept to consider the hypothesis of a fault against social justice.
The right of my neighbor to live is prior to my right to property. So too
is his right to a just wage.

If the glory and the service of God is equal, I prefer to be poor with the
poor out of love for Christ, who accomplishes in them the mystery of his
poverty in view of the salvation of the rich and of the entire world (*cf.* LG
41), and to facilitate for the needy access to the vital minimum, rather than
to be rich in company with the rich.

If the glory and the service of the poor and humble Creator, Jesus Christ,
are equal, I prefer to be humiliated with the poor and with Christ poor in

them rather than to be honored with the rich and by them. I prefer to be humiliated for the honor of the poor and for the glory of Christ poor.

If the glory and service of the eternal wisdom are equal, I prefer to be foolish, ignorant, senseless, in the eyes of the rich according to the flesh or according to the spirit, with the poor and humble rather than wise and learned with the rich or all those who seek the glory that comes from men; to know less in order that the poor may know more. More than the friendship of the rich, I yearn for the favor of the poor and of the "dis-advantaged."

I yearn to be and to have less that the poor and the humble be and have more.

That Jesus increase in the world of today, I must decrease in the eyes of this world and in my own. That Jesus be known, loved, served and blessed in the poor, the despised, the Pariahs and the out casts of our society, I must prefer their lot and their company each time that his glory will be equal to that which would result for him from my association with the affluent, the learned and the "integrated" of our world.

Importance of the triple colloquy for obtaining the third kind of humility

After having explained the nature of the "third kind of humility" or of humble love, Saint Ignatius lets us understand the impossibility of acquiring or of conserving this gift of God without a persevering recourse to prayer. Let us read over his text: "If one desires to obtain this third kind of humility, it will help very much to use the three colloquies at the close of the Meditation on 'The three Classes of Men' mentioned above. He should beg our Lord to deign to choose him for this third kind of humility, which is higher and better, that he may the more imitate and serve him, provided equal praise and service be given to the Divine Majesty" (Ex. 168, Note).

Ignatius reveals himself here as *a man of desires.* Yet this man knows that his supernatural desires will be fulfilled only by the gratuitous intervention of him who inspires them. Saint Gregory the Great said that God inspires us to ask for what he desires to give us.[21] The desire of man, in the measure in which it is achieved in prayer, manifests and reveals God's desire about him, the desire that God has to shower him with his gifts. So, the gift implored here is one of the greatest ever dreamed. We want as proof of it but the interesting variant in P2: "begging our Lord may wish to choose him, select him,[22] for this third and more perfect and better humilility." [23]

In a very real sense, God chooses among men those whom he calls more especially to exercise the third kind of humble love, those whom he *calls* to *choose*[24] this *more* perfect way (the second kind, by excluding, at any cost whatsoever, venial sin, signified the necessary choice for perfection). Such a grace is not, actually and efficaciously, granted to all[25] and implies the personal choice of a way of interior and exterior life in which it will be possible for the observer to recognize a sign (among others) of predestination.

Let us note finally that the conditional clause which ends the Ignatian sentence ("provided the service be equal or greater, or the glory be equal or greater that is given to the Divine Majesty" P2), suggests how exact is the interpretation we gave to the third kind of humility: the abstract notion of equal glory does not exclude the concrete and real existence of a greater glory of God obtained by the action considered. In the concrete reality, there is never an equal glory of God, but only one more or less great, in two actions considered.

In the development of such a view, we are forced to conclude that, in Saint Ignatius' eyes, the second kind of humble love is, in fact, unrealizable without the desire of the third. As, evidently, the old man in us desires riches and honors, we will not succeed in avoiding venial sin save in the measure in which we will cultivate, passionately, the desire of privations and humiliations, the folly of the cross. If it is true that we must beware of a romantic, illusory and masochistic desire of chimerical insults and indigence, wherein pride would be fed, it is not, however, quite exact, from a psychological point of view, to assert[26] that we can only desire the third kind of humility if we are already fixed in the state of the spirit of the second. Quite the contrary is true: we can only be fixed in the effective differentiation between poverty and riches, honors and humiliation if we cultivate, affectively, the preference for privations and insults.

Colloquies for acquiring the third kind of humility

"Virgin Mary, full of grace, Mother and handmaid of the Lord, should I not turn to you to obtain a share in the humiliations of your Son, covered with opprobrium? Did you not share his poverty in Bethlehem and during the flight to Egypt, his humiliations at the foot of the cross? You can, therefore, by a special power, communicate to me this treasure given you to distribute: privations and humiliations with Jesus, infinitely glorious wealth. You are full of grace not only because the Lord is with you and will be with you, but also because you have been with him, full of opprobrium. As you obtained for the bride and groom of Cana and their guests the best wine, so your all-powerful supplication will obtain for me to inebriate myself with what humanly is insipid and colorless, actual graces, graces decisively efficacious for preferring your Son's poverty and humility."

"Jesus, Lord and Spouse of my soul, you have prepared for me, for my proud heart, the remedy of contempts, a sure and efficacious remedy. If to bear them in silence is one of the most difficult sacrifices to offer in this life, is it not also the key which opens up to me the door, your Heart, and intimacy with your infinite love?

"Jesus so humble of Heart that it was impossible to humiliate you,[27] I beg you for the grace to suffer numerous and great adversities for you, for and in your love, since this grace contains so many others and conducts us along the shortest and surest road to perfection.[28]

"Inebriate me with your Blood[29] to such an extent that no created thing can cause my soul so great or equal a joy as that which it would receive by suffering for your glory.[30] "Words with double meaning or those which are hurtful or abusive do not cause either pain—but peace—when they are desired."[31]

"Holy and just Father, Father of mercy, God of all consolation, I offer You the poverty and humility of your Son as my thanksgiving, my petition, my oblation, my adoration and my expiation. Receive them as being all you desire I render you, since apart from them I have nothing to offer you worthy of you.[32] Through my privations and my humiliations may Your Son accomplish in me his redemptive *kenosis,* for the salvation of the world."

"Spirit of Jesus poor and humble of Heart, Spirit Paraclete, have you not confirmed me to confess before men the cross of the poverty and humility of your Anointed, Jesus? I have entire confidence that you will grant me the grace and the joy, in the gift of your wisdom, to prefer habitually and in acts poverty to riches and humiliations to honors, each time your glory from them will be equally served. Spirit of the Father and of the Son who mutually glorify each other by the cross, give me the grace to prefer them readily and even with a holy and ever growing passion, with that passion which the worldly have to prefer honors over insults.

"May the sacramental grace of your confirmation, Spirit of light and love, transfigure and transform my daily cross into light for my darkness, into a burning stick to be a living flame of your love, into a victorious might which neither demons nor men could resist. May the tree of the daily cross make of my soul a true paradise on earth,[33] a river of joy flowing over parched humanity."

"Oh privation, what have you become? I hope you will remain in my heart, for with you I will be consoled and will go to repose in the Heart of my Jesus crucified."

"Oh insults, why are you unmindful of me, I who do not forget you, I who love you so much and who desire to see myself in your company, abject with my Jesus humiliated?"[34]

NOTES ON CHAPTER TEN

1. *Cf.* B. de Margerie, S.J. CFW, Ch. XI, pp. 275, ff.: "The Coredeeming Church".

2. Note on Ex. 165, p. 182 of Puhl will explain the exclusive use of "Kinds" instead of "degrees", "modes."

3. The divine law is universal and indicates God's will may be only particular.

4. While Ex. 166, A and P2 make clear that it is not a question of deliberating on the act of committing a venial sin. Ex. 166, V (a parallel text) replaces the word deliberate by "*decernam.*" The translator of V doubtless has wanted to avoid creating the impression that the rejection of sin supposed necessarily an indeliberate act of the will. The making of these deliberate decisions is proper to man's discursive freedom.

5. The case of the order given by ecclesiastical authority. The Church has received from Christ the power to enact laws (LG, 27). However her positive laws do not bind "*cum gravi incommodo,*" except when the common good requires their observance. Likewise, the power of the state comes, in the last analysis, from God (*cf.* Rom 13:1-5). It can bind in conscience.

6. *Cf.* Jn 15:13: The political community may oblige its members to the sacrifice of their lives in defense of its common good.

7. *Cf.* GS, 79,2 which in no way contradicts the preceding note, since the raison d'etre of the state is the defense and promotion of the human persons of its citizens; *cf.* GS, 74,1.

8. Father I. Iparraguirre, S.J. rightly notes: "Saint Ignatius uses this term in the medieval sense given by Saint Thomas Aquinas (ST. II,II, 161–162) and Saint Bernard, as subjection and subordination." (*Obras completas de S. Ignacio de Loyola,* Madrid, BAC, 1963, note 104, p. 230. Such subordination is impossible without love.

9. The condition of an equal service of God implies that, in the opposite case, riches and honors will have to be preferred for the greater glory of God.

10. ST, II.II.72.3; *cf.* Jn 18:23. Here is the Latin text of the "Doctor Angelicus": *Tenemur . . . habere animum paratum ad contumelias tolerandas si expediens fuerit. Quandoque tamen oportet, ut contumeliam illatam repellamus . . . propter bonum ejus qui contumeliam infert, ut de cetero talia non attendet; alio modo, propter bonum nultorum quorum profectus impeditur propter contumelias nobis itlatas.*"

11. San Ignacio de Loyola, Obras completas, BAC, Madrid, 1963, *Autobiografia, #98,* p. 155, (Ch. XI).

12. Father R. Cantin, S.J., "Le troisième degre d'humilité et la gloire de Dieu," *Sciences Ecclésiastiques* 8, (1956), 237–66.

13. *Cf.* notes 10 and 11 of this chapter.

14. *Cf.* Jn 13:31,32; 17:1; generally, it is this Joannine perspective that the Greek Fathers, notably John Chrysostom, Andrew of Crete, and John Damascene, have developed in excellent texts.

15. *Cf.* our chapter III.

16. ST, III.50.6; 56.2.

17. We use here the Ignatian categories of the "Foundation."

18. Athought expressed by Pius XII in *Mystici Corporis,* 1943, 47: "The whole body of the Church, no less than the individual members, should bear resemblance to Christ . . . Embracing the evangelical counsels she reflects the Redeemer's poverty, obedience and virginal purity . . . She points out Christ deep in prayer in the mountain, or preaching to

the people or healing the sick and the wounded and bringing sinners back on the path of virtue, or in a word doing good to everyone. What wonder then if, while she walks the earth, she be persecuted like Christ, hounded and weighed down with sorrows" (*df.* also 38).

19. *Cf.* Saint John of the Cross, *Ascent of Mount Carmel,* I, 13: "When the soul applies itself constantly not to what is more, but to what is less . . . not to wish something but to wish nothing, not to seek what is better in things but what is worse . . . These practices must be whole heartedly embraced and applied to subjecting the will to do this. He who submits himself to this lovingly, intelligently and prudently will not have to wait long before he finds many delights and consolations." In the same chapter, the Carmelite Doctor describes three practices one after the other (against the conspiscences of the flesh and the eyes and then against pride of life), the structure and final polarizarion of which are remarkable like those of the three kinds of Ignatian humility: "1. to strive for self-contempt and to desire that others condemn me; 2. to speak of self with contempt and to strive that others speak the same way; 3. to have a low feeling toward self, to despise self and desire that others do the same." (*cf.* ST, II.II.161.6.3.)

20. *Cf.* Saint Peter Canisius, *Exhortationes Domesticae,* collected by Schlosser, S.J., Ruremonde, 1876, p. 19.

21. Saint Gregory the Great, *Dialogues* I,8; ML,77,188; *cf.* ST,II.II.83.2.

22. We translate the Latin *eligere* of Ex. 168, P2 by these two terms.

23. Here is the complete Latin text quoted partly in the preceding note: "*petendo ut Dominus noster velit eum eligere ad hanc tertiam et perfectiorem et meliorem humilitatim.*"

24. It is well to note the great difference between readings of the text of Ex. 168 in the Autograph and in P2 on the one hand (where one begs God to choose for us), the Vulgate on the other (where one begs God to bring us to the choice of the third humility: *poscamus ad talem perduci electionem*) (In Puhl the text reads; "He should beg Our Lord to design to choose him for this third kind of humility). Actually, there is no contradiction between these requests which complement each other: we ask God to choose us for the third kind of humility by inspiring us with the choice.

25. We mean: this grace is not granted everyone as an efficacious grace. That is why we use the adverb: efficaciously. We do not deny, of course, the relative efficaciousness of sufficient grace, which is a salvific reality in the divine plan.

26. *Cf. Los Ejercicios de San Ignacio a la luz del Vaticano II,* Congreso Internacional de Ejercicios, Loyola, 1966, Madrid, 1968, conclusion 50: "In order that this third kind of humility be not illusory, it should be preceded by the acquisition of the second kind of humility, on which the director should especially insist."

27. We may say that only pride, of which Jesus had absolutely none, feels humiliated by "humiliations."

28. We are inspired here by the attitudes and words of Saint Ignatius as related by Father de Ribadeneira, S.J., in his life of Saint Ignatius, Bk. V, Ch. 10 at the end, in the edition of this work by Father de Dalmases (MHSJ, vol. 93, 1965, Rome). These facts are mentioned in the place indicated, #170, pp. 881–883. Here is the text of Ribadeneira: "One day a Father (Nadal) asked him (Saint Ignatius) what was the shortest and surest road to attain perfection. He answered: To suffer numerous and great adversities for love of Christ. Ask our Lord, he said, for this grace, because, on granting it, he gives many others which are joined to and comprised in it."

It is important to note here that, more explicitly than in the Exercises, perhaps, Ignatius does not recommend only to accept humiliation and sufferings, nor even only to desire them, but also to ask for them. Here, there disappears every mention of a condition (equalness of the devine glory).

Is a desire completely such and completely engaged if it does not end up with the explicit petition for the object desired, in prayer?

29. *Cf.* the invocation "Blood of Christ, inebriate me" taken from the "*Anima Christi*" which is strongly encouraged by the Exercises (Ex. 63,147,253,258) and to which we shall return in a later chapter.

30. An Ignatian thought quoted in Ribadeneira's text, *cf.* note 28.

31. *Saint Ignatius of Loyola—Letters to Women,* Hugo Rahner, S.J., 1960, p. 266, letter to Isabel Roser, November 1, 1532.

32. *Cf.* Saint Margaret Mary, *Ecrits,* Gauthey, vol. II, Paris, 1915, pp. 135; *cf.* pp. 145, 149.

33. Thoughts inspired by the *Lettre aux Amis de la Croix,* of Saint Louis-Marie Grignon de Montfort: "Carry your cross patiently and by this cross you will be lighted in your spiritual darkness; for he who suffers nothing by temptation knows nothing. Carry your cross joyously and you will be fired with divine love; for no one lives without sorrow in the pure love of the Savior . . . The real earthly paradise is to suffer something for Jesus Christ . . . Let us imagine all the greatest joys here below: that of a crucified person who suffers much includes them all, surpasses them all."

34. Extract from the famous "canticle of suffering," of Saint Alphonsus Rodriguez, the humble brother porter of Majorca (1548–1617). We can also quote in the same sense this beautiful elevation of Father de Clorivière, during his tertianship, at Ghent, in 1766: "Oh my Jesus, of what price are the sufferings and opprobrium, since you have taken them on! I prefer them to all the pleasures of this life, even spiritual, and today in the presence of your divine majesty, I choose them as recompense and sole consolation of all that I will have been able to do that is pleasing in your eyes. Yes, Lord, even should I be able to save myself by a less arduous way, nevertheless, to have more conformity with you, I embrace with all my heart the way you have walked and I choose it forever. I confess that I am the weakest al all men, but you will be my strength and my life."

11

THE ECCLESIAL
SALVIFIC AND THEOCENTRIC
DECISION OF THE ELECTION

Many authors have seen in the election the main purpose pursued by the retreatant who is faithful to the intent of Saint Ignatius. We do not share
this view.[1] Yet the fact that it has been able to be maintained with some
semblance of truth shows quite well the central significance of the election
in the Ignatian retreat. Is it not one of the essential steps by which the disciple of Ignatius "seeks to dispose his life for the salvation of his soul" (cf.
Ex.1)? "Conquers himself and regulates his life in such a way that no decision is made under the influence of any inordinate attachments" (Ex. 21)?

The principal election (concerning state of life) and secondary elections
in the course of the retreat and throughout entire existence, structure and
divinize the natural dynamism of created freedom in its journey toward
the Absolute Freedom which created it, dwells within it, moves it and gives
it its purpose. This exercise of freedom tends toward true and authentic freedom,[2] toward its own definitive expansion in the never to be lost embrace
of eternal and infinite Freedom. The theocentric and ecclesio-centric election
the Exercises promote is the salvation of freedom.

Not without putting aside a detailed analysis of quite a few aspects of
Ignatian thought and text, we will limit ourselves to try to sketch its essential outlines: why submit to a process of election the choice of a state of
life and quite a few others of lesser importance? What are the matter, the
times and the methods of this human-divine decision? In what does the
confirmation of the election consist? What is the importance of the decision
of self-reform in the frame of the state of life already chosen? And what are
the norms of its implications in the matter of social justice and charity?

A. Our choice is to be rationalized, "ecclesiasticized," divinized.

Let us recall first of all the importance for man, as a rational being,
of the choice of his profession and of his state of life.

149

If man, a being provided with a rational mind,[3] should give to each one of his actions a purpose which corresponds to this nobility, if the Christian should structure all his enterprises not only under the light of his reason but also under that of his supernatural last end, how much more is it necessary to make a rational and supernatural decision when there is question of choosing a profession or a state of life, since on this choice will depend almost every action of life! A faulty choice will render faulty too all the means employed for its realization.

In the second place, the Christian belongs, through the grace of his baptism, to the mystical body of Jesus Christ, the Catholic Church, which unites, for the glorification of her invisible head, a great multiplicity of members and a great diversity of functions, grades and states. All the members of the body cannot be eyes or feet, but it is the Holy Spirit, the Spirit of Jesus Christ, soul of the mystical body, which divides and distributes among the members these diverse functions for the good of the whole body which is its own. Whence it follows that, as employers assign their task to each of their employees, so the Lord of all lords, Jesus Christ, invisible head of the mystical body, has his divine plan about the way according to which each of its members will participate, in charity, in the construction of this entire social and mystical body. Consequently, the human person ought not hinder what the Spirit of Jesus wishes to operate in it for the common good, but on the contrary serve faithfully the divine design in the profession or state desired by this Spirit.

Finally, the properly understood interest of the Christian demands also that the choice of profession and of state of life be rational, supernatural, ordered to the good of the Church[4] and of human society. Is not the eternal salvation of each one at stake, in some way, through this choice? In fact, although God refuses to no one the assistance necessary for salvation, without any doubt he communicates more abundantly his light, his grace and his strength, not to intruders who have put themselves arbitrarily in any profession whatsoever or who have embraced in the same way any state of life at all, but rather to those who, after attentive consideration, have assumed the one that has seemed to them the most conformed to the divine pleasure.

Further, if we wish to follow our own judgment (often blinded as the result of original sin and its consequences) and our own will (more often perverted for the same reasons), we will fall easily, under the influence of the "father of lies" and of his temptations, into great and pernicious illusions and errors.

God, on the other hand, prepares nothing for us that is not suitable, useful and salutary. He knows better than we ourselves what is most suitable for our eternal salvation and wishes to make it known to us for the sake of saving us through ourselves. The Creator knows his creatures. He is the supreme author of all natural gifts, of human professions worthy of this name[5] as well as of states of life.[6]

These considerations (of which every Christian of good will is capable) do not hinder a great number of them[7] from inverting the order of values and, as Saint Ignatius emphasizes, "many first choose marriage, which is a means, and secondarily the service of our Lord in marriage, though the service of God is the end" (Ex. 169). How does the Saint evaluate this situation? "Such persons do not go directly to God, but want God to come straight to their inordinate attachments. Consequently, they make of the end a means, and of the means an end" *(ibid)*. Their blindness, explains Saint Ignatius a bit further on (Ex. 172) goes so far as to make them represent to themselves as it were "a vocation from God," as many erroneously believe. They make a divine call out of what is in reality only "a perverse and wicked choice," and so the response to a diabolical appeal (in many cases)! This pseudo-election combines the twofold tendency of the fallen human being, one whose redemption is still but imperfectly accomplished,[8] to magic (by making God a means, one tries to make him serve us) and to idolatry (by making of the means a supreme end, one devotes to it the cult of worship due exclusively to God).

The bad election, therefore, tends to transform religion into superstition.

In the face of this, Ignatius of Loyola recalls to us that in every good election, our intention should be simple, considering only the purpose for which I have been created: "the praise of God our Lord and the salvation of my soul." Marriage is a means, not an ultimate end,[9] and it is a means not only of temporal happiness, but also and above all of eternal salvation for those who are divinely called to it. It is a means which, as a sacrament, is capable of conducting the souls of the husband and wife to the end of the praise of God and the salvation of their souls.

What is meant by saying that our "intention should be simple", "the eye of our intention ought to be simple, " (A, V, P2 Ex. 169)?[10] By this "pure eye" (Ex. 169, V) of our intention? From the whole context (Ex. 169) we may conclude that what is meant is the intention enlightened by the sole light of the creative, redemptive and consummating love of the Trinity which dwells therein and moves it. If the eye is the symbol of the intention, the body is the symbol of action and of election. "The eye is the lamp of your body. When your eyesight is sound, your whole body is lighted up, but when your eyesight is bad, your body is in darkness. Take care, then, that your light is not darkness. If your whole body is lighted up and not partly in darkness, it will be as fully illumined as when a lamp shines brightly for you" (Lk 11:34–36; *cf.* Mt 6:22, 23).

With many, the eye of the intention is not simple, and so the body of their election and of their action is in darkness. That this body become luminous, there must be a return to health of the soul now ill and in need of the simplicity of pure love. Saint Francis de Sales writes: "Simplicity seeks naught but pure love of God, which is not found save in self mortification. Simplicity is but an act of charity pure and simple, which has but one purpose: to acquire love of God. The pure love of God is its sole intent."[11] This commentary seems to us in perfect harmony with the Ignatian text which we are studying now: the pure and simple eye desirable for the human election to be a response to a real divine vocation, and not to a diabolical appeal, is but the tendency toward the pure love of the divine majesty and the service of God which it motivates (Ex. 370).

It might be objected that the entering into the unitive way would be conceived as the condition *"sine qua non"* of an authentic and not "oblique" election! The objection would not cause us great difficulty if it meant that the tendency toward the unitive way is the condition of a good election. In fact, the "four great meditations" of the second week (the Kingdom, the two standards, the three classes, and the three kinds of humility) have as their purpose to help the retreatant center himself on the spirit of Jesus Christ, the spirit of abnegation.

The Exercises, as the gospel itself, teaches the Christian the gratuitousness and disinterestedness of love and of charity. These qualities are the soul of love and of charity, which will bring about death to self and spiritual resurection, just as they brought about the death and Resurrection of Jesus Christ . . . The Christian formed by the second week of the Exercises searches for the gratuitousness and disinterestedness of love as a decisive norm, one that is alone, the norm for his resolutions,[12] briefly the pure love of God. And if it is true that the election is set even in the second week, a period of the illuminative way (Ex. 10), it is not less true that it has a place at the threshold of the third week to which the unitive way corresponds.

Fruit of an *act*[13] of pure love, the election has precisely as its aim to fix us in the *habitual state* of perfect charity, the end of the Exercises. It is an act which, along with others should facilitate entrance into a state.[14] It is the gate to the unitive way.

It is quite remarkable that Saint Ignatius foresaw explicitly the application of methods of election not only with a view to a better choice of a state of life, but also to make any decision whatsoever, secondary in relation to that one. Purity and simplicity of the eye of the soul, fixed on the service of God and eternal salvation, are in his eyes a condition necessary for any human decision to be presented as an authentic response to a truly divine call. He understood every human decision worthy of this name as having to be a response to a divine vocation, an act of pure love for the creative, redemptive and consummating love of the eternal Trinity. Particular and changeable decisions just as the immutable election of a permanent and definitive state of life are, in his eyes, a gift of the free divine, eternal, uncreated love, operating within the depths of created and purified freedom, a theandric synergy (*cf. Ex. 169: "in every* good choice" 15; 171–74, 184).

Such is, in his eyes, the situation of created freedom when it puts no obstacle in the way of divine action on it. But he recognizes, too, as we have already stated, that most of the freedoms do not permit themselves to be purified by the infinite purity of God and so are not entering into the delicate process of the elections[16] "Take care, then, that your light is not darkness" (Lk 11:35). In other terms, impurity of heart, of eyes, of in-tentions is often too great for the retreatant to be able to be admitted to the election as Ignatius understands it.

B. Subject matter of the election

Let us come back here, in the light of Ignatian texts and of contemporary developments of Church structures, to some points to which we have alluded already in the preceding section.

Saint Ignatius envisages one after another, in two parts of the Exercises, two choices which seems to us quite different.

On the one hand, he gives us a remote introduction to the whole subject of elections immediately before the meditation on the two standards, in an "Introduction to the consideration of different states of life" (Ex. 135). On this occasion, he contrasts "the first state of life, which is that of observing the Commandments," to the "second which is that of evangelical perfection, when he remained in the temple and left his foster father and mother to devote himself exclusively to the service of his eternal Father" (Ex. 135). Here, the author of the Exercises seems inspired by the traditional distinction between a common state and a state of evangelical perfection, the way of the commandments, and the way of the counsels.[17] He then suggests that his retreatants "investigate in what kind of life or in what state his divine majesty wishes to make use of us." He thus seems to have in mind the necessary choice between lay Christian life and religious life or at least a life of the counsels. There is no question of marriage a propos of the first, nor of priesthood in the context of the second. And this is not surprising, since the prelude is found set in relation to a succession of examples given by the child Jesus, in the temple, when he was twelve years old.

On the other hand, in the "Introduction to making a choice of a way of life" (Ex. 169), there is question of making a choice between marriage and the priesthood (it must be said, only in the Vulgate is this choice explicit, but the choice is again presented explicitly in both the Autograph and in the Vulgate[18] in Ex. 171). Nothing is mentioned clearly about the evangelical counsels as such. Consecrated celibacy is understood in the context of the priesthood. Religious life, though existing for a long time, is not mentioned, in contrast to Introductory Observation 15.

How explain the passage from the pair "commandments-evangelical perfection," of the prelude to the investigation into different stages of life, to the pair "marriage-priesthood" of the prelude to the election itself? How, too, explain the passage to two social sacraments? A variety of explanations might be proposed. While emphasizing that there is no contradiction between the two pairs considered, we think that the first prelude is undoubtedly a part of the first stratum, the "Manresan," of the Exercises, which did not admit of a very elaborate presentation of the election and of its rules, while the second prelude is in line with the new editing of these rules, just as of the "Foundation" (of which they are the logical and stylistic corollary), in the course of the Parisian period.[19] At Manresa, preoccupation with the priesthood did not yet exist in Ignatius' spirit; after his return from the East at Barcelona and later in Paris it became dominant. Furthermore, contact with elite Christians to whom he gave the full Exercises (never having given them thus to women) led him to accentuate the priesthood,[20] viewed, too, in the context of the religious life, rather than of the priesthood by itself.

We do not, however, wish to overemphasize these subtle nuances, still less since Saint Ignatius himself, between 1553 and 1556, made his thinking more precise in his autograph directory and complementary notes, by putting fresh emphasis, no longer on the pair marriage-priesthood, but on the other, commandments–counsels. Rather let us read his text:

"The object of the deliberation is: first, counsels[21] or precepts?; second, if one opts for the counsels, shall it be in religious life[22] or outside of it? in hospitals.[23] for instance, or elsewhere? thirdly, if one opts for religious life, for which Institute? fourthly, when and in which way? If, on the contrary, one opts for the precepts, in which manner and in what state"?[24]

This text is very suggestive since it shows us the extent to which the author of the Exercises was aware of the variety of possibilities which, already in the Church of the sixteenth century, were offered the retreatant. Ignatius already knew by reflection what Pius XII will underline in our century: one can follow privately as an individual in the world the evangelical counsels, without becoming a religious. Yet he could not divine there would be a choice of a "Secular Institute," as would be necessary to add today, and in which one professes to observe the evangelical counsels no longer privately, but publicly, in the world. He knows, too, that the choice of the way of the precepts does not necessarily presume the choice of the state and sacrament of marriage, but can be realized in the category of a celibate not consecrated by vow. He is also interested in the choice of profession at least implicitly, for he invites the retreatant to ask himself in what way he will be involved in the way of the precepts. And indeed, one who chooses this way, recognizing in it his divine vocation, might ask himself: Which secular profession is better suited to me for my aptitudes, inclinations, previous studies, personal needs or needs of the civil community, the local parish or the universal Church? None of these questions could leave indifferent one who seeks perfection, which is the obligation of every Christian.

Outside of the choice of state of life or of profession, the election, as Saint Ignatius conceives it, can be particularly concerned with the use of temporal goods (as is evident from the meditations on the two standards, the three classes and Ex. 189, to which we shall return later). Without saying so explicitly, he does not exclude the election from being made on the acquisition of a virtue or on its being more deeply rooted in the soul. Moral virtues are not indeed the ultimate end, but means to attain it. And it is under this title they can be made the object of an election. One may say as much, a fortiori, of the exercises of infused virtues: faith, hope and charity, which the human free will cannot acquire by its own means, but which it can accept and decide to exercise intensely, to be more certain of not losing them. It must be added that, no matter what the particular object of the election may be, it will always have as its subsequent end the increase of charity, which Saint Ignatius calls consolation (Ex. 316). The precept of charity sums up all others, just as the virtue of charity sums up all virtues (*cf.* Gal 5:14; Rom 13:10; Col 3:14). The love which makes one choose such a thing flows from the love of God, it has God for its only objective and wishes, by the particular choice decided upon, to increase to the point of becoming perfectly pure (Ex. 184, 316, 370). Every election that is authentic is always, for Saint Ignatius, an exercise and a development of the virtue of charity and of its diverse modalities.

C. Times and ways of election

At first sight, it might seem that the Ignatian expression which distinguishes "three times when a correct and good choice of a way of life may be made" (Ex. 176), means purely and simply three different ways of divine action in the soul which chooses. Certainly, this meaning is implied; but it is not excluded that the author of the Exercises wishes also to allude to the temporal sequence of divers ways according to which the divine agent acts in the human agent, in the course of one and the same election. In the first time, the divine agent reveals himself most: "When God our Lord so moves and attracts the will that a devout soul without hesitation, or the possibility of hesitation, follows what has been manifested to it. Saint Paul and Saint Matthew acted thus in following Christ our Lord."[25]

This first time corresponds to the consolation given to the soul "without any previous cause" (Ex. 330) which is not abnormal in the second week, nor in the unitive way.[26] It is the moment of the immediate action of grace on which often follow moments of mediate action. As it is not always easy to make the distinction between these different moments (*cf.* Ex. 336), one understands that Saint Ignatius foresees for the uncertain or quite simply for the soul that does not believe it has benefitted from this first time and mode of divine action, the possibility of having recourse to other types of election. He considers, however, the certainty of the first time as sufficient if the retreatant knows well how to distinguish it from other concomitant actions.[27] The other forms of election ought to be employed if the first is faulty.[28]

If one thinks, with Father Clemence,[29] that consolation without any previous cause becomes more and more frequent as the soul advances, if it is considered the soul's normal state in the unitive way, it will turn out that one will judge, too, that this first time of election is the normal one for the decisions made by the Christian purified by God. One might say that the Lord, the Spirit which breathes, where it will, and of whom one does not know whence it comes nor where it is going, draws the will of the saint and moves it from within without this saint hesitating, nor even being able to hesitate, to follow the path which is manifested to him, the way of the cross and of abnegation, which is also that of beatitude.

Just as it is permissible for us to aspire to the unitive way, and just as we have the obligation to do so, we can and must desire and ask of God this very precious gift which would take our thoughts, words and deeds away from their chill confusion and plunge them into the burning clarity of the divine Spirit, for his greater service: the clear, frequent, immediate manifestation of the divine will in order that our human choices can more perfectly realize it.[30] Not only more perfectly, but also more immediately.

Still, it belongs to the design of divine wisdom not to will always to manifest to us in this immediate way its salvific will, but rather to permit that we do not recognize the benefit, the light of such an immediate manifestation with all the clarity we would judge desirable. In this case, the same divine wisdom has at its disposal a second time "when such light and understanding are derived through experience of desolations and consolations" in the measure in which it is accompanied by that which discerns the spirit and movements constituting these consolations and desolations. God is not the only one acting. Devils and angels, the free will of each one of us influence in diverse ways the movements of our affectivity (although God alone can move our will to the point of changing it, which neither angels nor devils can do). By helping us discern the hour of the power of darkness and the luminous hour of his consoling grace, with their respective effects, Providence gives us the information and the clarity necessary for recognizing its will and its action.

God, the angels and the devils can, however, hide themselves to the point of delivering us over to the sole and troubled clarities of our reason. Our reason can, by an elaborate discursive process (which Saint Ignatius describes at length, differing from the immediacy of the first time in # 178—188 of his Exercises) and not without the help of the grace obtained by prayer, discover the divine will, "the state of life within the bounds of the Church" which "will help him in the service of God our Lord and the salvation of his soul" (Ex. 177) or every other object of this will. It is the third time. A time of psychic clarity, if we may be so bold, in contrast with the two preceding times, which were times of pneumatic and mystical clarity.

The second time corresponds, then, to an exercise of discernment of spirits and of consolations (angelic or diabolical: Ex. 331, 332) with a view to find out the divine will. Although the third time may not be a moment of desolation (Ex. 177) since "it is a time of tranquillity," one can, however, apply to this moment of reason an aspect of the observations by Saint Ignatius on the subject of one in desolation: "He can resist with the help of God, which always remains, though he may not clearly perceive it. For though God has taken from him the abundance of fervor and overflowing love and the intensity of his favors, nevertheless, he has sufficient grace for eternal salvation," to work out his election "begging God our Lord to deign to move his will, and to bring to his mind what he ought to do to promote his praise and glory with regard to the matter in question" (Ex. 320, 180).

If Saint Ignatius presents us these three times starting from their *"analogatum princeps"* which is the first, which he prefers above all and which is in his eyes the one which permits the surest choice for the recognition of the divine will, nothing forces us to identify this order with the real, historical one of the times of election in the case of those who have not as yet attained the unitive way but who, nevertheless, are tending there. We can perfectly think that the laborious third way corresponds to the purgative way, the second time to the illuminative and the first to the unitive. Thus it seems that the rational, not sentimental (*cf.* Ex. 182) election of the third time disposes one for the greatest grace of the election-discernment of the second time, and the second in turn disposes for the election of pure consolation without previous cause, for the election in a state of pure love of the first time. In other words, the process of election becomes more simple as the soul progresses.[31] Fidelity of reason to measure the pro and con in relation to the greatest glory of God, then fidelity of heart and spirit to discern the attachments and the consolations, appropriately merit at last the grace of consolation without previous cause in which ·God manifests, with all clarity possible here below, his burning will of salvific love.

We might even say, just as we have suggested before, that the sequence of the third, second and first times, in the face of the same decision to make, forms part of the supernaturally normal regime of Christian choice. After reasoning about the *objective* facts of the problem, comes the discernment of its *subjective* aspects which constitute often, in the concrete providential economy, the prior conditioning of the *transcendental manifestation* of the divine will. "But he who acts in truth comes into the light" (Jn 3:21); "He who obeys the commandments he has from me is the man who loves me . . . . I too will love him and reveal myself to him" (Jn 14:21); "He comes into the light, to make clear that his deeds are done in God" (Jn 3:21).

The soul which has long practiced rational (Ex. 181) and affective (Ex. 176) discernment acquires progressively a "supernatural *habitus*," made up of intellectual and moral acquired and infused virtues, and is therefore much more disposed to make quickly, under the influence of the gifts of counsel and of wisdom, decisions which are presented as savory fruits of the Holy Spirit.[32]

To put it in other words, the soul is more disposed to receive, perceive, and embrace the fresh manifestation of the divine will thanks to this ascetic of the mind and of the heart. The divine will *manifests* itself to the intellect[33] about the way to follow while the human will,[34] feels *drawn and moved* by the saving love, by and toward this divine will, in the clarity (without vision) of an absence of doubt, of a moral certitude quite sufficient. The process of election integrally considered, with its three moments, logically integrated and distinguished, appears, therefore, as an existential divinization, [35] at the same time contemplative and active, of the superior faculties, intellectual and volitional, of the human person.

We see a twofold confirmation of this entire interpretation in the Exercises and in the Ignatian election concerning the poverty of the professed houses.

In the first way of the third time, the retreatant is invited to "beg God our Lord to deign to move my will, and to bring to my mind what I ought to do to promote his praise and glory with regard to the matter in question. Then I should use the understanding to weigh the matter with care and fidelity, to make my choice in conformity with his most holy will" (Ex. 180). [36] Now, the terms employed by Saint Ignatius to signify the manifestation of the divine will in the course of the first time corresponds very exactly to those of this request of the third: it suffices for understanding them to compare the concepts and the terms of the two texts (Ex. 180 and 175). [37] In both cases there is question of an illumination of the intellect which sees itself shown the divine will and of an "impulse" of the human will by the latter. How can we help but conclude that, ordinarily, the manifestation of the first time is presented as a response to the prayer of the third? And that the third time is thus intrinsically ordered toward the first?

Such a conviction is reinforced when one considers the first rule of the second way of the third time: "The love that moves and causes one to choose must descend[38] from above, that is, from the love of God, so that before one chooses he should perceive that the greater or less attachment for the object of his choice is solely because of his Creator and Lord" (Ex. 184). Such a description of the state of the will and of the affections after the third time is substantially identical with the state in which they are found after the first. The use of the verb "perceive" (sentir, A) supposes also an intellectual knowledge already attained and a propos of which the "feeling" is exercised. Decidedly, the third time seems oriented toward the first!

The very experience of Saint Ignatius in the deliberation on poverty and in the spiritual diary, in 1544, furthers our interpretation. Just as Father Iparraguirre has emphasized, the deliberation constitutes a thorough examination of the advantages and disadvantages presented by the two possible solutions of the problem under consideration, while the spiritual diary, while it takes up these considerations (February 11 and 16, 1544), more ordinarily employs discernment of spirits and above all manifests the mystical illuminations and graces proper to the first time. [39]

It seems these things might even be explained thus: Saint Ignatius began with a profound examination, written down, of the reasons for and against each of the two solutions envisaged, analyzing them in the light, not of reason alone, still less of the senses, but of the reason itself enlightened by faith and absorbed by concern for the greatest glory of God (Ex. 179 and 181). Then, for forty days, he subjected the resolution to which he has thus come to a screening of consolations and desolations, after prayer, during preparation for Mass, its celebration and thanksgiving, all the time taking fresh notes. Above all he confronted his resolution with consolations without previous cause which occurred to every moment.[40] The three times were relived within the space of each of the forty days, more or less.[41]

It seems, then, permissible to consider the three times as three distinct and successive moments of a whole and unique act of election. From this point of view, the two distinct ways, the first more deductive, the second more inductive, of the third time (Ex. 178–183) are no longer exclusive the one of the other, but rather complementary and successive. Note also in this context that the integration of the consideration on death and judgment (Ex. 186, 187) confirms that the third time belongs to the horizon of the first week (cf. Ex. 71, V[42] and 74) and to the exercises of the purgative way (cf. Ex. 70) which correspond to it.

Briefly, if the third time, with its two distinct modalities, places the existential decision or election[43] of the human person on the rational[43] and ecclesial visible horizon, the second time or moment places it on the confines of the angelical and diabolical world, in the sphere of the ecclesial-invisible, while the first time receives it wholly from the eternal transcendent Trinity, which is besides immanent to the play of reason as well as to that of discernment of spirits. The living God appears thus as sole supreme cause of a process which places and assumes the human person in relations with the entire visible and invisible universe of matter, of mankind, of the angels and (indirectly) of the devils, finally, of the Divine Persons.

In the oblation in which this election ends (Ex. 183, 188), there is, implicitly but really, the whole universe, jointly with human freedom, which returns to its Creator. It suffices to say that such an oblation (Ex. 97, 98) is part of that offered by Christ to his Father. And as the Father accepted the sacrifice of his Son's death raising him up, so too the sacrificial election of the member of his Son ought to be offered through him to the Father to be accepted and confirmed by him in the gift of the confirming Spirit, if and in the measure it redounds to the greatest glory of the three Divine Persons (cf. Ex. 183)[44]

Colloquies for obtaining the grace of a good election

"Angel of the Trinity, you who are my guardian, obtain for me and give me true happiness and spiritual joy, for the good of my soul that it may advance and rise to what is more perfect, banishing all the sadness and disturbances which are caused by the enemy of mankind (Ex. 329, 331). Help me to discern the feelings which agitate me: the good movements to admit them, the bad to reject them (Ex. 313). Guide me in my election touching my soul delicately, gently, suavely, as a drop of water falling into a sponge. My doors are wide open to you, enter as into your own house (Ex. 335). Direct me in my choices as my invisible director" (*cf.* Ex. 7).

"Immaculate Virgin, my sister, heart and mother of the universal Church, mother of good counsel, obtain for me from your Son, from your Father and your Spirit that charity which abounds more and more in knowledge and in all understanding, to discern what is of most worth, in order that I be pure and blameless up to the day of Christ, filled with the fruits of justice by Jesus Christ, your Son, for the praise and glory of God the Father, in the bond of their Spirit. Oh daughter, mother and temple of God, following your example and relying on grace through your powerful intercession, may I not model myself on the present world, but rather renew my judgment to transform me and to make me discern what is God's will, what is good and pleasing to him, what is perfect, what is most perfect (*cf.* Phil 1:9-11; Rom 12:2; Ex. 339). Through you may my intellect and free will become for your well-beloved Son, an intellect and free will of superabundance in which he renews and prolongs his mysterious election for the glory of his Father."

"Lord Jesus, light in my darkness, Word and splendor of the Father, grant me abundantly (*cf.* Tit 3:6) your Spirit that I may be able to think, reason, examine, discern (Ex. 181, 182, 176) the signs of your will. Grant me above all by this Spirit of love a love so purified by you and so pure of all admixture of self love that you shine out in the motives which will make me prefer this or that person or thing (Ex. 370, 189, 338, 184), and that it be clear, not only to me before making my decision, but afterward to all, that the love which makes me choose comes clearly from you, without admixture of an inordinate attachment (Ex. 169) and is ultimately addressed to you, my Creator and Lord. (Ex. 184).

"As I do not know what I ought to do and am even unworthy of knowing it, I have no other recourse than to lift up my eyes to you, eternal wisdom. Deign to move my will and make known to my soul what I should do to be of use to your praise and glory by a choice in conformity with your good pleasure and your most holy will (2 Chr 20:12; Ex. 180).

"Loving and merciful Father, God invisible and incomprehensible, I adore your eternal and mysterious election concerning my created, temporal, human and visible election. Manifest to me your holy and sanctifying will. Work in me what is most pleasing to your divine goodness" (Ex. 151).

"Spirit, you who are the eternal bond between Father and Son, Spirit of counsel, soul of the Universal Church, enlighten my reason that it discern, distinguishing diabolical wishes, carnal desires of others and my own from your holy will which ever associates my good with that of other members of your Church. Your particular and actual will for me is ever tied to the permanent good of that universal Church of which you are the soul, the principle of unity, the uncreated bond, the sanctifier, the consoler and the joy. Show me the sanctifying and divinizing splendor of what you have eternally chosen for me and on my behalf. Draw my will that I may un-hesitatingly (*cf*. Ex. 175) follow and embrace yours. Oh eternal kiss ex-changed by the Father and the Son, dispose my soul to your service and your love, by the most suitable way, communicating yourself to it in the flame and kiss of your love (Ex. 15). Inflame it to such a point of your divine love that it can no longer love any creature on the face of the earth in itself, but only in you (Ex. 316). May my resolve and my choice be so received by you, Spirit of my sacramental confirmation, that they may be confirmed by your light and your power and thus confirm my perseverance in your service, in your grace, until your final encounter."

D. Confirmation of election by and in the effusion of the sacrament gift of the confirming Spirit."

Concluding the first way of the third time of election, Saint Ignatius ex-plains to the retreatant that "he must turn with great diligence to prayer in the presence of God our Lord, and offer him his choice that the Divine Majesty may deign to accept and confirm it if it is for his greater service and praise" (Ex. 183, A, P3, Puhl). What does this seemingly simple text show us? Thus: the total and single act of the election is to be ended by a last "time" or "moment" integrating a prayer of oblation and the petition directed to what this offering of the decision—received (Ex. 180, A) and taken—is oriented, that is that the election be accepted and confirmed by the Divine Majesty.

This text, so brief, is not fully understandable except in the light of the graces of "confirmation" received by Saint Ignatius after his election and es-pecially his confidences in the "spiritual diary." Only this document per-mits us to grasp the "pneumatical" dimension of the confirmation of the election in the eyes of Inigo de Loyola.

On February 11, 1544 Ignatius wrote: "On offering or on praying God our Lord, that the oblation made would be accepted by his Divine Majes-ty,[45] an offering made with much devotion and many tears, and afterwards, conversing with the Holy Spirit to celebrate his Mass, with the same devo-tion and tears, it seemed to me that I saw him in the dense light or in the color of a flame of fire, in an unusual fashion. With all this was confirmed in me the election made."

The election, then, is confirmed in the vision of the gift and of the fire of the Holy Spirit. Manifesting himself the Spirit confirms Ignatius in the decision with which he had inspired him.

Let us continue the quotation from the Ignatian text:

"Next, wanting to think over[46] and to go into the choices, and after hav-ing taken out the notes I had written down, to think them over,[47] I prayed to our Lady,[48] then to the Son and the Father that he would give me his Spirit to think over and discern.[49] I nonetheless from that moment spoke of this matter as of something already resolved, feeling much devotion and knowing certain things with some clarity of view . . . I no longer had any desire of seeing any reasons.[50] At this moment came to my mind other illuminations, that is, how the Son first sent his apostles in poverty to preach, and afterwards the Holy Spirit, giving his Spirit[51] and tongues, confirmed them, so that the Father and the Son, sending the Holy Spirit, all three Persons confirmed such a mission."[52]

The passage just quoted is decisive for understanding the Ignatian concept of the confirmation of the election. The prayer of petition for a divine confirmation manifests here the splendor proper to it: it is a triple colloquy asking successively of Mary, of her Son and his Father the effusion of the Spirit in view of discernment. The Spirit is given in the *clear understanding* which renders useleless a fresh examination of the *reasons. Reasoning* cannot but fade away before *intuition*:[53] This inner effusion of the Holy Spirit evokes, in the eyes of the mystical founder, the non-sacramental confirmation[54] of the apostles through the gift of the Spirit symbolized by the wind and the tongues, after the first Pentecost of the New Testament.

Let us clear up what is implied in Ignatius' thinking, and of which perhaps he was not even conscious but which is nonetheless demanded as a logical development of his thinking. The grace of a luminous and stable clarity in the recognition of the divine will (embraced by the election) is the grace of the confirmation, that is an irradiation and an actualization of the sacramental grace of confirmation (when that takes place). If the election, as we have already partly seen, and as we will go into more thoroughly shortly, is an ecclesial act in its origin, its importance and its purpose, it is not surprising that it is particularly favored by the profound grace of a sacrament conferred to render more perfect the tie which binds the Christian to the universal Church and to make of him a true witness of the faith of the Church in Christ, before the world, helping this Christian to defend her and to propagate her.[55] In the sacrament of confirmation, is realized the personal Pentecost of each Christian, filled afresh[56] with the Spirit of Jesus to proclaim before the world his faith in the Son of Man and in his body, the Church. This is what is ever an aspect of the election, in the Ignatian sense.[57]

The prayer for obtaining the grace of the confirmation of the election is, then, objectively, a petition made to the Father and the Son that they send again, on a new invisible mission, the Spirit visibly given and received the day of confirmation. It is an "obsecration," begging the three Divine Persons to give themselves more abundantly to the sacramentally confirmed, in a fresh effusion of the sacramental grace of confirmation. The grace of the confirmation of the election is, then, a sacramental grace, a new penetration of the human intellect and free will by the confirming Spirit coming to manifest and increase its hold by sacramental possession. A grace of strength and light, oriented toward a firm perseverance in the service of and the grace of Christ as Redeemer until his day, after his coming with all his saints (*cf.* 1 Cor 1:8; 1 Thes 3:13).

Thus one glimpse that this sacramental grace of confirmation in a Christ-like election is not unrelated to "confirmation in grace," when this is granted by God.[58] All actual graces are ever, in the divine plan, oriented toward the grace of perseverance, continual and final, in sanctifying grace. Their dynamisim is always eschatological. The graces of confirmation of our elections, in the Ignatian sense . . . can quite well be an aspect of confirmation in grace, an indissoluble bond between God and the soul, not physical and internal (as that which is the base of the beatific vision) but moral and external, absolute however, since, founded on an absolute decree of God and on a flow of grace, which, while safeguarding human liberty, continues perpetually its action to prevent all sin.[59]

Briefly, confirmation in grace is an efficacious grace, which includes a whole series of others, among which must be counted the graces of confirmation in human elections made under the inspiration of the Spirit. The graces of confirmation as confirmation in grace, therefore, all appear as effects of the sacramental grace of confirmation. But we do not intend to go deeply here into this theological opinion which would doubtless present some difficulties and merit a separate study.

The sacramental grace of confirmation, source of those of confirmation in the grace of the election, is transmitted by the Church in view of her full development. We are not surprised to find in Saint Ignatius a clear consciousness of the ecclesial nature of the actual grace of confirmation in the election.

For the author of the Exercises, the election is ecclesial in its origin, since it is the fruit of the intercession of all the saints (Ex. 58, 151), in whose presence it is made (Ex. 98). Its object is set within the bounds approved by the Church (Ex. 177). Finally, its raison d'être and its purpose is naught but the salvation of the one who makes it spiritually as well as the salvation of all other souls, for the greatest glory of God (Ex. 16). To promote the salvation of souls, is it not the same as to wish for the advancement of the Church, sacrament of salvation, that is, the instrument of Christ the Savior in his salvific work?

If the election, then, seems to be a fruit of the intercession of the heavenly Church, and an expansion of the Church on earth, is it not true that in the eyes of Saint Ignatius this ecclesial decision ought also to be approved by the visible Church, represented by the director of the Exercises? Is not the confirmation thus obtained, in his eyes, a supreme sign of the Trinitarian confirmation desired?[60]

If the ecclesial community can have a role in this confirmation, this role does not go beyond that of a certain preparation of the terrain,[61] while the decisive role is assumed by the official representative of the Church, even the visible head of the Church. "The hierarchy of the confirmation follows that of the visible representatives of Christ."[62]

Ordinarily, however, the director of the Exercises will represent adequately the Church and the Trinity in confirmation of the election.

Confirmation is indeed for Inigo de Loyola, a Trinitarian grace. We cannot help but be moved when we read the urgent prayer of his Spiritual Diary: "Eternal Father, confirm me; eternal Son, confirm me; eternal Holy Spirit, confirm me; Holy Trinity, confirm me; one and only God, confirm me; . . . and Father eternal, will you not confirm me?" These urgent petitions of February 18, 1544 were heard.[63]

Also, at the close of a lengthy analysis of the Ignatian concept of confirmation, Father Bottereau was able to conclude: "In Ignatius's words, confirmation is a superior degree of light and power concerning a disposition, a decision, a commitment. It results from an increase of faith, hope and charity, establishing the soul in the peace and joy of its Lord on the matter considered. According to the expression so frequent in the Spiritual Diary, one who is confirmed 'sees and feels' that he ought to keep his resolution." Moreover, the analyst adds, the confirmation "will be able to be reduced to an argument, *sufficing in time of trouble for remaining firm,* to a rememberance of a spiritual experience."[64] Consoling confirmation does not exclude the nuance of a desolation.

Except in the case of a vision or a private revelation, it only provides for the retreatant a moral certitude; still one important, concerning the divine will. Before the beatific vision, there is not necessarily absolute certitude about it, not even in the first time of election.[65]

Light not without shadows, the confirmation of the election shares the darkness and the light of the paschal mystery to which it introduces the retreatant. In a very real sense, Ignatius expects from the entire third and fourth weeks of the Exercises, from the contemplation on the Passion and Resurrection of Christ, the grace of confirmation for his retreatant.[66] Due to a quite profound reason, furthermore, although Jesus, the infallible man God, has no need at all of seeing himself confirmed, is not the Resurrection the highest of confirmations, the full effusion of the gift of the Spirit even into the body of the man Jesus, the ratification by the Father of the sacrifice of the only son? To the election of Jesus choosing a sacrificial death, announced at the Supper, maintained throughout his agony, responds the confirmation of this election (rendering possible its sacramental renewal) after the glorious reanimation of the corpse of the Word of Life.

Appendix: Method of amendment and reform of individual and social life in the state of life chosen. The ministry of almsgiving.

For those who cannot or will not make a properly called election on a change to be made, the author of the Exercises foresees the possibility of an election in the broader sense.[67] "It will be very profitable . . . to propose a way for each to reform his manner of living in his state" (Ex. 189).

What will be the *object* of this election of reform? It will consist, as in the case of the basic truth and the first way of the third time, in orienting his manner of living and position to the glorification and praise of God the Creator[68] and to personal salvation (*ibid*).

What will be the objectives of the reform intended, its *subject matter*? Saint Ignatius points out a triple objective: the way of life (we would perhaps more appropriately say the standard of living) of the family according to the flesh and the spirit,[69] next, "how he ought to govern (his family), how he ought to teach its members by word and example:" in other words, the apostolate in regard to his own; finally, how his income is to be distributed. Granted that the first and third objectives are attained, the objective presented consists essentially in a salvific and theocentric organization of family life and of the use of material resources.

The first of these two objectives are today vested with an importance which it did not have in Saint Ignatius' day. It is not wrong to think that our author, when he asked the retreatant to envisage *"quam amplam domum et familiam aequum sit se habere"* (Ex. 189, V, A, P2), did not exclude the determination of the number of children, since total continence, during a part or throughout the marriage, was a perfectly licit means for this determination of the size of the family. At any rate, today,[70] the determination made jointly by the married partners, the regulation of births could and should certainly become a matter for a decision reflected on together and before God. It is, as a matter of fact, something that belongs neither to the Church nor to the State but to the husband and wife alone, to decide the number of their children, while nevertheless relying on the teachings of the Church and informing themselves, as the case may be, in regard to the State, or States, about demographic problems.[71] It is evident that such a decision is, either for the married couples themselves, or for the Church, or for the States, the most important they could make for the salvation of their souls and for the greatest glory of God. If, then, there is any one decision that should be subject to an election (at least in the broad sense) it is clearly this decision relative to the number of children.

Such a decision finds its logical counterpart in the choice to be made about the way to teach "by word and example," the children and the household. We have here a priceless indication. Does it not mean that, if Saint Ignatius insists on silence during the Exercises (Ex. 20: "one must withdraw from all friends and acquaintances . . . in order to serve and praise God our Lord") it is precisely in view of obtaining such praise and service by foreseeing what one will *say* and do after the Exercises in regard to his friends and acquaintances," in order to receive from God himself, in the silence of contemplation," the *words*, no longer mixed up, cold and troublesome, but warm, clear and just"[72] which will draw others to the selfless service of the pure love of God (*cf.* Ex. 189 at end; Ex. 370)?

As to the salvific and theocentric organization of the use of material goods and of money, the author of the Exercises does not explain precisely the way and the *means* which will enable us to attain this end.

Such a determination, however, is the object of the "rules for the distribution of alms" (Ex. 337f.) These rules represent with several verbal nuances the four rules of the second way of the third time of election (Ex. 184-187) by adapting them to the particular case under consideration.

Their title is characteristic: the distribution of alms is conceived of as a *ministry*. The word evokes the idea of a sacred service, in view of the spirutal good of others, following on a divine mission (*cf.* Ex.344 b: there is involved "service and ministry of the temple") and presupposes the mystery of the Church. Understood is not only ecclesiastical benefices, but also every ownership of earthly good as belonging in the first place always to God, so that the human owner is always only as an administrator who will have to render an account for the use of goods entrusted to him by the Creator of the universe.[73] The goods of the rich (ecclesiastics and married persons) are always "the goods of God our Lord" from whom the rich receive a call and a "vocation for distribution if a person be called by God our Lord for such a service" (Ex.343). That the election be not questionnable, mixed with some carnal or inordinate attachment (*cf.* Ex. 172), but a response to the divine appeal ever pure and limpid, God must be resplendent (Ex.338) in the motives which make us prefer this or that beneficiary. To be more certain I am not deceiving myself and have not been deceived by the enemy of mankind, in this choice, I will give myself the advice I would give to a stranger, and will decide as if I were at the hour of death and judgement (Ex.339-41), desiring to make the most perfect decision for the glory of God.[74]

Among the beneficiaries I may prefer, for the greatest glory of God the Creator, I cannot leave myself out a priori. Here the author of the Exercises reminds us that "It will always be better and safer. . .if he imitates as closely as he can our great high priest, model, and guide, Christ our Lord" (Ex.344). The imitation of Christ implies the limiting of our desires out' of concern for the service of the poor. It encourages us to think that Christ's needs in others are greater than his needs in ourselves. In this way we will be more inclined to cut down on the part of our income reserved for our own use for increasing the part set aside for the poor, on the one hand, and for the specific works of the Church (symbolized by the temple; *cf.* Ex. 189, 344) on the other.

It is on this occasion that Saint Ignatius formulates concisely one of the key texts of the Exercises: "For everyone must persuade himself[75] that in all that concerns the spiritual life his progress will be in proportion to his surrender of self-love and of his own will and interests" (Ex. 189).

Thus is presented the conclusion: the last sentence is at the same time the ensemble of the treatment of the election and the summary of the second week of the Exercises. This remarkable text includes, in the Spanish Autograph as in the Latin versions,[76] a "*tanto quanto, tantum quantum*" which

French translations render as *"dans la mesure où"* and English translations render as "in porportion," rather colorless in comparison with the Spanish and Latin translation which adequately render and enable us to comprehend the profound meaning involved already beforehand in the "Principle and Foundation." "Hence man is to make use of them in as far as they help him in the attainment of his end, and he must rid himself of them in as far as they prove a hindrance to him" *(tantum quantum)*. The ordered use and detachment in regard to created things, to earthly realities presupposes the rejection of every inordinate attachment for self, "the surrender of self-love and of his own will and interests" (Ex.189), in view of the "salvation of his soul" (this last phrase mentioned earlier in the same number), in view of an ordered love of self.[77]

These reminders not only concern (we see it better today undoubtedly, because of the very evolution of property)[78] our obligation in regard to our own personal goods, but also our personal responsibility in the use of collective goods. The vow of poverty does not in any way signify, for the religious or for the member of a Secular Institute, the renouncing of all responsiblity in the administration and use of earthly goods. For he remains, for his part, indirectly responsible before God, the Church and the world for the use that his Order or Institute makes of its fortune.[79] The virtue of poverty demands that the goods of the collectivity be,[80] to the maximum, put in the service of the poor, indirectly or directly. The simultaneous "explosions" of population, communications and poverty oblige us to assume our responsibilities vis-a-vis the Third World[81] and all mankind in the disposition of our collective revenues.

Was not all this already present in germ in these Ignatian sentences of the last rule on the ministry of distributing alms: "That the furniture of the bishop should be cheap and poor.[82] This consideration applies to all stations of life, but attention must be given to adapting it to each one's condition and rank "(Ex. 344). So Saint Ignatius invites every rich person (out of love for the poor and for Christ poor) to adopt a manner of life despised and poor."

NOTES ON CHAPTER ELEVEN

1. The balanced article by S. Gomez Nogales, S.J. may be consulted on this controversy, "Cristocentrismo en la teleologia de los Ejercicios," Manresa 24 (1952) 33-52.

2. *Cf.* DH, 8; GE 1:

3. In contrast with the purely intuitive intelligence of angels.

4. Saint Ignatius does not say this explicitly, but the whole contemplation of the Kingdom of Christ suggests it.

5. *Cf.* Pius XII, *Sedes Sapientiae*, AAS, 48 (1956) 357: "*Omnium statuum, omniumque sive naturalium sive supernaturalium dispositionum donorumque principalis auctor ipse est Deus.*"

6. This traditional expression (*cf.* ST, II.II.183.1) designates the permanent obligations assumed in contrast with varying and extrinsic circumstances (such as riches and poverty). In the preceding paragraphs we have drawn on the official Directory of the Exercises, Ch. 22 (MHSJ, vol. 76, Rome, 1955, *Directoria Exercitiorum Spiritualium*, pp. 682-85). It is also to be noted that Vatican II (GS, 26) has emphasized that "There must be made available the right to choose a state of life freely," a right that is exercised most perfectly in the course of the Ignatian retreat of election.

7. *Cf.* Ex. 169 and P2. ("*ut evenit multis*"); the Vulgate drops this allusion to a great number here, but picks it up again later (Ex. 172: *non pauci errant*).

8. *Cf.* Rom 8:23, "We groan inwardly while we await the redemption of our bodies."

9. *Cf.* Ex. 169. It is precisely because marriage and the priesthood are only means and not the ultimate end that they can be the object of a choice; *cf.* ST. I,II,13,3; The entire 13th question presents the Thomist doctrine on election, summed up by R. Orlandis, *Manresa* 11 (1935) 291–298.

10. Transl. Puhl has simplified the expression as quoted in text.

11. Saint Francis de Sales, "Entretien XII on simplicity," *Oeuvres complètes*, Paris, 1899, vol. 3, p. 425ff.

12. J. Clémence, "Le discernement des esprits dans les Exercices spirituels de Saint Ignace de Loyola," *Revue d'Ascétique et de Mystique*, 28 (1952) 77.

13. Without the Christian having already necessarily attained the corresponding state.

14. *Cf.* ST, I.II.51.2.3.

15. Ex. 169, A,P2: "*In omni bona electione*"; V: "*ad quippiam bene eligendum.*"

16. *Cf.* "The Autograph Directory of the Exercises by Saint Ignatius de Loyola," *Obras completas*, Iparraguirre, 1963, Ch. 3, #22, p. 281.

17. This classical distinction, without being rejected, is not mentioned in the documents of Vatican II, which underlines the universal appeal to perfection, obligatory on each and everyone in his state of life: LG, Ch. V, esp. #40 and #42.

18. Transl. Puhl's translation has the same distinction as A and V.

19. For the development of this reflection *cf.* C. de Dalmases' explanation of the genesis of the Exercises, "Exercitia Spiritualia," MHSJ, vol 100, Rome, 1969, pp. 32,33; Father V. Larranaga, S.J. would date, without doubt, these texts of the Roman revision of the Exercises (*cf.* San Ignacio de Loyola, *Estudios . . . Saragossa*, 1956, Ch. II, pp. 139–56; AHSJ, 25 (1956) 396–415).

20. After the last retouches made, at Rome, to the text of the Exercises, Saint Ignatius had in no way at all in mind to admit into the Society of Jesus candidates not intending to become priests. He will only admit them later on.

21. The way of the counsels means that of the evangelical counsels of poverty, chastity and obedience. Let us recall on this subject the general norm given by Saint Ignatius: "Let the director take care that the retreatant is aware that there must be greater signs of

God in order to know that one is called to the precepts" (MHSJ, vol. 76, Rome, 1955, p. 72).

22. The official Directory, of 1591, Ch. 25, warns us against the election of a "religion" (that is of a religious order) which is decadent, corrupted, in which observance would no longer prevail. It also recommends the choice of the religious institute where observance is most perfect. It quotes norms for choosing given by Saint Thomas Aquinas (II,II.188,6) *Cf.* MHSJ, vol. 76, p. 679.

23. The insertion taken from notes by Polanco is undoubtedly inspired by experience, Polanco's notes concerned Saint Ignatius' desires in regard to the Exercises. *Obras Completas,* 1963, p. 283.

24. Saint Ignatius, *Autograph Directory*, #22, *ibid.,* p. 247.

25. Ex. 175. A number of commentators (such as Gagliardi and the official Directory) have seen in this early period an extraordinary grace, a kind of miraculous revelation of no interest for the immense majority of retreatants. Father Coathalem, whom we follow, sees in it rather a very elevated spiritual motion, a consolation without previous cause (Ex. 330), a motion carrying with it its certitude, not a properly so-called extraordinary grace (*Commentaire du livre des Exercices,* Paris, 1965, p. 214), but a rare favor (*ibid.*). This last point does not seem at all evident to us; this favor does not seem rarer than the tendency to the unitive way. We may read more on this problem in M. Giuliani, S.J., "Se décider sous la motion divine," *Christus* 4 (1957) 172,173. *Cf.* also Ex. 330, where Saint Ignatius quotes ST, I.II.9.1.6; 10.4 (in P2).

26. *Cf.* the preceding note and also the remarkable commentary by J. Clémence, *art. cit.* 64–67. The letter of Saint Ignatius to T. Rejadella, June 18, 1536, confirms the frequency of the first time in the eyes of the Saint. *Saint Ignatius Loyola—Letters to Women,* Rahner, pp. 331–35.

27. *Cf.* Ex. 336.

28. Autograph Directory, #18,19 (Iparraguirre, *op. cit.* pp. 280,280). Further, let us note that the personal example of Saint Ignatius (*cf.* note 34) is the best norm for a broad interpretation of these paragraphs of the Autograph Directory, which takes up in a more detailed manner a sentence of the Exercises: "*If* a choice of a way of life has not been made in the first or second time, below are given two ways of making a choice of a way of life in the third time" (Ex. 178). The conditional proposition does not indicate an obligation to begin by seeking an election in the category of one of the first two times, but underlines that which results if one begins in vain by one of the two. And it is what Saint Ignatius, as we shall see, did not do after his election on poverty.

29. Let us quote these remarkable lines: "It is very difficult to state with certainty the immediate nature of God's action in the soul or in nature. But in proportion as the soul continues its progress, that is to say that its entire interior and exterior conduct will be more and more under the governance of abnegation, that is of gratuitous and disinterested love, it will be more and more capable of recognizing the immediate action of God by making an experience of it, but by the very fact of its progress this consolation without previous cause will cease, at least will have to cease being a psychological happening individualized, numbered among other psychological happenings and interrupting their normal course, to become more and more a continuous experience which impregnates and in which is immersed all the happenings of psychological life of which it is the soul. Then the soul discovers in all consolations—and everything is then for it consolation—an inferior part which is explained by previous causes and a superior part which is consolation without previous cause, become continuous, of which God alone is the immediate cause. It does

not hesitate to attribute this joy to the immediate action—which does not mean: exclusive—of God" (art. cit. p. 68). Let us not forget, on reading this text, that in the eyes of the author (p. 67, no. 99) the election of the first time is a consolation without previous cause. From this there results, for him, that all the elections of the soul which is in the unitive way or almost all are made during the first time, without exclusion of the role of the two others, before, during or afterwards.

30. Cf. the letter of Saint Ignatius to Saint Francis Borgia, of September 20, 1548, "Letters of Saint Ignatius Loyola," Young, S.J. pp. 179–82; Obras completas, Iparraguirre, 1963, pp. 711–14.

31. Just as the prayer is simplified, on passing from a greater to a lesser multiplicity of acts, while tending toward the total unity of the unique, indefectible act, of the beatific vision.

32. It might be said that the election is an act of the moral, acquired and infused virtue of prudence, informed by charity and radiated by the gift of counsel; cf. ST, II.II.52.1.2 (ad 1m). It is even a fruit of the Holy Spirit, at the same time a fruit of human reason and of the Holy Spirit, a delicious fruit and a flower ordered to the supremely savory fruit of eternal life (cf. ST, I.II.70.1.2). In the third time, the election is made under the domination of infused virtue and in the first under that of the gift of counsel and of the other gifts of the Holy Spirit. There is, in fact, a wonderful coincidence between the Thomistic theology of the gifts of the Holy Spirit (to which, at least as far as I know, Saint Ignatius does not allude) and the first time or consolation without previous cause. In both cases, the soul is moved rather by God than by itself. "In donis Spiritus Sancti mens humana non se habet ut movens sed magis ut mota" (ST, II.II.52.2.1). Whereas human virtues perfect man according to his moving himself by his reason, the gifts of the Holy Spirit are infused perfections and given by God to dispose man for a greater mobility under divine inspiration, under divine movement (ST, I.II.68.1). And, precisely, what distinguishes the third time from the first, is that the former is characterized by man's rational motion, while the latter regards man as moved by God. Is not the transition from the one to the other one that is from deliberation (Ex. 183, Puhl, A,P2 identify election or choice with deliberation) to infused intuition?

33. Ex. 175 A,P2 (Puhl). The intellect is exercised in the examination of the reasons for and against the decision in view, and also of the dispositions of the will itself.

34. Cf. Ex. 175: The will is also exercised in the examination of the reasons pro and con (third time) and in the discernment of consolations (second time). It wishes the clarity of intellect which it applies to its object. Let us recall the interaction of the intellect and of the will so well analyzed by Saint Thomas Aquinas (ST, I.II.9.1.3): the truth is a particular good, to which the intellect is applied.

35. We mean that grace does not divinize only the essence of the soul or its faculties (theological virtues) but also its action (in view of its own perfection) and so its psychic dynamism.

36. Observe the order of the faculties in the Ignatian prayer: it asks for a divine action on the will, then that God bring to my mind (put in my soul, Ex. 180,A), that is in my intellect, what it ought to do. Saint Ignatius brings in and presumes the Thomistic analysis of the influence of free will (always in the measure of choosing among objects which solicit its attention) on the intellect. We note also that the text of the Vulgate (Ex. 180), inverting the Ignatian order, returns to the more classical thought of conditioning of the will by the intellect by inviting the retreatant to "pray the clemency of God deign to instruct his spirit and move his will." The mention of the clemency of God introduces furthermore a subtle nuance not found in the Autograph: we no longer deserve to know the divine

will, its unveiling manifests the divine mercy towards us.

37. However we must recognize there is a difference, Ex. 175 makes no allusion to a "reasoning", or a "discourse", even "pious" and "faithful", found in Ex. 180 (A,V). But rightly it omits it since the rational phase has been but a means for leading to further transition into intuition.

38. The Text of the Vulgate uses here the technical term "infused" affection. Observe . especially that there is a certain ambiguity involved in the meaning of the words: "love of God": Does it concern the infused love we have for God and from which would flow our love for others? We do not think so. Rather is meant the love that God is and has for us, for our love for such a person or thing flows from the infinite love God is and has for us, it is sharing. This interpretation results from the comparison with Ex. 237 where the same Spanish terminology is employed and where "*arriba*," "from above," is applied to the divine perfections whence our goods and gifts descend like the rays of the sun.

39. Iparraguirre, *op. cit.* 1963, p. 294. (Introduction to the deliberation on poverty).

40. I. Casanovas, S.J., *Comentario y Explanacion de los Ejercicios espirituales,* Barcelona, 1945, vol. II, pp. 275,276. Besides it must be observed that the prayer before Mass, the Mass itself and the thanksgiving, each took Ignatius a whole hour.

41. On the "unity of the three times" M. Giuliani, S.J. may be consulted. "Se décider sous la motion divine," *Christus* 4 (1957) 181–86. These pages contain very fine analyses and insinuate the orientation of the third and second times toward the first.

42. It is important to remark that these considerations of the Vulgate are without parallel in the *Autograph* and in the *Versio Prima*.

43. A text by Nadal makes this point quite clear: "This tranquil elevation of the soul and this union of power and light from on high are habitual with Father Ignatius. He almost constantly receives, from contact with a superior power, his method of knowing and disposing things, and other methods of knowing seem inferior to him. If, however, this superior method fails, one ought to have recourse to a natural method, without forgetting that, even if this superior method is effective, nevertheless it must always be conformed to the Holy Scriptures, to the virtues, to right reason, to edification, in a word, to the Church." This text is taken from M. Nicolau, S.J. *J. Nadal, Sus obras y doctrinas espirituales,* Madrid, 1949, p. 258, no., 8 and p. 311. It has been commented on by H. Rahner also in these terms: "The Church is the ensemble of everything visible, from the Scriptures to reason." (*Christus* 5, 1958,166: "Spirit and Church"). It might be added that this text permits us to understand that, according to Nadal, Ignatius lived ordinarily and made his decisions in the area of the first time of election.

44. It might be objected to our interpretation of the ensemble that the Exercises and the Autograph Directory seem to presuppose the existence of elections made solely by the first time. Of course. But actually typical Ignatian elections (the deliberation on poverty; the "Spiritual Diary") are clarified by the interplay of the three times. Further, our hypothesis admits of exceptions.

45. We will note the words used here and in Ex. 183 are identical: offering, prayer, divine majesty etc.

46. An allusion to the deliberation of Saint Ignatius on poverty, before the publication of the "Spiritual Diary." *Cf.* the text in: S. Ignacio de Loyola, *Obras completas,* Iparraguirre, 1963, pp. 293ff.

47. Note what seemingly is a return to the third time whithin the first; *cf.* note 49.

48. As and more than any other Christian, Mary possesses the Spirit which has been given here; *cf.* note 49.

49. The Spanish text says literally: "that he would give us his Spirit to think over and discern." The expression, paradoxical, shows that in the eyes of Saint Ignatius the natural play of human reason exercising itself on a supernatural matter is in no way divorced from the motions of the Holy Spirit.

50. Before supernatural intuitions, the desire for discursive reasoning, even illumined by the Holy Spirit, disappears.

51. The translation respects the paradox of the Spanish original: "*el Espiritu Santo dando su espiritu.*" Evidently Saint Ignatius intends to allude to the powerful wind on the day of Pentecost, sent by the Holy Spirit as its sign (*cf.* Acts 2:2).

52. Saint Ignatius of Loyola, Spiritual Diary, February 11, 1544; *Obras completas,* Madrid, 1947, vol. I, pp. 689,690 (ed. Larranaga).

53. *Cf.* ST, II.II.8.I.2: "*discursus rationis semper incipit ab intellectu et terminatur ad intellectum; ratiocinamur enim procedendo ex quibusdam intellectis; et tunc rationis discursus perficitur quando ad hoc pervenimus ut intelligamus id quod prius erat ignotum.*"

54. *Cf.* ST, III.72.2.1: "Christ, in virtue of the power of excellence he has over the sacraments, has conferred on the Apostles the fruit of this sacrament, that is the plenitude of the Holy Spirit, without the sacrament" (*rem hujus sacramenti sine sacramento*).

55. LG, 11; Pius XII, *Mystici Corporis,* AAS, 35 (1943) 201.

56. Under a new title, for the Holy Spirit had already been given in baptism.

57. The Ignatian election, as it appears in the Exercises and in the life of their author, is most often oriented, through poverty, to witness before the Church and the world.

58. On confirmation in grace, see the important and remarkable article by J. Gummerbach and Viller, DSAM, II,2 (1953) 1422-41.

59. *Ibid.* col. 1438; the authors state that the basis of this privilege of exemption from grave sin is a function or a dignity, in the Kingdom of God, with which sin is irreconcilable. Might it not be said that Saint Ignatius himself has enjoyed a confirmation in the grace of infused chastity, linked to his mission as founder of the Society of Jesus? Is it not this that seems to result from what is related in *St. Ignatius' Own Story,* Ch. I, #10? The passage relates the vision of an image of Mary with the Child Jesus, who made Ignatius forever disgusted with his past life and especially with things of the flesh, to the point of never thereafter giving the slightest consent to them. The paragraph begins with the following characteristic statement: "His holy desires *were confirmed* by a visit." This confirmation in grace of infused chastity is interpreted by Inigo as a confirmation of his former desires to imitate the saints (#9) and so of an election itself made under the action of grace. F. V. Larranaga (S. Ignacio, *Obras completas,* Madrid, 1947, vol, I, p. 137) quotes an interesting comment taken from *The Ascent of Carmel* (II, 17) where Saint John of the Cross makes use of a concept of "confirmation in good" by means of divine favors, which is quite close to the Ignatian concept.

60. For instance, he resolved to abide by the decision of his Franciscan confessor, Father Theodore de Lodi, concerning his election as General of the Society of Jesus (Iparraguirre, *op.cit,* pp. 290ff.).

61. *Cf.* M. de Certeau, S.J., "The days following the decision," *Christus* 4 (1957) 197. We do not think, however, that the community can, as such, confirm, but only prepare the superior's confirmation.

62. *Ibid.*

63. Saint Ignatius' "Spiritual Diary" of February 18, 1544, Iparraguirre, *op. cit.* pp. 332ff.

64. G. Bottereau, S.J., "La confirmation d'après le journal spirituel de Saint Ignace de Loyola," RAM 93 (1967) 35-51. The passage quoted is taken from pp. 50,51. Another like study on confirmation in the autobiography and in the correspondence of Saint Ignatius would be very helpful.

65. The absence of even the possibility of hesitating, mentioned by Saint Ignatius as a characteristic of the first time (Ex. 175) may well be understood as related to a moral not a metaphysical or absolute certitude.

66. The maxim in which our predecessors summed up the four weeks of the Exercises is will known: *deformata reformare, reformata conformare, conformata confirmare, confirmata transformare.*"

67. *Cf.* R. Orlandis, *art. cit.,* pp. 305,306.

68. We think it possible to translate in this way Ex. 189 P2. (the same sense in A): "*proponendo illorum creationem, vitam et statum debere esse ad gloriam et laudem Domini Dei nostri.*"

69. Ex. 189 is directed to married couples and also to church dignitaries. So the term *family* when it deals with the latter signifies not only the family according to the flesh (for instance, a nephew) but also their entourage, often designated at this period as "family." We may also understand thus the complex sense of the phrase: ". . . what part of his means should be used for his family and household" (Ex. 189).

70. After the discovery of scientific laws according to which the sexual act is only periodically, not always, fertile.

71. *Cf.* GS 87, 3; and our book: "*Sacraments and Social Progress* (Franciscan Herald Press, Chicago, 1974); and GS, 51,3.

72. *Cf.* Saint Ignatius' letter quoted in note 30.

73. Pius XI, *Divini Redemptoris,* #44, AAS, 29 (1937) 88, 124.

74. These rules offer us priceless information on the norms of fraternal charity and of charity toward self in Saint Ignatius' thinking. The first requires that there be desired, even for a stranger, "*all perfection possible in his state of life, the greatest perfection of his soul.*" (He would not be satisfied, then, with wishing for him worldly prosperity, or even eternal salvation at the last moment.) The second norm measures the true good desired for self (a demand of charity) whether in the light of death which detaches us from this world, or in the light of judgment which makes us fear hell and aspire to heaven. Death and judgment enable us, in particular, to acquire a more just view of the good we ought to desire for our body. Apart from the perspective of death and judgment, our love for our body is in danger of being false and pernicious.

75. Text of the Vulgate.

76. Ex. 189: The "*tanto quanto*" of the Autograph of the "foundation" was translated by the vulgate by "*eatenus . . . quatenus*" (Ex. 23).

77. *Cf.* ST, II.II.26.4; Mt 22:39.

78. GS, 71,3.

79. PC, 13: "Communities as such should aim at giving a kind of corporate witness to

their own poverty . . . to the support of the poor"; they "can rightly possess."

80. PC, 4: "Superiors should in appropriate manner consult the members and give them a hearing."; *cf.* also B. de Margerie, S.J. *op. cit.* Ch. XVI; *cf. Ecclesiae Sanctae,* 43,4, AAS, 58 (1966) 776.

81. This is the whole subject of the Encyclical *Populorum Progressio* of Pope Paul VI (1967) and of GS, 85,86; *cf.* also de Margerie, *Christ for the World,* Ch. XVI; and by the same author, *Sacraments and Social Progress, passim.*

82. The Latin adjective *"vilis"* from which the Spanish *"vil"* is derived, means here: common, ordinary, despised.

12

THE SACRIFICIAL SUPPER
OF THE NEW CONVENANT

Saint Ignatius introduces us to the third and fourth weeks through the contemplation on the Lord's Supper. This exercise can and should be called the exercise of the "third foundation."[1] After the first foundation, by which Saint Ignatius introduced the retreatant to the purgative way, after the second, that of the Kingdom, which served as entrance to the illuminative way,[2] we have here now the contemplation on the institution of the Eucharist for setting us on the unitive way, and for confirming us in the grace of the election.

After having commented on the principal aspects of the Ignatian text,[3] we will briefly show that they point to the consecration to the Eucharistic Heart of Jesus. Is it not in and through the Eucharistic sacrifice and communion that we find and choose the supreme "means," this *mediator* who conducts us to our last end and that we become prompt and diligent to listen to his call (*cf.* Ex. 23,91)?

The grace sought: sorrow and shame.

The third prelude makes me, here as before, "ask for what I desire," that is, "sorrow, compassion, and shame because the Lord (of the Universe)[4] is going to his suffering for my sins" (Ex. 193).

Are we not astonished on seeing Saint Ignatius invite his retreatant to ask for shame and confusion in the consideration of his sins, on the threshold of the "unitive way"? Are we returning to the first week?[5]

There are, nevertheless, profound reasons for doing so.

On the one hand, this subjective feeling of shame corresponds to a profound reality: it is on account of my sins, on account of his love for me, a sinner,[6] that the Lord goes to his Passion and that the Eucharist is an expiatory sacrifice.

On the other hand, by humbling myself with him and before him, I

175

dispose myself better for sharing in his exaltation. "Everyone who humbles himself shall be exalted" (Lk 18:14).

Finally, the reconsideration of my sins and of my unspeakable and incomprehensible unworthiness (Ex. 59,69,74,94) disposes me the better to perceive the infinite and unmeasurable love with which the Lord has offered, then, shed his precious Blood, the price of his priceless Blood (cf. Ex. 191; 2 Pet 1:19) to expiate my crimes and make of it a beverage for me.

The Eucharist-sacrifice is the expiation of all my sins, mortal and venial. The Eucharist-sacrament is the remission of my venial sins, and even, accidentally, of my mortal sins. The Eucharist, sacrifice and sacrament, preserves me from sin. The permanent Eucharist of the Real Presence introduces me into the nearness of my intercessor, of my advocate who prays constantly, mercifully, for me a sinner (cf. 1 Jn 2:1; He 7:25) in every tabernacle in the world.

Pardoned as I be, advanced as I can be along the unitive way (?), I remain, by the weakness of my own forces, capable of falling again into sin, of disdaining the Son of God, thinking the covenant-blood by which he was sanctified to be ordinary, and insulting the "Spirit of grace" (Heb 10:29). From all these evils, only the grace of the Eucharist, acting powerfully on my free will, can preserve me.

See, hear, look at the persons, who eat, their words, deeds and actions (Ex. 194)

"Then, taking bread and giving thanks, he broke it and gave it to them saying: This is my body to be given for you. Do this as a remembrance of me. This cup of the new covenant is my blood, which will be shed for you (Lk 22:19,20), "the blood of the covenant, to be poured out on behalf of many" (Mk 12:24) "for the forgiveness of sins" (Mt 26:28).

On pronouncing these words, Jesus proclaimed his will to make of his own death a sacrifice for the sins of the world and he offered it already, in advance, in sacrifice. The Supper, just as our "Mass" today, is a truly sacrificial action. The separated signs of the bread and of the wine are figures of the separation of the Body and Blood of the Savior in his death.[7] This non-bloody immolation of Christ, priest and victim, at the Supper, and at the suppers of our Masses, is the type, the model and the cause of our immolation in union with him. "Put to death whatever in your nature is rooted in earth: fornication, uncleanness, passion, evil desires, and that lust which is idolatry" (Col 3:5). "Those who belong to Christ Jesus have crucified their flesh with its passions and desires" (Gal 5:24).

Each time I offer the sacrifice of the Supper, I should renew my will to immolate my "old man" (Col 3:9) and, in this manner, my covenant with the Father in the Blood of the well beloved Son.[8] It suffices to say that my sacrificial immolation is inseparable from the exercise of my universal priesthood as baptized. I am inseparably, as a member of Christ, priest and victim. The two essential acts of my close participation in the Lord's Supper, each day of my life (if possible) are my offering of Christ and that of the whole Church, including myself, to the Father, in the Spirit, in a sacrifice of adoration, of expiation, of thanksgiving and of petition. It is not enough for me to ask for the good things that God, by inspiring me with this petition, wishes to give me. I must also offer everything, offer myself, in adoring and giving thanks.[9] From the capricious love of the child, I must constantly "pass on" to the sacrificial love of the adult, in Christ who passes on from this world to his Father.[10]

This sacrificial passage takes place when, receiving communion, I listen closely to these words of our Lord: "Take and eat . . . All of you must drink from it" (Mt 26:26-27) Communion is not a simple eating and drinking of the body and blood of the God-Man but a sacrificial eating and drinking of a Body and Blood offered by him in sacrifice. Communion is a participation in a sacrifice. To receive Communion is to become one victim with Christ for the glory of the Father and for the salvation of the world. Communion is not only to receive the present of the ineffable Presence, but also to unite myself and associate myself most intimately to the action of this Presence, and even to his Passion, and so to commit myself to transform my whole life in a holocaust in which selfishness is ever consumed in the flames of charity. Christ is not sacrificed to dispense me from immolating myself, but on the contrary to give me the strength to do so joyously and perseveringly.

"This is my Body which will be given up for you . . . this is the cup of my Blood . . . it will be shed for you." By adding: "Do this in memory of Me," Jesus sets the basic program and the permanent structure of my life.[11] If I do not want to "die in my sins,"[12] my life must be concentrated around the Eucharist, sacrifice and sacrament, around this eucharistic Christ who is the superabundant expiation of my sins.

Am I a eucharistic teacher? What do I do to help those who are about me to see in Communion the chief remedy (through the particular examination of conscience which strengthens it) for my dominant fault, the best means for acquiring the moral virtues and the desired dominant virtue (all present in Christ) and above all the intimate union with the members and the invisible head of the universal Church? What do I do then to help them see in the Eucharist the burning coal of divinity, filled with the fire of the Spirit, the the coal which purifies, enlightens, inflames the Christian with divine love?[13]

Am I an apostle of the Eucharist? What do I do to inculcate the ideal of the daily visit to the eucharistic Christ,[14] this visit which is moreover the response (on the plan of private devotion) to the mystery and dogma of the real and whole Presence of Christ, the intercessor, on our behalf, and which facilitates the exercise of mental prayer, preparation for sacramental Communion, the act of spiritual communion, opening up thus new horizons to the action of eucharistic graces as well as to the activity of charity toward the lowly, the poor, toward all those the world despises and abandons as it despises and abandons the "tabernacles," the tents of Him who is eternal Life?

Do not the age old tradition of the Church, and the writings and lives of so many saints—do they not echo this thought of Father Lallemant:[15] "We should love above all else to visit him often in the Holy Eucharist and make of it the first of our duties and needs"?

In the face of all this love in which Jesus envelopes us and with which he constantly pursues us, in all the tabernacles and on all the altars throughout the world, we can but repeat with Saint Ignatius: "He institutes the most holy (sacramental) sacrifice[16] of the Eucharist, the greatest proof of his love" (Ex. 289,3).[17] But this supreme sign is also, in the eyes of Saint Ignatius, as a realist, supremely efficacious for avoiding sin, for the conservation and augmenting of grace and so of charity (Ex. 44, V)[18] when one consents to eat it and to drink it.

However this sign seems to have left Judas cold. The Exercises strongly emphasize the conflict between Judas and Jesus, at the Supper. Jesus announces the betrayal of which he will be the victim, washes the feet even of Judas, who immediately after the Supper leaves to sell his master (Ex.289). In announcing the treason of one to whom he will give power over his Body and Blood (Lk 22:19), Jesus has before his eyes the thousands of priests who, in the course of centuries, would be unfaithful to the order of saving love, to the command with which they had been initially identified either by celebrating it in a state of sin or by no longer celebrating it at all.

In presenting me so forcefully Judas' betrayal, does not the author of the Exercises wish to make me reflect on what I could become if I abandoned myself to the hour and to the prince of darkness? Does he not wish me above all to see my ingratitude toward the supreme sign of his love so often received, eaten and drunk and realize that it puts me in a very real sense, below Judas?[19]

"Take this, all of you, and eat it: this is my Body. . .Take this, all of you, and drink from it: this is the cup of my Blood, the Blood of the new and everlasting covenant. It will be shed for you and for all men so that sins may be forgiven." These words of Jesus are acts, an action which expresses and manifests a suffering. On adoring, in faith, these words, we adore the twofold action, eternal and temporal, divine and human, uncreated and created, by which the Word made man wishes, on instituting his Eucharist for the expiation of our crimes, to give himself to us as food for and victim of our growth in him. We adore this twofold action which is a twofold love.[20]

At the sight of what our Lord suffers, shedding tears

Since the fruit sought is sorrow and confusion, it is not enough to see and to hear, nor even to look at what my pontiff and my victim is, says and does. I must also look at what he suffers. "This will be to consider what Christ our Lord suffers in his human nature,. . .what he desires to suffer.

Then I will begin with great effort to strive to grieve, be sad, and weep" (Ex.195), to suffer "condole and have compassion," "sympathize" with the Lamb of God.[21]

An amazing paradox: Saint Ignatius wants us "with great effort to strive to weep," nonetheless at the same time admits that this precious gift is beyond our powers. God permits us to be in desolation, dry-eyed, deprived of the consolation of shedding tears over our sins and over Christ's Passion, and "wishes to give us a true knowledge and understanding of ourselves, so that we may have an intimate perception of the fact that it is not within our power to acquire and attain tears[22] or any other spiritual consolation;[23] but that all this is the gift and grace of God our Lord" (Ex.322). And, also, doubtless, to show us that there is more perfection to be found from devotion without tears, as the angels,[24] that our charity is not the better if we receive this gift, that tears are not necessary and, above all, that he who has compassion for souls has no need of them.[25]

How to resolve this paradox: to strive to acquire a gift beyond powers? Elsewhere, Saint Ignatius offers us the key to the enigma: a prayer of petition preciseley intended to obtain the gift of tears, a gift which, though not necessary, is still precious: "to ask for what I desire. Here it will be to ask for a growing and intense sorrow and tears for my sins" (Ex.55). Prayer enables me to obtain from God, should it be pleasing to him, what is beyond my own powers. The effort itself to make myself shed tears will then be above all an effect of humble prayer, in acknowledgement of my unworthiness to receive this priceless gift. This effort at supplication will, however, integrate all my psychological powers, mobilized in compassion, and in consciousness of the precious nature of this gift even though it be not necessary.

Why? Because to convert into horror attachment and inclination for my sins and the disorder of my actions which have, indirectly, caused (occasioned) the Lord's Passion, should be the undertaking of an efficacious and passionate will which renders for me bitter and unbearable my sins. Such a will is more readily had when God grants also a feeling of shame, of confusion, of contrition which is translated into supernatural tears.[26]

If we must make an effort[27] to weep over and with Jesus suffering, while we beg him for the precious gift of tears, it is because—and to the extent— these tears help us increase in love of the Redeemer. Precisely, the tears of the third week, in contrast with those of the first, (at least theoretically) combine the different reasons for tears enumerated by Saint Ignatius in the Exercises and mentioned in a letter to Saint Francis Borgia: "I call it consolation when one sheds tears that move to the love of God, whether it be because of sorrow for sins, or because of the sufferings of Christ our Lord, or for any other reason that is immediately directed to the praise and service of God" (Ex. 316).[28] For tears of compassion toward Christ suffering are caused at the same time by sorrow for the sins which brought Christ to his Passion, by meditation on that Passion[29] and contemplation of the Father who hands over his well-beloved Son for the salvation of the world, that is, that this world be filled with the Spirit of love: is it not especially in this meditation on the Passion that the divine Persons are considered and that their love for sinful mankind shines out?[30] The Father and the Spirit, are they not inseparable from the Word who suffers and dies?

It may, then, be said that the fruit of tears synthetizes the graces desired and asked for in the course of each of the four weeks of the Exercises. It does so by unifying and, if we may say, liquifying the three ways, "purgative, illuminative and unitive," of the spiritual life. Tears, in Saint Ignatius' eyes, purify, illumine and unite with God. We understand, then, that the author of the Exercises, who was one of the greatest shedders of tears in the history of the Chruch,[31] wishes to encourage "the exercises of tears" during the last *three* points of the first contemplation of the third week: "In this way I will labor through all the points that follow" (Ex.195 at end).

The omnipotent Divinity hides itself in non-violence

The "sorrowful" consideration of the fourth point should now be extended into the fifth: "to consider how the Divinity hides itself, for example, it could destroy its enemies and does not do so, but leaves the most sacred humanity to suffer so cruelly" (Ex.196).

Jesus could have annihilated Judas, slain him who had, more gravely than Uzzah, profaned the Ark of the Covenant (*cf.* 2 Sm 6:3-7). He did not do so though he could have, but preferred to offer himself as a victim of expiation for the salvation of Judas.[32]

When he expelled the buyers and sellers from the temple of his Father using a whip he himself had fashioned of cords, Jesus, without warning, exercised a certain physical violence. When he enveighed against the Pharisees, he exercised a certain moral and psychological violence (*cf.* Jn 2:15-17, 8:21-55; Mt. 23). Now has come the hour of mortal violence by his enemies, the hour of his own physical and moral non-violence.[33]

Today, too, Jesus, non-violent God that he is, hides himself when he could destroy his enemies. Have I not been perhaps one of the worst?[34] God hides himself to save us, to save me. God hid himself to suffer for the sake of our salvation, of my salvation.

The Word would have been able to destroy me at the moment I crucified his humanity. He has preferred to let me pierce him to manifest to me in his opened Heart, the scar of which will never heal, his eternal love for me. The allpowerful has become the allweak, for the salvation of all the weak.

What am I going to answer to the saving silence of the Word,[35] to the passion of the pure act?

Response made to the hidden, non-violent God

Here is the third and last "consideration"[36] to which Saint Ignatius invites me: "This is to consider that Christ suffers all this for my sins, and what I ought to do and suffer for him" (Ex.197).

I asked myself already: "What have I done for Christ? What am I doing for Christ? What ought I to do for Christ?" as I behold Christ in this plight nailed to the cross. . .that he might die for our sins" (Ex.53). Much more is involved here: not only what I ought to do, but also—and especially—what I ought to suffer for Christ the Redeemer. The suffering Christ's silences, his pierced hands and feet answer me: "*Be, as much as possible, non-violent.*"

"For this reason, all Christians are urgently summoned to "practice the truth in love" (Eph 4:15) and to join with all true peacemakers in pleading for peace and bring it about. . . .We cannot fail to praise those who renounce the use of violence in the vindication of their rights and who resort to methods of defence which are o'herwise available to weaker parties too, provided that this can be done without injury to the rights of others or of the community itself. . . . But to the extent that men vanquish sin by a union of love, they will vanquish violence as well, and make these words come true: "They shall beat their swords into plowshares and their spears into pruning hooks; one nation shall not raise the sword against another, nor shall they train for war again" (Is2:4).[37]

To fufill this wish relevant to our times expressed by Jesus, our Peace, and again by Vatican II, I must accept the silence and gentleness of physical and moral non-violence, and thereby be one of those who take over the kingdom of heaven by violence,[38] the violence of sacrificial love. To be violent before God, I must be non-violent before men.

Even when I could crush with a word those who insult me, I must tolerate them, bear with them, love them, wish that my sinful humanity suffer in the image of the saintly humanity of Jesus and to reveal it to the world. As the divinity of Jesus hid itself on the cross and hides itself in the Eucharist, so, too, must I hide myself in the open Heart of Christ to reveal it to the world. Executioner of the Lord, I must become his victim. Without ever putting limits on the word,[39] ever free, of the Word of Life, my silence must, time after time, proclaim his redemptive death.

My non-violence must also become a word to proclaim the flouted and violated rights of Jesus, suffering today in the victims of so many social, racial and religious injustices.[40]

Before the Passion of Jesus, now continuing in the world how can I not ask myself what I have suffered, what I am suffering for him and what I ought to suffer for his glory? Jesus "is in agony to the end of the world." Should I not wish to endure and suffer from him (and for his Church)?

"To consider what I ought to *do* and *suffer* for him:" action and passion for and with Christ are bound together in submission to his command: "Do this in memory of *me*" offer me and offer yourself with me on offering Mass to my Father and on receiving me in Communion,[41] on thus making of your bodily flesh with mine one sole victim with it for the Church and for the world. By the violence of your non-violence joined with mine, expiate unjust violences, save and rescue the violent from their violence!

Colloquuy with Mary, Christ, the Father, the Holy Spirit, the Trinity

The author of the Exercises suggests these successive colloquies at the close of this contemplation: "to end with a colloquuy with Christ our Lord. . . he may engage in only one colloquuy with our Lord, or, if the matter and his devotion prompt him to do so, he may use three colloquies, one with the Mother of our Lord, one with her Son, and one with the Father'" (Ex. 198, 199). After his sojourn at Manresa, the saint not only prayed daily to each one of the three Persons separately, but also to the Holy Trinity.[42] Here, inspired by these data and these examples, we shall address ourselves successively to Mary, to her Son, to the Father, to the Holy Spirit, to the Holy Trinity.

"Oh Immaculate Virgin, by your consent to the Incarnation and to the Passion through the tears of your compassion, you have given us the great, pure fish[43] of the source,[44] which you caught and which you offer us to eat. You have also, along with the bread[45] given us the delicious wine mixed with water. Give us what you offer us: tears shed for our sins which have separated the Body of your Son from His Blood, expiation of our crimes. Adore in us the Lamb you give us.[46] Is it not your intercession and your presence we invoke that ever obtains the sacrificial renewal of the wedding of the Lamb and our sober inebriation as eucharistic victims?[47]

"Jesus, hidden God, you could annihilate your enemies and you do not. Grant me to have compassion, weeping in shame and confusion over your Passion brought about by your immense love for me, a sinner. Grant me to weep for my sins, not out of wounded self-love, but out of love of God. You, my Creator and my victim, give me the grace to make a vigorous effort to weep. Break the hardness of my heart, that I, weeping with you, avoid the eternal tears of hell.

"Eucharistic Heart of Jesus, you are the whole treasure and spiritual good of the Church. You are my constant companion, my teacher of adoration at the Tabernacle, my pontiff and my victim who constantly immolate yourself for me at Mass, my daily food in Communion.

"When I adore You, I adore the two acts of eternal and temporal, uncreated and created, infinite and finite love, by which you have instituted the sacrament of your Presence, of your Union, of your sacrifice and with which you make them continue among us, in the power of your Spirit, to the glory of your Father, in order to love in me and by me all men, your brothers, always with a sacrificial love.

"Adoring you I adore also the twofold act of love by which you have instituted the sacrament of orders for the remission of my sins and that I may associate myself with your sacrifice, eat your Flesh and drink your

Blood, adore your real and permanent Presence.

"May I, manifesting you to the world, help the young to respond in numbers to your double call: "Come, follow me!" "Do this in memory of me!"

"Father, the hour is come, glorify your Son that he may glorify you. You have given him power over all flesh that all those whom you have given him, he give life eternal. For eternal life is that they know you, you, the only true God and him whom you have sent, Jesus Christ (Jn 17:1-3). [48] Your Son, in the Eucharist, is life, our life.

"Father, I beg you, in the name of your only Son, give us our daily bread, your Son, the bread of life, the living bread come down from heaven. The bread he gives, is his flesh, given up for the life of the world. It is Christ for the world (Jn 6: 48,51). Give us, then, the ardent desire for daily Communion, the true daily bread. Give us the grace to follow the supreme evangelical counsel: No one can come to your Son unless you draw him (Jn 6:44). May the hidden inspiration of your grace, may the breath of your Spirit help your son's disciples to proclaim to all the existential decision, in a supreme sense, of eating and drinking daily, cost what it may, the Flesh and Blood of the Son of Man, the true bread from heaven that you give (Jn 6:54, 32, 33) and the grace of renewing daily, with ever greater love, this supreme decision." [49]

"Spirit of the Son, on drinking the Blood of the Son, who sends you, it is you I drink, [50] to the glory of the Father. Through me, give witness to Jesus and to his Eucharist, glorify the glorifier of the Father. [51] Perfect and divine counsellor, counsel others through me to attend Mass and receive Communion daily, to make frequent visits to the blessed Savior of the world present among us, thereby making spiritual communion. Put on my lips, Spirit who speaks through the prophets, words of light and fire which inflame hearts with charity and eucharistic desires.

"Each time I receive Communion, I receive you anew, Spirit whom the world cannot accept, since it neither sees you nor recognizes you." "I solemnly assure you, he who accepts anyone I send accepts me, and in accepting me, accepts him who sent me" (Jn 13:20). You dwell among us, Spirit sent, as the Father and sender, through the flesh of the Son sent and sender."

"Eucharistic Trinity, Trinity present in the Eucharist, Trinity to which is offered the Eucharist, [52] Trinity giving yourself to the world in and through the Flesh and Blood of the Son of Man, give us to shed tears for our sins to blame for their separation and grant us to receive in Communion the full remission of them: grant us that perfect charity which remits all temporal punishment due to sins, confirmation in the sacramental grace [53] of your Eucharist. Through it, fix yourself in us and fix us in you.

NOTES ON CHAPTER TWELVE

1. This view is suggested by Gagliardi, S.J., "*Commentarii seu explanationes in Exercitia spiritualia,*" Bruges, 1882, pp. 99, 100.

2. *Cf.* Ex. 10 "When the one who is giving the Exercises perceives that the exercitant is being assailed and tempted under the appearance of good, then is the proper time to explain to him the rules of the second week. For commonly the enemy of our human nature tempts more under the appearance of good when one is exercising himself in *the illuminative way.* He does not tempt him so much under the appearance of good when he is exercising himself in the *purgative way,* which corresponds to the Exercises of the first week."

3. We will not comment on all aspects of the Ignatian contemplation "from Bethany to the last Supper" (Ex. 190), but only on those which seem to us more important here. The Supper is also treated by Saint Ignatius in Ex. 289.

4. Ex. 193,V. The text of the Vulgate is here vested in Joannine majesty "The Lord *of the universe* . . . torments so considerable," this evokes Jn 13:1.

5. *Cf.* Ex. 48,50: the first exercise also asks for the grace of confusion.

6. "In the strict sense of the term, the cause of Christ's death is not sin, neither his own which was non-existent, nor ours. The cause of his death, is his love on the occasion of our sins, love of his Father and love of us." Father Philip of the Trinity, O.C.D., after these reflections (*What is Redemption,* New-York, 1961, pp. 72-73), mentions in this sense the commentaries of Saint Thomas Aquinas on Jn 14 (lectio 8, ed. Marietti, nos. 1974-76). He adds: "Sin can do nothing against Christ, who is innocence itself. On saying that sin did not cause Christ's death, Saint Thomas speaks in a strictly theological sense. It may, however, legitimately be said and preached that Christ died because of my sins (*Roman Catechism*), so long as it be properly understood. There is involved solely indirect causality, that of an "occasion" and not of an efficient cause (ibid.). "This is the way Saint Ignatius proceeds. *Cf.* Ch. III, note 27 where this text was quoted already.

7. *Cf.* Pius XII, Encyclical *Mediator Dei,* AAS, 39 (1947) 548,549.

8. Vat. II (SC, 10) speaks of "the renewal in the Eucharist of the covenant between the Lord and man," stressing that this renewal "draws the faithful into the compelling love of Christ and sets them afire."

9. Pastoral inquiries, rather limited however, have convinced us that a number of the faithful, during Mass, ask only for "graces" (often temporal favors) without making an offering, adoring, or asking for forgiveness. This is so especially during the double elevation. *Cf.* LG, 11,34.

10. Here is a magnificent passage from Bossuet: "let our passage be perpetual. Never let us stop. Let us not tarry but pitch our tents everywhere, like the Israelites. Let all be a desert for us as it was for them. Let us as they ever dwell in tents, our home is elsewhere. Let us march on, march on, march on. Let us pass on with Jesus Christ. Let us die to the world, die every day. Let us say with the Apostle: "I face death every day (1 Cor 15:31), I am not of this world, I pass on. I care for nothing" (Meditations sur l'Evangile, La Cène, 1ère partie, 2ième jour, fin).

11. Even of a simple communicant. *Cf. Mediator Dei* AAS, 39 (1947) 564.

12. *Cf.* Jn 8:21; Ex. 18:20; 33:12-20.

13. The Eucharist which is the sacrament of the unitive way, is also offered for the re-

mission of sins and for progress in Christian life. Viewed thus, it can be seen as the synthesis of the three ways of purgation, illumination and union. *Cf.* Ex, 44. quoted in note 18.

14. *Cf.* PO, 18. "Priests should prize daily conversation with Christ the Lord in visits of personal devotion to the most Holy Eucharist." It is well known that Saint Alphonse Liguori has written a classical book on "*Visits to the Blessed Sacrament.*"

15. *Vie et doctrine du P. L. Lallemant,* S.J., ed. Pottier, Téqui, Paris, 1924, p. 272. (principle IV, Ch. V, art. 6).

16. A speaks of sacrifice; V and P2 of sacrament.

17. Our translation synthetizes the diverse data of A, V, P2: "*signum summae dilectionis*" (V); "*maximum signum dilectionis suae*" (P2).

18. We quote here the concise Latin of the Vulgate (Ex. 44: *Eucharistiae (sumptio) maxime confert et ad fugam peccati et ad gratiae receptae conservationem et augmentum.*" *Cf.* SC, 10; PO, 5.

19. In fact Saint Ignatius invited the retreatant during the first week, to regard himself as less than the devils (Ex. 50), so it is not surprising to think he invites us, at least implicitly, to regard ourselves in the third week as less than Judas (Ex. 52).

20. *Cf.* B. de Margerie, *Christ for the World,* Ch. XIV; Pius XII, following Leo XIII, has shown that, in honoring with a special devotion the Eucharistic Heart of Jesus, we pay devotion "to the act of supreme love by which our Redeemer, opening up all the riches of his Heart, instituted the adorable sacrament of the Eucharist in order to remain with us to the end of time" (AAS, 48 (1956) 351).

21. *Cf.* Ex. 48 V: "*ad compatiendum Christo patienti*"; Ex. 195 P2: "*sic incipiam cum magno affectu condolere, contristari et plangere.*"

22. The text of the Vulgate speaks here of the impossibility of shedding "abundant tears" at will (Ex. 322 V) "*abundantiam lacrymarum.*" Did the translator intend to suggest that our *total* dryness was the result of insufficient effort on our part?

23. The complexity of the Ignatian concept of the meaning of tears is to be noted: they signify a suffering (Ex. 48 and 78) yet at the same time also a consolation, even when shed on account of our sins or of the passion of Christ (Ex. 316). We would be inclined to think that the consoling aspect of tears is explained thus in the life of Saint Ignatius: When he wept over his sins or over the passion of the Lord, he was already in the unitive way. His tears were at once sorrowful (morally and phsyically) and consoling because they sprang from a love already pure, while still increasing it.

24. Note by Saint Ignatius in his Spiritual Diary of March 29, 1544. (*Cf.* Iparraguirre, *op. cit.*)

25. Saint Ignatius, letter of November 22, 1553 written in his name by Polanco. It partly explains the gift of tears by the natural facility of the overflow of the superior affectivity over the inferior zones of the psyche and the personality.

26. We are inspired here by J. Calveras, S.J., "Comentario a la quinta adicion," *Manresa* 8 (1932) 2–27, esp. 15. We do not accept, however (in the light of the letter quoted in the preceding note) this exaggerated statement: "There can be deduced from Ex. 316, 322, 87, 89, 4 that Saint Ignatius regards consolation and in particular tears as something essential for the fruit sought, as something the retreatant is to seek and find by taking appropriate means" (*ibid.*).

The author thinks, too, that "to attain the substratum of the will to the point of transforming affective dispositions of the heart, these intense graces of devotion and consolation are necessary" (ibid.). Is not this contrary to what Saint Ignatius thought at the time of writing the Exercises, including the Roman period of their final composition? Nor is it evident, especially in the light of the letter to Saint Francis Borgia quoted above. The letter of 1553 shows a final development of Ignatian thought, set in the presence of a situation which has not been examined before: a lengthy period during which this gift of tears was absent. This development in the teaching on tears seems to correspond to a personal development, revealed by Father da Camara's Memorial and which seems not to have been analyzed up to now: "Father shed tears so continually that, if he had not wept three times during Mass, he felt he was in desolation. *The doctor ordered him to stop weeping and so out of obedience he stopped.* And so . . . he is now much more in consolation than before, without weeping. Father admitted this to Polanco as Dr. Olave has told me" (Memorial, #183, February 22, 1555, MHSJ, 66, 1943, FN I, pp. 638–639). There is room for thinking that this order by the doctor was given during the period from 1550 to 1556, a period in which Saint Ignatius suffered several serious illnesses, and so quite a while after the composition of the *Spiritual Diary* (1544,1545), or otherwise the directives concerning tears would be inexplicable. We would place it even between the *Diary* and the letter written by Polanco in Saint Ignatius' name, November 22, 1553, but after the letter of 1548 to Saint Francis Borgia (*Cf.* note 30). The letter of 1553 as a whole is much more easily explained following the change of attitude of Saint Ignatius as a result of the doctor's order. Let us pay special attention to this sentence in the letter of November 22, 1553 to Father Floris (Gaudeno): "To some, even if it was in my power to give tears, I would not give them, because they do not help their charity and cause harm to body and head, and consequently hinder every exercise of charity." Here there is, certainly, an attitude different from that of the Exercises, (without, however, any contradiction) and which is the result at once of the crisis in Saint Ignatius' health and his obedience to his doctor's orders. We can measure how heroic that obedience was, since Saint Ignatius, as the *Spiritual Diary* reveals, still regarded tears as the very incarnation of consolation. God asked of him the supreme renounciation. Can we not see therein an ultimate purification?

In any case, it is certain that neither the Exercises nor the *Spiritual Diary* of Saint Ignatius show the concept of "interior tears" of compassion toward the neighbor with which the letter of November 22, 1553 to Father Floris states he is satisfied.

27. To have a concrete idea of what Saint Ignatius means by "with great effort to strive to weep," this point must be clarified by the additional directions of the first week: external penances, in the matter of eating, sleeping, chastizing the body (Ex. 83–86). These penances can be employed for securing three effects: to make satisfaction for past sins; to overcome oneself; to obtain some grace or gift that one earnestly desires. Thus it may be that he wants a deep sorrow for sin, *or tears,* either because of his sins or because of the pains and sufferings of Christ our Lord; or he may want the solution of some doubt that is in his mind" (Ex. 87). Tears are, then, a gift so precious, so useful for obtaining a more profound contrition and compassion that Saint Ignatius encourages physical penance for obtaining it. Besides, one can see in the gift of tears an effect, and an aspect of man's victory over self, by which it is given him to subject the lower part of his sensuality to the higher part of his reason, to penetrate his soul with contrition and compassion (Ex. 87, 2). (*Cf.* note 25, at end.)

28. Saint Ignatius very clearly distinguishes the effect and the cause of tears. Their effect is to move the soul to the love of God, and that is why they can be called "consolation," combining it thereby with the definition immediately preceding: "an interior movement is aroused in the soul, by which it is inflamed with love of its Creator and Lord, and, as a consequence, can love no creature on the face of the earth for its own sake, but only in

the Creator of them all" (Ex. 316). Tears are an *external* movement combined with and fostering this interior movement. Their cause is or can be threefold: sins, Passion, service and praise of God.

29. Cf. Ex. 316 V: *"Lacrymas funduntur . . . ex meditatione Passionis Christi."* The word meditation (rather than that of contemplation) implies the arduous task of reason wishing to incite itself to tears.

30. On September 20, 1548, Saint Ignatius wrote Saint Francis Borgia that he ought to prefer "to shed tears than to shed his blood." He gave the gift of tears as a unique example (here) of seeking "his most holy gifts" such as the gift of tears. He then lists three categories of tears distinguished by their object: 1) because of our own sins or the sins of others; 2) while contemplating the mysteries of the life of Christ either here or in heaven; 3) from a loving consideration of the three divine Persons. "This distinction is clearer and better formulated in this letter (*Letters,* Young, p. 181) than in the Exercises. He adds: "Thus the higher our thoughts soar, the greater will be their worth." This is the *"tantum quantum"* of tears.

31. A point stressed by many authors, particularly Father de Guibert and Father Larranaga. The latter seems not to have compared Saint Ignatius' experience and teaching about tears with those of Saint Catherine of Sienna, *Dialogue,* II, Ch. V: "Categories, values, and fruits of tears." Saint Catherine distinguishes five different categories of tears, starting from carnal egotism, to those shed for love of God. Did her doctrine influence Saint Ignatius? It is quite possible, especially as to what is found in the Letter to Saint Francis Borgia mentioned in the preceding note. At any rate, it does not seem to us that the Ignatian doctrine on tears, viewed against the background of his experience, has been the object of sufficient study. *Cf.* the word *"lagrimas"* in Iparraguirre, *Obras completas,* p. 997; Larranaga, p. 849.

32. Jesus died for all men, including Judas, although the latter refused to profit by the grace of salvation to be found in this death which he particularly caused: "except for Judas, it cannot be said of any person that he is damned", writes M. Richard quoting Acts 1, 25; Jn 17, 12; Mt 26, 24 (DTC V.1 (1913) 99: art. *Enfer*). See on this subject the thesis of R. B. Halas: *"Judas Iscariot: A scriptural and theological study of his person, deeds and eternal lot,"* Washington, 1946.

33. Nevertheless, it is true that Judas and the enemies of Jesus "retreated slightly and fell to the ground" (Jn 18:6) when He said "It is I" (*ibid.*), and that the physical non-violence of Jesus during his passion did not exclude a certain moral violence ordered to the salvation of his enemies: "Those who use the sword are sooner or later destroyed by it. Do you not suppose I can call upon my Father to provide me at a moment's notice more than twelve legions of angels?" (Mt 26:52-53).

34. Cf. Ex. 58-60; 95.

35. *Cf.* Mt 26:63; 27:64; Jn 19:9; Is 53:7.

36. The last three points (Ex. 195-97) in contrast with the first three points, stress the verb *"considerar"* which was already strongly stressed by the meditation on the "two standards."

37. GS, 78 (#4-6). At the same time it encouraged non-violence, the Council maintained firmly the principle of legitimate defense in case of war and not only in an individual situation: "As long as the danger of war remains, and there is no competent and sufficiently powerful authority at the international level, governments can not be denied the right to legitimate defense once every means of peaceful settlement has been exhausted" (*ibid.* 79, #4).

38. *Cf.* Mt 11:12; Lk 16:16.

39. *Cf.* 2 Tm 1:9,10.

40. NA 5; cf. GS 75,6: "They will fight with integrity and prudence against injustices."

41. *Cf.* Saint Anselm, *Cur Deus Homo,* II, 20: "Can one conceive of conduct more merciful than that of God the Father saying to the sinner condemned to eternal torments and deprived of what could redeem him: 'Take my only begotten Son and offer him in your stead.' (*Accipe Unigenitum meum et da pro te.*) And that of the Son himself saying: 'Take me and redeem yourself. (*Tolle me et redime te)*? There truly, we may say, is what they say to us when they call us to Christian faith and draw us to it" SC, 12, and 48.

42. Saint Ignatius of Loyola, *Autobiography,* Ch. III, #28.

43. An allusion, in the text of Abercius (cf. note 45), to Christ.

44. A probable allusion to the Father, source of the Son and of the Spirit (*ibid.*).

45. We make here use of the famous epitaph of Abercius, of the end of the second century. The Greek text and the French translation is found in the *Dictionnaire d'Archéologie chretienne et de Liturgie,* I, 1 (1942) col. 74ff. (*art. "Abercius"*) of Cabrol-Leclercg. There is no reason at all for not seeing in this inscription, as we do in our text, a very ancient affirmation of Mary's virginity, and also of her mediation and her intercession in the celebration of the Eucharist, if the immaculate Virgin who offers the "delicious wine and the bread" is the same as she who has cought the great and pure fish, Mary.

46. Cf. Saint Louis-Marie Grignon de Montfort, *Traité de la Vraie Dévotion à la Vierge Marie,* #266–273.

47. *Cf.* LG, 50 at end; 10; 34.

48. We quote here the priestly prayer of Jesus, pronounced precisely during his discourse at the Last Supper, and which might be used in its entirety during this colloquuy. (We would furthermore desire to see it inserted into a possible fifth canon of the Roman liturgy. It constitutes the best possible commentary on the Christian meaning of the *Pater noster,* which, in contrast to it, does not make any explicit mention of the Son, the sole mediator.)

49. *Cf.* B. de Margerie, *Christ for the World,* Ch. XVI, *passim.*

50. *Cf.* 1 Cor 12:13 "All of us have been given to drink of the one Spirit." Saint John Chrysostom understands this of the Eucharist: PG, 61, 251; *Cf.* CFW pp. 462-463, 472, 480n. 28.

51. Jn 15:14; 7:18; 17:2; 8:49.

52. A doctrine explained at length by Saint Fulgentius, against the semi-Arians, as we show in our book: "*La Trinité chretienne dans l'histoire*" Ch. IX, Paris, Beauchesne, 1975.

53. The Church, in her ligurgy, seemed, before the post-conciliar reform, to invite us to ask for the grace of confirmation in grace; cf. J. Gummersbach, and M. Villier, *Confirmation en Grace,* DSAM, II, 2 (1953) 1431. We have been unable to verify whether the new *Roman Missal* of 1969 is oriented in the same sense and whether it is possible to quote prayers from this missal which ask for the grace of confirmation in grace.

13

PERSEVERANCE IN PRAYER
IN TIME OF DESOLATION AND
IN UNION WITH CHRIST IN AGONY

By the "third foundation" of the contemplation of the sacramental Supper, the author of the Exercises wants to dispose us to enter upon the unitive way of which the Eucharist is the sacrament. This unitive way corresponds to the third and fourth weeks, which simultaneously have for their object to establish us firmly in the grace of the election by acquiring its confirmation. Pricelsss graces all inseparable from perseverance in prayer, especially in the midst of trials and desolation. We have already had the occasion of considering the importance of perseverance in prayer when we discussed method.[1] Here we contemplate the mystery of the prayer of Jesus in agony, the prototype of our desolate and triumphant prayer.

What fruit do we want and ask for in the course of such a contemplation? In what does the agony of prayer consist? What are its results? Must we not accept and offer up in advance all the agonies and trials of our existence?

A. To wish for and ask for sorrow, distress, tears, in view of what Christ has suffered for me.

Christ, between the Supper and his Crucifixion, "began to experience sorrow and distress" in the Garden of Gethsemani (Mt 26:37,38): "My heart is filled with sorrow to the point of death. Remain here and stay awake."—Mk 14:33 makes clear that the Lord felt fear: the fear of death. It is that Jesus, who in anguish cries out imploring with tears and begging on his knees the one who can save him from death (Heb 5:7), that we ask for what we wish, that is, Ex. 203, P2: "sorrow[2] with Christ in sorrow, anguish with Christ in anguish, tears and deep grief because of the great affliction Christ endures[3] for me."

We find here, now more precisely and more poignantly expressed, a theme already considered,[4] There is no longer only a question of asking

189

for sorrow and tears or of arousing them by mobilizing all one's psychic forces to this effect, but it is also a question of desiring, wishing and requesting distress and heart break, in union with Christ. The king of the universe is presented to us in anguish and heartbroken. This term is perfectly exact: the body and soul of the Incarnate Word are on the point of being separated in death. In this sense death breaks the unity which exists *in* the Incarnate Word, although it cannot break the unity *of* the Word with either its soul or its body (a point to which we shall return).

So then, we, who, as a rule, desire and ought to desire inner peace and unity, we wish and beg here the anguish and heart break which conditions them and with which they remain mysteriously compatible. Christ agonizing wishes to teach us to find his peace in anguish itself, inner unity in contrition and the breaking of a crushed heart.

In this mystery of majesty and mercy[5] which is his agony, the only Son of God has wished to know our distress, as a conflict between the lower and the higher psyche of his holy humanity, a conflict in which his divine love, source of the distress in his Heart of man, masters it, without there being, however, at any moment, between his human will and his divine will, an unthinkable conflict.[6] On contemplating the adorable anguish of him who is our peace, we share in it: the anguish of the old man in us vanishes, leaving us no longer but that of the new man!

When we ask for a broken heart in the image of the Heart of Jesus, we, by this very fact, ask for tears of love, of compassion for the Savior. To offer them, along with his own, and with all the tears shed with and out of love for God down through the ages, to the Father, in reparation for all hardness of hearts.

If we desire and ask for sorrow, distress and tears for and with Christ in agony, will we not truly be better disposed to persevere with him in prayer, at the times of desolation and trials?

B. *The agony of prayer, struggle against Satan*

Agony is a struggle. The agony of Jesus in the Garden of Gethsemani is a struggle against Satan, who would prevent Jesus from carrying out the redemption of the world paying so painful a price: his death and his blood, and would attempt to convince him to save the world in a less costly manner.[7] But Jesus' struggle against Satan takes on (contrary to that of the first Adam, in another garden) the form of prayer, of a humble persevering petition addressed to the Father, prostrate in prayer (Mt 26:39): "In this anguish he prayed with all the greater intensity "(Lk 22:44).

What does Jesus ask of his Father? "My Father, if it is possible, let this cup pass me by. Still, let it be as you would have it, not as I "(Mt 26:39)! "My Father, if this cannot pass without my drinking it, your will be done" (*ibid.* 42)!

In this agony, Jesus fights against Satan to the point of shedding blood: "And His sweat became like drops of blood falling to the ground "(Lk 22: 44), a touch that specially moved Saint Ignatius: "This supposes that his garments were saturated with blood "(Ex.290). Faced with this "copious flow of blood" (*ibid.*), how would we help but evoke, on hearing it explained to us, the disillusioned reflection of the author of the epistle to the Hebrews: "In your fight against sin you have not yet resisted to the point of shedding blood (Heb 12:4)"?

Perseverance in prayer is an agony, that is, a struggle against Satan, a struggle which must go to the extent of a bloody confrontation, a psychic conflict between the lower and the higher man.[8]

Before the angelic world, even fallen, mortal man has unequal weapons[9] unless he prays: "Be on guard and pray that you not undergo the test" (Mt 26:41).

To avoid entering into conversation with Satan as the first Adam did, we must through and with the second Adam address ourselves to the Father.

Rejection of prayer is the sleep of the soul, the beginning or rather the condition for entering into the dialogue of damnation with Satan, the opposite of the dialogue of salvation with God.

"Asleep, Simon? You could not stay awake for even a hour" (Mk 14:37)?

C. The holy hour of persevering prayer

"So you could not stay awake with me for even an hour? Be on guard, and pray that you may not undergo the test. The spirit is willing but the flesh is weak "(Mt 26:40.41).

Christ in agony, fighting Satan to the shedding of his blood, invites me to pray one hour with him.

Christ is in agony to the end of the world. Through Saint Margaret Mary[10] and the Church,[11] Christ invites each Christian to join with him (each month, even each week) in his holy hour of reparation for the Sin of the World. We might even say; each day.

Through Saint Ignatius, and during the retreat with some of the exercises: five times a day: "He who is giving the Exercises must insist with the exercitant that since he is to spend an hour in each of the five exercises or contemplations which are made every day, he must always take care that he is satisfied in the consciousness of having persevered in the exercise for a full hour. Let him rather exceed an hour than not use the full time. For the enemy is accustomed to make every effort that the hour be devoted to a contemplation, meditation, or prayer should be shortened "(Ex.12).

He wants to convince us that prayer is useless, that many other occupations therefore would be more useful, more urgent, more efficacious!

The result is that "We must remember that during the time of consolation it is easy, and requires only a slight effort, to continue a whole hour in contemplation, but in time of desolation it is very difficult to do so. Hence, in order to fight against the desolation and conquer the temptation, the exercitant must always remain in the exercise a little more than the full hour. Thus he will accustom himself not only to resist the enemy, but even to overthrow him" (Ex. 13).[12]

Just as it is the prayer in desolation of the agonizing Christ which has saved the whole world, so the Christian's persevering prayer in time of desolation, his holy hour, united to that of Jesus praying in tears and shedding Blood, will merit from Christ the Redeemer the application, to the world of today, of the merits of his past agony. The holy hour of persevering prayer is therefore the salvation not only of the one praying, but also of the world which does not pray.

The prayer of the Christian, struggling perseveringly for the world against Satan, prolongs and reproduces that of the agonizing Christ: "I was given a thorn in the flesh, an angel of Satan to beat me and keep me from getting proud. Three times[13] I begged the Lord that this might leave me. He said to me: "My grace is enough for you, for in weakness power reaches perfection" (2 Cor 12:7-9).

Does not Christ call me, not only to participate personally in the holy hour of his agony in the Garden, but also to invite others to participate in it with me, to intercede with him for the world, to make reparation thereby to him for the sleeping of so many Christians and so many men, to console him[14] in this way? Will I refuse to interced with Christ in agony for sinful mankind? Will I choose to sleep while Christ is agonizing?

"When one is in desolation, he should be mindful that God has left him to his natural powers to resist the different agitations and temptations of the enemy in order to try him. He can resist with the help of God, which always remains, though he may not clearly perceive it. For though God has taken from him the abundance of fervor and overflowing love and the intensity of his favors, nevertheless, he has sufficient grace for eternal salvation" (Ex. 320).[15] Desolation is an abondonment, a trial, which invites us to go beyond feeling in faith, without changing our resolves, in particular on the subject of even the length of prayer, but rather to "insist more on prayer[16] and "make an effort to do some penance" (Ex. 319).

If we love God above all, we seek, not his consolations, but the God of consolations, the God who can ever be found even in darkness: "No follower of mine shall ever walk in darkness: no, he shall possess the light of life.[17] "This is what Nadal grasped so thoroughly. He tells us about himself when he was sent to a certain college where he felt such desolation on the first day that he could not pray. This was something he found habitually easy to do. But now he knew that he was to wish positively to be in desolation rather than in consolation, according to the principle which with he was familiar, of the third degree of humility of which Father Ignatius speaks in the Exercises. The next day. . .he received such light that he was called to savor and contemplate Christ crucified, meanwhile shedding copious tears.[18]

D. In the hour of darkness and of desolation, to anticipate the light of consolation

If we are ready to prefer desolation with Christ desolate to consolation of diabolical or even divine origin, the allpowerful Christ comes as consoler into the desolate soul, where he is ever master, able to "come into a soul, to leave it" at will "as one coming into his own house" (Ex. 330,335).

In this game of hide-and-seek by the Creator with the soul he loves while wishing to purify it by desolation, the one in desolation[19] should "strive to persever in patience, [20] thinking that "consolation will soon return "(Ex. 321). Just as Jesus was fortified during his agony by an angel (Lk 22:43) which appeared to him coming down from heaven and which is the real symbol of God the consoler illuminating darkness.

If men have partially[21] failed Jesus, the angels never did so. God is always present in the midst of his apparent absences. In the desolation and passion of Christ, we find all the lights, all the consolations, all the strength we need. Its contemplation should be the ordinary food of the soul, that which restores its balance. Thus in our desolations, we will always be able to find God's peace if we prefer to console spiritually those more desolate then ourselves, rather than look for carnal consolations.

It is not prohibited, however, rather the contrary, to look for, within the limitations of divine good pleasure, spiritual consolations from spiritual men, that is to say Christ the consoler. If Jesus asked His apostles to pray with Him to the Father whose will he adored, we too can seek God in man.[22] We thus acknowledge our weakness and our dependance in respect to the dispositions of divine Providence. Such a seeking should not, however, be pursued at length, under penalty of changing its nature and becoming a disorderly seeking of earthly consolations as opposed to divine ones, instead of being instruments of them. Jesus readily left the three favorite disciples, his friends, to go to pray alone, and this he did three times (Mt 26:39ff). To deserve to be the only friend who would never fail us, he accepted the denial of consolation when Peter, James and John, instead of watching and praying with him, fell asleep.

Nonetheless, neither the prayer of Jesus in agony addressed to men: "My heart is nearly broken. Remain here and stay awake with me" (Mt 26:38) nor that addressed "three times" to his Father: "My Father, if it is possible, let this cup pass me by," (Mt 26:39) were rejected. Quite the contrary. Not only all generations of Christians since then have stayed in prayer and watched for countless holy hours with Jesus in agony, but also the Redeemer, prostrate before his Father, was "heard" because of his piety, and "saved from death" by a glorious and prompt Resurrection (cf. Heb 5:7), which caused the "cup" of death to pass "far from" him. The angel, who fortified the Lord in his agony, symbolizes this twofold consolation from men his brothers, so num-

erous, and from his Father. If Jesus suffered in advance a mortal sadness
before the sin of the world, before the sins we had not yet committed, but
which he already knew, why not recognize also that we have today the marvellous power to console him retrospectively He who rules over all times and
knows what there is in man (cf. Heb 13:8; Jn 2:25) which he sees in his
Father (Jn 6:46)? Why not recognize that we can, by our works of reparative
consolation toward his desolate Heart, along with and through the angel sent
from heaven, fortify and comfort the Son of Man in His agony? [23]

In the measure in which we will dream of consoling Christ who continues,
in his members, to agonize to the end of time, we will be able to forget
our own desolations and anticipate his consolations. We will dispose ourselves also by anticipated and knowing acceptance of all the trials of our
existence, of those secret crosses which await each of our days to come as
so many real consolations, destined to manifest to us in an ever renewed
manner the love of the Son of Man, who will wish to associate us constantly with his salvific Passion for the world.

E. Colloquy: acceptance and offering of my future consoling desolation.

"There will be hours in my life when you will conceal, Lord Jesus, momentarily, of course not from the eyes of my faith but from those of my mind,
the luminous rays of your infinite might, of your eternal wisdom, of your
incomprehensible love. I will have, however, and always, sufficient light to
know through faith and adore your luminous darkness.

"This will be precisely in these hours of trial and desolation that you will
act more deeply in me. [24] Often, my action nourishes my self-love (my suffering
can feed it too). But when I suffer, if I let you act without opposing your
action, I no longer act and become the subject of your most purifying action.

"May I by way of my daily cross become, Lord Jesus, a contemplative
not only of your Passion, through my action, but also (not to say especially)
of your action through my passion.

"Savior of the world, I accept in advance all the trials to come which
your loving Heart prepares for me, without any exception. I thank you beforehand for manifesting to me through them your infinite love. I offer them
to you, in union with your own agony, oh Word, for my future trials. How
would I not drink, with you, as you, the bitter and merciful chalice your
Father prepares for me and wishes to give me? All these trials, which affect
my health, my work, or my reputation, all without exception, I accept as a
gift from the Father passing through your Heart and I offer them in order
that you unite them to the eucharistic oblation of your redemptive Blood,
which will render them fertile.

"That I may remain in these dispositions at the hour of trial, I supplicate
you, Jesus in agony, to grant me the favor of visiting you frequently (cf.
Lk 22:39) in the Garden of Olives. Make of me a contemplative of your

mysterious and prayerful struggle against Satan, of your agony, especially every Thursday of the week.[25] Not my sinful will, oh Jesus, but your twofold will, human and divine, created and uncreated, be done, since both your wills are ever holy and sanctifying. May my human will become, like yours while still retaining its defective image, a perfect instrument of your divine will, for the salvation of others.

"For that, give me the grace to persevere in prayer at the hour of trial, in the darkness of desolation. By this perseverance, continue to overthrow through me the prince of this world of darkness.

"My heart is hardened, prompt to follow the inclinations of the flesh, resisting the movements of your Spirit. Break its hardness by the influences of your grace, received in persevering prayer. Without it, I cannot discover nor follow the road to the means of salvation and perfection. Apart from it, I can neither meditate nor contemplate the eternal, invisible and supernatural truths concerning my duty to save myself. Without persevering prayer, I would not know how either to acquire stable and persevering habits of virtues, nor, consequently, to persevere in you. Without persevering prayer, I will not even suspect the dangers which menace my salvation, nor be aware of my spiritual needs.[26] Without persevering prayer, am I not exposed, not only to the most varied temptations, but even to that most particularly perilous, of tempting you by putting myself, out of my own initiative, without sufficient reason, in the proximate occasion of mortal sin?[27]

"Lord Jesus, God perfectly adored and man adoring, may the individisible unity, even in your agony, of your two natures in your person make the unity of my soul in and by prayer. Unify my soul by the bond of holy prayer as the nerves unify my body.[28]

"By the intercession of the consoling angel of your agony and that of your apostles Peter, James, and John, make of me, Heart of Jesus, a companion, a worshipper, a loving and persevering contemplative of your persevering prayer in the Garden of Gethsemani."

NOTES ON CHAPTER THIRTEEN

1. See our Chapter II.

2. It is not to be excluded (cf. Ex. 85, 86) that Saint Ignatius asks for physical sorrow. The Vulgate, however, (Ex. 203), has understood there was only question of a petition for "interior sorrow." It is, therefore, at least this kind of sorrow the retreatant is invited to seek.

3. The First Version (P2), in contrast with the Autograph, which uses the past tense, uses the present. It wants, doubtless, to stress thereby that the retreatant places himself in the presence of the suffering Christ.

4. Cf. our comment on Ex. 195, in Ch. XII.

5. A formula used by Saint Leo the Great. It manifests clearly the transcendance of the salvific action of the one in agony.

6. *Cf.* ST, III.18.6.

7. It is thus that, not without great depth of spirit, and in the context of Luke 4:13, Saint Cyril of Alexandria understood the mystery of the agony of Jesus.

8. The inner man in Saint Paul (Eph 3:16) corresponds to what we call the higher psyche, versus the lower.

9. *Cf.* Heb 2:7, 16; Eph 6: 10–18.

10. Saint Margaret-Mary, "Autobiographie," #57; *Vie et Oeuvres,* ed. Mgr. Gauthey, Paris, 1915, vol. II.

11. Pius XI, *Miserentissimus Redemptor,* AAS, 20 (1928) 173.

12. *Cf.* "*agere contra,*" Ex. 97.

13. *Cf.* Mt 26,44: "He left them again, withdrew somewhat, and began to pray a third time."

14. *Cf.* note 21.

15. There is no question here of "sufficient grace" in opposition to "efficacious grace," as in the theology of grace. There is involved rather a contrast with "sensible grace" in some way. The Vulgate was careful to avoid the Latin expression of sufficient grace . . . It introduced thus a nuance absent from the Autograph: a grace which suffices for operating here below, and not only for eternal salvation.

16. It might also be translated: "Pray more insistently."

17. *Cf.* Jn 8:12.

18. J. Nadal, S.J., *Journal,* text quoted by *Christus* 1 (1954) p. 97. Saint Ignatius, who does not seem as a rule to extend the third degree of humility to the area of consolations and desolations, is not, however, completely unaware of this viewpoint. Does he not ask, in his *Spiritual Diary,* March 16, 1544, that "visitations and tears not be given if the services of the divine Majesty is equal" (*Obras compl.* 1962, p. 317)?

19. *Cf.* Ex. 319.

20. Ex. 321 P2.: "*desolatus laboret totis viribus possidere animam suam in patientia.*" The fine allusion to Lk 21:18 (Vg.) "*in patientia possidebitis animas vestras*" is to be noted.

21. The consoling angel presents to Christ in agony all the reparations offered by generations to come; *Cf.* Pius XI, *Miserentissimus Redemptor,* AAS, 20 (1928) 174.

22. Expression of Father Claude Judde, S.J. (1661–1735) in one of his retreats.

24. *Cf.* Le Gaudier, S.J., "*Introductio ad solidam perfectionem,*" Avignon, 1829, Ch. 29, #2, pp. 355, 345: "*In omni actione nostra necessario aliquid nostrum est quod secreta familiaritate, delectatione nunnulla tamquam pabulo amorem proprium nutrit. At cum quid patimur, nihil necessario nostrum est praeter ipsum pati, id est, esse subjectum illius actionis qua Deo, vel agente, vel permittente, patimur . . . Quare quidquid hic invenitur Dei agentis opus proprium est. Quid igitur mirum si in eo sibi complaceat? Atque inde etiam fit ut perfectionum suarum splendorem amplius et perfectius diffundat.*"

25. While meditating on the words, actions and sufferings of Christ in agony.

26. *Cf.* Saint Alphonsus Liguori, *Praxis Confessarii,* #217ff. It is the teaching of this doctor of the Church that meditation on the eternal truths is morally necessary for all Christians to persever in sanctifying grace. It is morally impossible (that is, very difficult) for one who does not meditate not to fall into grave sins. Why? Because this person will not be concerned with taking practical measures for avoiding sin, nor for carrying them out. He will have little consciousness of his need to pray, will stop praying and so will perish.

27. *Cf.* Saint Alphonsus Liguori, *Theologia Moralis,* V. 63: the saint adds: "If man does what he can to avoid sin, God helps him do what is beyond his own powers and what he humbly asks him in prayer. Now, he who, without sufficient reason, exposes himself to the proximate danger of serious sin, does not do what he can. So, God does not help those who expose themselves rashly to the danger. (*Deus non adjuvat temere se periculo exponentes*)."

28. Simile used by Saint John Chrysostom.

14

UNION
WITH THE DEATH OF
THE CRUCIFIED LORD

The Christian is one whose eyes are fixed on Jesus crucified. He wants to know nothing among men but Jesus Christ and him crucified (*cf.* 1. Cor 2:2). Spiritually born of the pierced Heart of the Lamb of God, he comes back constantly to the foot of the cross.

Such is the movement too which guides Saint Ignatius in his Exercises. He provides on the one hand a whole complex of contemplations on various events which, together, constitute the passion and on the other hand (Ex. 209) an overall[1] contemplation which constitutes as it were a synthesis of it. So we are going to consider here the seven words of Christ on the cross[2] as so many structures of a Christian existence oriented toward compassion for the crucified Lord and toward a death united, in love, to his, for the glory of the Father. A death of one crucified-with-Christ, a death by which He can achieve the mystery of his own: "I have been crucified with Christ, and the life I live now is not my own; Christ is living in me" (Gal 2:19,20).

More than ever, what we want to obtain from God and what we ask of him, is sorrow with Christ sorrowing, on the cross, to be crushed with Christ crushed, tears and inner suffering for the so great sufferings that Christ endured on the cross for us (*cf.* Ex. 203). Are not the last words of Christ on the cross his testament, the revelation of his suffering Heart, the words of eternal salvation he wishes to address ever through us to mankind and which he addresses to us ever from the chair, the altar and the throne of his cross?

"Father, forgive them; they do not know what they are doing" (Lk 23:34).

A prayer answered (*cf.* Jn 11:42): eight thousand Jews (many of whom had heard Jesus' sermons, even were present at his death) were converted after Pentecost and asked to be baptized (Acts 2:42; 4:4). The death of Jesus merited for them the grace of a more attentive consideration of his pre-paschal message.

199

Often, what we say even to our friends in favor of Jesus and of His saving love seems rejected and useless at the moment. But, in the context of a
trial, the Spirit puts back in their memory our words and the cross of Jesus,
putting them on their knees before the crucified (*cf.* Jn 2:22) and then they
believe in the Son of Mary.

A sublime prayer offered for us, for me. Have I not, so many times,
been guilty of voluntary ignorance (*cf.* Jn 15:22), without excuse because I
have not kept Christ's word passed on by his apostles? and by his Church?

A prayer I must make my own, must say over and over on behalf of
sinners, whose sins I have indirectly caused by depriving them, through my
infidelities, of the superabundance of the graces which would have preserved
them from so many faults!

"Father, pardon them. Give them the perfect gift of the Holy Spirit who
comes down from you and from your Son (*cf.* Jn 1:17; 15:26) that they may
acknowledge their sins and not die in them (*cf.* Jn 8:21).

"Father, in the name of your dying Son, in him, by him and with him,
give me the Spirit who is the remission of all sins (Jn 20:22,23) that I may
die in the grace of your well-beloved.

"Father, in the name of your Son, pardon me, me who knew what I was
doing in crucifying your Son (*cf.* Heb 10:29). Father, pardon all those who,
in the course of my life, in any way at all, have crucified me. I feel that
I am even guilty indirectly of their faults in my regard.

"I assure you: this day you will be with me in paradise" (Lk 23:43).

The "good" and the "bad" thieves symbolize at one and the same time
the common destiny of all men: to be crucified with Christ and for his glory;
and the choice offered each one: to justify Christ crucified or to insult him,[3]
especially at the moment of death. If I do not consent, with the good thief,
to call upon Jesus dying, at the hour of my death, I condemn myself to ac-
cuse and insult him. There is no other choice: either to ridicule him by
treating him as powerless or to invoke his omnipotence at the very hour of
its manifestation: "We deserve it after all. We are only paying the price for
what we have done, but this man has done nothing wrong. Jesus, remember me, when you enter upon your reign."

"Jesus, you are king precisely through and upon your cross. Transform
the cross of my death into the altar of my sacrifice united with yours, into
a throne on which I shall reign with you (cf. Rv 3:21; 2:26) over the nations. May my death united with yours be fecund in grace for all others
dying! Jesus, you have come into your Kingdom. Remember me, at the hour
of my death. Grant me the grace of perseverance,[4] and the plenary indulgence
in the moment of death, to be thus preserved from purgatory through your
merciful love: "from today" to the evening of my life, that I be, through
the intercession of the good thief, with you in the vision of your glory and

of your reign.''

"Blessed 'criminal' hanging on the cross (*cf.* Lk 23:39) be my benefactor: canonized by Jesus dying, you are with him in paradise. Intercede for me, who have insulted the dying Christ by my sins, near to him, obtain for me the grace of a good and holy death, for his universal reign. May I die, as you with him, in the exercise of pure love (*cf.* Ex. 370).''

"Pardon, Lord Jesus, in the gift of pure love, all the temporal punishments still due my sins, at the hour of my death. Just as you fully pardoned[5] the 'good thief.' ''

"Woman behold your son."

Jesus, Saint Ignatius says (Ex. 297) recommended Saint John to his mother, and his mother to his beloved disciple (Jn 19:26) "I give you to each other as a pledge of the love I have for both of you. Be one to the other what you have been for me and what I have been for you."[6]

John, the well-beloved disciple of Christ, is at the same time the virgin and privileged disciple on the one hand, the one who represents, symbolizes, sums up all the disciples on the other.[7] It is he on whom Jesus chose to confer his mother, and it is in this twofold quality that he entrusts her to him. John represents here all the disciples, even all men (all destined to be the Lord's disciples). It is to all these that Jesus makes a gift of *his* mother proclaiming and revealing that she is *their* mother in the supernatural order.[8] "Oh Virgin, Mother of Jesus, you are the triumphant woman, prophesied by God, who breaks the head of the serpent since your immaculate conception and, more than ever, when you stood at the foot of the cross of Jesus (*cf.* Gn 3:15).[9] It is at this moment when your Son, calling you "woman" at the very instant he proclaims you mother of John, shows us in your spiritual maternity your triumph over Satan, and your mission as privileged associate of his redemptive work.

"You suffer intensely with your only son, maternally associated with his sacrifice. You give your consent to the immolation of the victim, born of your flesh, a consent born of your love, for our salvation. Upon suffering with your son dying on the cross, you bring to the work of the Savior an absolutely unique cooperation, by your ardent love, for rendering to us the supernatural life of grace. This is why you have become for us, in the order of grace, our mother: 'Woman, behold Your Son.'[10]

"Holy and blessed Mary, who doubts that you have believed the word of your God, you who have been so humbly submissive to the word brought you by his angel?[11]

"Mother of the Redeemer and of the redeemed (you yourself more sublimely redeemed in order to cooperate in a unique manner in our redemption)[12] in the name of the merits of your faith in the truth of your spiritual motherhood, which your crucified son reveals to you, obtain for us too to participate in your own faith in your spiritual motherhood throughout our whole life and especially at the hour of our death. Obtain this so precious grace for all those whom you have engendered in tears at the foot of the cross! Do not contemn the fruits of your tears:[13] Bring together all your children in the recognition and proclamation of your maternity of grace, shining with your tears, stained with the Blood of the Lamb.

"For the suppliant omnipotence of your transfixed heart,[14] the very obstacles, including the reactions of certain of our Protestant brothers and your children, are means for bringing spirits and free wills to cooperate with the most sublime ends of Your Son:[15] your increasing glorification in the Church and in the world, oh parousiac virgin![16]

"Inspire us, then, mother of perpetual help, and of good counsel, to do all in our power, by pen, by word, by deed, and by suffering, to make known, loved, venerated and defined by the Church[17] the salvific privilege of your spiritual motherhood, to the greatest glory of your son and Redeemer. The Church and each Christian, faithful to grace, do they not share in it in their own way? On proclaiming with much greater clarity and solemnity this truth already acquired by faith,[18] would not the Church and each Christian progress also in the unveiling of their own co-redemptive mystery, made more manifest to their eyes, and above all in a dogmatic deepening of their knowledge of the mystery of the Redemption and of Christ the Redeemer?[19]

"Too many Christians do not know the depth, the amplitude and the splendor of your suffering love, so merciful and co-redemptive, most holy Mother of God! To make reparation for our sins toward your Immaculate Heart and for the sins of others, should we not do all we can that there echo in the hearts and in the souls of all your children the words of your first-born in agony: "Behold thy mother!" "Behold thy son"? Should we not do all we can to open up to men the secret and the mystery of their supernatural genesis, of their birth from you and from the Holy Spirit?

"Sorrowful Virgin, you have loved me to the folly of the cross. To save me, you have accepted to be considered the mother of a criminal. This is how you have engendered me for his divine life. Give me the grace to be considered a fool, and senseless on account of my love for you and my desire to make you known and acknowledged as being, in and through the Spirit of your only Son, the spiritual mother of all men. To confess this truth of faith before them, I would be happy to sacrifice my earthly life. You have sacrificed your rights to the life of your Son[20] that he live again in me. Would it not be a joy to sacrifice my life that men acknowledge that they owe you, in Jesus, their supernatural life?

"You love me, Mother of God and of the Church, with a perfectly pure and unselfish love (cf. Ex. 16), without any inordinate affection. It is through pure love for your Son, your Father and your Spirit that you have engendered me for divine life. Communicate to me a share too in the grace to love the Church your daughter and your sister, the Church like you a virgin in her faith and a mother through her love, the Church of whom you are the type and in whom you engrave your likeness.[21]

"No one is worthy to be called your son, oh Mother of God, if he is not, as you, pure, if he is not as you, a disciple of Christ, if he does not stand, as you, at the foot of the cross. That is to say: if he does not ever have before the eyes of his spirit your son and Lord crucified, if he himself is not crucified by compassion, by the mortification of concupisence and of sinful passions.[22] Co-redemptive Virgin,[23] may your powerful intercession obtain for us, especially at the hour of death, but also during our whole life, the constant remembrance of the passion of your Son, in order that we be less unworthy of being called your sons!

> "Eyes of Mary, gaze upon me.
> Mouth of Mary, pray for me.
> Hands of Mary, bless me.
> Heart of Mary, love Jesus for me.
> Feet of Mary, direct my ways.
> Sufferings of Mary, intercede for me.[24]

"I hail you, Mary, full of sorrows; Jesus crucified is with you; you are worthy of compassion among all women and worthy of compassion is Jesus, the fruit of your womb.

"Holy Mary, Mother of Jesus crucified, it is we who have nailed your divine Son Jesus to the cross. Obtain for us tears of repentance and of love, now and at the hour of our death. Amen.[25]

"Jesus, realizing that everything was now finished, said, to fulfill the Scripture: 'I thirst'" (Jn 19:28).

The thirst of Jesus dying is not only that of one crucified and exhausted from shedding blood. It is also the thirst of the Savior thirsting to save eternally the souls he has created and whom he loves to the point of giving his life for them. The thirst of the Creator who wishes to communicate to immortal souls, threatened with eternal damnation, a share in his life. The infinite and eternal thirst of a God desirous of giving himself, at the same time the created and finite thirst of his human will desirous of being loved and causing love: to be loved by men his brothers, and make God his Father loved by them. Our Lord said to Saint Margaret Mary: "If you knew how much I thirst to make myself loved by men, you would spare nothing for that! . . . I am thirsty, I burn with the desire to be loved."[26]

Alas, this thirst finds often, today as on Good Friday, but gall and vinegar, ingratitude and blasphemous hatred from his creatures: "There was a jar there full of common wine. They stuck a sponge soaked in this wine on some hyssop and raised it to His lips," and Jesus took the wine (Jn 19,30).

Had he not told Peter: "Am I not to drink the cup the Father has given me?" (Jn 18:11). And He drank it down to the dregs.

"Lord Jesus, give me to share in your thirst for my salvation, and for the salvation of all men. Give me to satisfy your thirst to be loved. Give me the living water of your Spirit, which flows from your pierced Heart, that I may give to you to drink (*cf.* Jn 4:10; 7:37-39). Give me to love you by keeping your commandments (*cf.* Jn 14:21-23; 15:9; 16:27). You thirsted to be drunk in the Eucharist and you have poured out your precious Blood but to make of it a beverage for my soul (*cf.* Jn 6:53-55). Is it not above all in drinking your precious Blood that I will be able to quench your thirst to be loved and manifest efficaciously your salvific love? and make you loved by loving more?

"You fulfill the prophecy of the Old Testament: 'and in my thirst they gave me vinegar to drink' (Ps 69:22). Inebriate me with your precious Blood that I may be able to give you, in the poorest of your members, the glass of fresh water, the delicious wine of pure love (*cf.* Mt 10:42), at the same time accepting to drink with you the vinegar of hateful ingratitude.

"Then toward the afternoon Jesus cried out in a loud tone: 'Eli, Eli, lema sabachthani?', that is, 'My God, My God, why have you forsaken Me?'" (Mat 27:46).

God in some way has abandoned his well-loved Son, while at the same time being ever in him and with him, and without ever leaving him alone (*cf.* Jn 8:29; 10:38; 16:32)—when, as a result of my faults and my infidelities to the inspirations of His Spirit, the treasures of Redemption have been rendered useless for me and for others. It is, therefore, through me that the Father has, in some way, abandoned his only Son.

"Lord Jesus, you are still hungry and thirsty, you are ever a stranger, you stay nailed, you do not cease being a prisoner, you continue sick, in the lowliest of my brothers who are yours (*cf.* Mt 25:34-40). More than ever,[27] you hunger and thirst, you are naked, a stranger, sick and in prison. Each time I refuse to welcome you or visit you, I abandon you and cause this mysterious partial abandonment you have suffered, on the part of your Father, during your Passion.

"So it is then rather to me than to your Father that you say: 'Why have you forsaken me? And because, instead of remaining in my Heart, you have turned back to your self-love, which you should renounce (*cf.* Ex. 189). But if you love me, my Heart will be your treasure (*cf.* Mt 6:21) and it will be easy for you to tear yourself away from your self-love (Ex. 16,157), and arouse in yourself compassion for me in agony, forsaken, in the prisons, the hospitals, the chambers or lonely apartments of the elderly. It is there I await your visits and those of others encouraged by you.'

(Visiting hospitals, prisons, the abandoned, is this not the complement, the token of the authenticity of visits to the Blessed Sacrament?)

"Jesus, on accepting to be forsaken at the same time by men and, in a certain way, by your Father who still remains in you, you have reconciled God and men. There will perhaps be hours, in my life, in which I will have the impression of being forsaken at the same time by God and by men: I offer them to you beforehand for their reconciliation.[28]

"When Jesus took the wine, he said: 'Now it is accomplished'" (Jn 19:30).

Shortly before, in an anticipation of his sacrifice, Jesus had been able to say to his apostles: "I have finished the work you gave me to do" (Jn 17:4). To accomplish the work of the Father who has sent him, such has been his food during his public ministry (Jn 4:34). This work, is the establishing of the Kingdom of the Son, the Church (*cf.* Mt 13:41; 16:18). The Church, spouse of Christ, is going to be born, like a new Eve, from the pierced side of the new Adam, with the water of the baptism and the Blood of the eucharistic covenant. And in this Church, Christ on dying achieves the formation of his supreme member,[29] in which, at this painful moment, is concentrated in all its perfection the whole loving and hopeful fidelity of saved mankind:[30] Mary Immaculate, the pre-ransomed Virgin to be co-redemptress, the chef d'oeuvre of the Redeemer.

"Jesus dying out of love for me, grant me the grace to accomplish the work you await from me for your Kingdom and for the continuous establishing of your Church (*cf.* Eph 4:16). At the hour of my death may I be able to say, upon thinking of my co-redemptive cooperation with your work of sole Redeemer, in you, with you, out of love for you: 'Now it is accomplished.' Achieve, through the sacrifice of my death, the consummation of all into one, in the unity of your Spirit, for the glory of your Father (*cf.* Jn 17:23). May my death be, in the likeness of yours, a holocaust offered that "all may be one, as you are in the Father and as the Father is in you," that all the baptized celebrate together your Eucharist around one altar, you yourself, in the one and universal Church,[31] in order that the non-Christian world believe that you have loved it as the Father has love you(*cf.* Jn 17:23) before the creation.

"Jesus uttered a loud cry and said: 'Father, into your hands I commend my spirit.' After he said this, he expired (Lk 23:46).

The cry of the dying Jesus, many times stressed by the quadriform Gospel,[32] is certainly not a normal thing at the hour of supreme weakness. It is rather the magnificent shout of triumph of the new Adam, Redeemer, who thus signifies his triumph over Satan, over the world, over sin. It is, then, a cry of love for each human person. The cry of tenderness of the liberator.

This cry of love is also a cry of sorrow, in which are summed up and condensed all the outcries of the poor. It is the cry that recapitulates all suffering[33]before all injustices. It is the cry of the poor man par excellence, the cry of the developer who undergoes and sums up in himself all the trials of the under-developed. The cry which assembles and divinizes the cries of the majority of men of all times and especially of today, justly rebelling against undeserved misery[34]which is inflicted on them by the prince of this world. On hearing the cry of the dying Jesus, on the point of expiring, I hear the cry of anguish, of disgust, of sadness, of disturbance and of fear which Jesus makes his own by remitting to his Father his created spirit, so filled with his uncreated Spirit, for the salvation of all immortal souls.

"Oh Jesus, unjustly accused, therein including your members, I wish to defend you. Jesus silent before the unjust accusations of your enemies, give me the strength to be silent before unjust accusations when your greater glory is not involved. Jesus pierced by the nails of my pride and my sensuality, pierce me. I am crucified with you; the life I now live is not my own, but you live in me, you who have loved me and who have given yourself for me (Gal 2,20).

"At the hour of my death, call me, Lord, by a supreme efficacious grace, crowning the entire series of efficacious graces of contrition, of faith, of hope and of love. *In hora mortis meae voca me.* Call me giving me, by the anointing of the sick, the sacramental grace which prepares your athletes for the supreme combat.[35] Defend me against the treacherous enemy, especially at the last hour: *ab hoste maligno defende me.* May no temptation separate me from you: *ne permittas me separari a te.*

"Lord Jesus, receive my spirit" (Acts 7:59).

"Jesus crucified and crucifying, I accept from your pierced hands the death which it has pleased you to choose for me from all eternity and which your death, in time, has mercifully merited for me. I accept to die in illness or by an accident, suddenly or even deprived of the use of reason. I accept also to be importuned at the hour of death by temptations, and thus to take part in your struggle against Satan. I offer you my death in reparation for my life, for the sake of my own salvation and that of all men of all times.[36] May I thus become a perfect holocaust, consummated and consumed in the flames of charity.[37]

"Hide me, at the hour of death, in your sacred wounds: *intra vulnera tua absconde me.*" Hide me from myself, immersing me in you."

"Father, into your hands I remit the created soul of your Son, whom you have given me. Father, I offer you this holy and sanctifying soul for my salvation. I remit it into your hands, that is to your Word and to your Spirit.[38] I offer you, also to your Word and to your Spirit, the sacrifice of this created soul assumed by your Word and filled with your Spirit.[39] I offer you the sacrifice of your well-beloved, who is the sacrament, the sacred and efficacious sign of our supreme sacrifice.[40] Do not refuse, Father, to give Him to me in viaticum. That I may, with His soul, offer You forever my own. Amen."

NOTES ON CHAPTER FOURTEEN

1. This evokes the application of the senses (Ex. 121-26).

2. Following Saint Ignatius' suggestion (Ex. 297): "He spoke seven words upon the cross: he prayed for those who crucified him; he pardoned the thief; he recommended Saint John to his mother; he said with a loud voice: 'I thirst,' and they gave him vinegar to drink; he said that he was forsaken; he said: 'It is consummated'; He said: 'Father, into thy hands I commend my spirit,' " we shall, in our commentary, follow the same order adopted by Saint Ignatius. Besides, this seems, in general, more in keeping with the logic of the narration. Finally, the title (*cf.* Ex. 297, V, A): "mysteries accomplished on the cross" brings out very clearly a profoundly true view: the words of Jesus on the cross are "mysteries," and these mysteries are an integral part of the sacrifice of our Redemption. These seven words have merited for us, in a very special way, eternal life.

3. This is what a text of Saint Irenaeus seems to suggest. "The sentence (of condemnation of Christ) has been received by some for salvation, and by others for their damnation. The latter support the sentence and thereby are condemned; the former have received it and therein find their salvation. Now, those who have crucified Christ have supported the sentence ratifying it in themselves, and by acting thus in regard to Christ, have not believed in him; for it is because of the way in which they have accepted the sentence that they will perish in punishments. The sentence has also been received by those who have believed in him and it no longer hangs heavy on them" (*Demonstration of the Apostolic Teaching.*" no. 69).

The French translation by Father J. Bartholot, S.J., which appeared in *Recherches de Science Religieuse,* vol. VI, 1916, is quite different from that by L. M. Froidevaux, 1959 (SC, 62, Lyon, 1959, pp. 136, 137). The differences are not surprising, for the Greek original is lost and it was necessary to translate an Armenian version. The translation given here is better understood in the context of a possible allusion to the two thieves crucified with Jesus.

4. *Cf.* CFW, pp. 132-134.

5. *Cf.* Ex. 297: "He pardoned the thief." The pardon consists in the fact of admitting the "good thief" immediately after his death, into paradise.

6. Blessed Claude La Colombière, S.J., *Réflexions chrétiennes,* "Of Saint John, the friend of Jesus Christ." See *Oeuvres Complètes,* Grenoble, 1901, vol. VI.

7. *Cf.* F. M. Braun, O.P., *La mère des fideles,* Tournai, 1953, pp. 124-29.

8. It is from the Incarnation, by accepting to become the mother of Christ, that Mary has become spiritually the mother of all his members, as Saint Pius x clearly saw (Enc. *Ad diem illum,* Ensignements Pontificaux, Notre-Dame, Tournai, 1957, #230); Pius XII could therefore say with precision: "Jesus himself from the height of the cross wished to ratify by a symbolic and efficacious gift the spiritual maternity of Mary in regard to men, when he pronounced the memorable words: 'Woman, behold your Son.' " (*ibid.* #648, allocution of July 17, 1954).

9. *Cf.* LG 55: "The mother of the Savior is already prophetically foreshadowed in that victory over the serpent which was promised to our first parents after their fall into sin."

10. Here we have transformed into a prayer the teaching contained in LG, 58, 61.

11. Bossuet, *Panégyrique de saint Jean.*

12. *Cf.* B. de Margerie, S.J., *Le Coeur de Marie, Coeur de l'Eglise,* Paris, 1967, Pt. I, #7.

13. *Ibid.* #8: "The heart of Mary, at each Mass, even today offers in union with the Blood of her Son, her past tears, her sufferings and her love at the foot of the cross, to the Father, in the Spirit, for the salvation of the whole world."

14. Mary, at the foot of the cross, was transfixed by the sword of sorrows foretold by Simeon (Lk 2:34, 35; *cf.* LG, 57). It is of interest to note here the great devotion Saint Ignatius had toward the "*Virgo perdolens,*" Our Lady of the Seven Sorrows, a picture of which he carried about with him for a long time. Upon sending Father Araoz to Spain, he took it out of his bosom and gave it to him saying: "Take this image and esteem it highly. Do not give it to anyone. Know that, on all the pilgrimages I have made, I have always carried it with me. And God our Lord has done me great favors and shown great mercy through it" (MHSJ, 85, FN III (1960) pp. 405-9, Rome).

15. *Cf.* Pius XII, *Sumni Pontificatus,* AAS, 31 (1939) 508; *cf.* also 497.

16. *Cf.* Saint Louis-Marie Grignon de Montfort, *Traité de la Vraie dévotion envers la Vierge Marie,* #49-59; the saint shows that the second coming of Christ will be prepared by the reign of Mary, just as she prepared his first coming.

17. *Cf.* DS, 2802: Pius IX wrote in the Bull defining the Immaculate Conception: "The Church endeavors to perfect the formula (of the deposit of revelation) so that these ancient dogmas of the heavenly doctrine receive *evidence, light, distinction,* at the same time retaining their plenitude." It is thus that the dogmatic definition of the Immaculate Conception, on making clear, with this truth, its foundation, that is the doctrine of the new Eve associated with the new Adam, has conditioned the entire subsequent development of Marian doctrine, including its magnificent fulness in Chapter VIII of the dogmatic Constitution *Lumen Gentium* during the Second Vatican Council. There is there an historical precedent which suggests the great consequences which might be had, including ecumenical ones, from the dogmatic definition of the spiritual motherhood of Mary.

18. Paul VI explicitly affirms in his apostolic exhortation *Signum Magnum* that the spiritual motherhood of Mary is a revealed truth, believed by the faith of the Church: "*(Maria) coelitus nunc materno pergit munere fungi quo ad gignendam augendamque vitam divinam in singulis hominum redemptorum animis operam confert. Haec veritas . . . e libera voluntate Dei sapientissimi pars est expletiva mysterii salutis humanae; quam ob rem ab omnibus christianis debet fide teneri*" (AAS 59, 1967, 468). It could not be said more clearly (*ab omnibus christianis*) that all the baptized, all those who call themselves Christians, must hold this truth as revealed to all men and not only to Catholics. Besides, Luther still admitted this on Christmas 1529, ten years after his break with Rome: "Mary is the Mother of us all." This he said in a sermon. (*Cf.* Thurian, *Marie Mère de Seigneur et figure de l'Eglise, Taizé,* 1963, p. 251.

It would not be forbidden to Catholics to suggest to their Protestant friends a conditional Marian prayer of this kind: "Oh Mary, if you are my mother in Christ, make me know it." Nor would it be improper to ask them whether they are sure they are not personally envisaged in the statement of Jesus dying: "Behold your mother." Are they truly certain that these words do not mean: "Behold her, who by her intercession and her association with my sacrifice, has given you the spiritual life of faith"?

19. *Cf.* CFW, 220, 299-303: we outline there what might be the work of an eventual Vatican III.

20. *Cf.* Pius XII, *Mystici Corporis:* (Mary) "exempt from all personal and hereditary fault, ever straitly united to her son, presents him on Golgotha to the eternal Father,

while joining therewith the holocaust of her rights and love as mother, as a new Eve, for the sake of all the children of Adam . . . thus she who was corporally the mother of the head became spiritually the mother of all his members, through a new title of suffering and glory" (*Enseignements Pontificaux, Notre Dame,* Tournai, 1957, #383; AAS, 35, 1943, 247, 248). This text stresses the role of the maternal compassion of Mary in the mystery of her spiritual and universal maternity: and thus anticipates the declarations quoted above (note 10) of Vatican II.

21. *Cf.* E. Schillebeeckx, O.P., *Marie, Mère de la Rédemption,* Paris, 1963, pp. 128, 129: "The type is not reduced merely to being a model . . . it does not only refer to a static image . . . it rather represents something dynamic, a force for salvation. The archetype, Mary, is personally engaged in accomplishing in the other members of the ecclesial community what Christ has typically realized in his life for her. Being, as mother, type of the Church, she collaborates maternally in the edification of the Church undertaken by Christ."

22. We are inspired here by the very beautiful thoughts of Saint Dimitrios of Rostov, Orthodox Bishop in the Russia of the 18th century (*cf.* I. Kologrivoff, S.J., *Essai sur la sainteté en Russie,* Bruges, 1952, p. 320).

23. An expression explicitly used by Pius XI: "We invoke her under the title of co-redemptress" (Discourse of November 30, 1933, *Enseignements Pontificaux, Notre Dame,* Tournai, 1957, #326). See also Benedict XV (*ibid.* 267).

24. Invocations dear to Saint Therese Courerc, foundress of the Cenacle. They bring to mind the first method of prayer of the Ignatian Exercises, a propos of the five senses of the body: "If he wishes to imitate our Lady in the use of his senses . . . (Ex. 248).

25. Formula of the *Ave Maria of the Seven Sorrows.*

26. Saint Margaret Mary, *Vie et Oeuvres,* Ed. Gauthey, Paris, 1915, vol. II, p. 680, *cf.* CFW, pp. 223-224.

27. The relationship between increase in world population and the problems of development justify our "more than ever": *cf.* GS, 8, 47, 64, 87.

28. Is not this, at least somewhat, the theme of G. Bernanos in his "*Journal d' un curé de campagne*"? And the sacrificial recognition of the co-redemptive meaning of human suffering is it not the most powerful instrument for avoiding or surmounting neuroses which often accompany the failure, which can be voluntary, to recognize the meaning of suffering in human destiny?

29. *Cf.* this thought of Augustine: "Mary is a part of the Church, a holy, excellent, outstanding member, but still a member of the whole Church" (ML 46, 938). Schillebeeckx (*op. cit.* p. 129) comments: "in this Church, (Mary) is the spiritual-corporal womb. As mother, she gives it life." Vatican II explains (LG 53) that Mary "is hailed as a pre-eminent and altogether singular member of the Church," her "model in the matter of faith, charity and perfect union with Christ" (LG, 63).

30. *Cf.* Binder, *Maria et Ecclesia,* Academia Mariana Internationalis, Romae, 1959, vol. III, pp. 389-499 (esp. p. 427 on Mary heart of the Church, and p. 486; Mary standing alone at the foot of the cross, preserves perfectly faith in redemptive love: an important theme of medieval Mariology).

31. *Cf.* UR, 4: "little by little, as the obstacles to perfect ecclesiastical communion are overcome, all Christians will be gathered, in a common celebration of the Eucharist, into that unity of the one and only Church which Christ bestowed on his Church from the beginning".

32. The expression "quadriform Gospel" is from Saint Irenaeus (*Adv. Haer.* III, II, 8; PG, 7, 885); Mark mentions two loud criew of Jesus dying (15:34, 37) and Matthew likewise (27:46, 50).

33. Jesus knew them by his infused knowledge (*Cf.* DS 3924).

34. We are inspired here by the apostolic exhortation *Evangelica Testificatio,* of Paul VI, who underlines the importance of the outcry of the poor (Ps 9:13; Jb 34:28; see DC 68, 1971, 655: #17, 18 of the exhortation) and of the French translation of the Encyclical *Populorum Progressio,* #9: the text speaks of "undeserved misery," quoting Leo XIII, *Rerum Novarum,* but the Latin text confines itself to speaking of "*miserae-calamitosae fortunae*" (*Acta Leonis XIII* vol. II, 1892, 261) which is quite different. The concept of "undeserved misery" is, however, explained by Jn 9:3.

35. The anointing of the sick is not only a sacrament intended for the sick in danger of death, but also, and above all, according to the Council of Trent, the sacrament of the dying, the "*sacramentum exeuntium*" of those who "*tam periculose decumbunt, ut in exitu vitae constituti videantur*" (DS, 1698), the sacrament not only of those who are in danger of death, but also of those who are *in articulo mortis,* to bring them to eternal life, as an oil of hope. This doctrine is implicitly evoked by Vatican II when the Council recalls that "By the sacred anointing of the sick and the prayer of her priests, the whole Church commends those who are ill to the suffering and glorified Lord, asking that he may lighten their suffering and save them. She exhorts them, moreover, to contribute to the welfare of the whole People of God by associating themselves freely with the passion and death of Christ" (LG, 11). Is it not especially at the hour of death that we can associate ourselves with the death of Christ? On the anointing of sick, see B. de Margerie, *Sacraments and Social Progress,* Chicago, 1974, ch. V.

36. *Cf.* CFW, Ch. XI *passim* and especially p. 270. We show there how every Christian has a role in the distribution of the fruits of Redemption to all men of all times. He has a part in the subjective Redemption, while Christ alone has acquired for mankind the treasure to be distributed or objective Redemption. *Cf.* DS 3805 (Pius XII, *Mystici Corporis,* AAS 35, 1943, 212).

37. *Cf.* Saint Ignatius of Loyola, Letter on obedience, a propos of the holocaust of obedience of judgment (Letter of March 26, 1553, *Orbras completas,* 1963, p. 806).

38. It is known that Saint Irenaeus often presents the Word and the Spirit as the creative hands of the Father: *Adv. Haer, IV, V, passim; Demonstration of the Apostolic teaching,* #11, cf. J. Lebreton, S.J., *Histoire du Dogme de la Trinité,* Paris, 1928, vol. II, pp. 579–81; J. Mambrino, S.J., "Les deux mains de Dieu dans l'oeuvre de saint Irénée," *Nouv. Rev. Théol.,* 1957, 355–70.

39. Pius XII, *Mystici Corporis,* AAS, 35 (1943) 219.

40. *Cf.* CFW, pp. 263-264.

15

THE PIERCING OF CHRIST'S SIDE
AND THE BURIAL OF THE HEART
OF THE LAMB BEFORE THE EYES
OF MARY HIS MOTHER

Saint Ignatius after having contemplated "the mysteries of the seven last words" of Christ on the cross considers successively the piercing of the Redeemer's side, the burial of his corpse, and the mysterious separation, in the state of death, of his soul and body. The solitude of the Virgin and her sorrow are ever present in his mind as we shall see. On passing from the contemplation of the act of dying to the state of death of Jesus, we desire and ask for the grace to feel our hearts pierced by the sword of sorrow which pierced the Immaculate Heart of the Mother of God, that they may be hidden and given asylum in the wound, ever open, of Christ's side and be buried in the Heart of the Lamb.

A. The piercing of the Heart of the Lamb of God

Right after he has had us listen to the seven words of the divine testator, the author of the Exercises sees "at the moment when Jesus expires,"[1] "the sun darkened, the rocks rent, the graves opened, and the veil of the temple torn in two from top to bottom." and "his side pierced with a lance, and blood and water coming forth" (Ex. 297, V).[2]

Nature, the dead, history, all together at once seem to crumble, to break down and open up to honor and glorify the salvific opening up of the Heart of the Lamb in whom all is recapitulated. Henceforth the water of baptism and the Blood of the Eucharist can flow in floods to drown the sin of the world in a deluge of mercy. A deluge that will never stop: the Heart of Jesus is ever open. It is the sanctuary of the New Covenant, the new temple of the new Jerusalem (cf. Rv 21:22), and the torn veil of his dead flesh is of greater use than the torn veil[3] of the ancient temple.

Christian life consists of entering into the Heart of Jesus by reparative contemplation, of going out from that Heart by apostolic action while still remaining within. "I am the gate. Whoever enters through me will be safe; he will go in and out, and find pasture" (Jn. 20:9).[4]

As Nadal emphasizes, Christ's wounds are our gateway to come to God.[5]

We have an asylum in all our trials and tribulations. Who would not hasten to enter with full trust and confidence into that Heart of Christ which is wide open? Who would not, tranquilly and securely, set his hope, his salvation and his life in the opening in the rock which is Christ (*cf.* CT 2:14)?[6]

From the meditation on Christ's five wounds there flows over us a divine energy: from his hands, power to carry out in him our works; from his feet, strength of will to follow them; from his side, the help needed to apply our hearts to these works by gentle and ardent acts of charity and other virtues.[7]

So it is not surprising that the devotion to the Savior's wounds, including that of his side, has led to an explicit devotion to his Sacred Heart toward which the Spirit[8] has guided the Church, devotion to the Heart from which she was born.[9]

Rahner tells us: "The pierced Heart of Jesus Christ is the center of the world in which all the powers and all the currents of world history are, as it were, bound together into one." But repeating forcefully papal thinking, he adds: "If properly understood, the devotion to the Sacred Heart of Jesus belongs to the very essence of Christianity."[10] The pierced Heart of Jesus is "the ultimate meaning of the awesome multiplicity of all the things God has created and his most comprehensive statement"[11] about them is the Heart, in which" his love was pierced through."[12] It is the greatest sign of divine love and of truly human love in the world. It confers a supreme intelligibility on all other signs of divine love, which in a way fade away before it.

It depends on us that this sign be known in all its meaningful value. Following the expressed will of the Redeemer[13] ought we not display widely images of his wounded heart?[14] have them set up in public places so that the man in the street, the mass man, the depersonalized man of our great urban conglomerations can, on seeing them, overcome his despair and be reminded that he is the object of a personal, eternal, infinite, merciful love?

Let us renew ourselves in the cult of love, of adoration, of thanksgiving and of reparation toward the wounds of Jesus, most especially that of his pierced side, kissing each day our crucifix as Saint Joseph Cafasso constantly urged his Italian penitents to do in the nineteenth century.

If we ought to "show our esteem for the relics of the saints by venerating them and invoking them" (Ex. 358), how much the more ought we venerate statues and pictures of the crucified and of his heart, as well as crucifixes, kissing them and llving with all our feelings him whose heartfelt love for us has been so painfully manifested? Why would the man Jesus be the only one whom we would not love with feeling?

The contemplation on the piercing of the Heart of the Lamb and of the wounds of his hands and his feet lead us also to a rediscovery of the value of the "Sign of the Cross" and of its importance in our lives.

As early as the Fourth Century, Saint Cyril of Jerusalem wrote: "Let us not be ashamed to confess loudly him who has been crucified for us. Let us imprint confidently the figure of his cross on our foreheads and not only on our foreheads, but on everything we use, on the bread we eat, on the beverage we are going to drink.[15] Let us fortify ourselves with this sign when we go out of our homes, when we return home, before going to sleep, when we rise. It is a powerful protection, given gratuitiously to the poor as well as to the rich. This sign is the glory of the faithful, and, when one is confidently covered by it, the terror of demons. Before this sign they are forced to remember the crucified who has crushed the head of the dragon.''[16]

The sign of the cross, kissing the crucifix, the veneration of pictures and statues of the Heart of the Lamb of God, all this manifests and increases out faith in the redemptive and reconciling love of Christ Jesus, our Savior even in his state of death, and not only in his act of dying,[17] a love signified in the wounding of his side.

"Lord, instill in our hearts, the pious feeling for the wound you were given after your death. The lance pierced your divine Heart. May the force of the same lance, and the force of your wound, and the force of your Heart, penetrate the very inwards of mine, may it transfuse it with holy fear and with the spur of compunction and love.

"Blessed the heart thus pierced by this lance and which receives, under the cross, the stream of water and blood to bathe itself in these limpid sources. Oh! Christ Jesus, receive me into your ever opened Heart![18]

"Once fixed and set within your pierced Heart, we will the better be able to grasp with Saint Lutgarde d' Aywieres our vocation of reparators toward and with you.

"She sees you, you, the head of our salvation, with your wounds which appear just inflicted and bleeding, standing before the face of the Father, pleading with the Father for sinners.

"You say to her: 'See how I offer myself wholly to the Father on behalf of my sinners. I wish that you, too, offer yourself wholly to me for my sinners and that you turn away the wrath which is prepared to take vengeance on them.' Almost each day, at the sacrifice of the Mass, Lord Jesus, you told her again the same thing.[19]

"As Christians, we are washed, justified, baptized, pardoned[20] in your Blood, Lamb of God, then our thirst is quenched by this precious Blood in the Eucharist. We are ourselves[21] consecrated priests and victims by you, consecrated consecrator. The victimal and reparational vocation is not for us an accident super-added contingently and artificially to our Christian vocation, it is its very essence, its raison d'être.[22] No one can be fully and authentically your member, oh Christ priest and victim, if he does not offer himself to you and with you as a victim of reparation, of thanksgiving and of suppliant adoration for all mankind.[23]

"I want to fill up in my flesh what is lacking in your sufferings for the sake of your body which is the Church (Col 1: 24). I no longer wish to see, to have and to know aught but you and you crucified (cf. 1 Cor 2:2).

I have now appraised as loss in your sight what I used to consider gain. I have come to rate all as loss in the light of your surpassing knowledge, Christ Jesus, my Lord. For your sake I have forfeited everything. I have accounted all else rubbish so that you may be my wealth and that I may be in you, not having any justice of my own. I wish to know, you Christ, and the power flowing from your Resurrection and, sharing in your sufferings, to be formed into the pattern of your death (*cf.* Phil 3:7-.10).''

B. The Burial of the Heart of the Lamb

The Heart of Christ, now a corpse, no longer beats with love for us, it has even stopped, but, as the corpse of the Word, it remains the instrument of our salvation. In the tomb, this Heart which has loved men so much is ever the instrument of saving love, and its incorruptible instrument.

For Christ's corpse is still the corpse of the Divine Person of the Word. It is not an ordinary corpse, depersonalized. It is not the corpse of a saint, but of the saint of saints.[24]

Why? Even though dead, this body, instrument of divinity, acts not as dead but in virtue of the divinity which is united to it. Its action is in its image. Since death is privation of life, Christ's death tends toward to the removal of what is contrary to our salvation: the death of the soul and the death of the body.[25] It buries us in him and with him.

The incorruptible Heart of the Redeemer's corpse manifests to us evermore his saving love for our souls and for our bodies, while inviting us to bury ourselves in him.

We have been buried with him at the time of our baptism (Col 2:12): we are dead and our life is from now on hidden with Christ in God.[26] It is in the Heart of the buried Savior that we must hide ourselves as in a vivifying and divinizing tomb: "Through it, the world has been crucified to me, and I to the world" (Gal 6:14).

Just as Christ's corpse, obeying, does not resist, the men who bury and anoint it (*cf.* Ex. 298), I can manifest to the world Christ's salvific obedience unto the death of the cross (Phil 2:8; Rom 5:19) only by obeying all my life, unto death, as a corpse—just like a corpse[27]—according to the moving comparison made by Ignatius in the context of the patristic tradition, a comparison which does not take on full meaning save in the face of the corpse of Jesus crucified.

"Buried Heart of Jesus, my life, make me a sharer in your incorruptibility by granting me the grace of your obedience. It is through your obedience unto death that you saved me making me accept my radical, initial and continual dependence in relation to your twofold human and divine liberty. Your dead Heart reveals to me how far the perfect submission of your Human will to your divine liberty led you out of love for me.

"Never will I save others by disobedience to your Church. It would be a

scandal to them and their loss.[28] On the contrary, by offering you out of love
for them the trials, the privations, the silences and submissions of obedience,
I will merit for them the application of the supreme merit of your redemptive
death. You will carry out in me and through me your salvific obedience unto
death. I will be able in you and with you to raise up the spiritual corpses
of sinners.[29] I will be able to do this not necessarily by word and deed but
at least by silence and prayer in suffering. Though "what we will be," that
is, universal co-redeemers, "has not yet been manifested" yet "we know
that when it comes to light we shall be like him" (*cf.* 1 Jn 3:2) in the
measure in which we will have reproduced in us his obedience unto death,
and with the death of the cross, unto the tomb.

"Oh Word, we can only be your disciples by savoring you in the love
of suffering. The soul which refuses to accept suffering will be forced to experience it. But if on the contrary it is willing to bear it in concert with the
sun of light, it will experience no bitterness, no more than the divinity in
the Word was touched by the Passion, the torments of which it willingly
bore. My sinful soul blushes with shame at never having known you. For
I have ever vivid in me the love of sensuality. I have ever been dead to life
according to reason. May it, then, please today your infinite charity to
clarify the outlook of my intellect and that of every rational creature.[30]
May this my co-redemptive obedience be buried in yours, Heart of the
redeeming Lamb."

*C. The desolation and sorrow of the Virgin Co-Redemptrix
alone before the tomb wherein lay the Redeemer's corpse.*

After the last cry and sigh of Jesus crucified, Mary's sorrow grew with
her love.[31]

1) The body of Jesus "was taken down from the cross by Joseph of Ari-
mathea and Nicodemus in the presence of His sorrowful Mother" (Ex. 298,
A, V).

Mary remained standing, in suffering and in love, until the corpse of
her son and Savior was returned to her maternal adoration.

"Here the passion comes to a close and compassion goes on. Christ
is no longer on the cross. He is with Mary who has received him. As she
accepted him as promised, so she received him as consummated.

"Christ who has suffered in the eyes of all is once more hidden in his
Mother's bosom."[32]

His Mother's arms and Immaculate Heart are the first and deepest tomb[33]
of Christ crucified, taken down from the cross.

2) After the burial of her only, virginal and beloved son, our Lady re-
tired to her home (Ex. 208, 6th Day) which is none other than that of
the beloved disciple John, proclaimed her son by her only Son: "From
that hour onward, the disciple took her into his care" (Jn 19:27). This

text is highly symbolic.[34] Each Christian, no matter to which church he belongs, is he not "the beloved disciple of Jesus?" Should he not, as Leo XIII[35] said so well, offer Mary the hospitality of his stained heart, therein welcome the Heart of Mary, transpierced by the sword of his own sins, in a devotion of reverence, thanksgiving, reparative love and imitation? "His own": is not this John's home, the dwelling of the disciple, the priest and the apostle of Jesus, who welcomes Mary? Is it not the symbol of the universal Church which welcomes in faith[36] the Heart of Mary?

Yet there are so many Christians, in all churches, who refuse to welcome in their hearts Mary's Heart. Do they refuse to be beloved disciples of the Lord?

"Immaculate Virgin, sorrowful Mother of the Lord, I wish, like John, to receive you and take you to my own, in my heart, as my mother, honoring you, invoking you, desiring you, loving you, giving myself over to you, acknowledging the rights you have earned, by your tears, to my love, and doing so in order to be a true disciple of your son. The inestimable gift of the memory of you becomes the summit of an imperishable joy which associates me to your joy, superabundant in the midst of all tribulations, at the foot of the cross and during the paschal triduum. With what joy, with what benefits is not filled one who makes of his spirit the hidden dwelling of your holy memory?"[37]

3) During Holy Saturday, the desolation of the Virgin co-redemptrix did not disappear because John received her into his home. St. Ignatius, then, contemplates[38] "the most sacred Body of Christ our Lord isolated and separated from his soul . . . the solitude of our Lady in her great sorrow and fatigue, her desolation and affliction as well as the solitude of the disciples" (Ex. 208f). Mary's sorrow is brought about not only by the death of Jesus, so atrocious, but also, one would say, almost especially by the sin of the world which is indirectly its cause, without forgetting Peter's desertion, Judas' betrayal, the abandonment by the other disciples except John.

However, Mary's desolate suffering is thoroughly steeped in love of God and men who were the executioners of her son. Like the Passion of Jesus, and thanks to it, it is a loving suffering. Rather, its deepest source and, in one sense, its unique source, is her love for the divine and. human persons. Sin, denial, treason, abandonment only wound her for she loves with an ineffable purity the God offended and the offenders. Her suffering comes from love and increases love in her (instead of erasing it as happens so often with us). She feels she is crucified as and with her Son, by the conflict between God and men (cf. Gen 2:19).

In her solitude, in her desolation, she is more than ever united to the Father who delivered up his Son to death, to his Son who is her God, to men her brothers and her sons, who are so much more alone than she because of their sins. Sin separates the sinner from himself, from others and from God (cf. Eph 2: 14–18). The Immaculate is alone but not separated.

If we want to have an idea, of course but a dim one, of this loving and compassionate sorrow of Mary during Holy Saturday, we must turn toward that great mystic of the redemption,[39] St. Paul of the Cross and his moving description of his own prayer:

"Her soul, wholly immersed in pure love without images,[40] in most pure and naked faith, finds itself all at once, when it pleases the sovereign good, plunged equally in the sea of the sufferings of the Savior.

"At a glance, she understands them all without understanding them, for the Passion of Jesus is wholly a work of love.

"And as her soul remains totally lost in God, who is charity, who is all love, it becomes a mixture of love and sorrow, for the spirit is wholly penetrated by it, wholly plunged in a sorrowing love and in a loving sorrow."[41]

Elsewhere the Saint explained: "Bound by ropes, enchained, buffetted, whipped, wounded, crowned with thorns, bearing the cross, united to my Savior's death, I fly with him to the bosom of the divine Father, where the gentle Jesus ever remains. I let myself be fully immersed in his immense divinity!"[42] For St. Paul of the Cross the exercise of prayer consists in "putting on the sufferings of Jesus Christ."[43]

Thus Mary, after her son's death, is fully clothed in the sufferings of Jesus, plunged into the bottomless abyss of his Passion, to the point that her own compassion becomes for us an unplumbed mystery of suffering and love. Of her, in particular, can be said what is predicated in general in the Byzantine liturgy of the Mother of God: "Unplumbed depth in the eyes of the angels, inaccessible height for the mind of men." It is this creature whose love and suffering are of a purity, of a profundity, of a unique intensity which keeps on saying to us, in her solitude so filled with solicitude: "Behold your Mother! It is for you I suffer and it is for your sake I weep."[44]

What will we answer her who gives us all in giving us her only son and in offering him, with the immolation of her maternal feelings, for our sake? What will we answer the Immaculate Virgin who gives us divine life while immolating herself, with her son, as a victim for our salvation? What will we give her who has denied us nothing?[45]

After the fifth century, and without any doubt after the sixth, Christian tradition perhaps at first in the West, at any rate somewhat later in the East, has responded to the love and total self-giving of the Virgin Mother of God to mankind by total consecreation. Pope John VII already called himself the slave of holy Mary, and St. John Damascene[46] in the East as well as St. Ildefonsus of Toledo[47] in the West, have left us admirable testimonials of their respective total consecration to the Mother of God.[48]

For one who has understood the unique role played by Mary in the mystery of our Redemption by Christ and in the Church, consecration to the handmaid and Mother of the Lord[49] is assuredly more than a mere possibility. It could be naught but the indisputable and beatifying obligation of the loving heart, while at the same time an important stage in the salvific pilgrimage of the child of Mary in returning to Christ and to the Father in the Spirit. If Christ came to us and comes to us constantly through Mary, how would we return to him save through her?

The total consecration to the co-redemptive Mother of a crucified God will necessarily take on a reparatory aspect.[50] Mary cannot be loved without one's suffering from the offenses committed against her, without one's being willing to do everything to make her known and loved. Consecration as reparation to the Immaculate Heart of the Mother of God, in view of her service, out of love for the glory of the Divine Persons, is the answer which her son offers Mary repeating to her: "Behold you son!" If Mary repeats to us constantly, after Calvary, the testimonial words of her Lord "Behold your Mother", we should repeat to her with ever greater love the complementary words "Behold your son!" by renewal of reparatory consecration to her heart of mediatrix.

This service of reparation and of love of the Mother of God is manifested especially by the recitation of the mysteries of the Rosary. By contemplation of the sorrowful mysteries, we become in some way companions and comforters of our desolate mother at the foot of the cross on Calvary and during the paschal triduum. We love her and invoke her in the name of and on behalf of those who are unmindful of her.

The Rosary is a wonderful instrument of prayer,[51] especially in the empty moments of existence, a veritable school of contemplation as Leo XIII has emphasized,[52] "a synthetic symbol of Christological faith under the form of meditative prayer. It is a prayer which sums up the whole redemptive dogma" (Schillebeeckx[53]). Is not the Rosary, then, the expression and the means for daily renewing our consecration to God's Mother, the crown of roses offered her in homage and the bond of our servitude of filial and liberating love in her regard?[54] Is it not the "cord" to which we should "hold fast" for ascending to the Immaculate?[55]

"Oh crown of my mother's Rosary! I clasp you to my heart and reverently kiss you. You are the way to attain all virtue, the treasure of merits for paradise, the pledge of my predestination, the firm chain which holds back the enemy, the source of peace for the one who honors you in this life, the presage of victory for the one who kisses you at the hour of death. At this final hour, your appearance, Oh Mary, will be the sign of my salvation. Your Rosary will open up for me the gates of heaven!'[56]

"Queen of the holy Rosary, mother of sorrows, obtain for me the grace to spread your Rosary and to invite others to recite it, in testimony of gratitude for your co-redemptive compassion, as a sign of renewed consecration to your Heart, in reparation for so much forgetfulness in your regard. Your intercession has made me share, at the hour of my baptism, in the grace of your Immaculate Conception and of your immaculate charity for God and for men. May the recitation of the Rosary, in time of solicitude, of trials, of darkness, make me persevere in consecration to your service unto death. May my last hour be spent, as yours, in pure love of God. Pray for me, now and at the hour of my death, that I accept perfectly the loss of my mastery over my body delivered up, as that of your son and your own, to death. Into your hands, oh my queen, I remit my spirit that you may hand it over to your son.[57]

"Oh sovereign, Mother of God and Virgin, we attach our souls to the hope that you are favoring us, as an absolutely firm and fixed anchor. To you we consecrate our spirit, our soul, our body, each one of us, our entire person. We want to honor you by psalms, hymns, inspired canticles (cf. Eph 5:19; Col 3:16) in so far as we can, to render you honor according to your dignity, even though it be beyond our strength. If it is true, according to the sacred word, that honor rendered to other servants is a proof of love toward the common master, the honor which is rendered you, the mother of our master, can it be neglected? Must it not be sought zealously? Is it not preferable even to the breath of life and does it not give life?[58]

"Holy Mary, mother of our hearts, make our heart be like yours and like the Heart of your sweet son, our Lord!"[59]

NOTES ON CHAPTER FIFTEEN

1. Peculiar to the Vulgate, Ex. 297, 3: "*sol obscuratus est, ipso expirante, et petrae scissae sunt.*" The Autograph does not mention here the Lord's death.

2. There is to be noted the curious difference, in the arrangement of the three points of Ex. 297, between the Vulgate and the Autograph. It seems evident that the Vulgate has intended to stress (cf. the preceding note) the symbolic meaning of the cosmic earthquake, splitting the rocks, and its relationship with the separating, in death, of the Lord's soul and body.

3. The hymn is well known: "*Cor, arca legem continens*" of the office of readings for the Feast of the Sacred Heart of Jesus (new Roman Briviary): "*Cor, sanctuarium novi—intemeratum foederis—templum vetusto sanctius—velumque scisso utilius*; we allude to this text here.

4. Cf. J. Nouet, S.J., "*L'Homme d'Oraison,*" Oeuvres, vol. 2, Paris, 1890, pp. 348–50: "Enter into the Heart of Jesus by prayer . . . Come out of the Heart of Jesus to go and work for Jesus. Bring Jesus with you to put him in the hearts of those with whom you meet. Come out of Jesus as a ray comes from the sun without cutting itself off from the sun and as Jesus himself went out of the heart of his Father without separating himself from him. Enter in, come out, go in again into the Heart of Jesus thus. Set up in it your dwelling place, Christian soul. But when you are there, you are not content to stay there alone: draw there all those you can."

5. "H. Nadal Orationis observationes," ed. Nicolau, MHSJ, 90a, Rome 1964, #973, p. 299.

6. H. Nadal, S.J., *Adnotationes et Meditationes in Evangelia;* Anvers 1594/5, *in medit. de emissione spiritus,* Adnot. 368 b; *cf.* M. Nicolau, S.J., "Para la historia de la devoción al Corazón de Jesús: Jeronimo Nadal (1507-1508)," *Manresa* 15 (1943) 134–47.

7. "H. Nadal Orationis Observationes," *op. cit.* #873, p. 267.

8. *Cf.* Pius XII, *Haurietis Aquas,* AAS 48 (1956) 338–40: There the Pope stresses that Mary and the apostles were models of devotion to the wounds of the Savior and sees in the cult of the Heart of Christ a development of this original devotion. We have made a thorough study of this subject in our work (*ad usum manuscriptum*) on *The Heart of the Lamb of God,* Apostleship of Prayer, Rome, 1972, #40.

9. *Cf.* CFW, 464-466.

10. Rahner, S.J., *Spiritual Exercises,* N.Y., 1965, p. 242.

11. And also, we would add, the most comprehensible.

12. *op. cit.,* p. 242.

13. See the texts of Saint Margaret Mary Alacoque assembled by L. Garriguet, *Le Sacré-Coeur de Jesus, Exposé historique et dogmatique,* Paris, 1920, Ch. XI: "role of the representation in the practice of the devotion to the Sacred Heart," p. 421. The author notes here especially letters 131 and 133 of the Saint to Father Croiset.

14. *Cf.* Ex. 360: "We ought to praise not only the building and adornment of chruches, but also images and veneration of them according to the subject they represent"; *cf.* B. de Margerie, S.J., *The Heart of the Lamb of God,* Apostleship of Prayer, Rome, 1972, #56.

15. It is known that for Saint Ignatius prayers before and after meals should be recited as attentively as the words of consecration; *cf.* Ex. 214,215.

16. Saint Cyril of Jerusalem, Catechesis 13, #36; MG 33, 816. Also, Tertullian wrote: "We make the sign of the cross before going, and coming, on dressing, on retiring, on every occasion" (*De Coron.milit.,* ML 2,80).

17. *Cf.* CFW, pp. 261-262.

18. Nadal, continuation of text quoted in note 6 of this chapter.

19. Quoted by Father Debongnie, C.SS.R., Commencement et Recommencements de la Dévotion au Coeur de Jesus, *Le Coeur,* Etudes Carmélitaines, 1950, pp. 155, 158. Saint Lutgarde d'Aywieres lived from 1182–1246.

20. *Cf.* Rom 8:30; Ti 3:5-7.

21. *Cf.* CFW, 170-172; 222; 233-235; and de Margerie, *The Heart of the Lamb of God,* Rome, 1972, #61.

22. *ibid.* #59 p. 60; 64–68.

23. There is involved the highest exercise of fraternal charity.

24. *Cf.* CFW, 266-268.

25. *Ibid.;* ST, III.50.6, c.1.3.

26. Col 3:3.

27. Saint Ignatius of Loyola, *Constitutions of the Society of Jesus,* VI,1,1; Par 547.

28. *Cf.* Saint Ignatius, Letter on obedience, March 26, 1553, *Obras completas,* p. 806.

29. It is known that the resurrection of Lazarus has been interpreted by patristic tradition as the real symbol of the spiritual resurrection of the sinner; *cf.* Jn 20:22,23.

30. Saint Catherine of Sienna, Prayer of March 27, 1379, *Prayers and Elevations,* French transl. Bernard, pp. 117–24.

31. As we bring together here what concerns Mary, we go back to the viewpoint of the course of events, quoting the Ignatian text on Mary's sorrow when Jesus was taken down from the cross by Joseph and Nicodemus in her presence. St. Ignatius proceeds thus from time to time in the Exercises (when he proposes the contemplation of Christ's appearance to St. Paul (Ex. 311), and only after that of the Ascension (Ex. 312) and above all no where does he state that the order of contemplations is to follow rigorously that of history or of the Gospels.

32. Paul Claudel, "Chemin de la Croix," *Oeuvres complètes,* II, Trèizieme station, quoted by R. Halter, *La Vierge Marie dans l'oeuvre de P. Claudel,* Paris, 1958, p. 168.

33. *Cf.* St. Jean Eudes, *Le Coeur admirable de la Mère de Dieu,* livre III, ch. 6.

34. F. M. Braun, O.P., *La mère des fidèles,* Tournai, 1953, pp. 124–29.

35. Leo XIII, Encyclical *Augustissimae Virginis,* Sept. 12, 1897 We quote the very moving Latin text: *"Ingravescente aetate . . . facere non possumus quin omnibus et singulis in Christo filiis nostris Ipsius cruce pendentis extrema verba, quasi testamento relicta, iteremus: Ecce mater tua. At praeclare quidem nobiscum actum censebimus, si id nostrae commendationes effecerint ut unusquisque fidelis mariali cultu nihil habeat antiquius, nihil carius, liceatque de singulis usurpare verba Joannis quae de se scripsit: 'Accepit eam discipulus in sua' "* (*Leo XIII, Lettres apostoliques,* B. Presse, T.V., p. 168.).

36. *Cf.* B. de Margerie, S.J. *Le Coeur de Marie, Coeur de L'Eglise,* Paris, 1967. first part, #8: the heart of Mary, the heart of the eucharistic life of the Church.

37. *Cf.* St. John Damascene, "Homélie sur la Dormition," I. 14, *Sources Chrétiennes,* vol. 80, Paris, 1961, p. 119. Mary's joy at the foot of the cross is not surprising if it be recalled that her charity rejoiced over the salvation of the world wrought by her son's death. Furthermore, this beautiful thought of St. Robert Bellarmine may be applied to her: *"Si ulla est in hoc mundo vera consolatio, illa est in hac solitudine, ubi desunt omnes terrenae consolationes"* (*Opera Oratoria posthuma,* Rome, 1948, Vol. IX, p. 453). Finally, the death of Jesus did not deprive her of the divine Word, who constantly increased his presence in his mother through grace. To her particularly, whom St. Ignatius depicts to us often as so "sorrowful" (*v.g.* Ex. 208 and 298) is applied a reflection from his correspondence: "It would not be possible for anything to befall us which would occasion so much distress, because all affliction arises from losing or fearing to lose what one loves" (Letter of January 20, 1554, to Maria Frasoni del Gesu, *St. Ignatius Loyola, Letters to Women,* Rahner, p. 193). Mary had lost the humanity she had given to her son (hence her ineffable sorrow) but in no way had she lost the in-dwelling in her of his Person and divine nature, nor not even faith in his imminent Resurrection. As she loved in Jesus the divinity more than the humanity, it may be said she had a superabundant joy in the midst of all tribulations, not only in truth, but more so in fullest fidelity to the deliberate nuances of Ignatian thought.

38. In our translation we synthesize the Autograph and the Vulgate texts of the Exercises.

39. Cf. J. Lebreton, S.J., *Tu Solus Sanctus.*

40. Here St. Paul of the Cross describes a moment of his prayer. As is shown by the text quoted somewhat later (note 42), he presented the pains suffered by the holy humanity of the Savior.

41. St. Paul of the Cross, *Lettres*, III, 149.

42. ibid. 831.

43. P. Gäetan, *Oraison et Ascension mystique de S. Paul de la Croix*, p. 62. Bossuet had already profoundly treated analogically the relationship between love and suffering in Mary: "Love brought forth her sorrow and this sorrow was to give her death. And love came to her aid to make her live in order to make her sorrow live also . . . She ever saw Jesus Christ in the agonies of his cross, ever not only her ears but also the depths of her soul were pierced by that last cry of her dying beloved Son, a cry truly terrible and capable of rending her heart" (Sermon II on the Assumption, First Point, *Oeuvres complètes*, Paris 1885, Vol. III, pp. 488,489). Furthermore he thought of Mary's entire earthly life after the Crucifixion up to her Assumption.

44. It cannot be excluded that Mary, at the foot of the cross and during the paschal triduum, enjoyed an infused knowledge of the sins of all those of whom she was to be the co-redemptrix. *Cf.* Cardinal A.M. Lepicier, O.S.M., *Tractatus de Beatissima Virgine Maria*, Paris, 1912, p. 314: "*Beata Virgo divinitus accepit cognitionem de illis omnibus quae ad ejus dignitatem et officium, quatenus Dei Mater et Christi cooperatrix exstitura erat, spectabant, unde congrua esset Mater Dei et redemptrix generis humani,*" The author makes even clearer his thought: "*Hoc modo dici potest Maria apprime cognovisse sortes totius Ecclesiae, cujes mater erat constituenda, quatenus pro hominibus, suis filiis, quorum necessitates probe notas habebat, pati et intercedere efficaciter posset*" (*ibid.*).

45. *Cf.* Rom 8:32; would not the rejection of consecration to Mary be then objectively ingratitude as well as infidelity to movements of the Spirit? *Cf.* note 48.

46. Pope John VII, reigning from 705 to 707, called himself "*servus sanctae Mariae.*" The text of John Damescene's consecration to Mary will be quoted later on (*cf.* note 58) Then, too, does not the Ignatian expression "our Lady" imply, through its chivalrous connotation, consecration to Mary?

47. St. Ildefonsus of Toledo, *Tractatus de perpetua virginitate*, ch. 12, ML 96, pp. 105-10.

48. The Church, on instituting the feast of Mary's queenship in the Latin rite (now fixed on August 22) intended to show the importance of consecration to Mary. Pius XII in 1942 consecrated the world to her immaculate heart. Countless Pontifical texts, (*cf. Les enseignements pontificaux, Notre Dame*, Tournai, 1957, Tables logiques, #132), have stressed the presuppositions and consequences of consecration to Mary. St. Louis-Marie Grignon de Montfort, in his *Traité de la Vraie Dévotion*, (# 134-82) has expounded at length it motives in the framwork of the economy of salvation.

49. "*doule kai meter*" says St. John Damascene, *op. cit.*, Homélie sur la Dormition, III, 5, p. 195. The two words are from the Gospels.

50. *Cf.* DS, 3926: Pius XII there underlines the propriety of reparation toward her, since the divine life is received from Christ.

51. *Cf.* Luke 18:1: on the necessity of praying always.

52. A thought expressed by this Pope in his letter: "*Diuturni Temporis*" (1898) and in several other of his numerous encyclicals on the Rosary: also by Benedict XV Encyclical "*Fausto Appentente,*" AAS, 13 (1921) 334.

53. E. Schillebeeckx, O.P., *Marie, Mère de la Rédemption,* Paris, 1963, p. 171; The author treats beautifully the subject of the Rosary in pp. 168–76 and particularly stresses the importance of the family recitation of the Rosary on pp. 173,174.

54. St. Louis-Marie Grignon de Montfort in *Traité de la vraie dévotion,* explains at length the doctrine of the enslavement of love toward Mary and exalts the Rosary, Nonetheless he does not expound it explicitly as the chain of slavery of Mary; yet such a comparison is quite consonant with his thought.

55. Paul Claudel, *La Rose et le Rosaire,* Paris, 1946, pp. 145–48. *Cf.* P. Halter, *La Viergo Marie dans la vie et l'oeuvre de Paul Claudel,* Paris, 1958. The author underlines the importance of the role played by the Rosary in Claudel's life. He wrote J. Rivière on the 25 of May 1907: "Recite the Rosary; make the Stations of the Cross" (p. 31). He confides in his *J'aime la Bible* (Paris, 1955, p. 110): "How often the smoking jacket seemed a hairshirt and I would have preferred a rock in the Pacific to this place of honor at an official dinner at which it occurred to me to say the Rosary under the table cloth between two wives of American senators!" (p. 70). P. Halter explains that Claudel used to say the Rosary also "in his lodge at the theater . . . every evening at five o'clock or in some church or chapel nearby his lodging . . . This recitation so frequently made, accompanied by contemplation of the mysteries of the life of Christ and of his mother, turned out to exercise a profound influence on his thinking" (*ibid.* and p. 71).

56. Pius XI, in a Brief of July 20, 1925, quoted by A. Royo Marin, O.P., *La Virgen María,* Madrid, 1968, p. 425. The same author emphasized (p. 465) that Vatican II (LG 67), urging all Christians "to treasure practices and exercises of devotion toward her as recommended by the teaching authority of the Church", had in mind especially the Rosary, for no other devotion to Mary has been as strongly recommended by it. Furthermore it is in this sense that Paul VI gave an authentic interpretation of this conciliar text in his Encyclical *Christi Matri Rosarii,* AAS, 58, 1966, 748.

57. Venerable Bernard de Hoyos, S.J., (1711–1735) in his *"Instrucíon"* published by Father Abad, Comillas, 1948, #74.

58. St. John Damascene, Homélie sur la Dormition, I, 14, *Sources Chrétiennes,* vol. 80, p. 119.

59. Invocation attributed to St. Ignatius.*Cf.* E. Letierce, S.J., *Etude sur le Sacré-Coeur,* Paris, 1890, vol. I, p. 44. A propos of the marian devotion of St. Ignatius, note also that he habitually carried about with him a Rosary. *Cf.* D.F. Zapico, "El Rosario o corona de S. Ignacio de Loyola," AHSJ, 14 (1945) 131–37.

16

THE EMPTY TOMB
THE TRIUMPH AND GLORY
OF THE RISEN CHRIST.
HIS FIRST APPEARANCE TO HIS
HOLY MOTHER, THE VIRGIN MARY

The second part[1] of the above title is intended to emphasize the two-fold originality of the first contemplation of the fourth week which, we feel, has not been adequately recognized heretofore. St. Ignatius sets the fact and the mystery of the glorious Resurrection of the *body* of Jesus Christ our Lord between the mystery of the descent of his *soul* to hell and the mystery of his appearance in *body* and *soul* to his mother before any one else. This setting seems fraught with meaning, and we shall scrupulously respect it. We shall, therefore, borrow from the first prelude (Ex. 219) the structuring of the subject matter of this first contemplation for adequately treating the three distinct and successive contemplations after we have commented on the second and third preludes.

Composition of Place: Our Lady's home (Ex. 220).

St. Ignatius invites us "to see the place or house of Our Lady. I will note its different parts, and also her room, her oratory, etc." According to various approved texts of the Exercises, we are not merely to see in passing but to "dwell on" and contemplate[2] the disposition of the whole dwelling[3] including her room or oratory.[4] Our Lady's home is that of John who "took her to his own" (*cf.* Jn 19:27).

As we mentioned before,[5] Mary's home is the symbol of the universal Church through and in which the Lord's Immaculate Mother is to be welcomed. The Church was already represented at Nazareth by the house in which, in the name of mankind and especially of all Christians to come, the Virgin Mary consented to the redemptive Incarnation. (*cf.* Ex. 103, A, V, P2, Puhl contrasting: "to see the great extent of the surface of the earth, inhabited by so many different peoples., and especially to see the house[6] and room of our Lady in the city of Nazareth in the province of Galilee.")

Upon accepting the twofold yet single mystery of the redemptive Incarna-

225

tion and of her own spiritual maternity, Mary chose a dwelling in the universal Church. If her oratory, in a more profound sense, is the pierced and buried Heart of her son, her room is her own immaculate soul filled with the Spirit of Christ. In her soul dwell, permanently and never to be lost, the Son and the Father. (*Cf.* Jn 14:17,23). We "see" Mary's home with eyes of faith, to visit her who herself is the home, the dwelling place of the Three who are one, in the Church. The universal Church is the house which receives the ark of the new and eternal covenant.

In this Church, the heart of each beloved disciple of Jesus becomes a loving son who receives as a heritage his Mother, Mary. And this reception is presented as a reparation, for this desciple and beloved son has by his sins, by the sword of sorrow of his sins (*cf.* Lk 2:35) pierced his mother's soul and Immaculate Heart.

May our souls, as is the Church, be oratories where Mary co-redemptrix continues[7] to sing the *Magnificat* of her thanksgiving for our salvation.

Petition for grace: joy in Christ and His Mother (Ex. 221), third prelude):

The object of this first contemplation is to obtain, by asking for it, "the grace to be glad and rejoice intensely because of the great joy and the glory of Christ our Lord." When we synthesize the texts: A, V, P2, we see that the joy asked for is a joy with Christ, a participation in the joy, not only of Christ, but also of Mary, in their reciprocal[8] joy: *"gratia congaudendi et collaetandi"* (P2).

From the text of the Latin Vulgate of the Exercises we glean that the object of this contemplation is not only to share in the joy of the glorified Christ but also in that of his mother on beholding this glorification. And Mary's joy on beholding the glory of the risen Christ, is the joy of her own redemption and salvation. Christ redeemed her in a most sublime way precisely: that she might be our perfect co-redemptrix.[9]

Joy, in a profoundly Biblical manner,[10] is linked with glory. We ask God for what St. Peter described in his first epistle: "Without seeing him you now believe in him, and rejoice with inexpressible joy touched with glory" (1 Pt 1:8); it is what Christ himself asked for us, before his Resurrection, of his Father: "That they may share my joy completely" (Jn 17:13).

"Lord Jesus, you are resurrection and life, divine and human joy, infinite and finite, uncreated and created, eternal and temporal, voluntary and even sensible. You are divine joy, you have human joy.[11]

"Grant that I may willingly and ever rejoice because of your divine and infinite joy present in the innermost core of my soul. Grant that I may rejoice in the created joy of your soul, triumphant over my sins and my death, and also in the sensible joy of your heart which I receive daily in Your Eucharist for the assuaging of my inordinate grief.[12]

"Grant, Lord, that I rejoice, with your holy soul, in your eternal joy (as God's only Son, a joy received from the Father and communicated to the Spirit with the divine nature with which it is one). Grant me to rejoice in your human and essential joy,[13] of seeing the divine essence in your Father, and the joy of causing the accidental beatitude of your holy soul, of being the cause of your human happiness.[14]

"While begging you for a share in your joy, I beg you, by this very fact, rejoice in us. The fulness of your human joy in me will grow out of my own. I must accomplish, through my joy, what is still lacking in yours.[15] No one better than Mary, "cause of our joy" can help me do so. No one as she, as much as she, participated in your joy of Risen Lord. No one, as she, as much as she, caused your joy.

"While sharing your joy, Lord Jesus, I will manifest and reveal it to others, by my smile, by my words, by my actions. I wish thus to make them happy so as to make your holy humanity happy through them and through me, O you who, as Word, are infinitely and eternally happy to the extent that I cannot cause the joy that you are, but only that which you have.

"Heart of Jesus, plunge me into the abyss of your triple joy, linked to your triple love."[16]

a. *Descent into Hell of the glorified soul of Christ, Liberator of the souls of the just (Ex. 219).*

The author of the Exercises proposes, with a great theological preciseness and exactitude, this mystery as the very first of the glorious mysteries of the fourth week, even prior to the Lord's Resurrection. Let us read the text again: "Here it is how after Christ expired on the cross his body remained separated from the soul, but always united with the divinity. His blessed soul,[17] likewise united with the divinity, descended into hell.[18] There he sets free the souls of the just." Further on (Ex. 311), St. Ignatius makes clear that the Lord "appeared also in soul to the fathers[19] in limbo"[20] suggesting thus that their liberation must have consisted essentially in the "appearance"[21] of Christ.

1) The soul of the Lord, separated from his body, is still the soul assumed by the divine Person of the Word from which it is not at all separated by death. It is most accurately characterized as *blessed* for it is in no way unconscious of its hypostatic (personal) union with the eternal Word, but on the contrary sees it face to face at once as a distinct object from it and as the subject which has assumed it: such is the essential beatitude it possesses from the first moment of the Incarnation[22] which has now, in regard to it, if we may dare say so, become *inanimation.* Yet this soul is also blessed with an accidental beatitude, blessed because it is loved by the just in limbo, whether by the ancestors of the Incarnate Word, or also by his brothers in humanity.

The mystery of the beatitude of the separated soul of Christ, de-humanized[23] but in no way "de-divinized" by death, reminds me that my body, indispensable to my full beatitude, is not necessary for my essential beatitude. After my death, my soul, if it is admitted into the vision of God, will be *perfectly* happy, although the separated soul cannot enjoy *full* happiness. In the likeness of the hypostatic union, my union with God is indestructible by death and by other creatures. On the part of God, it ends only (and in this it differs from the mystery of Jesus) by the sinful initiative of my own free will.

2) The blessed soul of the Lord, now dead, not yet risen, comes to manifest itself in a salvific manner, to the souls of the just, of the fathers in "hell," that is to say, rather than in a place, in the state of waiting for beatitude. This Biblical language[24] evokes another fact of the Old Testament: Jesus joins the fathers,[25] his fathers, that is to say also all the just who died, addresses himself to those who died in the state of grace. By way of the simile of a lower place (the etymological meaning of the term "infernal") the descent into the lower regions signifies the concern of the Savior for the *inferior condition* of the dead.[26] It means also that Jesus communicates salvation and manifests his love to all who by his grace, before his coming, believed in him, even implicitly, and acted according to his commandments though but obscurely known. *Cf.* Ex. 71: "Those who were lost before the coming of Christ; those who were lost during his lifetime because they did not believe in the coming of Christ; others, though they believed, because they did not keep the commandments."

In other words, the "descent into the lower" refers us to those waiting in the lower regions. These just had, despite temptations, persevered unto death in loving and hopeful faith in Christ the Savior, under whatsoever name they knew and awaited him. They now see manifested to them the one who merited and bought at the price of his Blood their fidelity, the very one whom they were awaiting in the shadows.

The mystery of the descent into limbo is of much greater significance for us[27] than for Ignatius of Loyola and the men of the 16th century for two reasons. On the one hand, we know that pre-Christian mankind was more numerous and ancient than they could have believed. We know that man goes back millions of years. On the other hand, we are more inclined to think that the Blood of Jesus has been efficacious for salvation, not necessarily of their totality, but of a great number among their dead.[28]

We are dealing here, then, with the moving encounter of the Savior of the world with all the just of all "ancient testaments," not only that of Israel but also, without denying the imperfections of the analogy,[29] of the dead just of China, India, and of many other "pre-Christian"religions and cultures.

The first Adam recognizes the second and true Adam, his son and Savior and hastens to receive the recompense for an entire life lived, after original sin, "in many labors and great penance" (Ex. 51). Abraham, ancestor of Jesus (*cf.* Lk 3:34), "rejoiced more than ever on seeing his day" (Jn 8:56). Moses and David behold the one whose passion they foretold. Elias once again converses with the transfigured one of Thabor, about his exceedingly great love, now fulfilled, about his "departure" at Jerusalem (*cf.* Lk 9:31). Isaiah once again beholds the glory of the son of man (*cf.* Is 6:2-4; 9ff; Jn 12:41), while the Isaiahan prophet of the exile recognizes the suffering servant who has justified him and taken on himself his sins. And the servant himself sees, in a new way,[30] the spiritual posterity of his carnal ancestors. He is overwhelmed for he has given himself up to death. He sees the multitudes of sinners for whom he has interceded now become the trophies of his loving and humble triumph (*cf.* Is 53:6-12).

To all, the blessed soul of the Word of life announces, by his sole presence, his victory over the devil who held them captive, his triumph over their sins and over their death.[31]

3) Thus the eucharistic Christ, descending into the "lower regions" of our subconscience, into the *inferior zones of our psyche* weakened by original and actual sins, makes us understand today that we are no longer, thanks to his sacrifices, prisoners of our past, of our vices, of the bonds forged by our sins.[32] Everything can become new for us, thanks to the powerful freedom of the human soul of Christ the Savior whom we receive in the Eucharist, of this blessed soul which desires to make us share in his freedom and in his happiness.

4) More profoundly still, the Eucharistic Christ comes into us to accomplish through us the mystery of his descent into the lower regions, *making us descend through love into the mysterious prison and into the flames*[33] *of purgatory, by means of indulgences.*

Are we not, at least indirectly, responsible for the past sins,[34] who actually hold back from the beatific vision those paralytics of the supernatural life who are unable to help themselves and to free themselves, save by suffering, from their painful prison? Is it not then our duty in charity to gain, on their behalf, plenary indulgences when we can do so without great difficulty?

Why would we deprecate indulgences which reveal to us the indulegence of Christ suffering? If we considered indulgences with eyes enlightened by faith, we would perceive in them an application of the superabundant satisfaction of Jesus Christ, a precious flowing out of the divine springs of the Savior, springs never exhausted, an outgrowth of the virtue of his Blood, the least drop of which would have sufficed to redeem a thousand worlds. Would we not have reverently collected the drops of this adorable blood when it was shed for us on the cross?[35] Should we not collect with no less reverence the indulgences which permit us to help our brothers and sisters in purgatory and console them by obtaining for them the supreme consolation of the beatific vision (Ex.224)? Our charity for the living who can help themselves to a certain extent, would it be sincere and genuine if we did not love, not only in words but also in deeds, our dead brothers and sisters who are from now on unable to help themselves?

Do we love them as Jesus did, even to giving our blood and our life,[36] and consequently our prayers and our time for them? Will we not be judged on the love we owe our neighbor? "As often as you did (or did not) do it for one of my least brothers, you did (did not) do it for me" (Mt: 25:40.45). To love the souls in purgatory, is it not to love Jesus who lives in them, since they are justified, saved, predestined? To deliver them, by alms, prayers, Masses, indulgences, is it not to deliver Christ who lives in them and who will one day say to us: "I was in prison and you came to visit me. Come, you have my Father's blessing! Inherit the kingdom prepared for you from the foundation of the world "(Mt25: 36,34.)

We can understand why St. Ignatius, not content with asking us to "praise indulgences" (Ex.358), has insisted on this point in a text which is (in a broad sense) contemporaneous with the preceding: "The indulgences ennumerated in the bull are so many and so precious that I could not even begin to estimate their true value. I can only beg and beseech you, for the love and reverence of God our Lord, that you all hold it in the highest esteem and do all you can to promote and extend the devotion by having it preached to gatherings of people, by processions and other ways of moving people to devotion."[37] We can understand, too, that the post-conciliar Church, concerned as that of the early times of Christianity and of Vatican II[38] to offer her suffrages for the dead: "that they might be freed from their sins" (2 Mc. 12:46), has granted indulgences out of love for the living and the dead, for fasting, prayer, and alms-giving.[39]

"Blessed and holy soul of Jesus, I adore the mystery of your descent to the limbo of the fathers and of the just. I adore your love of the dead who are the truly living (cf Mt. 22:32).[40] I adore your liberating proclamation in regard to your dead brethren. I rejoice over the consoling mission you receive from your Father on their behalf. Consoler of your fathers in limbo, grant me, the grace and the favor of consoling you today in the souls of purgatory. May it please you to apply to them the indulgences which, under the inspiration of your Spirit, and following the counsels of your Church, I desire to gain for them. I resolve to gain every partial and every plenary indulgence[41] available for liberating you, you who are in some way through your members, a captive in purgatory. I will thus bring numerous saints[42] into paradise procuring for them that face to face vision compared to which all other knowledge of God is but ignorance.

"Lord Jesus, make of me the friend, the liberator, the apostle and advocate of souls consigned to purgatory and announce, through me, the mystery of holy indulgences, a magnificent synthesis of Christian truths.[43] May I thus imitate your descent into the lower regions."

b) *The glorious Resurrection of Jesus, visible sign of the invisible triumph of the Cross.*

The author of the Exercises relates "Christ's soul, likewise united with the divinity, descended into hell. There he sets free the souls of the just, then comes to the sepulchre." Then "the Christ-God uniting his body and his soul again"[44] is shown as having risen and raised himself.[45] The man Jesus Christ was raised by his Father through their Spirit,[46] yet as Incarnate Word he raised himself too. Before his Pasch Jesus said: "I have the power to lay it down, and I have the power to take it up again. This command I received from my Father" (Jn 10:18).

We can better understand thus[47] St. Ignatius' suggestion that we "consider the divinity, which seemed to hide itself during the passion, now appearing and manifesting itself so miraculously in the most holy Resurrection in its true and most sacred effects" (Ex.223), which are, according to the Vulgate (Ex. 223) the numerous miracles "performed by the risen Christ"[48]

The Ignatian expression "most holy Resurrection" corresponds with a similar expression used before: "the most holy Incarnation" (Ex.108, A, P2). The Resurrection, paschal stage of the Incarnation, is also worked by the Trinity, is a work common to the three Divine Persons, but the adjective "most holy" probably indicates that the Resurrection, just as the pre-paschal Incarnation, is attributed in a special manner, to the Spirit of Love.[49] The Holy Spirit fully takes hold of the Savior's humanity to act in the world: "Jesus who was handed over to death for our sins and raised up for our justification" (Rom.4:25).[50] That is to say: to give us himself in the Holy Eucharist.[51]

Just as the Savior's death is not at all a separation of his humanity from his Divinity, so the Resurrection is not their re-uniting, but rather the glorious and definitive reanimation of the corpse of the Word of Life by his blessed soul.[52] This union, inseparable from now on, of the body, blood and soul of Jesus, only Son of God, signifies and manifests the inseparable union of the Father, the Son and the Spirit who, together, work the Incarnation and the Resurrection.

The risen Christ is the glorious sign at once of the love which the Father, and the Spirit with the Son, have for us and also of the human and suffering love of the Son for us, during his Passion, the visible sign of the invisible triumph of the cross, to borrow an admirable expression from Father Garrigou-Lagrange. This sign shines out in all its brillance in the glorified wounds of Jesus.

In the light of the Resurrection and with the help of John's Gospel,[53] we better understand that the cross itself is "the glory of glories," to use the magnificent expression of St. Cyril of Jerusalem.[54] If, in the eyes of the flesh, Christ's divine glory appeared hidden during his Passion (*cf.* Ex. 223)[55] the eyes of faith, illumined by the Spirit of the crucified-Resurrected, recognize this triumphant glory of the crucified. St. John Chrysostom has sung it lyrically:

"The cross is the delight of the Father, it is the glory of the Son, the triumph of the Holy Spirit. The cross is more resplendent than the sun. The cross is the triumph of justice for it has torn up the sentance of our condemnation, it is the attestation of the divine bounty. The cross is the wealth of the poor.[56]

It must be admitted that Christians of the West today have often lost this awarness of the triumph of the cross, source of joy. Neither the cross of Jesus, not their own, seems adequately such. They rather are tempted to believe the cross is a sad defeat.

Nevertheless the liturgy of the East and of the West itself, the fathers of the Church, unanimously recognize, according to Scripture itself,[57] in the cross of him-who-was-to-rise a victory over sin, the world (in the most frequently used Joannine sense) and the devil. It is doubtless, in great part due to the diminution of faith in these invisible realities that there is a consequent loss of viewing the cross as glory and triumph. Is it not there, without doubt, that we find the finest of the "most holy effects" of the Resurrection in us: the renewal of the meaning and consciousness of the glory of the cross? Does not the Lord's Resurrection by glorifying himself in his wounds reveal for us the hidden glory of His Divinity? the glory which is prepared and hidden already in the mystery of our daily cross?

Logically, therefore, we ask for the grace to rejoice, with and in Jesus himself risen, in his triumph and victory on the cross, even, with him, in his past sufferings, when we ask for the grace to rejoice interiorly in the glory of his Resurrection (Ex. 221),[58] for the greater glory of the risen one. That is in order that all should recognize the glory of the crucified and his triumph on the altar—the throne and seat of the cross—that all see in their personal cross a sharing in this victory. The accidental beatitude which comes from creatures may fail us at any moment. Never, if we really wish it, will there be wanting to us the essential beatitude which comes to us in and through the Blood of the Lamb, from the Father, giver of the consoling Spirit.

Just as the separation, in death, of the body and soul of the eternal Son of God was the symbol of the desolations which separate us (in appearance) from the Divine Persons, so, the glorious reanimation of the corpse of the Word of life by his blessed soul is the symbol and the cause, in the objective order, of the subjective consolation, which consists precisely in union with the Father, the Word and Spirit.[59] Amidst the worst desolations, no one will be able to deprive us of the supreme consolation of the loving possession of the Divine Persons. Here is the hidden glory which the glorious passion of the only Son has merited for us and which gives us, as instrument of the Trinity, his humanity resurrected. Our faith in his love is the victory which has conquered the world (1 Jn 4:16; 5:4). If we heed Christ's words, if we believe in him who has been sent and if we love our brothers, we know that we have, we too, passed from death to life (cf. Jn 5:24; 1 Jn 4:14). We have risen with Christ for we have believed in the might of God who raised him from the dead. We were dead due to our faults. He has brought us back to life with him. He has pardoned all our faults (*cf.* Col 2:12-13).

"Lord Jesus, I adore your most holy and sanctifying Resurrection, the resolve of your human free will,[60] under the action of your divine Spirit, to glorify your Body[61] and the wounds which your love for me has therein engraved. I adore your human and free resolve to re-vivify your heart that it once more throb with love for me. I adore, in thanksgiving and total oblation of my free will to your divine and human glory, your will to humanize and divinize me.[62] You are resurrection and life, my resurrection and my life. May your most holy Resurrection render my soul blessed in the likeness of yours. Give me, through your Eucharist, in it, the glory, that is, the Spirit, whom your Father has given on raising you up, for he has loved you before the creation of the world (*cf.* Jn 17:22, 24).

"No one among mortal men has seen the glorious action by which you raised yourself and by which you entered forever into the glory of your Father. Yet may all see the action by which you continue, eternal and risen king, to enter into the glory of your Father through your members each time that, under the action of your Spirit, they follow you in suffering and in glory (Ex. 95).

c. *The apparition of the living Jesus in body and soul, first to His Blessed Mother.*[63]

We now come to the subject and the precise object of the first contemplation of the fourth week. The text, though brief, is fraught with meaning especially if pains be taken to fill it out with the indications furnished by St. Ignatius in the "mysteries of the life of Christ" (Ex. 299):[64] "Christ our Lord appeared to the Virgin Mary. Though this is not mentioned explicitly in the Scripture it must be considered as stated when the Scriptures say he appeared to many others. For Scripture supposes that we have understanding, as it is written: "Are you also without understanding?" Here St. Ignatius alludes to the reflection made by Jesus to his disciples after the second multiplication of bread: "Do you still not see or comprehend" (Mk 8:17)?[65] Mary's son could not fail to obey the divine commandment to honor his mother whose heart a sword has pierced. Assuredly, Mary, quite otherwise than the apostles, had no need of such an apparition of her risen Son, Creator and Redeemer, to sustain her faith and increase her love. From this standpoint, the testimony of other witnesses and of the apostles sufficed perfectly for her belief and her joy. Still, in the designs of the divine wisdom of her son, she had a certain right—also quite otherwise than other witnesses—to see her son risen, her son whom she had conceived and borne in the light of faith, assisted and in some way comforted during his Passion, as his generous associate[66] in the work of Redemption. If the holy women, all the apostles and as many as five hundred disciples assembled (1 Cor 15:6; *cf.* Ex. 308: tenth apparition) could see the risen Savior, how much more is it to be understood that the holy woman, holy above all others, the queen and mother of the Lord's apostles, his privilege disciple received his first visit after his Resurrection. [67]

St. Ignatius is perfectly correct in saying that Scripture takes for granted such an apparition, that it implicitly teaches it when it speaks of all the others, and that it would be senseless on our part to deny it. Besides, Christian tradition has emphasized this long before him. [68]

Jesus does not confine himself to appearing to his mother. He also speaks to her, as during his earthly life, and as he does to his apostles, he talks to her about the Kingdom of God which is his Kingdom and also hers, his mother's (cf. Acts 1:3; Mt 13:41; Lk 1:32, 33). We may even think that this first private apparition did not prevent Mary from benefitting from the other apparitions during the forty days (Acts 1:3).

More precisely, Jesus explains to Mary her mission to the Church born of him and of her, to the Church her daughter and her sister. The newborn Church is once more (cf. Jn 19:26) entrusted to her care and to her prayer (Acts 1:14). She will be the evangelist of Christ's infancy (Lk 1-2) during the infancy of the Church. It is precisely for being in part the evangelizer of the Lord's infancy that she will be the animator and, if we may so say, the instructor of the hidden life and infancy of the Church (Acts 1:14). Mother of the universal Church, which she has engendered in tears, after having conceived it joyfully in the annunciation, she hears once more: "Behold your son, the whole Christ!" If Magdalene received the mission of announcing the Lord's Resurrection, does not Mary receive that of making known the inhumanation of her son in her virginal womb, and so her own virginal motherhood? Does she not receive by this announcement the mission to teach the faith to the Church of which she is the virgin mother?[69]

Jesus, Mary's son according to the flesh, established as Son of God with power according to the Spirit of holiness by his Resurrection from among the dead,[70] appears to his blessed Mother with the body he received from her, as man, and which he gave her, as God, the possibility to engender, but in a state not due to her. This apparition is, then, an exaltation of the Divine Maternity of Mary at the same time as a reminder that Mary could do nothing without him (cf. Jn 15:5). Jesus appears to Mary as her Savior and Redeemer, risen to apply to her, to her in the very first place, the merits of his Passion, as the new and renewed Adam, in order that she might exercise perfectly her function as the new Eve, the true mother of the living, on becoming the evangelist of the Lord's infancy toward the evangelists of the Lord's public life and of his paschal mystery.

If St. Ignatius does not envisage in a precise way the conversation between the Savior and his Mother, he does, however, seem to bring out a point which commentators have quite missed, when he says that the risen Jesus "appears in body and soul to his blessed Mother" (Ex. 219, 1, P2, Puhl).

A minimizing interpretation of this text might simply see therein a statement of the living Christ's apparition, of Christ's body once more animated by his immortal soul from now on inseparable from it. Doubtless the translator of the Vulgate understood it thus: *"apparuit Beatae Virgini matri suae vivus"* (Ex. 219, V).[71]

However it is not certain that this exegesis corresponds with St. Ignatius' thinking. Assuredly the author of the Exercises accepted this translation without necessarily renouncing his earlier still valid thinking. We read, indeed, in the "mysteries of Christ" (Ex. 311) that Jesus: "appeared *in soul* to the fathers in limbo," a thought that is in no way adulterated by various official texts of the Exercises.[72] Relying on this parallel text, we may understand Ignatius' thinking concerning the apparition of Jesus to his mother thus: the author of the Exercises after mentioning that the blessed and separated soul appeared to the fathers and also that it later appeared to them after he had assumed his body, concludes synthetically that Christ appeared in body and in soul to Mary, that is, he manifests not only his body as living, but also, as he did to the fathers in limbo, his blessed soul. The Lord shows his body to Mary's eyes and his soul to Mary's soul. What St. Ignatius seems to tell us is that there is no reason to think that Mary received from her Son a lesser knowledge than that given the fathers of limbo.[73] We have only to read over the text (Ex. 219, A, P2 and Puhl) to conclude that this interpretation seems more appropriate. It furthermore is not at all alien to the theology of his times.[74]

The Church, which does not demand[75] us to accept it, does not forbid us to adopt this interpretation of St. Ignatius' thought. When Mary with the eyes of her maternal flesh sees once again the living body she gave her eternal son, she also beholds with the eyes of her soul, in an intellectual vision, the immortal soul she did not give him for it was created directly[76] by this Son who assumed it. Further, at least with the eyes of faith, if not, as is probable, with the eyes of her soul momentarily enlightened by a transitory beatific vision,[77] she beholds the Divinity of the eternal Word, her Creator.

St. Theresa of Avila trembled with emotion when, in a vision, she beheld the beauty of Christ's *hand*. What then did the immaculate virgin feel before his whole glorified Body, and more so before his most holy soul, and if so, especially before the infinite majesty and sweetness of the Divinity?[78]

Jesus' mother could have told of her beholding the risen body of Jesus and have related what she heard in human words from his lips as did the apostles about the apparitions they had seen. However, this vision of the soul and, probably, of the Divinity of Jesus, for Mary exceeded all the bounds of human expression.[79] She might have said as St. Paul later on: "I must go on boasting, however useless it may be, and speak of·visions and revelations of the Lord. I know a man in Christ who . . . was snatched up to the third heaven . . . up to paradise to hear words which cannot be uttered, words which no man may speak" (2 Cor 12: 1–4). Mary, like Paul, could not express the most sublime, the most beautiful in the vision received by her of the risen Christ, things even more sublime than received by Paul. That is why she remained enveloped in total silence.

"Holy Virgin, blessed Mother,[80] I rejoice with you, with your immaculate soul which has ever known, even at the foot of the cross, at its peak, the superabundant joy gushing from the presence of the well-beloved, a joy felt with your heart of flesh on beholding the glorious Resurrection of your son and Savior.[81] Your ineffable joy is mine, I enter into it, I share in it. It is a gift from your son for us. Your joy intercedes for me. Help me to watch over, as do you, the infancy of the Church in souls, to bring about the birth of the Church in souls[82] by the evangelization of the mysteries of the infancy of your son, the eternal and incarnate Word, and of your role played in these mysteries. May I thus be able to come to contemplate and see face to face the splendor of your soul and of your glorified body in heaven where you reign forever over the Church and over the world. May the joy of your Assumption be thus ever mine. Queen of the world, immerse me in the eternal and infinite joy of your son."

D. The risen Christ, consoler of Mary and the Apostles.

In this contemplation of the appearance of the risen Jesus to Mary, St. Ignatius invites us to try to "consider with what promptitude and generosity the Lord has performed his function as consoler of his own, comparing it with the way in which friends are wont to console each other" (Ex. 224, V).[83]

The Ignatian Christ of the fourth week is the consoling Christ, the first paraclete who consoles us and fills us with joy on promising and on giving us the second, the Holy Spirit;[84] he gives Mary and his disciples the grace of being "inflamed with love of their Creator and Lord" to the point of "being unable to love any other creature on the face of the earth for its own sake, but only in the Creator of them all" . . . whence there comes "an interior joy that invites and attracts to what is heavenly and to the salvation of one's soul by filling it with peace and quiet in Christ our Lord" (Ex. 316).[85] This joy is then an effect of the pure love of the soul for Christ, who pours it into that soul (cf. Ex. 370). It is the joy of the unitive way (cf. Ex. 10).[86]

There are in our world so many desolate, troubled souls, souls inclined to lower and earthly things, souls disturbed in the face of temptations, agitated, defiant, without faith, without hope, without love, souls plunged in darkness, lazy, tepid and sad,[87] whom Christ wants to console through me as I ought to console him in them. If the power of the risen Christ has taken me over, is it not in order to strengthen those in whom he is ever, to the end of the world, in agony? If the risen Lord makes me, through Mary, share in his immense joy, it is not in order that it radiate through my smiles, my words, my pen?

It is above all by his eucharistic action in me that Christ wishes to console me, and, through me, others. This twofold divine and human action, this theandrical[88] action places in me perfect acts of virtues which are fruits of the Spirit. Is not my virtuous action the very reason for being of the mystery of the distinct and inseparable divine and human actions[89] which is the Incarnation of the Word of the Father, Spirator of the Spirit? In the Eucharist, the pure divine action continues to assume, to divinize, to transfigure permanently and indestructibly the human, intellectual and volitional action of the Redeemer in order that this human action "action" mine in some way integrated with his, in view of the consolation of others. The sacramental grace proper to the Eucharist is it not that of the increase of fraternal charity? How can I better dispose myself to imitate Christ the consoler if not in eating and drinking him so as to be able with him, in him, through him, to give joy to others? that is, to lead them to the Eucharist?

If it is true that in comparison with consolations given by Christ as paraclete, through and in the gift of the consoler Spirit, the fruit of each Communion, consolations which come from creatures are so weak and null, nonetheless we have the opportunity to aid others in various ways to find and accept such consolations which Christ and the Spirit as paracletes wish to offer them. Rather, Christ and the Spirit are, par excellence, consolers, are themselves the consolations[90] they wish to be given. In the Eucharistic Christ is contained every consolation, every joy, all the treasure of the Church,[91] of humanity, and of each human person. The peculiar fruit of the Eucharistic Communion is to inflame the communicant with love for the Eucharistic Heart of Jesus, the Creator and Lord, to the point that it can no longer love any other human heart save in him, to please him, to rest in him and rejoice in him (cf. Ex. 316). It is precisely really to console others that "Love has but one science, one language, one desire, one pleasure, to make known, loved and served Jesus Christ in the divine Eucharist" (St. Peter-Julian Eymard).

"Eucharistic Heart of Jesus, you give in yourself the joy you bid us feel.[92] You give it as a fruit of your Spirit. Through me console my friends that they may also be yours. Let my lips, gleaming with your precious Blood, radiate the views and the lights of faith, the desires of hope, the flames of charity for the consolation of your desolate members.

"In the hours of my trials and desolations grant me, I beg you again, Jesus, the grace to rejoice willingly in your divine and infinite joy present to the very core of my soul, in the joy of your soul triumphant over my sins, in the sensible joy of your Heart which I receive every day, for the healing of all my disordered sadness. Give me this perfect inner and external freedom, vis a vis the outer and inner world, a freedom which is a sign of emotional maturity and a factor of perseverance in your love. May a quarter of an hour[93] close to you, with you, in you, suffice to render me happy, not despite, but through the trials which are occasions for growth in detachment and charity and so of my joy. Transform my daily cross into an inexhaustible source of joy.

"Let there thus shine in me and through me the devouring fire of your joy, risen Jesus."

NOTES ON CHAPTER SIXTEEN

1. This second part of our chapter heading is taken from the very title of the Ignatian text: "The apparition of Christ our Lord to our Lady" (Ex. 218). The text of the Vulgate differs in several points from that of the Autograph. It clearly brings out that the fundamental subject matter of the first contemplation of the fourth week is, not so much the Resurrection as such, as the apparition of the risen Jesus to his Mother.

2. Here we combine the terms used in the Vulgate and in P2: "see" "dwell on."

3. We translate freely thus "*reliquam dispositionem.*"

4. While the Vulgate interprets the Autograph's (*camara, oratorio*) as distinctive, namely "*ut cellulam et oratorium.*" P2 makes them the same "*cellulam seu oratorium,*" Mary's oratory or chamber as consecrated virgin. The term "cell" is properly applied to religious only. Its usage by the translators of the Autograph is surely not accidental.

5. *Cf.* Ch. XV; and M. Giuliani, S.J., "Le mystère de Notre Dame dans les Exercices," *Christus* #2 (1954) p. 33: "Our Lady's chamber is a meeting place between God who gives himself and humanity which receives him."

6. The Vulgate speaks here of a "small house" "*domuncula.*"

7. *Cf.* Saint Ambrose, on Luke 2:26: "*sit in singulis Mariae anima ut magnificet Dominum; sit in singulis spiritus Mariae ut exultet in Deo.*" (ML, 15, 1642; quoted by Paul VI in his great Mariogical discourse before the Council, November 21, 1964: AAS, 56, 1964, 1016,1017.)

8. Observe here the difference between the Autograph and the Vulgate: the former centers our joy, not only in the joy but also in the glory of the risen Christ, while the latter, while asking also for a share in the joy of the Virgin Mary not yet glorified by her Assumption, only mentions Christ's glory.

9. *Cf.* Pius XII: *Fulgens Corona,* DS, 3909; AAS, 45 (1953) 581; St. Pius X, *Ad diem illum, Actes de Saint Pie X,* Bonne Presse, Paris, vol. I, p. 86: "If the Virgin has been freed from original sin, it is because she was to be the Mother of Christ; now, she was the Mother of Christ in order that our souls may live again in the hope of eternal goods;" LG 54, 61; Pius XII, *Ad coeli Reginam,* AAS, 40 (1954) 635.

10. In St. Paul, glorification means joy (for instance, Rom 5:2; *cf.* Ps 31:11; 149:5). *Cf.* J. M. Bover, S.J., *Teologia de San Pablo,* Madrid, 1961, p. 91.

11. The divine perfections, such as beatitude, are identical with God's infinitely simple essence, while Christ's acts in his human nature are distinct from the essence and faculties (intellectual and volitional) of this nature. These acts are accidents which flow from the essence.

12. *Cf.* CFW, 412-413.

13. It is known that classical theology distinguishes essential beatitude (which comes to the human person from the possession of its Creator), from accidental beatitude (which results from the possession of a created good). This clear distinction is unfortunately too often forgotten today.

14. *Cf.*Lk 15:7; ". . . there will likewise be more joy in heaven over one repentant sinner than over ninety-nine righteous people who have no need to repent." The parallel text in Lk 15:10 shows that "heaven" means angels. If converted sinners cause the accidental joy of the angels, why not that of Christ? *Cf.* B. de Margerie, S.J., *The Heart of the Lamb of God,* Rome, 1972, #72 and note 128; Pius XI, *Miserentissimus Redemptor,* AAS, 20 (1928) 173; A. Koller, *Reparation to the S. Heart,* Hales Corner, 1971, pp. 124-126.

15. *Cf.* Col 1;24.

16. *Cf.* Pius XII, *Haurietis Aquas,* AAS, 48 (1956) 327,328, DS, 3924.

17. Here there is an interesting difference between the Autograph on the one hand, the Vulgate and P2 on the other. The Autograph reads: "The blessed soul of Christ descended into hell." The other texts replace the Spanish singular by the Latin plural, while the adjective "blessed" is omitted: *"descendit ad inferos."* The adjective"blessed" doubtless means that Christ's soul, after death, was freed from all suffering, especially in the lower areas of the psyche.

18. We are quite aware that many of our contemporaries, who find that the virgin birth and Chrit's Resurrection are myths, will find some difficulties, if not very great ones, in the face of the mystery of the descent of the soul of Jesus into the lower regions. None the less here there is a dogma of Christian faith, one professed by the Symbols of the Church (for instance, *cf.* DS 852) and proclaimed by her liturgical prayer. Nor should it be forgotten that this point has been abundantly illustrated by modern studies (shown by articles which contemporary dictionaries of theology devote to it). Above all, however, we are not addressing here an apologetic to unbelievers but rather a "retreat" to believers.

19. An allusion to the patriarchs of the old Testament, ancestors of Christ the Savior.

20. This term has here the same sense as "lower regions" as distinct from "hell." There is not a question here of what today we call purgatory, but rather of a state of waiting, *without* sufferings, of the justs deprived of the beatific vision before Christ's descent. *cf.* ST, III.52.2. Besides it might be said that St. Ignatius had read Question 52 of the Third Part of the *Summa* before he composed this contemplation.

21. Their complete liberation was inseparable from access to the beatific vision. *Cf.* ST, III.52.5. Our text quotes Ex. 311 thus: "He appeared also in soul to the fathers in limbo and after he had taken them from there and *assumed his body again."* The meaning is here the same in the Autograph, the Vulgate and in P2. The expression is not too fortunate. It might seem to suggest that (in the eyes of St. Ignatius) the Word would have abandoned his body at the moment of his death, which St. Ignatius explicitly denies in Ex. 219: "His body remained separated from the soul, but always united with the divinity." *Cf.* CFW, 268. There we have stressed that the death of the Lord was not (contrary to what certain Christians imagine perhaps) a separation between his humanity and his divinity, but one between his body and his soul, within his humanity. So Ex. 311 must be understood in the light of Ex. 219.

22. DS, 3812; CFW, 229-233; 159.

23. *Cf.* CFW, 266: the soul separated from the body is no longer a human person, a man, although it is ever endowed with an "ego."

24. The "lower regions" translate the Biblical "*sheol.*" *Cf.* Numbers 16:33.

25. *Cf.* for instance, Gn 47:30.

26. We employ the expression "an inferior condition" on account of the dehumnaniza-tion which results from the separation of soul and body.

27. The Dutch Catechism has seen this quite clearly. However it must be admitted that, by keeping silent about the fact that the mystery of the descent into the lower regions is a mystery of salvation for the just alone, the Dutch Catechism might well give the errone-ous impression that Jesus on descending into the lower regions communicated salvation to all the dead without exception, a thesis many times condemned by the Church; *cf.* DS, 587, 1011,1077. Though the exact meaning of these texts may perhaps not be easy to dis-cern they indicate a direction.

28. *Cf.* CFW, Ch. II, The Lord Jesus, salvation of pre-Christians.

29. As a matter of fact, there is no public revelation, including propositions, in the case of "ancient testaments outside of Israel."

30. In his Father, Jesus already saw his carnal ancestors, under the title of secondary object of his beatific vision, and also knew them, as man, by his infused knowledge. Fur-ther, of course, he saw them as God, with an infinite and eternal knowledge. *Cf.* Jn 2:25; note 22.

31. Indirectly it is the devil who held them captive through the as yet unremmitted orig-inal sin, the precise reason for their inability to enter into the beatific vision. *Cf.* ST, III.52.2.2,4;52.5. The blessed soul of Jesus Christ was, in the lower regions, liberating and sanctifying.

32. For us, today, one of the fruits of the contemplation of this mystery of the descent of Jesus among the dead, "to the lower regions," is to make penetrate the light of the divine Word as well as the light of that which participates in it, human reason, into the inferior zones of our psyche (imagination, feelings) submitting them fully to the superior zone (of intellect and will), in a word, to help us "overcome ourselves" by "making our sensual nature obey reason, and to bring all of our lower faculties into greater subjection to the higher" (Ex. 87).

33. *Cf.* Mgr. d'Hulst, on the fire of purgatory: "Fire of jealous love. Love avenges itself as befits love. Its vengeance destroys, not the object loved which has been unfaithful, but its very infidelity and thereby, punishing it, purifies it and makes it worthy of love" (Let-tres de Direction, Lettre 107; *cf.* DTC, XIII, 1, 1936, 1322–24, art. "Purgatoire"). It is known that the existence of fire in purgatory, though not defined by the Church, and dis-cussed in Florence with the Orthodox, is however traditional teaching of Catholic theology, maintained and mentioned by Paul VI in his Profession of faith of June 30, 1968: AAS, 60 (1968) 444, #28.

34. St. Francis Borgia *Tratados espirituales, Tratado tercero, Collirio espiritual,* Barcelona, 1964, p. 84: "Perhaps some souls are in purgatory on account of your bad example, be-cause you have been a cause of scandal for them; others, because you did not want to help them overcome their sins; and finally many due to your negligence or lack of charity, as a result of your failure to help them by prayers and suffrages. Be ashamed now of all you have done to send souls to purgatory and of the little you have done to liberate them. In this way you will regard your faults (for which you do not know whether you deserve to pay in purgatory) as greater than theirs."

35. *Cf.* Bourdaloue, Sermon pour l'ouverture du Jubilé, *Oeuvres complètes,* Paris, 1857, vol. III, p. 612. The entire sermon should be read.

36. *Cf.* I Jn 3:16, "We too must lay down our lives for our brothers."

37. St. Ignatius of Loyola, Letter to the Townspeople of Azpeitia, August-September 1540, Letter 26, pp. 42-45 (Transl. William J. Young, S.J.). It must be admitted, however, that this letter does not treat of indulgences in general, but of a number of indulgences promulgated by a pontifical bull. Yet the praise given them by St. Ignatius presupposes the same high regard of indulgences in general. St. Ignatius is then the first to observe what he recommends in Ex. 358 and 42.

38. *Cf.* LG, 50: "The pilgrim Church from the very first ages of the Christian religion, has cultivated with great piety the memory of the dead. Because it is "a holy and wholesome thought to pray for the dead that they may be loosed from sins" (2 Mc 12:46), she has also offered prayers for them."

39. In the recent *Enchiridion indulgentiarum* published in 1968 by the Holy See there is an application of the Apostolic Constitution *Indulgentiarum Doctrina.* There every prayer, alms, or work of penance receives a partial indulgence.

40. A thought often expressed by St. Theresa of Avila: our present life is but death in comparison with life eternal.

41. On this distinction, *cf.* the Apostolic Constitution of Paul VI *Indulgentiarum Doctrina,* and related norms, AAS, 59 (1967) 21.

42. *Ibid.,* p. 19: "As by means of indulgences, the members of the Church in a condition of purification (*Ecclesiae purgantis*) are the sooner integrated into the heavenly Church, indulgences intensively and rapidly advance the Kingdom of Christ."

43. In fact, the indulgence is "the remission of the temporal punishment due to sins already forgiven as to guilt" (Paul VI, *op. cit.* AAS, 59, 1967, 21). It illustrates the Catholic doctrine on the communion of saints, purgatory, the necessity of satisfaction, God's justice and mercy, the power of the Church in view of salvation. Luther himself, when he was still a Catholic, but already finding difficulty with the Church precisely on the question of indulgences, did not fail to grasp their spiritual usefulness, as the following excerpt from his short "treatise on indulgences" not too well-known, shows: "The granting and gaining of indulgences is a useful practice, despite the commerce and avarice which, we fear, they imply. Perhaps God wishes today to show a greater mercy toward the dead, since he sees them so forgotten by the living." Luther added at once another reason: "More souls are going to purgatory than before, because present-day Christians are lazier than those of former times. Many go there on this account, but few do anything for them since those still living are just as lazy as the dead. So at least in this way (by incouraging them to gain indulgences) the pope comes to their aid." This Latin treatise of 1517 has been translated into English and published by J. Wicks, S.J., "Martin Luther's Treatise on Indulgences," *Theological Studies* 28 (1967) 481–518. We have quoted an excerpt from #7 of the treatise (*ibid.* p. 516).

44. Ex. 219, V: "*rediens ad sepulchrum, corpus cum anima denuo univit.*"

45. We combine the two texts, the Autograph and P2. The Autograph does not state by whom "*resuscitado,*" the P2 text has "*suscitans seipsum.*"

46. Acts 2:24, "God raised Him up again"; Rom 8:11, "If the Spirit of him who raised Jesus from the dead dwells in you, then he who raised Christ from the dead will bring your mortal bodies to life also through his Spirit dwelling in you."

47. If indeed Jesus not only was raised but also rose, (perhaps) we see better that the Resurrection is not only an act of the Father, but also of the Word, the act common to the three Persons who indivisibly possess the one and the same divinity or divine nature.

It is this divinity common to the three which is manifested in the Resurrection.

48.Observe that the Vulgate seems to identify as miracles what the Autograph calls the "most holy effects of the most holy Resurrection" purely and simply.

49. As is known, Catholic theology attributes particularly to one of the Divine Persons a common perfection which has a particular affinity with the personal property of this Person in the bosom of the Trinity. So there is attributed to the third Person, who proceeds through love, what depends on divine goodness and makes it stand out, such as sanctification. Now, the Resurrection is ordered to the sanctification and salvation of mankind, to man's return in love to his last end. *Cf.* on this, ST, I.39.7; Leo XIII, *Divinum Illud Munus,* AAS, 29 (1896,1897) 646ff.; DS, 3326.

50. On the meaning of this text, *cf.* J. M. Bover, S.J., *Teologia de San Pablo,* Madrid, 1961, pp. 369–79.

51. Baptism is ordered to the Eucharist and constitutes an aspiring toward it. *cf.* ST, III.73.3; 65.3.

52. CFW, 238: The Resurrection is not the first of a long series of reincarnations.

53. Jn 12:32, "And I—once I am lifted up from earth—will draw all men to myself. "The elevation in question is at the same time the crucifixion and the Resurrection. The following verse, 33 confirms this: "This statement indicated the sort of death he had to die." The death of Jesus on the cross is, then, in his own eyes, an exaltation, a glorification. As a consequence, it is a triumph: "Take courage! I have overcome the world" (16:33). So it is therefore a source and an occasion of joy for Christ and for his disciples: "That my joy may be yours and your joy may be complete" (15:11; *cf.* 17:13).

54. St. Cyril of Jerusalem, *Catechese* 13, MG 33, 772: "*kaukema de ton kaukematon o stauros.*"

55. Note here a difference between the Autograph and the Vulgate. The Vulgate says purely and simply that the divinity hid itself during the passion and death of Christ. The Autograph adds a nuance: "The divinity seemed to hide itself during the passion." The meaning is actually the same in both. The Vulgate implies that the divinity was hidden in respect to the eyes of the flesh and of reason rejecting its own light. It does not at all say that the divinity hid to the eyes of Mary's faith, for instance, at the time of the crucifixion.

56. St. John Chrysostom, commenting: "*Pater, si possibile est . . .*"

57. *Cf.,* for instance I Pt 4:13,14; "Rejoice instead, in the measure that you share Christ's sufferings. When his glory is revealed, you will rejoice exultantly . . . for then God's Spirit in its glory has come to rest on you." An even better confirmation of our statement is to be found in the texts quoted in Note 53.

58. Here, in Ex. 221, the word glory does not mean, as it usually does with St. Ignatius and elsewhere in the Exercises, for instance Ex. 179, praise of God but rather the irradiation of divine perfection (*cf.* Autobiography, #29), the inner splendor of God which is manifested to the world: "The act of creation is but the overflow of the Father's glory" (*ibid*), writes Courel (DSAM, 6, 1967, 490-92: art. on "the greater glory of God)" Here in Ex. 221 we can also appropriate Courel's excellent comment apropos of the Father's glory in the Kingdom (Ex. 95): "(Glory) is the movement itself of the Word who passes through creation to transfigure it and make it rise up to God." (*Christus* 3, 1956, p. 335: "*la gloire plus grande de Dieu*"): the glory of the risen Christ means that he makes known to the world his divine perfection. It is the same as the Father's glory into which he enters (Ex. 95), that is, in which his holy humanity totally immerses itself. *Cf.* St.

Ambrose: *"tunc secundum carnem homo, nunc per omnia Deus"* (PL, 16, 1341). As we do somewhat later on, we can attribute this perfection which is common to the three Persons, particularly to the Person of the Holy Spirit (*cf.* Note 49).

59. *Cf.* Ex. 316: Consolation is when "an interior movement is aroused in the soul, by which it is inflamed with love of its Creator and Lord, and as a consequence, can love no creature on the face of the earth for its own sake, but only in the Creator of them all." On the other hand, in desolation (Ex. 317) "the soul is separated, as it were, from its Creator and Lord."

60. The resuscitating action of the Word, through his human soul, on his corpse signifies and implies the instrumental action of the human free will of Christ's soul. It may be said, it is a twofold will, divine and human, of the Word who works the mystery of his bodily Resurrection. At the same time we may think that the human soul of each one of us, with its free will, will serve as an instrument for the twofold will of the risen Christ to bring about our resurrection on the last day.

61. Finally, the risen Christ's Body is the perfectly translucent instrument of his created soul and of his uncreated Spirit. It is no longer subject to space and time but on the contrary masters them. It is therefore perfectly "humanized" while at the same time it is "divinized." *Cf.* the text of St. Ambrose quoted in Note 58.

62. In the glorious resurrection, the human person sees its body humanized and its soul divinized (by the beatific vision).

63. Ex. 219: The Vulgate has translated by *"vivus"* the expression *"en cuerpo y anima"* of the Autograph. We will have to come back to this point. Note the expression "his blessed mother." It seems to suggest Mary's right to see Christ risen, a right acquired by her unique and decisive contribution to the redemptive Incarnation. She who is "blessed among all women" has the right to receive the first blessing of her son.

64. Many modern Catholic as well as Protestant exegetes (for instance Zahn and Albertz) agree with this Ignatian reaction. Here is what Lagrange has to say: "The piety of the children of the Church holds as certain that the risen Christ appeared first of all to his most holy Mother. She nursed him, guided his infancy, as it were, introduced him to the world at the marriage feast of Cana, and stayed in the background until she stood at the foot of the cross. Yet Jesus consecrated to her alone with Joseph thirty years of his hidden life. How could it be that she would not have for herself alone the first instant of his life hidden in God? The promulgation of the gospel is not involved here. Mary belongs to a transcendent order in which she is associated as Mother with the Paternity of the Father in regard to Jesus" (*L'Evangile de Jesus-Christ,* Paris, 1930, p. 586). We shall introduce here a nuance. The apparition of the risen Jesus to Mary was not concerned with the Lord's public life, the death and Resurrection of the Lord, but it is not excluded (*cf.* Note 60) that it may have had as its object the spreading of the gospel of the infancy. We might well expand the reason given by Lagrange to justify the silence of the Gospels about this apparation by stressing with Roschini that the witnesses to the Resurrection presented to us by the evangelists started out by doubting as obviously was not Mary's case, yet this doubt increased their credibility. Furthermore, a mother's testimony would have been suspect in the eyes of many just as was that of the holy women in the eyes of the apostles. (G. Roschini, O.S.M., *La vita de Maria,* Rome, 1947, p. 343). Roschini deepens the whole question of the apparition of the risen Jesus to his Mother.

65. We may also see in St. Ignatius' words: "For Scripture supposes that we have understanding" (Ex. 299), a reference to Lk 24:25 (*cf.* Ex. 303,2) and the answer Jesus gives there to "the disciples of Emmaus": "What little sense you have! How slow you are to believe all that the prophets have announced! Did not the Messiah have to undergo all

this so as to enter into his glory?" In the New Testament a lack of understanding is equivalent to a want of faith (cf. Mt 16:8) It may also be said that in St. Ignatius' eyes the denial of an apparition of Jesus to Mary is the same as a lack of faith in the Savior's love for his Mother, in his predilection and gratitude in her regard.

66. Cf. LG 61: "singulariter prae aliis generosa socia."

67. Cf. Lk 7:15, "The dead man sat up and began to speak. Then *Jesus gave him back to his mother*," who was a widow and the mother of this one and only son. Mary's situation was the same. It is true that Jesus did not rise to die again as was the case with the widow of Naim's son, and that explains precisely, in part, why this first aparition was not prolonged by living on with Mary. (He had already renounced this common life upon entering on his public life). But the earlier instance of Naim strengthens the moral certitude we have of the apparition of the risen Jesus to his Mother, which reflects his farewell to his Mother before beginning his public life (cf. Ex. 273).

68. The oldest testimony is not that of the poet Sedulius in the fifth century, (*Carmen pascale*, 1.V, ML 19, 743) as Roschini (*op. cit.*) and U. Holzmeister, S.J. believe ("Num Christus post resurrectionem benedictae Matri apparuit," *Verbum Dei*, 22, 1942, 97–102). Or more exactly, though this is not quite certain, this testimony by Sedulius might be the oldest about an apparition of the risen Jesus to his Mother *alone*.

At any rate, the apocryphal gospel of Bartholomew, which goes back to the fourth century, at least, mentions this apparition of the risen Jesus to His Mother, as does St. John Chrysostom.

Furthermore, we quote the moving texts of the apocryphal gospel. In a narrative modelled on the apparition of Jesus to Mary Magdalene, Jesus replies to his Mother's declaration of faith by this salutation: "Hail, to you who have borne the life of the whole world! Hail, my Mother! My arch-saint! . . . Hail, my robe of glory with which I have garbed myself on coming into the world! Hail, you who bore the life of the whole world in your womb! All paradise rejoices because of you. I tell you, Mary, my Mother, he who loves you, loves life" (Quoted by E. Cothenet, "Marie dans les Apocrypes, *Maria*, Paris, 1961, vol. VI, p. 109).

Another fragment from the same gospel, first entitled "The Gospel of the Twelve Apostles," then recognized as identical with that of St. Bartholomew, shows a clear awareness, in the ecclesial community in which this apocryphal gospel flourished, of the connection between this apparition and the mystery of the Passion (and not only of the Incarnation).

"Know this, my Mother. This flesh is that which I received in you. It is the flesh which reposed in my tomb, the flesh that has risen today and which stands before you. Fix your gaze on my hands and my feet, oh Mary, my Mother! Know that it is I whom you nourished. Doubt not that I am your son. It is I who left you in John's hands at the moment I mounted the cross. Now, then, oh my Mother, hasten to let my brethren know and tell them . . . (*Patrologia Orientalis*, 1903, vol. II, p. 170).

St. John Chrysostom, for his part, perhaps influenced by an apostolic tradition which would be, according to Loisy (*Le quatrième évangile*, Paris, 1903, p. 908, n.1), due to an extraordinary exegesis of Tatian, believed that the Virgin Mary was the other Mary, (cf. Mt 27:6 and 28:1ff.) mentioned, who enjoyed with Magdalene the first apparition of the risen Christ (Homelie 88 on Mat.: MG 58, 777). As C. Gianelli rightly says (*Revue des Etudes byzantines, Mélanges Martin Jugie*, Paris, II, 1953, p. 108, in an article entitled: "Temoignages patristiques grecs en faveur d'une apparition du Christ ressuscité à la Vierge Marie"): "This erroneous exegesis presupposes correctly the belief in a meeting between the risen Christ and the Virgin and must have contributed not little to spread that belief." "Their exegesis has been determined by a pre-existing belief" (*ibid.* p. 109).

It is not at all excluded that the narratives of the apocryphal gospel of Bartholomew are based on this pre-existing belief and in fact it seems quite probable. At any rate, it seems clear that it is through this evangelical source, by way of Ludolph the Carthusian, that this belief reached St. Ignatius. For Ludolph, in his famous *Vita Christi* wrote: "The Gospel says nothing about this apparition, but it is piously to be believed since it is found frequently in a legend about the Lord's Resurrection. It was, indeed, most appropriate that he visit his mother before anyone else, since she had loved him more than others . . . had suffered more on his death than others, and, more stricken by sorrow, had more ardently awaited his Resurrection." (*Vita Christi,* Lyon, 1522, vol. II, Ch. 70, fol. 372; *cf.* H. Pinard de la Boullaye, S.J., Aux sources des Exercices spirituels, RAM 1950, 344 where is found the Latin original of the text.)

The same belief reached St. Ignatius also by way of Blessed Jacques de Voragine and his Golden Legend, Ch. 54. The Dominican Mariologist (*cf.* Lorenzin, O.F.M., *Mariologia Jacobi a Voragin, O.P.,* Rome, 1951) observes that, in his Golden Legend, Voragine writes: "If we do not believe in this apparition because no evangelist mentions it, we must perforce conclude that after his Resurrection Jesus never appeared to his Mother, because no evangelist tells us where or when. But we may not accept that such a son disrespected such a mother by such negligence." And he adds quite justly: "The evangelists did not mention this apparition perhaps because it was their function to present only the witnesses of the Resurrection, and it was not appropriate to present a mother's testimony on behalf of her son. If the holy women's testimony seemed delirious, what might have been said of that of Mary?" Voragine, however, differing from Ludolph, makes no mention of the apocryphal gospels.

So then the belief in the Church in a first apparition of the risen Jesus to his Mother is not based on the testimony of the apocryphas. On the contrary, this testimony is explained by this pre-existing (and even immemorial) belief. Suárez was right in saying: "Without any doubt, we are to believe that Christ, after His Resurrection, appeared first of all to his mother. This doctrine is so worthy of belief that it has been accepted almost without controversy by all the doctors and the faithful. Therefore it has been proclaimed by all Catholic writers who have treated of this question. It seems then that such has been the perpetual thinking of the Church (*perpetuus Ecclesiae sensus*) for we find no initial point in time when it began to be taught in the Church. And although the ancient fathers do not speak of it often, this is not because they might have thought the contrary (they have never denied it) but because they only related what had been written by the evangelists" (*Opera omnia,* Vives, Paris, 1873, vol. 19, Disput. 49, sect. I, p. 876).

So it is not surprising that Pius XI spoke of this pious belief in 1876 (*Les enseignements pontificaux, Notre-Dame,* Tournai 1957, #72 and 76).

69. Numerous modern exegetes agree with R. Laurentin that "Mary is directly or indirectly the primary source of the account (in Lk 1–2). This derives especially from the character of the scene of the Annuntiation of which she was the sole witness and from the explicit mention of her recollections (*cf.* Lk 2:19, 51). (*Structure et Théologie de Luc. I-II,* Paris, 1957, p. 190. See also on this subject, in the same work pp. 97–99.) Already St. Robert Bellarmine has written in a sermon of August 15, 1604 a propos of Mary's life after the Ascension: "She was ever engaged in prayer and in teaching. She taught, instructed, consoled the faithful. That is why she was left on earth though otherwise worthy to ascend into heaven with her son. We might say she was the nurse of the Church (*nutrix Ecclesiae*) which Christ had engendered on the cross. She taught St. Luke the mysteries of the Annuntiation, the Nativity, the Circumcision and the Purification." See St. Robert Bellarmine, *Opera oratoria posthuma,* Rome, Greg., 1943, vol. II, p. 99; and B. de Margerie, S.J., "La mariologie existentielle de Saint Robert Bellarmin," *Marianum* 26 (1964) 344–89, esp. p. 367. It is in this context we think we can conjecture the object of the post-paschal conversation between the risen Savior and his Mother: the function she would perform in the young Church, her daughter. We do not know whether other

authors have already developed this view when treating of the apparition affirmed by St. Ignatius.

70. *Cf.* Rom 1:3,4.

71. Observe, however, that the translation of the Vulgate, if it does not affirm it, does not exclude in any way the intellectual vision of Christ's glorified soul by Mary's soul.

72. Here we quote the Vulgate (Ex. 311): "*Apparuit etiam patribus in limbo, quoad animam.*" P2 says: "*in anima.*"

73. We imagine the reader's surprise at our interpretation which, to out knowledge, has never been proposed before. Let us reflect, however, on many incontrovertible facts: the whole series of thirteen "apparations" of the risen Jesus proposed by the author of the Exercises (Ex. 299-311) was a consequence of his own intellectual and imaginative visions of Christ described in his autobiography (#29). Later, after the final composition of the Exercises, St. Ignatius speaks quite precisely, in his spiritual diary, of the trinitarian mystery and of his visions involving it. If, for him, the Divine Persons are distinct and perceived as such, why would it not be admitted also that he does not confuse the risen Christ's body and soul when he clearly distinguishes them, just as he does not confuse them when he describes their separation in death, immediately before his presentation of Christ's apparition "in body and soul" to Mary? He was in no way obliged to use this astonishing and extraordinary expression: "*apparuit benedictae Matri suae in corpore et anima*" (P2, Ex. 219). It must further be noted that logically, perhaps, the expression suggests a transitory beatific vision of the divine nature and of the divine person of the risen Christ given to Mary, if we reflect that the souls in limbo were admitted into the beatific vision of Christ's divinity as soon as they saw his blessed soul (*cf.* ST, III, 52, 4,1: "*in ipso inferno eos luce gloriae illustrando;;*). *Cf.* note 77.

74. We note that St. Thomas of Villanova, with whom St. Ignatius corresponded, also preached to the faithful about the apparition of the risen Christ to his Mother. Many theologians, it should be particualrly observed, admitted already a transitory beatific vision to Mary. Long before Trent, they thought that Mary as much as and even more than Moses and Paul had been elevated to a sublime contemplation of God (*cf.* 2 Cor 12:1-6), that is, to the beatific vision at certain times, though they did not use the term. (After Trent, the thesis of the beatific vision prevailed.)

We note, before Trent, the names of Gerson and St. Bernardine of Sienna, among others who lived before St. Ignatius (*cf.* Roschini, *Mariologie,* vol. II, Pt. II, Rome, 1948, pp. 184-87). In fact they are the same authors who admitted the beatific vision of the risen Jesus given to Mary and his apparition in the flesh to his Mother after his Resurrection. Roschini, without referring (at this moment), to the Ignatian text, admits both together, not failing to mention the vision of Jesus' soul to Mary: "It may reasonably be believed that at this moment the risen Jesus made himself seen by his blessed Mother not only as to his body and soul but also to his Divinity" (*Vita de Maria,* p. 342). See also St. Bonaventure, *Collatis 6 de Donis Sp. Sancti,* 324.

75. However, in the eyes of many theologians, the denial of this (physical) apparition of the risen Jesus to his Mother would not fail to be rash. The apparition is supported by legitimate reasoning based on propriety, the famous "*potuit, decuit, fecit*" which the magisterium adopted a propos of the Immaculate Conception (DS 3908). It also corresponds with today's prevalent feeling of the faithful which is, following the happy expression of K. Adam, "Christ's breathing" (see Roschini, *La vita di Maria,* p. 338). To be sure, we would not say the same of the opinion concerning either the apparition of the risen Christ's soul to Mary, or her beatific vision of her son's Divinity after his Resurrection. Both of these opinions were not widely diffused among Christian folk, at least explicitly.

For it is not certain that the former opinion restricts Mary's vision to the physical aspect. Let us say a word also about a related subject: It may be perfectly accepted that Mary, after Jesus' Resurrection, saw as many others did (why would she here too be an exception?) the numerous risen bodies of dead saints who "came forth from their tombs and entered the holy city and appeared to many" (Mt 27:52,53). The text expressly stresses that this occurred after the resurrection of Jesus. There is involved here a certain number of fathers delivered from limbo by Jesus. It may be held they appeared to Mary with Jesus, and that among them was St. Joseph. Were they not all spiritual children of Mary? Their anticipated resurrection, due to her merits, was it not for Mary an immense joy? (On Mt 27:52,53, Benoit, O.P., *Passion et Résurrection du Seigneur*, Paris, 1966, pp. 230–32, may be consulted.)

76. Catholic faith teaches us that human souls are directly created by God (DS 3896). In this sense, the apparition of the risen Jesus' soul to Mary strengthened her humility, for she saw more clearly that her son owed it to her only indirectly.

77. *Cf.* Notes 74 and 75. Cardinal Lepicier finds even that the gospel implicitly confirms such a beatific vision for Mary, at this moment, setting her in an order apart (she does not go to the tomb, and no one is charged with bringing her the news: see A.M. Lepicier, O.S.M., *Tractatus de Beatissima Virgine Maria*, Paris, 1912, pp. 310,311). He quotes in support of his view a general principle of mariology accepted by St. Thomas Aquinas: "It is reasonable to believe that she who engendered the only Son of the Father, full of grace and truth, received, more than anyone else, the greatest privileges of grace" (ST, III.27.1). Suarez has expressed more succinctly the same general mariological principle: "It is impossible to measure the Virgin's privileges following ordinary law" (*De Mysteriis Vitae Christi*, d, 3, 5, 31). The magisterium of the Church adopted this principle on the occasion of the definition of the Assumption: "*Doctor Eximius, cum hanc de mariologia profiteretur normam, nempe 'mysteria gratiae, quae Deus in Virgine operatus est, non esse ordinariis legibus metienda sed divina omnipotentia, supposita rei decentia absque ulla Scripturarum contradictione aut repugnantia,' concludere poterat mysterium Assumptionis credendum esse universae Ecclesiae communi fretus fide*" (Pius XII, *Munificentissimus Deus*, AAS 42, 1950, 767). J. de Aldama, S.J. may be consulted on this subject, "Piété et système dans la mariologie du Doctor Eximius," *Maria*, vol. II, 1952, pp. 983,984. Suarez, basing his opinion on these principles, admitted also the thesis of a possible beatific vision of the risen Jesus by Mary. Lepicier (*loc. cit*) gives us the following reason for this: Apart from her greatest consolation (had she not suffered more than anyone else, after Jesus?) such a vision enabled her more fully and more efficaciously to intercede for mankind. As Roschini emphasizes (*Mariologia,*), this vision excluded momentarily in Mary the act and not the virtue of faith, the infused habit of faith which remained with her. Does not Scripture present her as an eminent believer? Vatican II, upon rightly exalting Mary's faith six times (LG 53, 56, 58, 61, 63, 65; and especially 58: "*B. Virgo in peregrinatione fidei processit*"), in no way intends to exclude this disputed thesis. (*Cf.* LG 54: "The Synod does not, however, have it in mind to give a complete doctrine on Mary, nor does it wish to decide those questions which have not yet been fully illuminated by the work of theologians.") *Cf.* ST, II,II, 175,3.

At any rate, all Catholic theologians agree in stressing that Mary has singularly and uniquely cooperated to our Redemption by her faith (LG 61) thereby becoming our mother in the order of grace. The merit of this unique faith has been clearly brought out by Laurentin (*Court traite de théologie mariale*, Paris, 1953, pp. 71,72). It might be said, in the context of the Exercise, that the risen Christ consoles Mary appearing to her to increase her faith (cf. Ex. 316), faith in the Divinity of her son whom she does not see habitually, faith in her own Divine Maternity, consequently, and also in her redemption by the Blood of her Savior. It is in this context that he manifests himself intimately to his Mother as dwelling within her (*cf.* Jn 14:21-23); *cf.* verses 19,20. It is thus that he increases in her the desire for the vision and the consummation of her own salvation (*cf.* Ex. 316). Whence Mary's immense joy which we should share: the joy of her sublime redemption, since she is redeemed perfectly in order to be our co-redemptrix. Does not Scripture itself testify (Lk 1,48, "All ages to come shall call me blessed.") to Mary's privileged knowledge in the bosom of her faith (Lk 1,45), presenting her as a prophetess?

78. *cf.* Ex. 124 A: "This is to smell the infinite fragrance, and taste the sweetness of the Divinity. Likewise to apply these senses to the soul and its virtues, and to all according to the person we are contemplating, and to draw fruit from this." There is question right here of the Incarnate Word. It is well to note that, in this application of the senses, the author of the Exercises distinguishes clearly the Divinity and the human soul of Christ.

79. This is what St. Bernardine of Sienna emphasized. For him there was involved an apparition of a superior, more sublime order, unable to be expressed in human words, an apparition therefore which could not be confused with others. (*Cf.* Roschini, *Vita di Maria,* p. 342.)

80. This beautiful expression is used only twice by St. Ignatius: here a propos of the vision of the risen Christ (Ex. 219) and Christ's farewell to his Mother before beginning his public life (Ex. 273). Is this only by chance? We do not think so. There is rather here an effort to bring out that the Son is now in some way returned to his Mother, or better gives himself back, in a new way, to her to whom he has never ceased giving himself spiritually (*cf.* Lk 7:15; *cf.* note 67). The expression "blessed Mother" (to which we have already referred, note 63) is perhaps an allusion to the first-gospel or protoevangelium and to Lk 1:42. Mary has perfectly escaped the divine malediction and original sin (as St. Ignatius personally believed: *cf.* "Fontes Narrativi," I, MHSJ vol. 73, Rome, 1951, p. 491). She was blessed to the extent of being: "an almost infinite treasure of the charisms of the divine Spirit, the seat of all divine graces, an inexhaustible abyss of the gifts of the Spirit," as Pius IX wrote in the Bull *Ineffabilis Deus,* defining the doctrine of the immaculate conception, and commenting therein in the light of tradition on Lk 1:28, and 1:42 (*cf. Enseignements Pontificaux, Notre-Dame,* Tournai, 1957, #49).

81. It is permissible to think that, on seeing her risen son, Mary kissed and adored her Savior and the Redeemer's glorious wounds, thanking him for having redeemed her and for having so intimately associated her with his redemptive work. Such a vision must have been followed by a *Magnificat* of the pre-redeemed co-redemptrix. Just as Jesus must have thanked Mary for having given him this now glorified flesh which permitted him to save the world.

82. Original expression by Romano Guardini.

83. The text of the Vulgate (*"prompto copiosoque . . . consolandi suos officio"*) is assuredly more eloquent here than that of the Autograph which does not have these indications of promptitude and abundance in consolation, nor the suggestion of best friend (*"ab amicissimo"*).

84. *Cf.* 1 Jn 2:1; Jn 14:26.

85. That is why St. Ignatius forged (Ex. 229, a propos of the seventh Additional Direction) the following admirable expression: "rejoice in our Creator and Redeemer," even better translated by the Vulgate and P2: "*Creatori et Redemptori congaudere, ad congaudendum suo Creatori et Redemptori.*" Such an expression implicitly contains an entire plan of life opposed to a negative pessimism.

86. *Cf.* Ex. 10: This Introductory Observation, stating that the first week corresponds to the purgative way, and the second to the illuminative, suggests that the third and fourth

weeks correspond to the unitive way. Further, as St. Thomas Aquinas has splendidly and profoundly stated, joy is an effect of charity, one provoked at the same time by the well beloved's presence and by the fact he himself is immutably happy (cf. ST, II.II.28.1).

87. Cf. Ex. 317. There can be no better description of the effects of atheism.

88. On the exact meaning of this word, see DTC, XV. 1 (1950) 205-16, art, by A. Michel on the theandrical operations of Christ, and DS, 268. "Theandrical operations" mean for the Catholic Church, the two operations, divine and human, of Christ, in their harmonious union.

89. Cf. St. Leo the Great, letter of August 17, 458 to the Emperor Leo I(DS, 317): the two actions, human and divine, of Christ are inseparable and inconfusible, we must distinguish them in the concrete works carried out by the Lord Jesus.

90. St. Ignatius constantly extolls the search for consolation: Ex. 2, 252, 254, 89, 133. We must flee desolation, even the thought of it: Ex. 319, 321. According to St. Ignatius, consolations are an effect of grace and a mark of divine benevolence which he always understands without any egotistical reaction, while, for St. John of the Cross, consolation denotes above all the subjective joy it brings. St. Ignatius, understanding consolations in so refined a manner, is able to identify them with God and have us seek after them. While it would properly be scandalous for St. John of the Cross to divinize his joys and make them the goal of his spiritual life. These reflections of L. Roy, S.J. ("Faut-il rechercher la consolation dans la vie spirituelle?" Sciences Ecclesiastiques 8, 1956, 110-31 and 165,166) cast much light on a delicate and difficult subject. It should also be said that St. Ignatius even praises "a discernment of consolations" which forms a part of "discernment of spirits," lest we fall victims of false diabolical consolations (cf. Ex. 331, 336). Besides, all the consolations described by St. Ignatius (cf. Ex. 316) bring about love of God and detachment from creatures as their consequences or lead to them as their effect and cause (cf. J. Calveras, "Commentary of the Fifth Addition," Manresa. 8, 1932, 3-27).

91. PO, 5; ST, III.65.3.1; 79.1.c, ad 1m: "in Eucharistia totum bonum spirituale Ecclesiae continetur" (PO,5).

92. Phil 4:4, "Rejoice in the Lord always"; Gal 5:22, "The fruit of the spirit is love, joy, peace . . ."

93. St. Ignatius told his doctor and Gonzalez da Camara that nothing could make him melancholic except the total suppression of the Society by the Pope and even in this case it would be enough for him to recollect himself for a quarter of an hour in prayer to be as happy and even more so than before! Besides, this was precisely his reaction upon hearing of the election of Paul IV. (Cf. Memorial of da Camara, 182 and 93, Fontes Narrativi, vol. I, pp. 638 and 582, MHSJ, vol. 66, Rome 1943.)

17

THE GIFT
OF THE SPIRIT OF TRUTH
TO THE SPOUSE OF CHRIST,
THE HIERARCHICAL, ROMAN CHURCH.
NORMS OF ORTHODOXY.

If the *Spiritual* Exercises speak relatively little about the Holy Spirit and if they do not propose a contemplation on the mystery of Pentecost, explicitly, it is doubtless because they do not come to a close but open upon the life of the Church, which is an awaiting for the return of Christ.[1] It is also because they give us doctrinal norms in view of this return and because these norms are expressly illuminated by the gift of the Spirit to the Church, manifested solemnly on Pentecost. "He who has been taken away from us" (Acts 1:11) is he who "is with us always, until the end of the world" (Mt 28:20), through and in his Eucharist, his Spirit and his Church, in a manner both visible and hidden. He "will return" in fulness of visibility on the last day (*cf.* Acts 1:11), when this radiant Morning Star will judge that the Spirit and the spouse will have sufficiently told him: "Come, Lord Jesus!" (Rv 22:16, 17,20).

To help us persevere, under the action of the Spirit, in this Church which is fully in expectation of the Lord's return, and also to help us build this Church (*cf.* Eph 4:16) by this very perseverance, the author of the Exercises, in times so troubled and perilous as we continue to live in after him (*cf.* Ex 369), has wished to leave us some rules and norms of orthodoxy. These rules constitute an application of the meditation on the "Two Standards" to the cultural, disciplinary and doctrinal domain. Of course, in contrast with what he had proposed for our reflection through this famous meditation, St. Ignatius here does not explicitly uncover what he judges are the ruses of the devil in doctrinal matters, but only the program of Jesus. However, Satan's ruses are implicitly exposed, since it is required to "praise" precisely what the enemy of mankind, Lucifer, disguised as an angel of light, attacks.[2]

In the doctrinal and disciplinary confusion which has plagued the life of the Church after Vatican II, we think it of the utmost importance to propose, following St. Ignatius, these rules of orthodoxy as an exercise of discernment of spirits in doctrinal matters. To be sure, some of them may appear, at first sight, anachronistic. Reflection, however, shows that almost all are relevant.[3] Here we should like to present a commentary, though incomplete, aimed at bringing out their spiritual implications and consequences as appropriate in the course of a "theological retreat." We will attempt to clarify them in the light of other texts of the Exercises, and of St. Ignatius, as well as Vatican II, in a context quite different, which is that of the ecumenical movement.

We will distinguish, along with many of the best commentators,[4] three groups among these eighteen rules. The first group is made up of the first nine rules and concerns the forms of ecclesial and liturgical life that are praiseworthy: Christian devotion and life. The second is made up of the next three rules and have to do with the attitude to be had toward authority. Finally, the last five rules touch on the verbal prudence to be observed in clearly doctrinal questions.

St. Ignatius, as to the first set of rules, was inspired by the context of the maxims of Erasmus; as to the last set, by the Lutheranizing preaching of an Augustinian in Rome, Mainardi,[5] who shortly thereafter apostatized, not without having beforehand caused much trouble for the author of the Exercises.[6] Furthermore, this last set of rules is more concerned with the way of preaching and explaining dogma.[7]

We shall not comment on each one of these rules but rather will supplement them by the famous "presupposition" (Ex 22) which quite well perfects and clarifies them. After we have recalled the view of the Church which underlies them, we will show the positive consequences (praises) and the negative consequences (no public or partisan controversies) as well as finally a consequence that is at the same time positive and negative: fraternal correction, in intellectual and doctrinal matters, extolled by the "presupposition."

Since we regard these rules as an exercise in discernment of spirits,[8] an extension of the meditation on the "Two Standards," the fruit we wish to garner from this exercise is that of knowing and detesting the doctrinal and devotional ruses of "evil spirits",[8] of a knowledgeable embracing of the sacred and salvific doctrine of Christ and of his Church (cf. Ex. 145), under the action of the sacramental grace of confirmation.[9]

Finally, let us note, before getting down to the heart of the subject, the complexity of the title if we consider the nuances in the various versions: "Rules to be observed for thinking and feeling surely and truly *with* and *in* the orthodox and militant Church, as we should" (Ex. 352).[10] The Church to which the retreatant belongs is both militant, (she fights against errors and lies sowed by the prince of this world who is the father of lies), and orthodox, endowed by the Spirit of truth with the true doctrine which is her principal weapon in this conflict. The retreatant, if he observes these rules, will think in conformity with truth, knowing with certainty, sharing thus, in a limited manner, in the infallibility of this orthodox Church. The judgment of the retreatant, his "feeling,"[11] will not only be externally conformed *with* the hierarchical Church, but also will be an intimate sharing *in* this judgment, under the action of the Spirit who assists the Church and moves the Christian to make her doctrine his own, carrying out this obligation with a luminous joy.

A. Firm adhesion to the Magisterium of the Church, Spouse of Christ, our Mother, ruled and governed by the Holy Spirit for the salvation of souls.

First, we treat of three rules (1,9,13) which describe the Church's role and which besides are the most important, for the others only bring out the consequences of the principles they pose. In them we see that every obligation that is proposed in respect to the Church, first of all, presumes that she is acknowledged as a mystery of love, of love obedient to Christ, a saving love in our regard, thanks to the gift of the Holy Spirit. "The true spouse of Christ our Lord, our holy mother, the hierarchical Church, which is the Church of Rome. . . [12] We must be convinced that in Christ our Lord, the bridegroom, and in his spouse the Church, only one Spirit holds sway,[13] which governs and rules for the salvation of souls. For it is by the same Spirit and Lord who gave the Ten Commandments that our holy mother the hierarchical Church is ruled and governed" (Ex. 353 and 365).[14]

What is the precise meaning of the two Biblical and traditional images of the Church as spouse and mother? Our answer will be given in the light of Vatican II (which has rendered us the great service of honoring these images), and of St. Augustine. Such a procedure seems proper for a better understanding of Ignatian thinking, for St. Ignatius wished to set himself in the great current of Biblical and traditional thought, now summarized by Vatican II.

The Church is the faithful spouse[15] indissolubly bound[16] to the Lord. She preserves intact the deposit of revelation[17] to return it on the last day to him who had entrusted it to her. She testifies to her fidelity to her spouse Jesus by faith, trustful hope and charity: "She preserves, by virtue of the Holy Spirit, in their virginal purity, an integral faith, a firm hope and a sincere charity."[18] If the Synagogue was unfaithful, the Church is faithful, thanks to the gift of the Spirit which her spouse has made her. None the less, each one of her members is not assured of the same fidelity,[19] and that is why St. Paul could write to the Corinthians: "I am jealous of you with the jealousy of God himself, since I have given you in marriage to one husband, presenting you as a chaste virgin to Christ. My fear is that, just as the serpent seduced Eve by his cunning, your thoughts may be corrupted and you may fall away from your sincere and complete devotion to Christ. I say this because when someone comes preaching another Jesus than the one we preached, or when you receive a different spirit than the one you have received, or a gospel other than the gospel you accepted, you seen to endure it quite well" (2 Cor 11: 2-4; Paul is referring to Judaizing Christians).

The Ignatian exhortation to fidelity toward the spouse of Christ is set in

a partially analogous context: if the fidelity of the universal Church toward
her Spouse (Eph 5:22–27; cf. Mt 16:18; "The jaws of death will not prevail
against it"), is divinely assured and guaranteed, the same cannot be said of
the fidelity of particular or local churches or of individuals. Ignatius invites
them, therefore, to discern, better than Eve, the deceits of the evil serpent,
and not to accept another gospel, another Jesus, and another Spirit than
those of the universal and Roman Church. In other works, St. Ignatius,
following St. Augustine[20] and Paul, invites *us* to become what we are, the
Church spouse of Christ, by fidelity toward the hierarchy.

If the image of spouse signifies the Church as a whole, including the hierarchy, that of mother more especially refers to the hierarchical Church. The
Church is mother in so far as she gives the spiritual life of faith, the supernatural life of grace, of charity and of virtues by her teaching and by her
sacraments. She is also mother in as much as she educates and nourishes the
faith already given. It is to her we owe our knowledge of and adherence to
revelation. It is through her, in her, with her and due to her that we know
and love Christ, that we remain in him and live for him. Without her, outside of her,[21] against her, there would be for us neither Christian life, nor
remission of our sins. We would still groan in the shadows of death.

Many texts of Vatican II, just as did St. Ignatius and tradition, harmoniously link the images of the Church as spouse and mother. This is but right,
for the Church is only Christ's spouse in order to bring forth, through him,
virginally, souls for the supernatural life of grace, in faith, hope and love
and for the glory of the consummated Kingdom.

The following quotations show this clearly: "The bride of the Incarnate
Word, and the pupil of the Holy Spirit, the Church is concerned to move
ahead daily toward a deeper understanding of the sacred Scriptures so that
she may unceasingly feed her sons with the divine words . . . ."[22] "The divine Office is the voice of the bride addressing her bridegroom; hence all who
perform this service are sharing in the greatest honor accorded to Christ's
spouse, for by offering these praises to God they are standing before God's
throne in the name of the Church their mother."[23]

When Vatican II underlines the educational role of the Church as mother:
"As a mother, the Church is bound to give these children of hers the kind
of education through which their entire lives can be penetrated with the spirit
of Christ",[24] it does not explicitly say that the Church gives divine life to her
children, it does say so in other words when it presents her as the sacrament
of salvation. More profoundly, the council even lets it be understood that it
is not only, in the Church, the hierarchy which plays a maternal role, but
also the body of Christians who by prayer and sacrifice united with those of
Jesus, contribute to the salvation of the world. "Let each one remember that
he can have an impact on all men and contribute to the salvation of the
whole world by public worship and prayer as well as by penance and voluntary acceptance of the labors and hardships of life. By such means does the

Christian grow in likeness to the suffering Christ (*cf.* 2 Cor 4:10; Col 1:24).[25]

That is to say, the Church as a whole, is the co-redemptive spouse of the Lamb, the mother of all mankind. She suffers and prays that all mankind be filled with Christ's Spirit so as to become his temple, the body of Christ and the People of God [26] The whole Church is to engender, in suffering and tears, all men to divine life, indirectly, or, as in the case of the hierarchy, directly. Yet, if all in the Church do not engender to divine life through the word of preaching and through the sacraments, they do have, as baptized and confirmed, the mission to evangelize and to teach others in the life of faith, to help them in the exercise of charity.[27]

So it is then that the Ignatian rules of orthodoxy are directed to each one that he or she observe them and make others observe them. This each one will do since it is his obligation to share in the role of spouse and in the maternal vocation of the Church, when he realizes more and more his filial debt, one that can never be paid, to that same Church.

If we owe to the hierarchical Church, to the bishops in full communion with the vicar of Christ, to those who are—exclusively[28]—the authentic interpreters of the deposit of revelation entrusted to the whole people of God,[29] a true and certain knowledge of Christ's gospel in its integrity,[30] we readily understand the insistence with which St. Ignatius enjoins on us the duty of total submission of our minds and wills to the magisterium of the Church, our mother, under the action of the Holy Spirit. "We must put aside all judgment of our own and keep the mind ever ready and prompt to obey in all things the true spouse of Christ, our holy mother, the hierarchical, Catholic, orthodox and Roman Church" (Ex. 353, First rule).[31] The thirteenth rule[32] explains: "If we wish to proceed securely in all things, we must hold fast to the following principle: What seems to me white, I will believe black if the hierarchical Church so defines" (Ex. 365).

If the first rule emphasizes obedience and the thirteenth faith, or teaching, both coincide in a disposition, a preparation and a promptitude. The background which makes relative the secondary elements in the comparison of these rules is the contemplation, in faith, of the mystery of the Church as Christ's faithful spouse, as mother who has given and continues giving us the life which is his, without which we would not know him. The attention of the mind, instead of concentrating on secondary elements, taken in themselves, which are objects of the Church's teaching, focusses first and foremost on the Church herself who teaches, to consider next particular points in the light of this universal, Catholic Church. The believer fixes his attention on the *mystery* of the Church, animated by the Holy Spirit who guides and directs her, on Christ who is her Lord and invisible head. He distrusts his own judgment (Ex. 59,60,63), aware of the partial corruption of his intellectual and volitional faculties (Ex. 51) which leaves intact, however, the essence of his soul.[33] He is desirous of finding the wisdom, the goodness and the power of God in the disciplinary and doctrinal determinations of his mother, assisted by the same

Spirit who animates the virginal mother-spouse. He also seeks out reasons which will justify her decisions, shuns considerations and attitudes which would render them incomprehensible[34] and thus arrives, by a joint, harmonious exercise of prudence, faith, obedience, and charity, to see with the Church as black what had just seemed to be white. His eyes are now illumined by faith (cf. Eph 1:17). His Pauline prayer is now heard: the God of our Lord Jesus Christ, the Father of glory, gives him a Spirit of wisdom and of revelation which illumines the eyes of his heart. His heart is changed and next his eyes are opened. He has the insight, in the Spirit, to know what the Church, under the action of the Spirit, wants to make him see.[35]

Of course, he knows that the "definitions" and "determinations" of the Church do not have equal import[36] and concern objects of unequal significance. He knows also[37] that the same truths may often be expressed in a variety of ways more or less adapted to communicate them to the men of his times. And finally, he knows that, if he has competence on the matter under consideration, he can have the right in due measure of his competence, or the obligation, to make known humbly and courageously his opinion[38] to modify, perfect or even to help her correct[39] her teaching (should the matter not come under the Church's infallibility). So it is in an atmosphere of "right liberty" that he lives and makes more profound his constant and ever-growing disposition to obey, in the luminous shadows of the faith, the Catholic Church of Christ.[40] It is the obscure clarity of the faith which has rendered its black appearance to what seemed to him white, at the very moment when he knows he can, either by his prayer, or by his competence joined to it, help the Church[41] see what she has not yet seen if he thinks, without certitude, that he has glimpsed it, and with reservation of his adherence to the Church's view.

Under the action of the Spirit who dwells in the whole Church, in the past, present and future, the believer makes his own the past view of the Church to the extent that this can help him better see the future while he anticipates his mother's future view and conforms himself to her present one. Thus, by perfect and "pneumatic" observance of the rules of orthodoxy (cf. 1 Cor 2:10-12), the believer receives more and more the thinking of Christ (cf. 1 Cor 2:16). His soul filially scrutinizes the depths of God the Father, progresses to the eschatological consummation of his spiritual marriage with the Son, becomes ever more the temple of the Spirit. The Christian knows that apart from perfect communion with the successors of the apostles united around Peter and Mary, there is no complete and definitive union with the Father and the Son[42] nor with the Holy Spirit who is their consubstantial and indivisible communion.

For him "putting aside all self-judgment," "keeping the mind ever ready to believe black what he sees as white," if the Church so defines (even not infallibly) becomes the easy and delightful breathing of his soul in which the Father and the Son spirate their eternal Spirit who constantly illumines him with His inspirations. This same Spirit breathes (cf. Jn 3,6-8) ceaselessly in

her the adoring love of the Father and of the Son and, by that very fast, sav-
of the world (*cf.* Jn 4:23,24; 4:42). For the disciple of Ignatius, at the close
of the retreat, to hear the voice of the Spirit which breathes in the Church
and speaks through her is no longer a problem, but a need and a joy. He
lets carnal or "natural" men[43] wrangle about black and white, about the precise limits of the rights and obligations of the Church, of magisterium and of
her faithful. While regarding this last kind of reflections as legitimate[44] when
it is not self-serving his own judgment, he knows that what is born of the
flesh remains flesh and prefers to keep, in the unfathomable depths of
the Church, his rebirth of the Spirit. It is thus that the Spirit in and through
the Church his body, "teaches us, governs us and directs us in view of the
salvation of our souls."

*B. Negative consequences of this contemplation on the Church: no public or
tendentious controversy with the hierarchy.*

From their illumination itself, the eyes of the heart deduce a practical
norm concerning relations with the hierarchy. St. Ignatius expresses it as follows in the tenth rule:[45]

"We should be more ready to approve and praise the orders, recommendations, and way of acting of our superiors than to find fault with them.
Though some of the orders, etc. may not have been praiseworthy, yet to speak
against them, either when preaching in public or in speaking before the people, would rather be the cause of murmuring and scandal than of profit. As
a consequence, the people would become angry with their superiors, whether
secular or spiritual."

We shall postpone treatment of the purpose of this rule for the time being.
We will come back to it when we comment on the "presupposition." Now
we will bring out how it is radically counter to the most spectacular aspect
of controversy manifested in all periods but so frequent and so "popular"
today.

This rule does not involve doctrine as does the one previously discussed.
We do not intend to separate the two, however, even though they are distinct. It is obvious that in our day of parliamentary democracy and universally
diffused information St. Ignatius, were he living in our times, would revise the
rule in regard to "temporal superiors." We are more sensitive today to the
need of checking abuses of power in view of the common good.[46] This does,
in no way, eliminate the obligation of obedience to just laws[47] and decisions
of political authority within the bounds of the moral order, as Vatican II
states. It is precisely on this account that the reticence of the Ignatian rule
on public controversy remains justified. Public controversy endangers the fulfillment of an obligation imposed by the divine, natural and positive law of
obedience toward lawful authority in the temporal order.[48]

This call for obedience echoes that found in Rom 13:1–7. However, it does not deny the legitimacy and the duty to "object" to orders or dispositions of authority. [49] Such objection may be fully public if all other means are of no avail, for it then pursues the common good of all, including those holding authority.

A much greater reserve is imposed on what involves a public and partisan criticism of ecclesial authority. Is not the danger even greater? The unity of the ecclesial community, assured by its spiritual leaders, and, in the last analysis, by the Holy Spirit, suggests rather recourse to means other than tendentious "controversy" to remedy abuses, a recourse that is always possible. Neither the conflict of classes, nor particular conflicts should penetrate within the Church, a communion of charity, of faith and of hope. Fraternal correction, an exercise of charity, need not be public in order to be efficacious. On the contrary, its publicity is more often harmful to its effectiveness. This correction is the best way to remedy abuses, a means which St. Ignatius mentions at the end of this rule and which we shall shortly treat.

Briefly, the author of the Exercises invites us to ask ourselves what is the spirit, behind this urge to object which, from time to time, tempts us. Is it because it is fashionable? Is it due to temptations from the enemy of mankind? Is it genuine concern for the common good? Or a revolutionary ideology? Is it out of charity toward those criticized and from a desire for their real good? Here we have an opportunity to practice discernment of spirits. For St. Ignatius the dominant tendency ought to be not to reprehend, to speak against, but to approve and to praise. In regard to authority, civil and ecclesiastical, the maxim of the "presupposition" is also to be applied: "Every good Christian ought to be more ready to put a good interpretation on another's statement thatn to condemn it as false." The one holding authority is my neighbor, too. The Holy Spirit incites the members of the same Church to reciprocal union. Is he not the eternal bond between the Father and the Son? . . . "with perfect humility, meekness and patience, bearing with one another lovingly. Make every effort to preserve the unity which has the Spirit as its origin and peace as its binding force" (Eph 4:2,3). Each time they are possible, this is what approbation and praise bring about.

C. Positive consequence: praising and speaking prudently.

In the face of the critical insinuations of Erasmus, who so scathingly denounced possible abuses endangering the very use of the gifts of the Holy Spirit, St. Ignatius reacted vehemently against unwillingness to praise what merited praise. When there was question of confession and weekly Communion, frequent attendance at Mass, lengthy prayers and the divine Office, religious vows and the religious state, veneration of relics and of the saints, indulgences, the lighting of candles in a church, external penances, statues or church ornaments, postive or scholastic theology (Ex. 351–60 and 363), he recommended always to praise all that was, in varying degrees, the object of the criticisms, of the insinuations, and of the biting irony of Erasmus.[50] In a more general way, the ninth rule (Ex. 361), recommends, after all these particular suggestions of praising, that "we must praise all the commandments of the Church, and be on the alert to defend them, and by no means in order to criticize them."[51]

This ever present attitude of constant praise in regard to the commandments, counsels, doctrinal and disciplinary, of the Church, spouse of Christ, mother of the faithful and temple of the Holy Spirit is stressed by the initial word of each rule, ever the same: *alabar, laudare,* praise.

Such an unwavering attitude is set in the over all context of the Exercises which singularly illumine it. Indeed, is not praise of God, Creator and Savior, as is formulated in the "Principle and Foundation" (Ex. 23), above all the way to realize the very vocation of the human person? If it is by praising God that man will save his soul, is it not also by praising the action of God, Creator and Savior, by means of sacraments, prayers, vows, veneration of saints and statues, lighting candles and gaining indulgences, study of orthodox theology, whether scholastic or positive, that man will express his praise of God's being, identical, in divine simplicity, with this action? How is it possible to praise the Creator without praising, on recognizing it as such, his salvific action through the sacraments and sacramentals[52] of the Church, the sacrament of universal salvation? Under this relationship, as we have emphasized, do not the rules of orthodoxy constitute a priceless commentary on and a deepening of the "Foundation"?

The contemplation of the trinitarian mystery of the Church, "the raison d'etre of the universe,"[53] the Church, a world holy, good, reconciled, saved in hope, a world which "wholly follows Christ," as St. Augustine so beautifully says,[54] opens up singularly widened horizons for the salvific praise of God, Creator and Savior, who dwells in it, acts in it, saves through and in the Church. The praise of the Church, mystery and sacrament of salvation, becomes praise of God, of the redemptive Trinity.

If "the perfect, due to constant contemplation and the enlightenment of the understanding, consider, meditate, and ponder more that God our Lord is in every creature by his essence, power and presence,"[55] the Exercises tells us how the retreatant in the fourth week is more disposed, by contemplation initiating him into the unitive way, to discover the divine action in the action of the Church. Is it not, besides, proper to a Catholic ecclesiology to look on the Church not only as the congregation of the faithful but also, even more, as the instrument of the salvific action of the Trinity in their regard?[56]

Next, and secondly, the attitude of praising God with, in and through the Church, adopted by the rules "for thinking with the Church", is logically in opposition to the attitude of destructive criticism.[57] This is the attitude of Satan and his ministers. Satan wants to build a Babylon on the ruins of Jerusalem; so, under pretext of abuses (whether possible or real) which men, under his deceitful influence, make of God's gifts, he invites them to despise and reject, out of pride, these gifts (*cf.* 140–142). He goads them on thus to look at the defects, the vices, the negative, the blameworthy, the evil, rather than the perfections, the virtues, the good, the praiseworthy, the positive. "If I reveal the defect of another, I manifest my own" (Ex. 41). He tries to turn our attention away from what is better in order to turn it toward what is less good (*cf.* Ex. 333 and 356, 357) and thence to what is evil. Instead of making us praise the good, for the glory of the author of all good,[58] he tries to make us criticize the possible or real evil which often goes along with it, in order thus to turn us away from the Supreme Good. In this way he will bring good men to prefer to criticize errors (an attitude that moreover may be necessary but one that is secondary: *cf.* Ex. 41), rather than praise and extol the good and the true.

The tactic of Christ, the wisdom of God, faced with this program of destructive criticism of his work, consists then in making us praise the ecclesial mediations of his salvific action before men. This he does in order that, despite demoniacal temptations, men may be able to benefit from them. His strategy is also to have proclaimed, without exaggeration or attenuation, his salvific truth. Despite the diabolical errors which seek to falsify truth by way of either embroidering or lessening it, Christ's object is to enable men to adhere to it in faith and deduce from it the consequences for their behavior.

In this way, for historical and contingent reasons which are not without ontological import, the author of the Exercises, after having described and enumerated the acts to be praised, shows the truths to be praised and proclaimed. These are those truths which constitute the necessary presuppositions of these actions, with a discernment such that their proclamation does not destroy the salvific action, the collaboration of human free will with divine grace. The human speech of the Christian should announce the sacred doctrine of salvation (Ex. 145, V). He is to proclaim in words the truths necessary, according to the needs of our times, for salvation (Ex. 363), starting out from the Scriptures, the fathers, medieval and contemporary doctors and councils, in view of bringing men to the worship and love of God, so that they love and serve him (*ibid.*) This announcing of the doctrine of salvation will have to include, secondarily, the analysis and refutation of mortal errors (Ex. 367, V) propagated by the father of lies to lead men to hell (Ex. 71) through unbelief or rebellion of will (*cf.* Ex. 363, 139, 141). There is question of unmasking them to bring out clearly the partial truth they contain.

To announce the doctrine of salvation, the sacred doctrine which saves,[59] is it not to announce—in moderation—the predestination of free will to faith and works brought about by grace, speaking little of predestination (without at the same time saying nothing about it) and much about grace[60] and free will (Ex. 366–69)?

Among the works of free will which are brought about, sustained, and crowned by grace, there is the acquisition of a sound doctrine which safeguards from the mortal errors of the denial of free will or of grace (Ex. 369, 366).

The salvific doctrine is the doctrine of predestination and of merit, of faith and of works, of faith which works by charity (Gal 5:6), of grace and of free will, of pure love and even of servile fear (Ex. 366-70). This salvific doctrine shows the value of natural good works of unbelievers and of sinners as dispositions to grace and salvation (Ex. 368), without failing to extol the mystery of predestination and grace (Ex. 366).

It suffices to say that Christ calls his disciple to the acquistion of this "doctrine of salvation" so necessary[61] for him to be able to speak of the mysteries of faith and to praise the orthodox action knowingly. The vocation to an orthodox apostolate and to praise, inseparably contemplative and social, becomes, in the bosom of the mystery of the taught and teaching Church,[62] a vocation to the study of divine revelation.[63]

Still, as this apostolic mission is entrusted to the Church as a whole, it presupposes the exercise of intellectual and reciprocal charity on the part of the witnesses of Christ and the Church in the Spirit.

D. Both negative and positive consequences: Benevolent dialogue, and if necessary, fraternal and ecclesial correction.

We are rightly concerned today to associate the orthopraxis of active charity with orthodox doctrine. If the "rules of orthodoxy" constitute the quasi-conclusion of the Exercises, they are begun with a "rule of orthopraxis" which is intellectual and doctrinal, traditionally designated under the term *"praesupponendum"* or a "necessary presupposition." Although at first sight restricted to relations between the retreat director and the retreatant, it has, actually, a universal amplitude[64] and constitutes the admirable chart for a dialogue, at once orthodox and charitable, in the bosom of the Church, a dialogue polarized by mutual concern to be set on the right road to eternal salvation by the saving or salvage of language in time. Here we have the complex formulation which we shall divide for greater clarity:

a) "To assure better cooperation between the one who is giving the Exercises and the exercitant (read 'Christians'), and more beneficial results for both, it is necessary to suppose that every good Christian is more ready to put a good interpretation[65] of another's obscure statement[66] than to condemn it as false."

b) "If he cannot save the statement, the one who made it should be asked how he understands it."

c) "If he is in error,[67] he should be corrected with all kindness.[68]

d) "If this does not suffice, every appropriate measure should be taken to bring him to a correct interpretation[69] and so defend the proposition from error" (Ex. 22).[70]

A favorable interpretation, a clarifying dialogue, kindly, direct fraternal correction and finally, indirect fraternal correction in view of the salvation of the neighbor and the saving of his proposition if these two "savings" can be simultaneously obtained, that is what the author of the Exercises asks. The text of the Vulgate, dropping the saving of the proposition, underlines that we ought to be ready to sacrifice our own judgment in order to save our soul (*cf.* Ex. 365). If the explanatory dialogue suffices, fraternal correction, even kindly, will not be necessary. If direct correction does suffice, indirect correction will be equally superfluous. At any rate, we see that the presupposition is far from being limited, as at times has been the impression, to a demand for an equitable interpretation of another's words. Further, it explicitly includes, each time it will be necessary for the good of souls (and for the common good, not only for the personal good of the party to the dialogue) fraternal correction, without excluding recourse to authority. Its aim is, thus, the salvation of those who dialogue by means of this effort to save the language employed.

A parallel text of the Exercises makes the Ignatian objective clear: "It is permissible to speak of a commonly known error that infests the minds of those with whom we live."

"It is permissible to speak of the sin or fault of another, if my intention is good . . . when it is revealed to some one with the intention that he help the one who is in sin to rise from his state. But then there must be some grounds or probable reasons for believing that he will be able to help him" (Ex. 41).

Although the aim pursued here by St. Ignatius be partly the same (the common good, fraternal correction), it must be noted that the measures envisaged correspond only to the fourth stage of the presupposition: indirect fraternal correction, and presuppose, each time that this is concretely possible, that recourse was had prior than this to the first three in succession.

This is precisely how St. Ignatius proceeded in 1538 when, during Lent, Mainardi, an Augustinian preacher of Lutheran tendencies, was gaining influence over the Spanish clergy. St. Ignatius apprised them of his erroneous ideas, but in vain. The Spanish clergy blindly admired the Italian preacher. They were hostile to St. Ignatius and his companions. Inigo then followed the evangelical counsel (Mt 18:15-17), of which the "presupposition" constituted an abstract and partial transcript. He and his companions asked Mainardi to retract or, at least, to explain in a Catholic sense certain of his scandalous propositions. When Mainardi refused to do so, they thought they were duty bound to preach the true Catholic doctrine to the people, against the errors spread by the Augustinian preacher, but without naming him. This, however, resulted in the fiercest persecution suffered by Ignatius, and finally led to a judgment by the Holy See wholly favorable to our saint.[71] It seems likely that the inclusion of rules 14-18 in the ensemble of "rules for thinking with the Church" was the result of this preaching by Ignatius and his companions against the errors spread by the Augustinian monk, who in 1541 became a Lutheran.[71]

It will be noted also that St. Ignatius, on avoiding all personal and public controversy with the Augustinian monk, applied in advance—if we may be permitted an anachronism—the norms laid down by Vatican II.[72] The recent Council, however, does not restrict itself to ask that controversy be avoided. It encourages bishops, and so, indirectly, all preachers, following St. Paul (2 Tim 4: 1-4) which it cites, to proclaim the word, to insist in season and out of season, to refute, to warn, to exhort, with tireless patience and concern to instruct: "For the time will come (has it not already come?) when people will not tolerate sound doctrine, but, following their own desires, will surround themselves with teachers who tickle their ears. They will stop listening to the truth and wander off to fables." The Council quotes this text only to justify its declaration of the obligation of bishops: "The bishops are to make faith bear fruit and vigilantly ward off any errors which threaten their flock."[73]

Among these errors, there is one which is very characteristic and widespread. It is that a positive explanation of the Gospel suffices and there is no need to denounce errors opposed to it. Besides the fact that this does not correspond at all to the thinking of the N. T., such a trend is certainly not in conformity with the explicit norms of Vatican II.[74] Does not the Council teach that: "the good news of Christ constantly renews the life and culture of fallen man. It combats and removes the errors and evils resulting from sinful allurements which are a perpetual threat"?[75] Does it not exhort the laity: "Since, in this age of ours, new problems are arising and extremely serious errors are gaining currency which tend to undermine the foundations of religion, the moral order, and human society itself, this sacred synod earnestly exhorts laymen, each according to his natural gifts and learning, to be more diligent in doing their part according to the mind of the Church, to explain and defend Christian principles, and to apply them rightly to the problems of our era."[76]

It is not possible to doubt, then, that, for the Church of Vatican II, as for St. Ignatius, "to snatch the neighbor from the slavery of error"[77] denouncing "a commonly known error that infests the minds of those with whom we live"[78] is a very great work of fraternal charity. It is still true that the denunciation of error, whether directed to the authors themselves, or to others and particularly to ecclesiastical authorities, is a very delicate task to carry out in the concrete. Catherine of Sienna clearly recognized this and provided a solution to the difficulty, a solution which bears the evident marks of the Spirit of Christ. God inspired the saint:[79] "Your correcting should be coupled with humility and follow the method I have indicated. You are to reprimand yourself at the same time you reprimand others." This is a perfectly justifiable consideration, even in the doctrinal area. Each one should say to himself in all truth that he has within him the root of all vices, the ten-

dency to embrace all errors, and, though unaware of it because of the falli-
bility of his mind, he has actually embraced and embraces more than one
error.

There remains in particular this fact: the initial assumption of the Ignatian
"presupposition," namely that "it is necessary to suppose that every good
Christian is more ready to put a good interpretation on another's statement
than to condemn it as false." This is what Vatican II wished to inculcate
and recommend in a special way. Besides such an attitude will preserve all
involved from quite a few errors and is what will principally contribute to
the dialogue the Church of today wants to promote, in the world, in the
Church, and between the Church and the world.

We think it well here to quote the texts at length. "Respect and love
ought to be extended also to those who think or act differently than we
do in social, political, and religious matters, too. In fact, the more deeply
we come to understand their ways of thinking through such courtesy and
love, the more easily will we be able to enter into dialogue with them. This
love and good will, to be sure, must in no way render us indifferent to truth
and goodness. Indeed love impels the disciples of Christ to speak the saving
truth to all men. But it is necessary to distinguish between error, which always merits repudiation, and the person in error, who never loses the dignity
of being a person, even when he is flawed by false or inadequate religious
notions."[80]

Love impels Christ's disciples to proclaim the truth which saves. For love
wishes to snatch others from the error which ruins them. They are, however, not to do so by any means whatsoever. "Truth, however, is to be
sought after in a manner proper to the dignity of the human person and
his social nature. The inquiry is to be free, carried on with the aid of teaching or instruction, communication, and dialogue. In the course of these,
men explain to one another the truth they have discovered or think they
have discovered, in order thus to assist one another in the quest for truth."[81]

Are not the Ignatian Exercises, in the light of the "necessary presupposition" which introduces them, a privileged means of dialogue in the world,
in the Church and between churches, in view of the search for a more ample
truth that each one actually possesses? Are they not an instrument for carrying out the wish of Vatican II which we have just quoted?

Let us say even better: is not there found one of their objectives, in view
of the glory of God, of the salvation of souls? Do they not intend to help
each one to eliminate the obstacles which are opposed to an authentic dialogue in doctrinal matters? Do they not propose the acquisition of a "sound
doctrine" through dialogue, to use an expression from the pastoral epistles?

For obtaining such a wondrous grace, vertical dialogue is more important
and efficacious than horizontal. It is above all through and in prayer and
dialogue with the Divine Persons, with angelical and human persons who
are established in divine glory forever, in the "spiritual exercises," that we

will be able to dispose ourselves to interpret well the propositions of our neighbor, "to correct him," not harshly but "with all kindness" and "to use all appropriate means to bring him to a correct interpretation and so defend the proposition from error." By so doing recourse to the ecclesiastical community and its authority will be rendered unnecessary, even useless. Among all the opportune means to deliver the neighbor from his error, is not prayer ever the most necessary, the most enlightening, the most opportune? This will be so, provided I am quite convinced that I too need this neighbor's intercession to enable me to adhere more wholly, my eyes cleared of the dust of my errors, to the plenitude of the universal and infallible Church. It will be so, also, provided I believe that I, who remain fallible, have need of being corrected with kindness by the Church, which is communion in truth and in love.

E. Colloquies for obtaining the grace to judge and to think with the Church in pilgrimage to the Heavenly Church.

"Most Holy Mother of God, you are the treasure[82] of all mankind, the inextinguishable lamp and the scepter of orthodoxy,[83] ever Virgin in your faith, your fidelity, your Heart and your body. Thus it is that you are the mother of the virginal fidelity of the Church. You are our mother in the Church, through her, by way of her, you imprint on her the true image of your person and of your mystery. She is as you, through you, a virgin, a spouse, a mother,[84] sanctuary of the Holy Spirit.[85] You are ever submissive, in humble love, to the Son of God whom you engendered. Thus the Church is wholly subject to the divine authority with which she is clothed in your eyes.[86] On submitting ourselves to her, with her, it is to you who gave us divine life, to whom we subject ourselves.

"You are the mother of the economy,[87] the mother of the Church. May your all powerful intercession obtain for us to praise, with your perpetual and nuptial virginity,[88] more than marriage, virginity and consecrated celibacy,[89] more than external acts, interior life and contemplation (*cf.* Ex. 355–357), the divine Office henceforth the prayer of the whole people of God[90] and the Rosary, the summary of the Gospels.[91]

"Lord Jesus, you are the priest, the Lord and Savior of your Church. You love her as your only spouse, indissolubly and faithfully bound to you. You give her the most precious gifts of your heart. It is to me in her that you offer these gifts, images, and indulgences, evangelical counsels and divine Office, prayer and penance, sacramentals and sacraments, magisterium and orthodox theology. There we have so many gifts of your Heart to each of your disciples, in and through her, your Mother, your word, your Spirit, your Eucharist.

"Through our use and our praise of the divine Office, lengthy prayers, vows, penance, relics, statues, sacramentals, sacraments, the teachings and precepts of your Church, [92] it is you whom we praise and it is you who praises, by your Spirit, in us, your Father. You continue, by means of us, your lengthy nocturnal prayers, your obedience, your poverty, your virginity, to death, your satisfactions offered in expiation. You are the light our candles honor, the supreme image of God which we wish to imitate by imitating your saints and honoring their images. When, as sovereign priest, you celebrate and renew in and through your Church your sacrificial Supper, you offer to the Father, united to your own adoration, all our praises of your works. Thus you become, ineffably, the universal praise of the glory of your Father, [93] in the Spirit of love which dwells and works in you as in us.

"Is it not at this moment, giving us yourself in the Eucharist, that you consummate your marriage with the Church, your spouse? Do you not anticipate, preparing it, the eternal consummation of your marriage with each one of us? Is it not, then, in the course of this sacrifice of the Church, in her, that you communicate yourself to our souls? Is it not then that you embrace them and accept us to your praise and to your love, dealing directly and immediately with each one of us, encouraging us to perfection (Ex. 15)? Is it not at this moment of our communion with you that you fills us with your pure love, you, the predestined predestinator, [94] our free liberator, the performer of our good deeds, the seer who gives us the faith of which you are the consummator"[95] (cf. Ex. 366–70)?

"Spirit of Jesus, flame of love of the divine spouse, [96] soul of his mystical body, you inspire the same thoughts and the same feelings in the invisible head, in the visible head [97] and in the members of his body.

"Through the spouse of your anointed, you teach us, you guide and govern us for the salvation of our souls. You who have given us the ten commandments, you are in person the new law. [98] He who unites himself to the Lord in you, is with him but one Spirit (cf. 1 Cor 6:17). We are the letter written through the attentions of the episcopal college united around the successor of Peter, not written with ink, but with you, the Spirit of the living God, to be read by the world (cf. 2 Cor 3:3). Raise up the veil placed over hearts by the devil who wants to prevent them from reading it. Our gospel is still veiled because the god of this world has blinded the minds of a number of our contemporaries so that they do not see the gospel radiating the glory of Christ on the unveiled countenance of the Church which reflects it as in a mirror (cf. 2 Cor 3: 23; 4: 6). And if the devil has placed over our own hearts a veil which prevents us from seeing the blackness of what the Church condemns, and the whiteness of what she approves let it fall, Spirit of truth, You who animate and assist the Church, by converting us and delivering us from the errors of our own judgment, [99] you who are the liberating Spirit (cf. 2 Cor 3: 16, 17). Are you not the only Spirit of the Father, of the Son[100] and of the only body, the Spirit who leads us by the one faith, received in one baptism, to the one Lord and, through him, to the one God and Father of all, who is above all, through all, and in all (cf. Eph 4:4-6)?

"You are the Spirit who speaks ever through the prophets, the Spirit, the breath, the unction who anoints us in order that, strengthened by your might, burning with your dynamism, we pronounce, thanks to you, the words of eternal life, the words which will not pass, the words which will convert the men to whom you send us.[101] Triumph in each one of us over the diabolic spirit of timidity and human respect, over the spirit of fear and of slavery, since we have received you, Spirit of might and of charity (*cf.* Rom 8:15; 2 Tim 1:6–7).

"You are not only the Spirit who makes resound in the Church and, through her, in the world the living voice of the Gospel.[102] It is also under your assistance that the divine word, entrusted by you to the apostles, is through holy tradition,[103] transmitted integrally from generation to generation to their successors that by them it be preached, explained and faithfully diffused. You are the enlightener and the supreme author of this transmission and of this tradition. Under your assistance, the magisterium listens to your word lovingly and draws on this one deposit of faith for all it proposes for belief as being revealed. It is under your action that holy tradition, Holy Scripture and the magisterium of the Church, indissolubly linked and joined, all together contribute to the salvation of souls.[104]

"Spirit Paraclete, Spirit of truth given by the Lamb paraclete,[105] give to priests, to all priests and to the faithful concerned with theological learning,[106] to nourish themselves with the sacred Scriptures, liturgies, the writings of the fathers and doctors of the Church who are witnesses and channels transmitting the divine and apostolic tradition. May they draw therefrom knowledge and love of the Church. Is it not "to the extent that he loves the Church that each one possesses you, Holy Spirit?"[107]

"That the catholicity and apostolicity of your Church be better manifested, Spirit of unity, nourish too the spiritual and ecumenical life of Catholics with the treasure of the multiple traditions, past or present, which flourish in other churches or ecclesial communities, such as the treasure of the liturgy, the monastic life, and the mystical tradition of the Eastern Christians, the devotion and piety of Anglicanism, evangelical prayer and Protestant spirituality.[108] Is it not true, in fact, that numerous elements of sanctification and of truth are still to be found outside the structures of the one Church of Christ, entrusted by our Savior, after his Resurrection, to Peter who was to be her shepherd? These elements belong properly speaking to the Church of Christ by the gift of God, and by their very nature call for Catholic unity.[109]

"That we may better be able to dispose ourselves to follow your inspiration for the restitution of unity among Christians, unifying Spirit, source of the ecumenical movement,[110] grant us, Spirit of Truth and of Love, to be more prompt to interpret in a favorable sense the words and doctrines of our separated brethren and the churches and ecclesial communities than to condemn them, when such an interpretation is possible. If it is not, ask them through us how they understand them. Establish thus a minimal communion in you, between us.

"Holy Spirit, you dwell in us. May your assistance prevent us from succumbing to the diabolical temptation of letting ecumenical concern degenerate into false irenism,[111] and may it make us, on the contrary, preserve in its integrity the good deposit, the sound words you have entrusted to the Church until the day of the Lord's return. In your infinite might, you are capable of preserving in us and through us this deposit (cf. 1 Tim 6:20; 2 Tim 1:12–14).

"Spirit of promise, you have marked us, from the time of our baptism and of our confirmation, with your seal. You constitute the earnest of our heritage, you in whom we have been bathed in a bath of regeneration and renovation. You have been spread over us in profusion by Jesus Christ our Savior in order that we obtain hopefully the heritage of eternal life. You prepare our corporal redemption for the praise of the glory of the Father. Give us, then, if we should come to forget through our faults your eternal love and the integrity of the deposit which you have entrusted to us through your body, the church, grant us servile fear of her anathemas and of sinning against you. We implore this of you, that you preserve us from separating ourselves from her and from you.[112] Once we are freed from danger, grant us filial fear of losing faith and love, the fear which is pleasing and dear to you, for it is but one with the pure love of your divine majesty (cf. Eph 2:13, 14; Ti 3:5-7; Rom 8:23; Eph 1:6, 12; Ex. 65; Gal 1:9; 1 Cor 5:4, 5; Ex. 370).[113]

NOTES ON CHAPTER SEVENTEEN

1. This perceptive observation is taken from J. Goussault, S.J., who also inspired our parallel with the Ascension (cf. Ex. 312).

2. cf. our Ch. VIII, notes 20, 21 and 22, as well as the corresponding texts, for our comment on Ex. 141. Here, we do not say that Erasmus or Luther (in the measure in which St. Ignatius criticized, implicitly, their propositions) were possessed by the devil. Nor do we deny the partial truth contained in their errors as in every other case of error. We state quite simply what is also implicit in the Ignatian text; there are "diabolical doctrines" (1 Tm 4:1) the diffusion of which is fostered by human minds.

3. Thus, for instance, the seventh rule (Ex. 359) on fast and abstinence has lost materially a part of its actuality as a result of the change in Church discipline. But it formally maintains its worth, in as much as it inculcates the importance of external penance, stressed anew by Paul VI in the Constitution *Poenitemini* in 1966. Likewise (cf. Ex. 358: sixth rule) the "Bulls of Crusade" have been replaced in our times by the encyclicals on the Rosary and development! Finally, our contemporaries are surely less preoccupied with the mystery of predestination (Ex. 366, 367). Nevertheless, save for certain aspects we have already mentioned of the sixth and seventh rules, they have all kept their material and formal truth.

4. Among them, in historical order we cite: Leturia, S.J., "Sentido verdadero en la Iglesia militante," *Gregorianum,* XXIII (1942) 137–68; J. M. Granero, S.J., *Sentir con la Iglesia y problemas modernos,* Madrid, 1956, Ch. I, pp. 11-36; G. Fessard, S.J., *La dialectique* . . . , Paris, 1966, vol. II, pp. 159-253; esp. pp. 161, 162 (on the structure of the rules).

5. See: *S. Ignacio de Loyola, Obras completas,* vol. I, Madrid, 1947, ed. Larranaga, *Autobiography,* #98, commentaries pp. 543-51.

6. *Ibid.*

7. Leturia, *op. cit.,* p. 160: in contrast with rules 2–8, the last five do not imply any particular practice of a devotional or disciplinary order.

8. *Cf.* Fessard, *op. cit.,* p. 163.

9. *Cf.* our Chapter VIII at end.

10. The Vulgate speaks of "thinking *with* the Church," while the Autograph and P2 read "*in* the Church." Granero and Fessard (*op. cit.,* p. 162) explain there is no contradiction between the two translations and prepositions, "both the one and the other were accepted and approved by Ignatius." Likewise, the Vulgate speaks of "the *orthodox* Church" while the Autograph and P2 prefer the term "militant." For the term *"sentir"* cf. the following note.

11. *cf.* Leturia, *op. cit.,* p. 141: *"sentido"* (from the title of the rules in the Autograph) is "a sort of instinct which is not only knowledge but knowledge a thousand time sasavored and assimilated, in the manner of thinking which seizes and satisfies the soul which is found in the second Introductory Observation (Ex. 2). We must have this "feeling" not only with the Church, obeying her precepts and directives, but also in the Church, feeling ourselves in her bosom as her children and members, and assimilating her thoughts and affections." The meaning of the expression is therefore indissolubly both intellectual and affective. We have expressed this in our translation by putting side by side the words "think" and "feel," "thoughts" and "affections."

12. The words "which is the Church of Rome" are from P2.

13. The text of Ex. 367 P2 sheds light on a text of the Autograph, rather difficult otherwise to understand. In fact, P2 reads thus: ". . . *cum credamus quod in Christo Domino et sancta Ecclesia idem resideat Spirit Sanctus, qui nos docet et dirigit in salutem animarum nostrarum,"* which is indeed clearer and more understandable than the text of the Autograph: "Between the Spouse who is Christ our Lord and the Church his spouse, is the same Spirit." The text of P2 suggests that the same uncreated Spirit dwells in the *created humanity* of the Incarnate Word and in the Church. Let us recall that it is also as man that Jesus is the head of the Church. It is the same Spirit who guides Christ as man (*cf.* Lk 4:1) and the Church (*cf.* Jn 14: 26).

14. It is extremly probable that this text ("the same Spirit and Lord," ("*per eundem Spiritum ac Dominum"*) contains an allusion to 2 Cor 3: 17, "the Lord is the Spirit." This statement is set in a context of contrast between the Old and the New Testaments, or rather contrasts the understanding by the "Jews according to the flesh." Such an allusion would singularly clarify the text. If, as St. Paul says: "But whenever he turns to the Lord, the veil will be taken away. The Lord is the Spirit, and where the Lord is, there is freedom, "so that the Old Testament becomes "unveiled" in and by Christ, we can make an analogy: The Spirit which has given us the precepts of the Old Testament, the decalogue, clarifies them in Jesus Christ, likewise will remove the "veil" which prevents us from seeing as black what we thought white and which the Church, moved by

that Spirit, tells us is black. How can we help but think here of that other text of Paul which follows closely upon the one we have just quoted: "If our gospel can be called 'veiled' in any sense, it is such only for those who are headed for destruction. Their unbelieving minds have been blinded by the god of the present age (that is, Satan) so that they do not see the splendor of the gospel showing forth the glory of Christ, the image of God" (2 Cor 4: 3, 4). Does not Satan blind one who refuses to see the blackness of what the Church condemns? We are sent back here to the discernment of consolations extolled by St. Ignatius (Ex. 331). Of course, let us not ignore that in the fifteenth rule of orthodoxy, the author of the Exercises has in mind the conscious contradiction of one Erasmian expression (cf. Fessard, op. cit., pp. 168-70). But we think there is question there of another part of the Ignatian text which also admits of several levels of interpretation. Fessard has seen clearly the symbolical meaning of the adjectives "black" and "white," but he does not seem to me to have noticed the inversion made by St. Ignatius in regard to the text of Erasmus. Erasmus thought: "White would not be black, even if the Pontiff of Rome should define it as such," that is, my doctrinal innocence would not become guilty even should the Pope express himself in this sense. (Cf. Fessard, op. cit., pp. 169, 170; Erasmus, opera omnia, vol. IX, 1706, p. 517.) The Ignatian text reverses the relationship of the two adjectives: "What seems to me white, I will believe black if the hierarchical Church so defines" (Ex. 365). There is a vast difference between the Erasmian statement of whiteness (not at all a nuance of "what seems to me") and the disparity introduced by St. Ignatius between what seems and what is. The discernment of spirits enabled Ignatius to keep in mind that the prince of this world of darkness disguises himself under the appearance of an angel of light (cf. Eph 6:12; 2 Cor 11:14), "black" into "white." It is not, then, surprising that St. Paul tells us also that the ministers of Satan disguise themselves as ministers of justice (ibid. 15). The difference between Erasmus and St. Ignatius is that the former does not seem at all to reflect on the circumstances of his "vision," while the latter knows that it is not independent of the dialectic of the "Two Standards." Ignatius knows that his interpretation is incited in different senses by Satan and by the Spirit of Jesus.

15. GS 43.6: The Church is "by the power of the Holy Spirit the faithful spouse of her Lord" remains so, and "has never ceased to be the sign of salvation on earth." Let us note here the connection between the topic of the spouse and the Holy Spirit, source of fidelity, supernatural, and not natural or simply human. If the Church had been, at a single moment of history, unfaithful to Christ, she would have ceased to be the sign of salvation and would have lost her very reason for being.

16. LG, 6: Christ "unites the Church to himself by an unbreakable covenant" which is precisely the New Testament, differing from the Old which has been abrogated ("quam sibi foedere indissolubili sociavit").

17. Cf. LG, 25: DV, 10: The Pastoral Epistles; P. Medebielle, DBS (art. Dépôt) 11 (1934) 374-95.

18. A frequent topic in the Fathers, quoted in this sense by LG, 64, used here. See, among others, St. Augustine, sermo 191, 2, 3 (ML, 38, 1010).

19. GS, 43.6: "the Church is very well aware that among her members, both clerical and lay, some have been unfaithful to the Spirit of God during the course of many centuries."

20. St. Augustine, Enarrationes in Psalmos, 147.10: "The Church is called a virgin. Few are virgins in the flesh. All must be so in their hearts. Virginity of the heart is a faith uncorrupted." ("Paucorum est virginitas in carne, omnium debet esse in corde . . . virginitas cordis, fides incorrupta.")

21. *cf.* LG, 14: The Church teaches faithful Catholics that she is necessary as the body of Christ, for salvation: "Whoever, therefore, knowing that the Catholic Church was made necessary by God through Jesus Christ, would refuse to enter her or to remain in her could not be saved." *Cf.* LG 16 on non-Christians; UR 3 on the separated churches.

22. DV 23: It is, therefore, to the Church that we owe our being nourished by the word of God.

23. SC 84, 85. The maternal office of the Church does not leave her children in a purely passive condition. They share her maternal function, praying in the name of their mother. We are mother Church, we engender through her, in her, thanks to her, with her, children for divine life. *Cf.* text quoted in note 25.

24. GE, 3: Therefore it is the Church to which we owe that our life is imbued with the Spirit of Christ. *Cf. ibid.,* Introduction: "In fulfilling the mandate she has received from her divine founder to proclaim the mystery of salvation to all men, and to restore all things in Christ, holy mother the Church must be concerned with the whole of man's life, even the earthly part of it insofar as that has a bearing on his heavenly calling."

25. AA, 16; *cf. Ad gentes,* 5; CFW, ch. XI in its totality, esp. pp. 281-285; on the motherhood of the Church, see H. de Lubac, S.J., *Meditations rur L'Eglise,* Paris, 1953 and J. Madoz Mater Ecclesia, *Est. Ecclesiasticas* 16 (1942) 433-452.

26. *Cf.* AG, 7: "This missionary activity finds its reason in the will of God, . . . that the whole human race is to form one people of God, coalesce into the one body of Christ, and be built up into one temple of the Holy Spirit." A beautiful trinitarian expression of ecclesiology.

27. *Cf.* LG, 33, 34.

28. DV, 10: "The task of authentically interpreting the word of God, whether written or handed on, has been entrusted exclusively to the living teaching office of the Church, whose authority is exercised in the name of Jesus Christ."

29. *Ibid.:* ". . . one sacred deposit of the word of God, which is committed to the Church."

30. UR, 3: "It was to the apostolic college alone, of which Peter is the head, that we believe our Lord entrusted all the blessings of the New Covenant, in order to establish on earth the one body of Christ into which all those should be fully incorporated who already belong in any way to God's People." In other words, non-Catholic Christians are not yet fully incorporated into the Church, the body of Christ. *Cf.* UR, 22: "But baptism, of itself, is only a beginning, a point of departure, for it is wholly directed toward the acquiring of fullness of life in Christ. Baptism is thus oriented toward a complete profession of faith, a complete incorporation into the system of salvation such as Christ himself willed it to be, and finally, toward a complete participation in Eucharistic Communion."

31. In the alignment of these adjectives we bring together various versions of the Exercises (A, V, P2). The addition of the word "Roman" (P2) shows that St. Ignatius was aware of the papal implications of the term "hierarchical." *Cf.* Fessard, *op. cit.,* p. 167, n.1.

32. Ex. 365. Fessard (*op. cit.* p. 199) presents us with a suggestive interpretation of this rule, especially from an historical angle. He is correct in saying that the Ignatian text sees in the Holy Spirit "the conjugal bond of Christ and the Church." We think, however, that 2 Cor 3:17-4:4 may be used to explain more clearly the text of the rule.

(*Cf.* our note 14 where we have attempted to do this.)

33. *Cf.* DS, 1521.

34. St. Ignatius of Loyola, Letter on obedience, of March 26, 1553: "that you be quick to look for reasons to defend what the superior commands, or to what he is inclined, rather than to disapprove of it." Later on, St. Ignatius gives another means to attain to the perfection of obedience of judgment, the famous "blind obedience" which presupposes conformity of the order given to the divine will and "proceeds blindly, without inquiry of any kind, to carry it out." He continues, "But this does not mean that there is no freedom to propose a difficulty, should something occur to you different from his opinion, provided it be done after prayer." In the thirteenth rule of orthodoxy, is precisely a certain "clairvoyant blindness," to use an expression of St. John Climacus from his *Scale of Paradise Cf. Letters of St. Ignatius of Loyola,* William J. Young, S.J., 1959, p. 287ff.

35. So there can be seen, in this obedience and doctrinal submission at once blind and clairvoyant, an activity due to the gifts of wisdom, counsel and understanding of the Holy Spirit. This submission will be fostered and shown by applying what is proposed in the Constitutions of the Society: "The doctrine which they ought to follow in each branch should be that which is safer and more approved, as also the authors who teach it." (*Const.*, George Ganss, S.J., 1970, #358, 4, p. 189).

36. *Cf.* LG, 25: "Bishops, teaching in communion with the Roman Pontiff, are to be respected by all as witnesses to divine and Catholic truth. In matters of faith and morals, the bishops speak in the name of Christ and the faithful are to accept their teaching and adhere to it with a religious assent of soul. This religious submission of will and of mind must be shown in a special way to the authentic teaching authority of the Roman Pontiff, even when he is not speaking *ex cathedra.* That is, it is acknowledged with reverence, the judgments made by him are sincerely adhered to, according to his manifest mind and will. His mind and will in the matter may be known chiefly either from the character of the documents, from his frequent repetition of the same doctrine, or from his manner of speaking. "This text clearly shows the need for and the existence of an interior, noninfallible, conditional, but none the less real and obligatory, adherence of the intellect and of the will to the teachings in which the Church's infallibility is not involved.

37. GS, 62 #2, 7.

38. LG, 37: GS 62, 7.

39. UR, 6: "Christ summons the Church, as she goes her pilgrim way, to that continual reformation of which she always has need, insofar as she is an institution of men here on earth. Therefore, if the influence of events or of the times has led to deficiencies of conduct, in Church discipline, or even in the formulation of doctrine (which must be carefully distinguished from the deposit itself of faith), these should be appropriately rectified at the proper moment."

40. The expression "Christ's Catholic Church" is used in UR, 3.

41. GS 44 as a whole, esp.: "With the help of the Holy Spirit, it is the task of the entire People of God . . . to hear, distinguish, and interpret the many voices of our age, and to judge them in the light of the divine Word. In this way, revealed truth can always be more deeply penetrated, better understood, and set forth to greater advantage."

42. *Cf.* 1 Jn 1:3; 2 Jn 9: "Anyone who does not remain rooted in the teaching of Christ does not possess God; while anyone who remains rooted in the teaching possesses both the Father and the Son."

43. 1 Cor 2:14: "The natural man does not accept what is taught by the Spirit of God. For him, that is absurdity. He cannot come to know such teaching because it must be appraised in a spiritual way."

44. *Cf.* notes 36 and 39 of this chapter.

45. Ex. 362. It is to be noted that the expression of the Autograph "common people" or "lower classes" and of P2 "ignorant" is in Puhl "people". A remarkable parallel text serves to clarify this point and to bring out the gravity of a violation of the tenth rule in the eyes of St. Ignatius due to an unjustifiable finding fault and criticizing the orders, recommendations and way of acting of superiors. Ex. 42: "By recommendations of superiors is meant crusade indults and other indulgences, such as those for peace on condition of confession and reception of Holy Communion. For to be the cause of one acting against such pious recommendations and regulations of superiors, or to do so oneself, is no small sin."

46. GS, 74 and 79.

47. CD, 19; DH 11.

48. DH, 8.

49. John XXIII, *Pacem in Terris,* AAS LV (1963) 273, 274; DH, 6: "The protection and promotion of the inviolable rights of man ranks among the essential duties of government." DH, 11: "At the same time, however, the apostles did not hesitate to speak out against governing powers which set themselves in opposition to the holy will of God: "We must obey God rather than men" (Acts 5:29). This is the way along which countless martyrs and other believers have walked through all ages and over all the earth."

50. R.G.-Villoslada, S.J. ("San Ignacio de Loyola y Erasmo de Rotterdam," *Estudios Ecclesiasticos* XVII, 1943, 76-82) has shown the extraordinary similitude of the first twelve rules of orthodoxy with the refutation of the propositions of Erasmus, condemned by the Sorbonne at the request of the theologian Noel Beda, which he quotes in detail.

51. *Ibid.* 82–88, illustrates this rule by the famous dialogue between St. Ignatius of Loyola and Louis Vives, a follower of Erasmus, at Bruges during Lent of 1529. Inigo defended against Vives lenten fasting and abstinence. Doubtless, some will be tempted to think that every defense of the Church is an apologetic and anachronistic attitude. But does not the Holy Spirit invite us to love the Church and so defend her when attacked? What should we say? Quite simply show those who attack that God, reason, their own good requires that they praise even what they unjustly attack. The text of the ninth rule directs the defense of the precepts of the Church toward positive praise of them, thereby going beyond mere defense. It is not at all forbidden by this rule to give consideration to criticisms which suggest modifications and improvements in the Church's positive legislation which form part of its human aspect and which therefore has need of continual reformation (*cf.* UR, 6). This is so without, however, compromising the minimum stability necessary for the life of the Church. Finally, Vatican II expressly requires us to defend the doctrine of Christ (DH, 14).

52. The divine Office, consecration of the religious state, statues, blessed candles, and so a notable part of the things the rules of orthodoxy tells us to praise come under the category of sacramentals. They are "sacred signs which bear a resemblance to the sacraments: they signify effects,   particularly of a spiritual kind, which are obtained through the Church's intercession. By them, men are disposed to receive the chief effect of the sacraments, and various occasions in life are rendered holy" (SC, 60). By the sacraments and the sacramentals, almost every honorable use of material things is sanctified by divine grace

and directed to the praise of God (*cf.* SC, 61). It may be said then that what the rules of orthodoxy intend to inculcate and preserve when they urge us to "think with the Church" is a sacramental view of the universe and the praise of God.

53. St. Epiphanius' thought: "*Ecclesia finis omnium. rerum.*"

54. St. Augustine, *Sermo* 96, ML, 38, 584–88.

55. It is worthwhile to compare this text (Ex. 39) with that of the eleventh rule of orthodoxy (Ex. 363): "Further, just because scholastic doctors belong to more recent times, they not only have the advantage of correct understanding of the Holy Scripture and of the teaching of the saints and positive doctors, but, enlightened by the grace of God, they also make use of the decisions of the Councils and of the definitions and decrees of our holy Mother Church." Text of Vulgate has: "for helping us save ourselves" ("*ad salutis nostrae subsidium feliciter utuntur*"). Note that on the one hand the discovery of God's universal presence, or on the other hand the activity of theologians placing the documents of the magisterium of the Church at the service of the salvation of souls, is attributed to the same illumination, in accordance with the norms of the "Principle and Foundation "(Ex. 23). In both (Ex. 23 and Ex. 363), there is question of putting creatures at the service of the salvation of man (even the use of the term "*utendum*" in the Vulgate of both texts). The eleventh rule opens up for us a wide horizon of the Ignatian view of the magisterium of the Church, which he regarded as an instrument at the service of the salvation of souls.

56. *Cf.* CFW, 283-285.

57. A certain constructive criticism, one based on competence, prayer, humility, charity, exercised preferably in private, is admissible; *cf.* LG, 37: "An individual layman, by reason of his knowledge, competence, or outstanding ability which he may enjoy, is permitted and sometimes even obliged to express his opinion on things which concern the good of the Church." The Council adds: "Let it always be done in truth, in courage, and in prudence, with reverence and charity toward those who by reason of their sacred office represent the person of Christ."

58. The formula: "God, the author of all good," appears frequently in St. Ignatius' letters, for instance in the letter to Ferdinand, King of the Romans, Epp., III, 401, 402, #1721, middle of April 1551. The author of the Exercises followed the advice found in his favorite book, *The Imitation of Christ:* ". . . refer whatever found in created things to the glory and praise of their creator" (Bk. III, Ch. 34, 2).

59. *Cf.* Rom 1:16, (The gospel) "is the power of God leading everyone who believes in it to salvation." For St. Paul the gospel is the synthesis of the entire economy of mystery, the body of the truths of Christian faith (*cf.* J. Bover, S.J., *Teologia de San Pablo,* Madrid 1961, p. 92). So we can identify "the sacred and salvific doctrine" (Ex. 145) and the gospel.

60. *Cf.* The seventh rule of orthodoxy: "Hence, as far as is possible with the help of God, one may speak of faith and grace that the divine majesty may be praised" (Ex. 369). The Autograph and P3 reads: "for the greater glory and praise of his divine majesty," while the Autograph has: *diffuse*: in an extended and developed fashion. On the other hand, the fifteenth rule warns that: "we should not make it a habit of speaking much of predestination" (Ex. 367). Thus there is a distinction between talking about grace "at length and with emphasis" (Ex. 369) and "habitually" about predestination (Ex. 367). Bourdaloue is an example of one who preached on predestination (*Oeuvres completes,* Paris 1864, vol. I, pp. 382–400, pre. vendr. de carême). As the text goes on to say, St. Ignatius wanted Christians to avoid the temptation of a certain fatalism due to excessive preaching

on predestination and so "become indolent and neglect the works that are conducive to the salvation and spiritual progress of their souls" (Ex. 367).

61. *Cf.* LG, 33, 35; AA, 6.

62. The whole Church including the hierarchy is taught by Christ, and the whole Church is teaching, including the laity: DV, 10 and the preceding note.

63. *Cf.* DV, 25; this study will be only oral for the illiterate.

64. *Cf.* Fessard, *op. cit.,* vol. II, pp. 259-79.

65. *"in bonam trahere partem"* (V), the words: "every good Christian" indicate the universality of the presupposition.

66. *"propositionem obscuram alterius"* (V).

67. *"si mal la entiende"* (A); *"si minus recte . . ."* (V).

68. *"con amor"* (A); *"benigne"* (V). As Fessard observes (*op. cit.,* pp. 266–68) at this third stage the formal dialogue ends. The fourth stage implies virtual recourse to the community, to authority, to God, through prayer.

69. " . . . *illum sanum intellectu ac securum reddat ab errore"* (V). The intellectual integrity spoken of here implies the exclusion of error, which "infests minds" and "poisons the free will," a mortal illness of the spirit (*cf.* Ex. 41, 369).

70. While the Autograph and P2 speak of the salvation of the neighbor, P1 speaks of "defending his proposition from error," in the words of the presupposition, both in the Autograph and in P2. There is not always a contradiction between the two: "salvation of the neighbor" and "saving his proposition from error." *Cf.* MHSJ, vol. 100, pp. 114-116, Rome, 1969.

70. *Cf.* San Ignacio de Loyola, *Obras completas,* Madrid, BAC, 1947 ed. Larranaga, pp. 543-51; MHSJ, vol. 66, FN, vol. I, p. 267; Rome, 1943. St. Ignatius followed his own advice given in the presupposition, but also in the tenth rule of orthodoxy, at the end: "But while it does harm in the absence of our superiors to speak evil of them before the people, it may be profitable to discuss their bad conduct with those who can apply a remedy" (Ex. 362). The Vulgate sees in this "private admonition" *"privatim admonere"* a worthwhile act (*operae pretium*). The text of the tenth rule covers in a general way the two different suggestions which crown the presupposition: direct fraternal correction, and indirect by recourse to the Church. We may consult on the question of fraternal correction ST, II.II. 33. The entire question might serve as an (anticipatory) commentary on the last part of the Ignatian presupposition.

71. *Cf.* San Ignacio de Loyola, *Obras completas,* I. Madrid, 1947, p. 546.

72. UR, 10: "Instruction in sacred theology and other branches of knowledge, especially those of a historical nature, must also be presented from an ecumenical point of view, so that at every point they may more accurately correspond with the facts of the case. It is highly important that future bishops and priests should have mastered a theology carefully worked out in this way and not polemically, especially in what concerns the relations of separated brethren with the Catholic Church." Nevertheless, it is clear (*cf.* the following note), that the desire of Vatican II to avoid polemics is not absolute or pure and simple, but relative and conditional, in so far as possible, and especially to the extent where polemics, especially, personal, bring on even greater evils than those they intend to remedy. Controversy, differing from dialogue, seeks conflict.

73. LG, 25.

74. *Cf.* Chaine, *Les Epîtres Catholiques,* Paris, 1939, p. 345: see the words *erreur* and *faux docteurs* in the analytic tables. The first letter of St. John combats Christological errors etc.

75. GS 58.

76. AA, 6; OT, 15: "The history of philosophy should be so taught that by coming to grasp the basic principles of the various systems, students will hold what is shown to be true among them, and be able to detect the roots of errors and disprove them." The same might well be said in regard to the teaching of the history of theology.

77. LG, 17.

78. Ex. 41. Let us note here that, in the eyes of St. Thomas Aquinas, subjects have the duty to "object" publicly to their prelate when faith is endangered. In other cases, fraternal correction of a superior by an inferior should remain secret. It is a work of charity, not of justice (ST, II.II. 33.4.2): Correction which is a work of justice belongs exclusively to prelates or religious superiors.

79. St. Catherine of Sienna, *Dialogue,* ed. Hurtaud, Paris, 1915, vol. I, Ch. 105, p. 383.

80. GS, 28; *cf.* DH 14.

81. DH, 3.

82. St. Cyril of Alexandria, Homily at Council of Ephesus on Mary, Hom. 4, PG, 77, 991; 77, 995, 996.

83. *Ibid.*

84. *Cf.* St. Fulgentius of Ruspe, Ad Probam, de Virg. et Hum. c. 5: "*Ecclesia sponsa est etc . . .* " ML, 65, 327.

85. *Cf.* LG, 53: "Mary (is) . . . the temple of the Holy Spirit"; LG, 4: *"Spiritus in Ecclesia et in cordibus fidelium tamquam in templo habitat"* (*cf.* 1 Cor 3:16; 6:19).

86. The authority of the Church, on a psychological plane, is so much the greater since it does not come to her from herself but from God. Parents who do not present the divine origin of their authority, with humility, far from adding to it, psychologically speaking, lessen their authority. The same holds true for ecclesiastical superiors. Roothaan, a General of the Society of Jesus in the nineteenth century, said: "*Ego obediens praecipio"* —I command obeying, I only command to exercise obedience in virtue of which I am a superior.

87. An expression found in the Greek Fathers. Theodotos of Ancyra (d. 446), MG, 77, 1393, 1394; St. Proclus of Constantinople, (d. 446) says: Mary is the "mother of Mystery" (PG 65, 791, 792).

88. By the expression: "nuptial virginity" we intend to emphasize that Mary's virginity was lived in the context of her real married life with Joseph, a type of virginity. It is through this type that her virginity is distinct from all others, in so far as her virginal marriage was destined for the virginal procreation of the God-man. It would therefore be more exact to speak of a maternal and nuptial virginity.

89. In the fifth rule (Ex. 357): "However, it must be remembered that vow deals with matters that lead us closer to evangelical perfection." St. Ignatius does not deny that marriage is good and praiseworthy (*cf.* Ex. 356) but presupposes that the vow can be made only about what is objectively better. Although spouses are called to perfection (*cf.* LG, 42), they are not called to what St. Ignatius calls the state of evangelical perfection or of the counsels (*cf.* Ex. 135).

90. *Cf.* SC, 100 "And the laity, too, are encouraged to recite the divine Office, either with the priests, or among themselves, or even individually." Paul VI spoke of this later in his apostolic constitution *Laudis Canticum,* in 1970; likewise, the "*Institutio Generalis de Liturgia horarum,*" published with the new divine Office, in 1971 (#21, 22, 27): families also are invited to recite the divine Office.

91. The divine Office, in general, does not present the Gospels read at Mass. The Rosary constitutes, in as much as it is a meditation and a contemplation of the mysteries of the gospel, a very useful complement of the divine Office.

92. We try here to bring about a "Christological concentration" of the first nine rules of orthodoxy (Ex. 353–61) by showing how each one of them concerns actually the mystery of Jesus and by recapitulating them under Christ; *cf.* Eph. 1:10.

93. *Cf.* Eph 1: 6, 12.

94. *Cf.* St. Augustine, *De dono perseverentiae* 24, 67 (ML, 45, 1034): ST, III. 24.3.4; CFW, 428.

95. *Cf.* Heb 12:2, "Let us keep our eyes fixed on Jesus, who inspires and perfects our faith."

96. st. John of the Cross, *Vive flamme d'amour,* I, 1.

97. *Cf.* Pius XII, *Mystici Corporis,* AAS, XXXV (1943) 211; CFW, 366 ff.

98. *Cf.* ST, I.II.106. 1.

99. *Cf.* LG, 17.

100. *Cf.* Rom 8:9.

101. *Cf.* Jn 6:68; Mt 24:35.

102. DV, 8.

103. G. Martelet, S.J., translates the Latin text of DV, 9 thus: "Holy tradition, became the word of God."

104. DV, 8–10. The Council speaks here evidently of the divine-apostolic tradition and not of whatsoever ecclesiastical tradition. The distinction between tradition and tradition is furthermore not easy to establish, since tradition grows subjectively and by way of traditions which explain it and develops into the "fullness of divine truth" toward which the Church constantly moves" . . . "until the words of God reach their complete fulfillment in her" (DV, 8, 2). Then all will vanish before the appearance of the one divine Word seen face to face. In the light of the text we shall quote in notes 108 and 109, it may be said that the desire, at least implicit, of Vatican II is that it be seen that the traditions of the churches and ecclesial communities still separated from Rome contribute, in all they present of truth, to the subjective development and the explanation of tradition in and through the Church until the return of Christ. This, in order that she might give back to him the deposit of revelation (entrusted to her) with the increment gained, that is, with such explanations. Consequently it becomes more and more obvious that the notion and reality of tradition are to be from now on elements of unity among all Christian communities rather than factors of division.

105. *Cf.* 1 Jn 2:1; Jn 1:29. We think the expression "Lamb paraclete" coupled with "Spirit Paraclete" (*cf.* Jn 15,26) makes clear the distinction between the two paracletes.

106. *Cf.* DH, 14: "The disciple is bound by a grave obligation toward Christ his master ever more adequately to understand the truth received from him, faithfully to pro-

claim it, and vigorously to defend it, never—be it understood—having recourse to means that are incompatible with the spirit of the gospel.''

107. St. Augustine, *in Jn. tract.* 32, 8: (ML, 35, 1646; OT, 9.

108. Ecumenical Directory promulgated by the Holy See, II, 70: DC, LXVII (1970) 521: *cf.* paragraphs 74 and 92 which indirectly explain the conditions of applying the advice given. Catholic students of theology can be authorized to attend courses given by non-Catholic theologians in institutions of other Christians if they have been sufficiently prepared, if they have the psychological and spiritual maturity demanded, not without taking into consideration the nature of the instruction given. The more this instruction is of a doctrinal nature, the more circumspect superiors should be in giving · them permission. It is evident that many students do not fulfill the conditions of adequate preparation and of maturity. They would not be qualified to partake of the riches found in Protestant spirituality without danger. These students, in the measure of their ignorance of Catholic doctrine on the precise points under consideration, would be incapable of recognizing errors or (and more so) of refuting them. For frequently the errors are mixed up with the riches. To such students might well be applied the precept of the natural law to avoid putting their faith in proximate danger without grave reason and without taking proper precautions for safeguarding their Catholic faith. All this does not in any way hinder that for a certain number of others the suggestion of the Ecumenical Directory be, on the contrary, the beginning of a great spiritual and doctrinal enrichment for a more profound personal Catholicity.

109. LG, 8; UR, 3.

110. UR, 1.

111. UR, 11: "It is, of course, essential that doctrine be clearly presented in its entirety. Nothing is so foreign to the spirit of ecumenism as a false conciliatory approach which harms the purity of Catholic doctrine and obscures its assured genuine meaning.''

112. *Cf.* LG, 14: Whosoever, therefore, knowing that the Catholic Church was made necessary by God through Jesus Christ, would refuse to enter her to remain in her could not be saved.'' He who should wish, up to the last moment of his existence, to separate himself in this way from the Catholic Church would sin by the very fact against the Holy Spirit (*cf.* Mk 3:29). It is well to recall here the teaching of St. Irenaeus: "Where the Church is, there is the Spirit of God; where the Spirit of God is, there is the Church and all grace" (*Adv. Haer,* III, 24, 1; PG, 7, 966). As the Church instituted by Christ is founded on Peter, we may add with St. Ambrose: "Where Peter is, there is the Church; where the Church is, there is no death, but eternal life" (*enarr. in Ps.* 40, 30; ML 14, 1082). *Cf.* Ex. 353; P. 2: (*sponsa Christi*) *est "sancta mater Ecclesia hierarchica, quae Romana est."* The Roman Church is the Church governed by the Spirit for our salvation.

113. *Cf.* Teixidor on the eighteenth rule of orthodoxy: servile fear and pure love in St. Thomas Aquinas and St. Augustine, (*Manresa,* VIII, 1932, 312–316). Fessard rightly observes, in his second volume, that this last rule of orthodoxy, with which the book of Exercises ends, constitutes also a recapitulation of the Exercises. It praises servile fear, which corresponds to the purgative way of the first week and which helps us overcome mortal sin (servile fear which Luther still praised in 1514; *cf.* his sermon, O. Scheel, Dokumente zu Luther Entwicklung), as well as filial fear, which no longer fears the punishment of sin but the possibility of offending God, and which corresponds to the il-illuminative way and especially, to the intense service of God our Lord out of pure love, which corresponds to the unitive way (*cf.* ST, II.II.19.11).

18

CONTEMPLATING
IN HUMAN ACTIONS AND BEYOND,
DIVINE LOVE

We have reached the summit which crowns and recapitulates the Ignatian Exercises. We shall follow step by step their author's thoughts presented us in this contemplation:[1] "to inflame within us spiritual love" in regard to God and to the world. In the course of this contemplation we shall intersperse, as he does, oblationary colloquies with the divine Persons. We shall, however, preface our commentary with an introduction which will show, we trust, the permanent meaning underlying what we think are the historical sources of the contemplation. We shall have it followed by a consecration to the Eucharistic Heart of Jesus, a synthesis of what we think is the hidden essence of the Exercises in general and of this last contemplation in particular.

A. Introduction. This contemplation, initially a method of prayer to obtain the grace of observing the first commandment, has become, without ceasing to be such, the summit of the Exercises and the start of the retreatant's return to the world. In it is expressed, without being consummated, his return to God.

It is known[2] that commentators are in sharp disagreement as to the function of this contemplation in the over-all design of the author of the Exercises.

Some see in it "the conclusion of the four weeks as the "Foundation" is their introduction."[3] Its four points are not unrelated to the four weeks. Each point takes up one of them in ascending parallel. The contemplation itself comes immediately after the fourth week and is distinct from it. Others,[4] on the contrary, think that it "seems to be rather on the same plane as the three methods of prayer.[5]

We think that, despite what has been written to the contrary,[6] both views are reconcilable. It seems that St. Ignatius has converted into a synthetic conclusion of the Exercises, at the moment the retreatant returns to God's world, what he had originally lived and presented as an exercise intended for the examination of conscience on the first commandment.

On the one hand, the inquests of Alcala in 1527 already show St. Ignatius' teaching how to meditate on the "the method of loving God."[7] As
early as Manresa, according to Polanco, he endeavored "to inflame others in
the love of God and formed them in the methods of prayer."[8] Later, the
"Summary of St. Ignatius' preaching on Christian Doctrine"[9] doubtless tells
about Inigo's past practices by showing him catechizing a propos of the first
commandment. This teaching includes that on the three powers of the soul
which are to be employed to love God whole heartedly by recalling His bene-
factions: creation, redemption, spiritual favors received (*cf.* Ex. 234). Here we
have the *memory* involved. Then there is the *will*. The whole soul is to be
engaged in loving God through the joy which the will strives to acquire in all
things, desirous of pleasing in all its Creator and Lord. Ignatius concluded the
catechesis on the commandment stating that there is love of God for himself,
and love of neighbor for God our Lord. For *understanding* this twofold love,
he added, it is very necessary to be indifferent to all changeable things such
as riches and poverty."

It is enough to read this text to perceive that there was a moment, in the
genesis of the Exercises, when a "method of prayer" on the first commandment covered a subject which the author afterwards divided between the
"Foundation" and the contemplation for inflaming divine love, revealing
thereby that, from start to finish, the Exercises intend to purify, enlighten and
enkindle by this love the retreatant's heart.

Fessard seems inclined to accept this hypotheses along with other arguments
not less convincing. The retreat notes of the English humanist John Helyar,
who made the Exercises in 1535/1536, present a preamble to the "Foundation", the content of which is identical with what was to become "Introductory Observation 5" (Ex. 5) and to provide also the essential element of
the oblation "*Sume et Suscipe*" (Ex. 234) in the contemplation "*Ad Amorem.*" In Helyar's notes, as in the oblation, there is to be noted insistence
on turning the memory, intellect and will to God.

Fessard adds: "The formal ressemblances in the Helyar text go so far that
there is reason to ask: would it be that this version testifies to a state of
Ignatius' thinking, or at least of the composition of the Exercises, in which
the "*Ad Amorem*" in germ is so slightly distinguished from the "Foundation"
that the "*Suscipe*" appears in the disposition in which the retreatant should
be when he is going to meditate on the "*Homo creatus est*"? Without doubt,
Helyar's text only represents the notes of one retreatant. Also it is not possible to derive any apodictic proof in favor of the identification we suggest.
Yet, in matters of this nature it is futile to look for more than such indications" (Dialectique. . ., vol. I, Paris, 1956, p. 189.). And Fessard adds in a
note that this identification had been suggested to him in the course of a
conversation with Father Giuliani.

We think that the dove-tailing of the data with the details which result
from the analysis of St. Ignatius' catachesis and of the first method of prayer,

in regard to the first commandment, is such that there is moral certitude as to the genesis of the "*Ad Amorem*." No one, to our knowledge, has suggested prior to this more parallels than we have presented here.

On the other hand, it seems clear enough that this final contemplation belongs essentially, as does the fourth week which it follows, to the unitive way (*cf.* Ex. 10).[10] It assumes that progression of the first three weeks and even that of the fourth, if we keep in mind the plenitude of the fruits it can produce. This does not prevent at all giving this contemplation even to someone who makes only the first week if we have understood the perspicacity and profundity of an observation by Nadal. He says that in the course of each exercise each retreatant should exercise himself successively in the purgative, the illuminative and finally the unitive way.[11] This makes it perfectly clear that it could have been given as early as the first week, after receiving Holy Communion.[12] Is not the grace proper to the Eucharist precisely "to inflame him with spiritual love" (*cf.* Ex. 44)? We cannot see any reason for depriving a retreatant of a meditation or contemplation on the exercise of the first commandment of God!

We think, therefore, that it is possible at least' to set forth the following working hypotheses which further research might weaken or confirm. It is this, that Inigo de Loyola was progressively led to distinguish, in a very early exercise which was a method of prayer-examination of conscience aimed at obtaining the grace to observe the first commandment (*cf.* Ex. 240), a more ascetic area, which became the "Foundation," and a more mystical area, which became this contemplation. The love of God, after having been detached from creatures, ends up by finding in them, with a joyous spontaneity, God's presence and action. The return to God opens up a return to the world filled with God.

Since love never finds that it is exercised to its full extent and with the intensity to which it aspires, we shall comment on this "contemplation for inflaming, attaining, obtaining and understanding[13] spiritual love," in respect to God and to the world in God, as being inseparably a prayer of petition to that effect, a method of prayer, of contemplating the first divine commandment, to which Christ has given its precise significance on applying it to himself,[14] the Incarnate Word. The *spiritual* love we seek thus to "inflame, attain, obtain and understand" is that of the *Incarnate* Word and, in him, through him, thanks to him, that of the Father and the Holy Spirit. We ask (*cf.* Ex. 240, A, P2) "for a perfect understanding of the commandment of divine love, in order to observe it the better for the glory and praise of the divine Majesty."

In other words, the object of this contemplation, already suggested by its title—*contemplation to inflame* us with spiritual love of God—is to put us in a state as constant and ordinary as possible of consolation, so as not to place an obstacle to all the intense[15] graces of consolation with which God wishes to shower us. It suffices, for understanding this, to compare this title with the description of consolation in the rules for discernment of spirits: "I call it consolation when an interior movement is aroused in the soul, by which it is inflamed with love of its Creator and Lord, and as a consequence, can love no creature on the face of the earth for its own sake, but only in the Creator of them all" (Ex. 316).[16]

The object of the contemplation which appears much more clearly in the light of the title of the Vulgate properly translated, is not then only to obtain divine love, but to obtain to be inflamed with it to the extent that this fire purifies us of all inordinate love of creatures and enlightens our hearts by making them perceive His presence in the whole universe (cf. Ex. 39). We only contemplate divine love in order to be set afire by that love in its very attainment.

B. Two Preliminary points (Ex. 230,1; 231,2)

Their purpose is to correct the egocentric notion that the old man tends to have ever and ever again, that is, to propose to himself about charity and love. Far from being first and before all a feeling, "love ought to manifest itself in deeds rather than in words." This is so for it depends more on the former than on the latter.[17] Ardent love is an active love. In what does action consist? It consists not only in receiving, as the old man tends to think and desire, but "love consists in a mutual sharing of goods, for example, the lover gives and shares with the beloved what he possesses, or something of that which he has or is able to give; and vice versa, the beloved shares with the lover." In other words, love implies reciprocity "of knowledge," and of freely sharing of "honors, or riches."

Assuredly, the author of the Exercises describes here the requirements of authentic love, love grasped in its inmost nature.[18] He wishes, starting out from the analogy of human love, worthy of the name, to make us reflect on the relations of love between the Creator and the creature and on their demands.

Indeed he exemplifies the manifestations of this reciprocity: "if one has knowledge, he shares it with the one who does not possess it; and so if one has honors, or riches. Thus, one always gives to the other" (Ex. 231).

Let us explain more in detail what is understood. The divine Persons, upon loving, ignorant, poor, ignominious humans (cf. Ex. 59; 1 Cor 15:43) make them sharers in their riches, and their glory.[19] The God, who had invited us to make our own the poverty and the ignominy of the humiliations he had assumed for our sake,[20] is He who offers us now a share in his wisdom, his possessions and his glory. Christ has never ceased to wish to have us enter with him into the glory of his Father (Ex. 95).

Furthermore, we must place the second preliminary point in the context of the trinitarian mystery. The Son receives everything from the Father (knowledge, glory) upon receiving from him, in his eternal passive generation, the absolutely simple divine nature, a nature common to them—everything, not only a part. And the Son, on loving the Father, in the act of thanksgiving, produces with him the one who is their eternal and mutual communion, the personal return of the Son loved and loving the Father, their very reciprocity. The Holy Spirit, in turn, receives from the Father and the Son all they have in common, their power and their action, their nature in a word. The exchange of intra-divine love founds the reciprocity of our human loves[21] as the exchange of love between each one of us and each one of the divine Persons.

After these preliminary points, come the *usual preparatory prayer and the first prelude or composition of place,* "which here is to behold myself standing in the presence of God our Lord and of his angels and saints, who intercede for me" (Ex. 232).[22] The Church of heaven joins with that of earth in prayer for me, especially at each Mass, each *"synaxis."* The saints and angels, under the action of the Spirit of love, pursue me with their love. In union with Christ, priest and king, with Mary, their queen, they intercede to obtain for me the grace I desire.[23]

The God in whose presence I am (whether I think of it or not) is the immense God who fills and overflows all places, the infinite God, present everywhere, everywhere and at all times loving me. Thus all places, all space, are filled with this simple being who is everywhere infinite and incomprehensible love for me.

By the *second prelude,* I ask "what I desire. Here it will be to ask for an intimate knowledge of the many blessings received, that, filled with gratitude, I may in all things love and serve the Divine Majesty" (Ex. 233).

So, then, it is a *twofold grace* I ask: light for the intellect, strength for the will. May my intellect know divine love, may my grateful will be inflamed[24] wholly with love of this Love, upon consecrating itself fully to its worship and service. May I thus (*cf.* Ex. 240) observe better the first and supreme commandment of this love, loving it in everything, thanks to a perfect understanding of God's precept of love.

Now, it must be noted that the perfect understanding and even, consequently, the perfect observance of the commandment of pure love is eschatological. In a sense, they are inaccessible here below and will not be obtainable if not after death. This statement at first sight is startling, yet is quite consonant with the explicit teaching of St. Augustine and of St. Thomas Aquinas.

On the one hand, it is true, of course, that charity, or love of God, is, even in this life, immediate, while knowledge of God the Creator, is always mediate, that is, through knowledge of creatures (ST. II, II, 27, 4). On the other hand, in the eyes of St. Augustine, concupiscence prevents the human person here below from loving God fully. St. Thomas reaches the same conclusion though by a different procedure. Due to the importance of the subject, it is well to quote what he says at some length. "A precept can be

fulfilled in two ways: perfectly and imperfectly. A precept is fulfilled perfectly, when the end intended by the author of the precept is reached; yet it is
fulfilled imperfectly, however, when, although the end intended by the author
is not reached, nevertheless the order to that end is not departed from . . .
Now God intends by this precept that man should be entirely united to
him, and this will be realized in heaven, when God will be 'all in all,'
according to 1 Cor 15:28. Hence this precept will be observed fully and
perfectly in heaven; yet it is fulfilled, though imperfectly on the way. Nevertheless on the way one man will fulfill it more perfectly than another, and
so much the more as he approaches by some kind of likeness to the perfection of heaven" (ST,II.II.44.6; cf. text quoted here of St. Augustine,
De perf. justitiae, cap. 8; ML,44,300, 301).

As is seen, in the very subtle conclusion of this instructive text, the "Eucharistic doctor" (Pius XI) explains that those on the way, though incapable of observing the precept of charity in its full perfection (since they cannot
love God with an ever actual love ST, II.II.24.8), nevertheless observe it
the more perfectly they approach, in fact, this eschatological ideal, by thinking as constantly as possible of God and by loving him in the same way,
as much as human infirmity permits, imitating (in a necessarily limited
manner) the angels and saints who are already in heaven, established in
the vision and love of God. It is precisely so because the earthly perfection
of charity is not purely and simply such that it can ever grow (ST, II.
II.24.8.3), "Perfectio viae non est perfectio simpliciter." It is concupiscence
which is partly the reason for this impossibility of keeping our minds constantly on God, with an ever actual love, from which we are still banished.
The sacrament of the Eucharist is the most powerful instrument given us
here below to activate, as constantly as possible, the virtue of charity, and
to bring us close thereby to our last and one act, lasting forever, of eschatological and total charity (cf. also ST, II.II.44.4.2). It is because he is the
"doctor of charity" that St. Thomas is at the same time the Eucharistic
and the angelic doctor.

Then, all at once there stands out the reason for the superiority of the
interior act of charity in regard to God relative to all external acts of the
same virtue, a point equally developed by the common doctor (ST,II.II.
27.6.3). It is by the former that man attains his last end, while the latter
are but means. Apostolic action will pass, but the love of God and of men
will not pass. If love ought to manifest itself in deeds rather than in words
(Ex. 230), it is to be shown more in interior works than in external actions. Transitory love will pass, immanent love will never pass.

Therefore it becomes clear: in the heart of Catholic tradition, the Ignatian petition in the second prelude of our contemplation means the desire
of and the petition for an earthly love as aware, constant, real and total as
possible for the Majesty of divine Love. Thus there flows a first implication
from the first and greatest commandment: "You shall love the Lord your

God with your whole heart, with your whole soul and with your whole mind"
(Mt 22:37, 38). So we understand how St. Alphonse Rodriguez could write:
"The principal study of the servant of God ought to be to make every effort
to stay united to God in prayer, by contemplation and actual love. The servant of God must keep firmly in mind that the principal foundation of his
spiritual life consists in this familiarity with God. He should firmly believe
that it is his treasure and all his good and exercise himself constantly in the
practice of his love. So he will keep his eyes closed to all the rest and put all
things under his feet. It is assuredly indeed, the end for which he has been
created, and a Christian could have nothing better to do. True love of God
is the best of all acts. St. Thomas says, in fact, that the interior act of charity is the most meritorious act man can perform" (*Union and transformation
of the Soul in Jesus Christ,* Ch. V). Whence comes the importance of "ejaculatory prayer."

However, the grace sought by the second prelude of our contemplation not
only implies the fullness and actuality of our charity toward God, but also its
purity and in some way its exclusiveness. There is question of loving God in
all things (Ex. 233) and of consecrating ourselves wholly to his love *(ibid.* V).
St. Francis de Sales helps us here to coordinate and better perceive certain
points of the Ignatian exercise, which he appreciates so much: "The price of
the love we bear God depends on the eminence and nobility of the motive
for which and according to which we love Him. It depends on the fact that
we love Him for His sovereign, infinite goodness as God and according to
which He is God" (*Treatise on the Love of God,* X, 3; *cf.* Ex. 370).

Now, our doctor observes: "There are souls . . . who love excessively and
with an over tender and passionate love what God wishes they love. These
souls love the divine goodness above all things, but not in all things . . . due
to causes and motives which are certainly not against God, but rather apart
from God. They love excessively, but do not at all love excesses, diverted
through loving outside of him and without him what they should love only
in him and through him" (*ibid.,* X, 4; *cf.* Ex. 316, 338, 184).

Other souls love God in all things, although they love many things along
with God and God along with many things (*cf.* Ex. 154; *Treatise,* X, 5). St.
Ignatius suggests and asks them to detach themselves as much as possible
from love of all creatures for concentrating all their affections on the Creator
of all, for loving him in all and loving all in him (*Const.* III, 1, 26, # 288;
cf. also ST, II.II.27.8).

St. Francis de Sales, while recognizing that "it would not be possible to
live at all without passing from one to the other of these diverse loves,"
presents to us the Virgin, both spouse and mother of Christ, as the sole
creature who has loved God "equally everywhere, apart from everything and
without everything" (*Treatise* . . . X, 5).

The petition for grace of the second prelude means therefore the petition
for a constant labor of purification of our motives for loving creatures out

of love for God. This love must be such that "the soul, as a consequence, can love no creature on the face of the earth for its own sake, but only in the Creator of them all" (Ex. 316).

This twofold grace of light and strength has a social, horizontal direction: I should acknowledge the love that the Trinity, in Christ, has manifested toward the Church and men, in order to be able, in all places, at all times, to love and serve Christ, the whole Christ.

C. Grades of Contemplation

1. First Point: the gifts and the gift of God.

The author of the Exercises asks me here "to recall to mind the blessings of creation and redemption, and the special favors I have received. I will ponder with great affection how much God our Lord has done (and suffered) [25] for me and how much he has given me of what he possesses, and finally, how much, as far as he can, the same Lord desires to give himself to me according to his divine decrees, (according to his good pleasure)" (Ex. 234). [26]

Upon giving me what he possesses, God has also given me what he is, within the bounds compatible with my mortality. In each of his gifts, God gives himself, the Infinite, the Eternal, to me, without being hindered by the very finiteness of his gifts. He gives himself to me "as much as possible" in so much as I place no obstacle in the way. [27] Yet, so long as I live in this world and have not been confirmed in grace, the Eternal cannot give me himself definitively. The gift God makes me of himself remains modified by the fragility of my free will which is, however, comprised in the design of his salvific Providence.

The gift of God is summed up, condensed, culminates in the Eucharist. "If God is for us, who can be against us? Is it possible that he who did not spare his own Son but handed him over for the sake of us all will not grant us all things besides" (Rom. 8, 31–32)? [28]

The object of this first point is to make me "ponder with great affection the very love which God has given me and with which He has given himself to me on giving me all that I have and all that I am. To inflame my love there is no means more powerful [29] than that which consists in contemplating the infinite, eternal, gratuitous, merciful, incomprehensible, uncreated and creative love of the Divine Persons for me. This is exactly what the providence of the Trinity has had in mind on asking man to honor and adore their love for us (a love identical with the Trinity itself), in and through the real symbol of the wounded and glorified Heart of Jesus Christ. The abundant multiplicity of divine gifts brings me back, in and through the Eucharistic Heart of Jesus, to the perfect simplicity of the eternal giver, who makes himself a one and supreme gift.

Yet this love symbolized and summed up in the Heart of the Redeemer not only manifests itself in the gifts of creation and redemption which are

common to all men, but also in "special and *personal* gifts" (Ex. 234, V),
made to each one. It is permissible to think, with Calveras, that in the Ignatian terminology "special gifts" refers to spiritual gifts (Ex. 322), offered by
the divine and sovereign goodness (Ex. 20) to those who place no obstacle
to it, that is, to consolation and to intense grace. All who have received the
grace to make a retreat with the Exercises constitute a restricted elite and
many of this number have received these intense graces of consolation.

Let us recall, in fact, that only these graces of intense consolation bring
about the effective conversion by which the soul enters upon the strait road
of true evangelical perfection and becomes capable of letting itself be carried,
full sail, by the Holy Spirit. Thus only can it come in all things "to love and
serve the Divine Majesty" (Ex. 233), which is precisely the grace sought in
our contemplation.

In other words, the author of the Exercises invites the retreatant to revive
in himself the inebriating recollection of the intense graces and consolations he
has received during his whole life, without which he would not have been
able to make the retreat and which have brought him to its culminating and
real point. He invites him to recall all the actions and *events* of his life
during which he has been "inflamed with love of his Creator and Lord, and
as a consequence, can love no creature on the face of the earth for its own
sake, but only in the Creator of them all" and "all interior joy that invites
and attracts" most vehemently "to what is for the salvation of his soul"
(*cf.* Ex. 316). This he is to do in order to establish himself beyond all superficial consolation, as much as possible, in a *permanent state* of consolation
and of spiritual love, a love, at the same time inflamed, for God and for
all things in God, especially for all men in God.

Briefly, to detach ourselves from every trace still remaining of carnal love,
the remembrance of the intense graces of spiritual love, without attachment
to these signal graces (*cf.* Ex. 322), seems particularly efficacious to the contemplative of Manresa. These intense graces, are they not so many water-wells
in the desert which give the pilgrim renewed strength on his journey toward
the supreme oasis of the Kingdom, toward the source at which he will at
last be able to sate his thirst for perfectly loving love in a manner no longer
habitual only, but ever constant and wholly present (*cf.* ST, II.II.184.2)?
Above all, are not these intense graces of consolation, this inmost experience
of the gifts of the Transcendant who make the Christians perceive the meaning of infinite and personal love, for him, inherent to the mysteries and sacraments of God, Creator and Redeemer? In short, is it not above all through
these "special gifts" that he perceives the personal love which shines out in
the "universal" and common "gifts"? Does he not also perceive that each
universal and common gift is offered by God in a special way, in an ever
singular context since it implies the whole and singular destiny of the beneficiary?

St. Ignatius proposes to us a special response to these special gifts. We shall comment on it after the fourth point.

2. *Second Point: The Presence of the Giver in His gifts.*

God who gives himself to me with and through creatures is not far from them, but is immanent to them. The contemplative of Manresa expresses this thus: "This is to reflect how God dwells in creatures: in the elements giving them existence, in the plants giving them life, in the animals conferring upon them sensation, in man bestowing understanding, So he dwells in me and gives me being, life, sensation, intelligence, and makes a temple of me, besides having created me in the likeness and image of the Divine Majesty" (Ex. 235).

God has created the elements, the plants and the animals only for man, for all men and for me in particular, in order that man glorify him. I sum up in myself all creation, since I am, I live, I feel, as do creatures inferior to me, but I am, with other men, the only being that knows that I am, that I live, that I feel. It is this microcosm of the universe which is man whom God has chosen to make his temple, to raise to the supernatural order, to a share in the intimacy of his own trinitarian life which neither human intellect nor free will could ever have guessed, desired and attained by its own power. God wants to dwell in each human person in such a way that not only his existence and his perfections but also the Trinity of his Persons be objects of this knowledge and love.[30]

God, present in the universe and in man is not, however, the "Wholly Other",[31] but is "Other." The immanent God remains transcendant to the universe and to man to which he is present. It is precisely as transcendent, superior to all, that he is present and immanent to all as "Other."

Not content with being present to me in the world and in the intimacy of my mind, as the author of nature and of my nature in its totality, he has wished further to make himself present, in a way much more intimate, to my mind as the object of my faith and of my filial and supernatural charity. "Anyone who loves me will be true to my word, and my Father will love him; we will come to him and make our dwelling place with him" (Jn 14:23). However, the Son and the Father make their dwelling in me in order that I may dwell in them: "Live on in me, as I do in you" (Jn 15:4). St. Ignatius of Antioch wrote to the Ephesians: "Let us perform all our actions with the thought that the Lord dwells in us. Thus we will be his temples and he himself will be our God dwelling in us. This is just what actually is and what we shall clearly see through the true love which brings us to him."[32]

In other words, to the measure we will love God as present in us and act in the loving presence of this Presence, will we let him enter ever more into us and render himself more intimate to our minds.

God who dwells in elements, plants and animals is always the God who loves me with an eternal and infinite, incomprehensible and merciful love. His love for me gives them being, life and feeling and puts them at my service. In a supreme manner he dwells in the temple of Christ's Body (*cf.* Jn 2:19, 21) and of his Soul, really present in the Eucharist in so many temples of stone just that my soul become ever more, through Communion, the temple of the Lord, of the Father and of their Spirit. It is through the Eucharist that we pass on from the image to the likeness of the Triune God, that we become an image ever more like the Trinity.[33]

"You willed, oh eternal Trinity, that man wholly share you. You gave him memory to recall your benefits, and through it he shares your power, oh eternal Father. You gave him intellect to know your goodness, and through it share your only Son's wisdom. You gave him will to love what the intellect sees of your truth and through it share the love of the Holy Spirit."[34]

In and by the exercise of the theological virtues, accrued and aroused by the Eucharist, memory is ever more like to the almighty Father, the object of its hope; intelligence ever more like to the Son in whom it believes; and will ever more like to the Holy Spirit who is their love and whom it loves. It is above all in contemplating, hoping and loving the Trinity that man passes from the image to the likeness of the living God who gives himself to him in the Eucharist, precisely for this object.[35] When I believe in the Word, the Father represents, prolongs and reproduces in some way in me the eternal generation of his Word. When I love the Father and the Son present in me by the intensified grace brought about by the Eucharist, both represent, prolong and reproduce in me, in some way, the mystery of their eternal active spiration of their Spirit become mine.[36]

As, on the natural plane, human love recapitulates being, life and feeling, dispersed throughout the universe, on the supernatural plane, charity is the summation of the whole law (Rom. 13:9). Lagrange writes:[37] "It contains the fullness of all commandments and all works." The two words "summation" and "fullness" are applied by Paul to define the place of charity in spiritual life and that of Christ himself in the supernatural economy of the world (Rom 13:8-10; Eph 1:10; Col 1:19; 2:9). It may be concluded that the same primacy which belongs to Christ in the supernatural economy of the world, belongs also to charity in each men's spiritual life.[38] Even better, it is through the gift of charity, in the Spirit (Rom. 5:5), that Christ exercises concretely his absolute and universal primacy.[39] It is through the exercise of love toward the Son, his Father and their Spirit that man is unified, inflamed, more and more in spiritual love under this same Spirit's action, the Spirit the bond of love between Father and Son. He thus becomes, in his memory, intellect and will, an image ever more like to the Three who are One, the temple and the manifestation of their power, wisdom and goodness. It is the sacramental grace of the Eucharist, a grace of increase in charity, which is the most powerful factor of this ever greater divinization.

"Lord Jesus, your Heart, your Soul, in the Blessed Sacrament, are filled with the gifts of the Holy Spirit and infused virtues. Thanks to Eucharistic Communion, a supreme accidental union, here below, between you and me, an incomparably more important and more vivifying union for me than that substantial union between my soul and my body, which you will dissolve at the hour of death—I receive from you not only the increase of the gifts of the Holy Spirit, especially of the gift of wisdom, but also that of infused moral virtues as well as the delightful perfecting of their acts, the fruits of the Spirit. You come into me to make me love your Father through my love for my brethren and yours.

"Eucharistic Heart of Jesus, you extinguish ever more in me, each day, by Communion, the fires of concupiscence, and you heal gradually my yet corrupted nature, preparing it, by communication of your divine character, for the splendor of the resurrection. You blot out recollections, images and impression which are the seeds of sin. You give me ever more abundantly the fruit of peace which excludes all inordinate fear and all anxiety. I possess you tending to the fullness of your own joy (cf. Jn 15:11). You are mine and I am yours (cf. Sg 2:16).

"Through the Eucharist, Lord Jesus, you are, you live, you act in me in order that I be, live, feel, think and act in you. To the extent that I may ever know you more in me, ever be mindful you are present in me, love you and embrace you there where neither the world, nor the flesh, nor the devil can penetrate, in the inmost depths of my soul, without ceasing to know you, adore you and embrace you as the Word Creator in your cosmic traces and in your human images.

"Oh almighty one dwelling in inmost depths of my free will, take it! Oh wisdom illumining my intellect, divinize it by contemplation! Oh love burning in my heart with an inextinguishable flame, consume it in your pure love, break down its hardness, permeate my will. Take, too, through hope my memory fixing it on you, its divine Host. You are the eternal in me. In you, in my inmost depths, are hidden everything best in my past and in my future, all brought together in your present."

3. Third Point: Action of the Giver in His Gifts

After having contemplated God as giver, then as giver present in his gifts, the author of the Exercises has considered his action through his gifts in favor of the beneficiaries: "This is to consider how God works and labors for me in all creatures upon the face of the earth, that is, he conducts himself as one who labors. Thus, in the elements, the plants, the fruits, the cattle, etc., he gives being, conserves them, confers life and sensation etc." (Ex. 236).

If the pure and eternal act works and labors for me in all creation from its first moment to the consummation of ages, is it not above all in, through and by means of men and women of all times that he acts out of love for me, for my benefit, since man exists and so long as he will come back toward God on his historical pilgrimage?

The Author of the history of the universe has guided it for my salvation. Every human act of all times, past, present and future, all this tremendous activity of man in quest of his salvation, was also a quest of my beatitude, which is an integral part of it, since I am destined to be an accidental beatitude of my most distant ancestors as also of the last men who will benefit from the parousia of the Lord. Every man, at any moment of history he may have lived or be destined to live, desires to know, in order to achieve thus his own beatitude, the unique reflection of God which, in the fresco of creation, I constitute. It is in this sense that I am, potentially, the happiness and the salvation of every man, as every man is destined to be my salvation and my happiness in Christ. I am not, therefore, a stranger to the basic project of every man, nor to that of Christ who takes on himself the projects of all men in as much as they are of worth. Through all these Christ has suffered and works for my happiness, as he also desires through them to find in me his own happiness, the accidental joy of his human intellect and will. Or rather, the eternal idea which he has of me, and which is identical with his divine essence and nature, constitute his essential beatitude. Poor creature so contingent and so limited, I have the obligation to think and believe that I am the human and divine, temporal and eternal happiness of Jesus Christ, the Incarnate Word![40]

Here is what God's universal action, visible in the elements, plants, fruits and cattle, in machinery and in history,[41] brings to my mind constantly. All is for me, in order that I be for Christ and that Christ find in me his own human and divine happiness (cf. 1 Cor 3: 22-23).

That the loving activity constitutes a much more intimate and personal sign that simple presence, is what the true story of the life of St. Elizabeth of Hungary shows us. Early in her reign she had the custom of sending gifts of clothing and food to the poor peasants of her domains. This was a token of her love. Later, she brought them these gifts herself. Finally, she goes to their homes, prepares their food with her own hands and personally takes care of the sick. No one will deny that this is a supreme testimonial of love.[42]

An eloquent symbol of the mystery of the redemptive humanation of the Son of God, though pale, since, if St. Elizabeth could prepare food for her subjects, she could not give herself to them as food and drink. Whereas Jesus has wished to give himself to me in the Bread of life and the Blood of Redemption, an efficacious sign of the co-redemptive sacrifice he inspired, inspires and will inspire on behalf of my salvation in all his members and at all times. From the beginning of human history, and down to its consummation through every man who accepts, even though obscurely, incorporation into him, Jesus suffers and dies, satisfies and merits for me, to make reparation for my sins and to obtain for me eternal life. If I am culpable for everything in regard to everyone, I am also indebted for everything toward all, in order that Christ be all in all. Saved by the one Savior through all the saved, I ought in turn to save all men,[43] merit and satisfy for the glory of Christ, source of all merit and all satisfaction acceptable to the Father. Gratitude toward all those who, under the inspiration of the Spirit of Christ, have been made my co-redeemers, oblige me in turn to assume the vocation of universal co-redeemer, at the service of the one Redeemer of all.

If all the angels and saints intercede for me (Ex. 234), it is under the action of the Holy Spirit (Rom 8:26, 27). It is to this intercession I owe so many benefits received (Ex. 233). My full gratitude should impel me to serve and love all the time and everywhere the whole Christ who has loved me, loves me and will love me from the beginning down to the end of time. The history of man is none other than the history of the meritorious love which through all his members Christ has not ceased and will never cease to manifest to me. The universal history of man is dominated by the communion of saints.

To contemplate divine love in human activity, is not only to consider and to love this love while it is acting through it, but it is also to love this love embracing the action of others in my behalf, to the point that all men of good will, throughout all ages, have loved me and communicated to me their spiritual goods, their riches in Christ (cf. Ex. 231).

"Father, on offering you the sacrifice of your whole Christ, the Supper of the new and eternal alliance, through which you unite men among themselves, I offer you all the acts and sufferings of all the members of your Son, in reparation for my faults, in thanksgiving for your benefits bestowed on me, and in adoration of your salvific will in regard to them and to me. Through him, with him, in him, to save them unto the end of time and to the limits of space, I reach men your children, under the action of the Spirit."

"Lord Jesus, I thank You for having associated to your death for me all the deaths and all the sufferings of my brethren who have been accepted as yours. My soul, bathed in so many human and divine tears, aspires to restore to you in all love, suffering and death. Of so many of my suffering and dying brethren, you had made for me so many benefactors and even benefits received (cf. Ex. 233).

"Your love impels me, for, alone, you died for all, that the living live no longer for themselves, that no one among us die for himself, that we live and die for you, that you yourself be the Lord of the living and of the dead (cf. 2 Cor 8:14, 15; Rom 14: 7-9). You died to merit from your Father to make yours all human deaths, to integrate all deaths into yours, and thus to make all men come to eternal life. So your love, your suffering and your death, impel me to transform my own death into a holocaust for my brethren as you have done. If I should, in you, with you and through you live, act and labor for them, I should above all suffer and die for them. I wish to transform the world to their benefit only so as to help them die with you in order to live ever in you, through you and for you.[44]

4. *Fourth Point: the infinite transcendance of the Giver in relation to his gifts.*

We have now reached the zenith of the Exercises, and of the contemplative life into which the fourth week is to initiate us. This God who gives us the universe, who is present to it, who acts through it on our behalf, is in no way confined by it. The universe of divine gifts remains finite and limited, but God himself is infinite, unlimited, eternal. Let us read the Ignatian text: "This is to consider all blessings and gifts as descending from above. Thus, my limited power comes from the supreme and infinite power above, and so, too, my justice, goodness, mercy etc., descend from above as rays of light descend from the sun, as the waters flow from their fountain. etc." (Ex. 237).

God does not cease to be the origin, the source of all his gifts, the sun which constantly illumines them. All human perfections are but pale rays of the divine, infinite perfections.

The contemplation of the created world inflames our souls with love of divine goodness in the measure that we recall all the perfections distributed in a particular way among diverse creatures are found universally gathered together in God as in the fount of all goodness. If then the worth, the beauty and the charm of creatures now attracts human souls, as so many streams, how much more, if they be compared to their source, the "wellspring of God's goodness" *(Dei fontana bonitas)*, will not that goodness draw to itself men's souls?[45]

This first aspect of divine transcendence[46] is inspired by "affirmative theology," It must be completed by the views of "negative theology." After St. Thomas Aquinas let us listen to St. John of the Cross:[47] "All the beauty of creatures, compared to the infinite beauty of God is but supreme ugliness. The soul attached to the beauty of any creature before God shares in its ugliness. This soul will not be able to transform itself in the divine beauty. All the graces and attractions of creatures compared with the grace[48] of God are but supreme disgrace and supreme displeasure.

"All the goodness of creatures compared to the infinite goodness of God is but supreme malice. "None is good but God alone" (Lk 18:19). The soul which attaches itself to the goods of this world is supremely evil before God. All the wisdom of the world and all the talents of creatures compared to the infinite wisdom of God is but pure and supreme ignorance (*cf* I Cor 3:18). Also every soul which relies on its knowledge and talent for· uniting itself with that wisdom is supremely ignorant before God and will remain far from it."[49]

The God immanent to the world and to the spirit of man remains, therefore, infinitely transcendant in his very immanence. It is not possible to "reduce" the Creator to creatures. There can never be question of seeking and finding God only in the world, the eternal only in time, for God is ever greater than all his gifts. No matter what the agrandizements of our heart and that of others, "God is greater than our hearts" (1 Jn 3:20). An infinite abyss ever separates God's created gifts from the uncreated Gift which is God himself. Even in Christ, an infinite abyss ever distinguishes his two natures,[50] the human and the divine.

St. Ignatius, upon underlining in this *last* point of his contemplation, the infinite transcendance of the divine perfections in relations to all shared created perfections, shows clearly that "conversion to the world" of God in no way is the supreme stage of the dialectical movement of the human spirit in its return to its Principle. On the contrary, return to the world, included in return to God present in the world, culminates in return to God who surpasses the world and will ever surpass it infinitely. After having been detached from the sinful world, the Christian turns toward it to save it while constantly turning toward the divine immensity which created nature never contains. After conversion to the holy God comes conversion to the transcendental God. There will never be any going beyond this supreme dialectical stage.

We must, then, modify and complete the "cyclical" concept of Nadal[51] and K. Rahner.[52] The latter expresses it as follows:

"In the Spiritual Exercises and throughout the life of St. Ignatius, there can be recognized a constant circular movement: from the world to God, from God to the world.

"The movement through the world and in the world constantly increases his love for God, and the movement in God and through God constantly increases his love for men who are in the world, since they are made in his image and likeness.

"His discovery of God has made him abandon the world to be more fully absorbed in God, but when this absorption was completed, his love flowed in the world as the love of God who is *"diffusivum sui,"* who gives himself.

"The more he saw the world, the more he was absorbed in God; the more he was wholly absorbed in God, the more he passionately embraced the universe out of love for God.

"His life became a reconciliation of contemplation and action, of flight from the world and insertion into the world, of devotion to God and dedication to the children of God on earth."

Such a reconciliation, as the *Spiritual Diary* shows, cannot be here but initial and imperfect, for it tends constantly toward its eschatological plenitude. It is only in the face to face vision that we will be able to grasp in a plenary and lasting way the truth concisely and vividly defined by the

Church: "between creatures and Creator there cannot be observed a likeness without observing a much greater unlikeness between them."[53] It is only in the beatific vision that God will fully manifest, in the bosom of and beyond the finiteness of the world, his inexhaustible incomprehensibility.

It may be said that this orientation at the heart of apostolic action toward contemplation of transcendence, in relation to it and to its object, divine goodness, has been, after St. Ignatius, stressed likewise by St. Francis de Sales in his *Treatise on the Love of God."* The fourth point tends toward what the French doctor calls "love of complacence by which we rejoice in God's goodness. The soul which is exercizing itself in the love of complacence cries out perpetually in its silence: "Enough for me that God is God, that his bounty is infinite, that his perfection is immense; that, whether I live or die, this means naught to me, for my dearly beloved lives eternally a fully triumphant life." The heart, steeped in this sweetness, "praises supremely the Divinity for what it can be adequately praised by itself alone." And when we proclaim: "it is not (so much) the glory of created praises that we desire for God by this aspiration, but (rather) the essential and eternal glory which he has in himself, by himself and of himself, which is himself (*Treatise* . . . V, 1, 3, 12).

Briefly, the fourth point brings us to the *admiration* of a God ever new, for he is infinite. Unlike most creatures, God is ever "astounding."

And if it is true that his contemplation renders us ever greater sharers of his saving love, and so sends us to men, it is in order to help them raise themselves up to him. For St. Ignatius, love-of-God-in-the-world would ever inseparably be a love-of-God-alone:

"I beg the same Creator and Lord, for whose love every other love should be embraced and governed . . . It is possible that the greatness of love which overwhelms the soul should find relief, even in things that are earthly and base, provided it does not make itself earthly or base but loves them all for God our Lord and insofar as they are directed to his glory and service. This is something which necessarily has to do with our last end, which is itself perfect and infinite goodness, which must be loved in all other things. To this end exclusively the whole weight of our love should be directed."[54]

In other words, the response of the creature to the goodness of the transcendant God could be only pure love for him (*cf.* Ex. 370). It is only upon loving God for himself that we can respond, in a finite manner, to the infinite gratuity of his love for us. Even if he did not shower us with gifts of this gratuitous love, he would still be infinitely loveable. Love is ever loveable.

D. The response of true love.

After each of the four points, St. Ignatius suggests turning back on ourselves, a "reflection," a "conversion to myself."[55] "Then I will reflect upon myself, and consider, according to all reason and justice, what I ought to offer the Divine Majesty, that is all I possess and myself with it. Thus, as one would do who is moved by great feeling, I will make this offering of myself." (Ex. 234).

Let us reflect on this text before commenting on the words it introduces. As God has given himself when he showers his gifts on us, so we ought, reciprocally, give ourselves to him when we give him and render him all we have received from him. Such a restitution is a work of judgment and reason (cf. Ex. 96), and at the same time of love. That is, the only way to be just in regard to God, is to love him for himself. This love not only includes deeds, but also feelings and words (Ex. 230). And even a "great affection," "cum summo affectu." St. Ignatius joins with St. Thomas Aquinas here for whom charity is not only benevolence, good will toward others, but also affective union.[56] Loving words addressed to God, are deeds, not passing but immanent, and, if they do not exclude others, constitute a "mutual sharing of goods" (cf. Ex. 231). Thereby an "activist," anti-contemplative interpretation of the Ignatian text is radically rejected. Contemplation "to inflame us with divine love" is not intended exclusively to foster external actions inspired by this spiritual love. The "deed" in which love consists can be not only psalm singing or lengthy prayers inside or outside churches (cf. Ex. 355), but also interior acts of the thological virtues (Ex. 316), as well as colloquies (Ex. 54).

Furthermore, although the term "contemplation" may not have here, necessarily, the technical sense (nor does it in other places of the Exercises have such a meaning, cf. Ch. II, note 1 of this work),[57] we must acknowledge that it is oriented[58] toward this sense and also does not exclude it at all. The love of God is assuredly, not only the object, but also the principle of the "contemplation for inflaming and arousing"[59] this very same love.[60] This contemplation is a spiritual exercise of spiritual love in search of its own growth, not only effective but also affective.[61] And as we are men, and not pure spirits, this increase, inherent to this contemplation, supposes the exercise of speech which is characteristic of the human person in his earthly existence. Today, perhaps, if St. Ignatius were composing the Exercises, he would express the first prelude (Ex. 230) of his contemplation quite differently. In our activist era, one of contempt for the interior life and lengthy prayers, would he not say that "love does not consist only nor principally of external deeds, does not exclude interior affections and includes especially immanent acts of the will?"[62]

That such may well be St. Ignatius' thinking, we have as proof of the comparison used by him to introduce the "Sume et Suscipe": "As one would, with great affection and in words . . . offer some present to another." Is it not true that human words characterize a gift as a gift? Most frequently, if not always, the present is accompanied by words which explain the intention to offer something to another. Without such words, the present might be regarded by the recipient as a simple loan or even, in some cases, as an insult! Only words confer a clear meaning on actions. Of course, God has no need of our words to know our intentions. But we do have need to speak to him in human terms to make clear to ourselves the meaning of our relations with him.[63] Thereby is explained the difference between oblation, promise and vow.

Here St. Ignatius does not invite the retreatant to take a vow (cf. Ex. 15, 57) which would be however a more total expression of his total oblation. While leaving him free, he suggests to him explicitly a simple oblation which displays the potentialities of the preceding oblations made from the very start of the Exercises (Ex. 5, 23; end of 98).

"Take, Lord, and receive all my liberty,[64] my memory, my understanding, and my entire will, all that I have and possess. Thou hast given all to me. To thee, O Lord, I return it. Dispose of it wholly according to thy will. Give me thy love and thy grace, for this is sufficient for me."[65]

This famous text integrates abandon, offering and petition. It expresses the will to refuse nothing to God, to surrender before the solicitations of his grace and to desire and ask nothing save himself or what leads to him.

"Lord Jesus, I want to love with a pure love, which can come only from you, your infinitely gratuitous love for me. You have no need of me, you who are my God, to be happy. I add nothing to your divine happiness—and you love me, me nothingness and sin.[66] Your love for me is so perfectly unselfish. How would not my love for you be pure of all self-love?

"When I adore your infinite love for me, I adore your eternal essence, with which it is one. I adore, in your infinite love for me, your infinite love for yourself, since the first act is one with the second, in the absolute simplicity of your divine essence. I recognize my total dependence in relations to this infinite love for me, and the rights over me of your infinite love for me. I regret and desire to expiate all the faults committed against this infinite love for me. I implore your infinite love to pour into me the pure love which desires to follow you in the poverty, humiliations, and sufferings which your Divine Majesty has embraced for love of me. May this very gift make me make reparation for all my faults against your infinite and gratuitous love.

"My act of thanksgiving to you consists in offering you my intellect, that it be purified by Faith.[67] Take my intellect, prone to so many errors, and purify it in the luminous shadows of faith. Take my ignorant and blind intellect and make it share your divine wisdom by total adherence to your Word.

"Take my weak will so perverse and wicked. Set it afire with your love. Grant my intellect the grace to know, by faith, in all that happens, your infinitely wise, powerful and loving will that I may adore it and embrace it.

"While the beginnings of my supreme unhappiness would consist in clinging to my own judgment, so fallible, to my own will, so unstable, my supreme happiness consists in sharing, in charity, the indefectibility and infallibility of your infinitely wise will.

"Your particular and actual wills concerning me are ever polarized by your general and constant will as a Savior: you will to introduce me along with others into the beatific vision of your love, into this vision where you will at last be able to give yourself to me according to your ordination, where you will take my will perfectly in order to inflame it with your love.

"Take, then, from now on my memory to flood it with the ardent and confident desire for the vision of your wisdom and of your love, with this confident desire, based on your fidelity, which we call hope.

"Take all that you have given me, and my body, in death, to possess it more profoundly again in the resurrection.

"Take my past, my present and my future. You wish to bring them together in your eternity.

"Give me your love. That is, to love you purely, supernaturally, in every creature, through and in the Spirit who is love between your Father and you.

"Give me your love everywhere present, your love which creates all and which conserves all, for me.

"Give me your grace, uncreated and created, habitual and actual, antecedent, helpful and cooperative, Your efficacious graces of pure love.

"Lord, give me the grace to reach here below "the promised land of divine union" (St. John of the Cross) and the efficacious graces of perfect conversion necessary to attain to the purity of your love. Of my own I have but the abyss of my malice and my perversity. Convert me, cost what it may. Give me to live here below, in the habitual exercise of pure love toward your love which dwells in me, in a light inaccessible to reasoning, to natural and psychological knowledge, but accessible to the shadow of faith and the flame of charity which flares therefrom. Are you not a devouring fire, a jealous God?

"Give me, with the grace of perfect conversion to you, that of your perpetual presence without which my deeds would be cold and dark, but with which they will be clear and warm,[68] for the joy and benefit of your other members and so for your greatest glory.

"Give me, Lord, your love and your grace. that is, the grace to persevere in your love and your grace. The grace of final perseverance,[69] confirmation in your grace. The grace to be fixed in you and of never offending you deliberately.[70] All is possible to your infinite might. I fully accept not to know here below the fact of this confirmation in your grace, and to discover its marvel only when fixed in your glory.

"In the measure in which I let you take my nature (intellect, will and memory), you will give me not only your infinite love eternally, but also the finite love of all the elect, not only your grace for me but also a plenitude of graces which will flow over all the predestined in the bosom of the mystery of the communion of saints. Through me, you wish to manifest your love to all men of all times by associating me, mysteriously, to the distribution of your grace to each and everyone of them.[71]

"In giving me your love and your grace it is, then, the souls, and even these angels and saints who intercede for me now (Ex. 232) whom you give me and will give me, to the extent of making me merit for them their graces. Just as it is also through them and thanks to them that I will receive your love and your grace. By your love, their grace and their glory are mine and I am exceedingly rich in me and in them, rich with all your riches and all your glory, merited by poverty and ignominy (cf. Ex. 234, 231, 147). The Mother of God is mine and the whole Church is mine.[72]

"If I ask nothing else of you, is it not because, on asking you for your love and your grace, I had asked you for the universe, the Church, you yourself? Without you, the universe and the Church are not; in them, you are enough for me.

"Lord Jesus, I am overwhelmed with joy in the midst of all my tribulations because you are, as Word, infinitely and eternally blessed,[73] present in me by your grace. You are joy, my joy which no one can take away from me."

Conclusion: Renewed Consecration to the Eucharistic Heart of Jesus.

"Eucharistic Heart of Jesus, you are the whole treasure and spiritual and corporal good of the Church, all my good, my treasure, my life, my passion, my sun, my joy; my all.

"You are my permanent companion of exile and adoration in the tabernacle, the pontiff and the victim I offer each day, my nourishment at the time of Communion.

"Adoring you, I adore the two acts of love, eternal and temporal, uncreated, and created, infinite and finite—voluntary and sensitive—by which you have instituted the sacrament of your presence, of your sacrifice and of your union and with which you make them live on among us, in the might of your Spirit, to the glory of your Father, in order to love, in me and by me, all men your brothers, with a sacrificial love.[74]

"Adoring you, I adore also the triple love, divine, spiritual and sensitive, by which you pursue each human person during his pilgrimage on earth. And I associate myself with it.

"Adoring you, I adore your glorious coming, when, all the veils falling, your multipresence shining forth, your created loving liberty, subjecting to itself the whole universe, will raise up all hearts to gather together all the predestined, through your Spirit, in a mutual translucence. For in you and thanks to you, all will shine as suns filled with the light of your love.[75]

"The whole universe is then suspended from you and as it were contained in you, Oh Eucharistic Heart of Jesus, and in your all-embracing sacrifice.

By it, you wish ceaselessly to fill with the infinite pleroma of your divine nature and of your action the finite cosmic pleroma of the world upon making your ecclesial pleroma share the plenitude of the graces of your humanity (Col 2:9: Eph 4:19; 2:23; Jn 1:14b), in order that finally, we all be filled in you (Col 2:9b).[76]

"Adoring you, I also adore the Father and the Spirit whom you sent for your glory and for that of your Father. Eating you, I receive anew the Father and the Spirit with you and let him make more profound their dwelling in me, inaugurated at the time of my baptism, strengthened when you confirmed me.

"I thank you for having placed me in the service of your sacrifice, for having made of me the consumer and adorer of your real presence.

"May I, on manifesting you to the world, manifest to it also the love of your mother Mary, whose purely human flesh has given us your theandrical body? May I thus help numerous youths to listen attentively to your calls: "Come, follow me! Do this in memory of me!"

"May you, bread and wine of eternal life, prepare it for me, granting me this plenitude of perfect charity which remits all debts and temporal punishments due to sin. Grant me, too, confirmation in the graces of your elections and in your sacramental grace and the assiduous contemplation of your presence of omniscient and almighty love in all creatures (cf. Ex. 39).

"I do not ask you for any revelation of these graces here below, but, with your Church, at Mass, I beg that nothing may separate me from you and that I live ever in the presence of your love, as the sacramental and daily celebration of my nuptials with you, the spouse of my soul,[77] the Lamb of my pasch, in you and with you, coming to the Father.

"Come then in me to continue to immolate yourself through me to your Father, in the fire of your Spirit, until the day when, raising me up from the dead, glorious, for your glory, you will consummate our union."

Anima Christi [78]
Soul of Christ, sanctify me.
Body of Christ, save me.
Blood of Christ, inebriate me.
Water from the side of Christ, wash me.
Passion of Christ, strengthen me.
O good Jesus, hear me.
Within your wounds hide me.
Do not permit me to be separated from you.
From the malicious enemy defend me.
In the hour of our death call me.
And bid me come to you,
That, with your saints, I may praise you,
forever and ever. Amen.

NOTES ON CHAPTER EIGHTEEN

1. The title of the Latin Vulgate (230) is: *"Contemplatio ad amorem spiritualem in nobis excitandum."* The word *"excitare"* means: light up, inflame. It is evident that the expression "spiritual love" is contrasted with "carnal love." This, together with the fact that charity toward God and the neighbor is a one and indivisible reality, not in its object but in its essence (GS, 24; LG, 41, 42; CFW, 245-248), makes clear that there is question also of inflaming in us, by means of this contemplation, spiritual love toward the neighbor and the universe which is inseparable from it. A carnal love of God would be meaningless. The existence of a carnal love for the universe and for men is only too common. Already this simple title constitutes an implicit protestation against every form of pantheism.

2. *cf.* a fine presentation of these different opinions in J.M. Diez-Alegria, "La contemplacion para alcanzar amor en la dinamica espiritual de los Ejercicios de San Ignacio," *Manresa* XXIII (1951) 171-93.

3. An expression used by J. de Guibert, S.J., *La spiritualité de la Compagnie de Jésus,* Rome, 1953, p. 118, n. 38, to summarize this view he does not share. He does, however say: "It (the contemplation) may very well form this conclusion in so far as it is an initiation into this life of constant prayer which makes us find God in all things."

4. Diez-Alegria, *art. cit.,* pp. 172, 173. He presents furthermore this view as exclusive of the preceding and linked to a more ascetical, less mystical view of the contemplation *"Ad Amorem."*

5. J. de Guibert, S.J., *op. cit.*, (n.3), *ibid.*

6. Diez-Alegria, *art. cit.,* p. 173; G. Cusson, "Pédagogie . . ." Paris, 1968, pp. 371, 372.

7. *Scripta de S. Ignacio,* vol. I, p. 612.

8. J. Polanco, *Chronicon S.J.,* vol. I, p. 21: ". . . *in his quae ad inflammandum amorem in Deum et varios orandi modos pertinent, proficiendi, perutilem operam proximis navare coepit . . ."* These words marvellously correspond, justifying it, with the view we are expounding here on the origin of the contemplation which they present in a similar way to its title in the Vulgate and linking it with the methods of prayer. On these points, see Codina A., S.J., *Los origenes de los Ejercicios espirituales de S. Ignacio de Loyola, Estudio historico,* Barcelona, 1926, pp. 41-53.

9. S. Ignacio de Loyola, *Epistolae,* vol. XII, pp. 666-73, MHSJ, v. 42, Rome, 1968.

10. This is what J. Nadal seems to say (Ep. P. H. Nadal, vol. IV, Madrid, 1905, p. 673: *"la vida unitiva . . . es el proprio della 4a semana en el exercicio de amor con Dios"*: these last words seems to be an allusion to our contemplation).

11. *Ibid.,* p. 685.

12. Directory of Fr. Miró, Ch. 3, n. 60; MHSJ, *Directoria,* Matriti 1919, p. 860, nota. Cf. Diez-Alegria, *art. cit.,* p. 172.

13. We translate by these three verbs the complex meaning of the Spanish word *"alcanzar"* (Ex. 230, A). They are to be included in the title as found in the Vulgate, in order to render integrally the Ignatian idea.

14. It cannot be excluded that in Matthew 22:37 Jesus meant that he is both God and the

neighbor to be loved at the same time; *cf.* Mat 10:37 and St. John Chrysostom, MG, 58, 661.

15. *Cf.* Ex. 320. The concept of "intense grace" in the Ignatian Exercises may be presented on the theological plane in this way: "Intense grace is an assistance given by the Holy Spirit which is not only remedial but also entitatively, ontologically supernatural. By such grace the Holy Spirit acts on the intellect or on the will or on both at once, actualizes infused virtues and gifts and thus produces an experience of God in the retreatant." "Every intense grace involves gifts of the Holy Spirit," actualizing them and making them pass from potency into act. *cf.* J.P. Domene, S.J., *Elementos teologicos en los Ejercicios,* Santander and Taichung, 1963, pp. 73, 74.

16. *cf.* Ex. 316 A: *"Viene la anima a inflamarse en amor de su Criador"*; V.: *Exardescit anima in amorem Creatoris sui"*; P 2: *"Anima accenditur in Dei . . . igneum amorem"*; "the soul . . . is inflamed with love of its 'Creator and Lord' " (Puhl).

17. However, let us note that St. Ignatius does not at all deny that love should be manifested in words. For other men (of course, not for God) deeds remain frequently ambiguous signs so long as human speech does not explain their meaning. This is what St. Thomas Aquinas stressed a propos of the matter of sacraments (*cf.* ST, III.60.6). Should it not be said that some words of forgiveness make charity stand out much more clearly than deeds? However, St. Ignatius' view is stressed frequently in the N.T., Mt 7:21; 1 Jn 3: 17,18.

18. *cf.* ST, II.II. 23.1: "The love of benevolence (which wishes for the good of others) does not suffice for friendship, which requires also reciprocity, *Mutua amatio,* and the mutual benevolence of friendship is founded on a communication. God communicates to us his beatitude. Here is the foundation of the friendship of charity between God and man." The Thomistic theology of charity has magnificently given depth to the datum of revelation by making use of the Aristotelian analysis of human friendship. And it might be said that St. Ignatius consulted this part of the *Summa* before he definitively drew up the preliminary remarks of his contemplation. St. Thomas had already, long before St. Ignatius, seen that "the essential" of the love of charity is an "existential and reciprocal relationship" and was not satisfied with a "scholastic definition" such as "benevolence of the loved for the loving" (a point which, perhaps, has not been perfectly grasped by Fessard, *La dialectique des Exercices,* vol. I, Paris, p. 148).

19. Fessard, *(ibid,* p. 148), observes quite rightly: "In this giving of the first place to knowledge, among the goods love wants to communicate, would not Ignatius' voluntarism be tempered by an intellectualism of sound alloy and one taken from the best source? To exclude all doubt it suffices to state that this list takes up inversely the gradation of the "snares and chains" (Ex. 142) against which the "Two Standards" are intended to put us on guard before the "Election." And that knowledge, substituted here for pride, is above all, for Ignatius, the knowledge of the You in which consists eternal life (Jn 17:3), a specific remedy for radical pride which is the fruit of the tree of knowledge (Ex. 51)?

20. Ex. 95,146.

21. For the exchange of intra-divine love founds the mystery of the communion of saints which implies the communication of spiritual goods among all members of the pilgrim, suffering and triumphant Church. Friendship, to the extent it is supernatural, integrates under a new title, in the communion of saints.

22. *Cf.* Ex. 60.

23. The souls of purgatory intercede also in a general manner for the living, even if they do not know exactly their needs or their petitions. These predestined souls go on

living in a state of charity toward the living. This does not mean that it is necessary to invoke their intercession (*cf.* A. Michel, DTC 13, 1, 1936, art. Purgatoire).

24. See above (*cf.* note 13) our comment on the title of the contemplation "for inflaming in us spiritual love."

25. The mention of Christ's suffering is here proper to the Vulgate ("*pertulerit*").

26. The phrase "according to his good pleasure" is also mentioned in the Vulgate ("*juxta divinum suum . . . beneplacitum*") but is not found in the Autograph.

27. *Cf.* statements by St. Ignatius made to St. Francis Borgia in his letter of 1545: "I am nothing but an obstacle . . . and I find this a source of greater satisfaction and spiritual consolation in our Lord because I can thus attribute nothing to myself which has any appearance of good . . . There are very few in this world—nay, I will go further and say there is not one—who during mortal life can properly judge how far he is an obstacle and to what extent he resists the workings of God's grace in his soul" (*Letters of St. Ignatius of Loyola*, William J. Young, S.J., p. 83 (1,339-43. Letter 101).

28. Bossuet has a fine comment on this Pauline text: "It is the same charity of the Father which liberates him, abandons him, sacrifices him and which adopts us, vivifies us and regenerates us . . . his inventive and ingenious love has fortunately inspired him to will the design of mercy and, in a way, of losing his Son to open the way to adoption and of bringing about the death of the one heir to enable us to enter into his rights. Children of adoption, what a price your eternal Father paid for you!" (Le Premier Sermon pour le vendredi de la semaine de la Passion, *Oeuvres,* Vives, vol. IX, p. 518). Long before, Salvien had written even more eloquently: "*Plus amat nos Deus quam pater filium . . . Propter nos Filio suo non pepercit. Et quid plus? Adeo et hoc Filio justo et hoc Filio unigenito et hoc Filio Deo. Et quid amplius dici protest? Et hoc pro nobis, id est pro malis, pro iniquis, pro impiissimis*" (*De Gubernatione Dei,* ML, 53,81). In this context, how could we not mention the daily crosses received from God as priceless benefits and great manifestations of his love for us?

29. There should be noted in this context the helpful reflection of Garrigou-Lagrange, O.P.: "The formal motive of charity is the divine goodness supernaturally known, in as much as it is in itself sovereignly loveable for itself. Thus to love God for his benefits (if these last words express the formal motive of our love and not only a means of knowing and preparing oneself to love the divine goodness), would not be an act of charity (*cf.* ST, II.II. 27.3). Charity brings us to love God more than all his gifts, for the goodness of the benefactor surpasses all his gifts" (*Synthèse thomiste,* Pt. VII, Ch. VI, Paris, 1946, p. 525).

It is to be observed that in the contemplation on which we are commenting. the first point prepares for the fourth, which exalts the amiability of God beyond all his gifts, and so the pure love, praised and esteemed "above all" in the last rule of orthodoxy, the conclusion of the Exercises (Ex. 370), is their last word!

30. *Cf.* ST, I.43.3; DS, 3815.

31. It is known that the expression designating God as "Wholly Other" is a favorite of Karl Barth. It is evidently irreconcilable with this doctrine. If God was not only "Other," as he is, but also "Wholly Other," we would not be able to have any real knowledge of him but only an equivocal concept. Too many Catholic authors have taken up this expression without adverting to its implications. It excludes logically *every* likeness between Creator and creature, without restricting itself to acknowledge that he is more unlike us than we are like to him (*cf.* DS, 806). So there would no more be any possibility, if this thesis were accepted, of showing or of proving the existence of God starting out

from created realities (*cf.* DS, 2004, 3538).

32. St. Ignatius of Antioch, Eph. XV, 3.

33. *Cf.* ST, 1.93.8 and 9. In St. Bonaventure (*cf.* n. 36) the passing from sign to likeness by the image is perhaps more clearly marked. Material creation is a trace of the Trinity, and so equally, is the human body. The human soul, on the natural level, is an image of the Trinity which becomes, by grace and charity, above all in the exercise of the theological virtues, its likeness. This likeness will be consummated in the beatific vision.

34. St. Catherine of Sienna, dialogue of October 1378, *Oraisons et Elevations,* trad. Bernard, p. 32. See also, in the same sense, her prayer for the feast of the conversion of St. Paul, January 23, 1377.

35. *Cf.* M. V. Bernadot, O.P., *De l'Eucharistie à la Trinité,* Juvisy, 1919.

36. These ideas may be justified in a more rigorous manner in the light of diverse aspects of the doctrine of St. Bonaventure, *cf.* O. Gonzalez, *Misterio Trinitario y existencia humana,* Madrid, 1965, pp. 564-98.

37. M. J. Lagrange, *Epitre aux Romains,* Paris, 1950, p. 317.

38. J. de Guibert, S.J., *Théologie spirituelle,* Toulouse, 1946, p. 317

39. *Ibid.*

40. *Cf.* ST, I.18.4.; SCG, IV, 13 at end; *de Ver.* 4,8. We have developed this theme in our article: "Relations humaines, Relations divines"; *cf. Divinitas.* 1974; CFW, 425-426.

41. St. Ignatius does not speak at all, in our contemplation, explicitly about the history of salvation. But it must be said that he speaks of it implicitly, in the third point on which we are commenting here, on presenting God as author and supreme operator of the action of creatures, of this action which is an accident distinct from their being.

42. *Cf.* W. Sierp, S.J., *Das goldene Siegel,* 1937, p. 60.

43. *Cf.* Clement of Alexandria, Strom. VIII, 2; PG, 9, 413: "starting out from one and by one alone we are saved and save (others)"; *cf.* CFW, 281.

44. Fraternal love is always subordinate to the love of God (GS, 42) and the very love which we owe our neighbor inclines us to desire him and procure, as much as possible, the knowledge and lasting possession of the living God. No one can really love another if he does not desire that the loved one love above all love.

45. SCG, II, 2.

46. The technical meaning of these expressions is very well expounded by J.M. Nicolas, O.P., *Dieu connu comme inconnu,* Paris, 1966, pp. 142–48.

47. St. John of the Cross, *Ascent of Carmel,* Bk. I, Ch. IV.

48. It could also be translated as "grace" in the sense of "charm."

49. We have doubtless here the most radical and most dramatic expression, at the heart of orthodoxy, of negative theology.

50. *Cf.* CFW, 201: doctrine of Chalcedon.

51. *Cf.* M. Nicolau, S.J., J. Nadal, *Obras y doctrinas espirituales.* Madrid, 1949, pp. 323-26 (on the "circle" between prayer and action).

52. K. Rahner, Die ignatianische Mystik der Weltfreudigkeit, RAM, XII (1937) 125; the

-same text may also be found in Theological Investigations, t. III, Baltimore, 1967, pp. 277-293.

53. *Cf.* DS, 806.

54. St. Ignatius de Loyola, Letter of May 18, 1547 to the Bishop of Targa, Manuel Sanchez. *Cf.* letter of Venerable Father Libermann, of July 27, 1832: "it is sometimes thought one loves his brother in God, while all our love falls on man, on the creature, on nothingness, and God is left out completely. As for me, my dear, without doubt I love you, I love you with my whole heart, but I am very much concerned lest I lower myself to the creature. So I love you in God, or rather, I love God in you. I endeavor not to leave God in order to come down to you, a creature. I love in order to raise you to the bosom of God, to love you only in him, through him and for him. Love me, too, in this way, I beg you!" (Quotation by Blanchard, *Le Vénérable Libermann, Paris, 1960, Vol. II, p. 187*).

55. *Cf.* Ex. 234, V.: *"vertam ad meipsum"*; A: *"reflectere in me ipsum"* (trad. Roothaan).

56. ST, II.II. 27,2; 184.2. See note 61.

57. Pius XII, Allocution of August 3, 1958 on the contemplative life. To be found in *Documentation Catholique.*

58. Such is certainly the object of this contemplation, the supreme exercise of the fourth week which itself is an introduction to the unitive way.

59. The word *"excitare"* employed by the Vulgate (as we have already mentioned) means also "awaken." Even on the natural plane, man tends to love God above all, by a natural inclination which, though inefficacious, is nonetheless helpful, and perfected by charity (*cf.* St. Francis de Sales, *Traité de l'Amour de Dieu,* I Chs. 16–18). The dynamism of this natural tendency is in some way "aroused" and "awakened" by the Exercises and especially by this supreme contemplation.

60. *Cf.* ST, II.II. 27.2: Love adds to benevolence an affective union between lover and beloved. The lover deems that the beloved is in some way one with him or that he belongs to him and is thus moved toward him.

62. Otherwise, it should paradoxically be said that the "contemplation to inflame with spiritual love" in regard to God does not concern "contemplatives." On the contrary, it might be said that its two preludes are in perfect harmony with the doctrine of St. Thomas Aquinas on the superiority of the mixed life relative as to either the active life, or to the contemplative life (*cf.* II.II. 182.2.3; esp. III Sent., dist. 35, q.1, a4, solut. 3). In this last text, St. Thomas explains that a "greater charity is shown when one sacrifices the consolations of contemplation to seek the glory of God in the conversion of others, as human friendship seeks more the good of the friend than the pleasure resulting from his presence."

63. *Cf.* ST, III.60.6.

64. In Ignatian terms, liberty here seems to include the faculties (memory, intellect and will) mentioned immediately after and to correspond with what scholastic theology would have called the essence of the existing soul.

65. Ex. 234. We have joined and integrated the various nuances of the Vulgate and of the Autograph. The word "rich" is found only in the Vulgate.

66. That is: I who have of myself but my nothingness and my sin; *cf.* DS, 392, with the explanations on this text on our Ch. III, n. 50.

67. We have tried to summarize the four weeks of the Exercises in the preceding sentences, under the aspect of the relationship of created liberty to the infinite love for it, of its Creator.

68. See the letter of St. Ignatius to St. Francis Borgia of September 20, 1548 which dealt with a theme analogous to the one the saintly Duke, still married, had treated in his letter to St. Ignatius, of January 16, 1548: "I beg you to ask of God for me a gift for the acquiring of which he is beginning to incline me. I see that he wants to give it to me and is beginning to grant it. That is: the exercise of constant contemplation for which we have been created. I know that I am asking much and that this grace of God in the name of the faith· and merits of your reverence. I hope to obtain it and that the Holy Spirit will communicate himself to the just in a manner that they can prepare sinners to obtain eternal life" (Suau, *S. Fr. de Borgia,* Paris, 1905, vol. I. p. 169). It will be noted that St. Francis does not disassociate his contemplative ideal from an apostolic objective, one that is polarized by the glorification of God.

69. We know that the grace of final perseverance, making us merit eternal life, the last free act of man on the way, is a "great gift," absolutely gratuitous, of the saving God; cf. CFW, 134-135. The grace of confirmation in grace is distinguished from it in that the former preserves mortal man from grave sin not only at the hour of death, but also during the whole of life, starting from the moment it is given.

70. The Church, upon condemning the proposition according to which the just man can, without a special privilege, avoid venial sin during his whole life (Trent, DS, 1573), does not forbid us to think that the just man who has already sinned venially can, without a special privilege, and in the fidelity of grace, avoid future deliberate sin.

71. "In the mystical Body," Pius XII wrote: "no member can do anything good and just, in respect to the communion of saints, that does not contribute to the Salvation of all. *"Mystical Corporis,* AAS, 15, 1943, 235; *cf.* Ex. 333 and CFW, 281ff.

72. St. John of the Cross, Prière de l'âme enamourée, *Oeuvres complètes,* Bibl. Européenne, Paris, 1967, pp. 978, 979.

73. A thought inspired by the works of St. Alphonsus Liguori. He thought that the highest act of charity man can perform here below, of course under the action of grace, is to rejoice because God is infinitely and eternally happy. Likewise, St. Paul of the Cross wrote: "My joy is that God loves himself infinitely. My joy is His essential beatitude, the beatitude which he has in himself without having need of anyone. Do you know what consoles me a little? It is the blessed certitude that our God is the infinite good that he is, and that no one can praise and love him as much as he deserves" (Letter to Agnes Grazi, November 15, 1737, quoted by S. Breton, *Mystique de la Passion,* Tournai, 1962, pp. 104–6). Likewise Charles de Foucauld wrote in 1903/1904: "I see everything under the light of the immense peace of God, of his infinite goodness, of the immutable glory of the blessed and ever tranquil Trinity. All is swallowed up in the happiness that God is God" (quoted by J. M. Six, *Itineraire spirituel de Charles de Foucauld,* Paris, 1958, pp. 375, 376).

74. *Cf.* B. de Margerie, S.J., *The Heart of the Lamb of God,* Rome, 1972, #18; v; CFW, 401. We renew here an Act of Consecration already indicated in part p. 182.

75. *Cf.* CFW, 441. Mt 13, 43.

76. *Cf.* B. de Margerie, *op. cit.,* #9; CFW, 322-323.

77. It may be said, baptismal grace directs towards the spiritual marriage which is the grace proper to the Eucharist, provided no obstacle be put in the way, if it be under-

stood that the increase of charity which it gives is entirely directed toward a complete transformation into the beloved in which both parties give themselves to each other in total possession by a union of love, consummated, in so far as possible, in this life. (Definition by St. John of the Cross of the spiritual marriage, *Cantique spirituel,* Strophe 27, no. 2; cf. CFW, p. 439, p. 439n.131). That baptism makes the Christian soul the spouse of Christ is what St. Paul suggests (2 Cor 11:2). St. Ignatius was not unaware of this (*cf.* Ex. 365 and 20).

78. The prayer *"Anima Christi"* which St. Ignatius appreciated so much that he suggests it be recited according to the third method of prayer (Ex. 260, 258) is a prayer of thanksgiving after Holy Communion. So it shares the eschatological character of the Eucharist itself, wholly directed toward the glorious coming of Christ. The grace of the Eucharist integrates, in its eschatological dynamism, the contemplation *"Ad Amorem excitandum"* which, on the basis of the recognition of the real presence of love in this world is intended to bring us, we who dwell in exile here below to the one and uninterrupted act of beatifying love by way of multiple acts of charity possible in this "vale of tears", to use a term found in the *Salve Regina,* a prayer equally recommended by the Exercises (Ex. 258). The fourth point of the *"Ad Amorem"* invites us to love God not only in the world, but also "beyond all and without all things," to repeat the terms already quoted from St. Francis de Sales. See also: J. Munitiz, S.J., *A Greek "Anima Christi" Prayer,* East. Churches Rev. 6 (1974) 170-180.

BIBLIOGRAPHY

A. Texts and Translations of the Exercises

Exercitia spiritualia, MHSJ, vol. 100, Rome, 1969; critical edition of Exercises prepared by C. de Dalmases, S.J. (English translation of Exercises by Louis J. Puhl, S.J., Newman Press, 1951)

B. Commentary and Ignatian Literature.

Bellecius (*cf.* DSAM art. Bellecius) *Exercitia spiritualia,* Madrid, 1945.

Brou, A., S.J., *Saint Ignace maître d'oraison,* Paris, 1925.

Casanovas, I., S.J. *Comentario y Explanación de los Ejercicios Espirituales de S. Ignacio de Loyola,* Barcelona, 1945.

Christus, review of Ignatian spirituality, starting from 1954.

Coathalem, H., S.J., Commentaire du Livre des Exercices, Paris, 1965.

Cusson, G., S.J., *Pédagogie de l'experience spirituelle personelle,* Paris, 1968.

Domene, J.F., S.J., *Elementos teologicos en los Ejercicios,* Santander, 1965.
Los Ejercicios de S. Ignacio a la luz del Vaticano II, Madrid, BAC, 1968.

Fessard, G., S.J., *La dialectique des Exercices spirituels de S. Ignace,* Paris, 2 vols, 1956–66.

Gagliardi, S.J., *Commentarii seu Explanationes in Ex. Sp.,* Bruges, 1882.

Giuliani, M., S.J., *Prière et Action,* Paris, 1966.

Iparraguirre, I., S.J. *Obras completas de San Ignacio de Loyola,* Madrid, 1963, BAC.

Nadal, J. S.J., *Adnotationes et Meditationes in Evangeliis,* Anvers, 1594–95.

―――. *Orationis observationes,* MHSJ, 90a, Rome, 1964.

Nicolau, M., S.J., *J. Nadal, sus obras y doctrine éspirituales,* Madrid, 1945.

Nonell, G., S.J., *Los ejercicios espirituales de N.P. S. Ignacio,* Manresa, S. Jose, 1896.

Rahner, Hugo, S.J., *St. Ignatius' Letters to Women,* Herder and Herder, N.Y., 1959.

————. *Ignatius the Theologian,* N.Y. 1968.

————. *Saint Ignace de Loyola et la genèse des Exercises,* Toulouse, 1948.

Rahner, Karl, S.J., *Spiritual Exercises,* NY., 1965

C. Other works

Enseignements Pontificaux: Notre-Dame, Tournai, 1957.

St. Alphonsus Liguori, *Theologia moralis, Praxis confessarii.*

St. Anselm, *Cur Deus Homo*
St. Augustine, *Confessions.*

Benoit, P., O.P., *Passion et Resurrection du Seigneur,* Paris, 1966.

Bossuet, *Oeuvres complètes,* Paris, 1885, esp.: *Méditations sur l'Evangile.*

Bourdaloue, *Oeuvres complètes,* Paris, 1857.

Bover, J.M., S.J., *Teologia de S. Pablo,* Madrid, 1961.

Breton, S., O.P., *Mystique de la Passion,* Toulouse, 1962.

St. Catherine of Sienna, *Dialogue; Oraisons et Elevations.*

St. Antoine-Marie Claret, *Escritos autobriograficos,* Madrid, BAC, Vol. 188.

St. Francis Borgia, *Tratados espirituales,* Barcelona, 1964.

St. Francis de Sales, *Traité de l'Amour de Dieu; Entretiens.*

Garriguet, L., *Le Sacré-Coeur de Jesus* (historical and dogmatic explanation), Paris, 1920.

Grandmaison, J. de, S.J., *Ecrits spiriuels,* Paris, 1953.

Guibert, J. de, S.J., *Leçons de Théologie spirituelle,* Toulouse 1946.

————. *La Spiritualité de la Compagnie de Jésus,* Rome, 1953.

Haulotte, E., S.J., *Symbolique du vêtement selon la Bible,* Paris, 1966.

St. Irenaeus, *Adversus Haereses: Demonstration of apostolic Preaching.*
St. John Climachus, *Lettre au Pasteur.*

St. John Damascence, *Homélies sur la Dormition,* SC, 80, Paris, 1961.

Kologrivoff, I., S.J., *Essai sur la sainteté en Russie,* Bruges, 1952.

Blessed Claude La Colombière, S.J., *Oeuvres complètès*, Grenoble 1901.

Lallemant, L., S.J., *Doctrine spirituelle*, Paris, 1959.

Laurentin, R., *Court traité de théologie mariale*, Paris, 1953.

————: *Structure et Théologie de Luc I–II*, Paris, 1957.

St. Louis-Marie Grignon de Montfort, *Traité de la vraie dévotion a la Sainte Viegre; Lettre aux amis de la Crois.*

Lubac, H. de, S.J. *Le drame de l'humanisme athée*, Paris, 1945.

————. *La foi chrétienne*, Paris, 1969.

St. Marguerite-Marie Alacoque, *Vie et Oeuvres*, ed. Gauthey, Paris, 1915.

Maritain. J., *Neuf leçons sur les premiers principes de la Philosophie morale*, Paris, 1951.

St. Robert Bellarmine, *Opera Oratoria Posthuma*, 11 vols., ed. Tromp., Rome, Gregorianum, 1942–69.

Scheeben, M.J., *The Mysteries of Christianity*, St. Louis, 1954.

Schillebeeckx, E., O.P., *Marie, Mère de la Rédemption*, Paris, 1963.

Vansteenberghe, E., DSAM, I (1936) 1017–25 art., "Aspirations."

I

ANALYTICAL INDEX

Angels 33 ff, 52 nn 11-14, 54 n 44, 81, 84, 87, 104 n 2, 120 n 19, 122 n 42, 156, 159

Animals 38, 42, 52 n 11

Apostolate 72 ff, 113, 116

Church: -time of: 63; as Kingdom beginning: 70 ff; 77, 78 n 10 and n 17;90 n 17; 106, 112, 114, 118, 119 nn 2, 6, 122 n 32, 146 n 5, 150, 171 n 43, 162-163, 205, 226, 234 ff, 254 ff; - poverty of: 93 ff; right of ownership: 102 n 16;

Compunction 57 n 81

Consolation 141, 147 n 19, 155-157ff, 179, 193, 236 ff, 249 n 90

Contemplation 164, 280, 305 n 62, 306 n 68

Counsels (evangelical) 124 n 57, 146 n 18, 153-154, 168 n 21, 169 n 22

Death 30, 137 ff, 141, 173 n 74, 205-206, 214 ff, 232, 239 n 21

Desires 127 ff, 135 n 24, 143; God as Desire: 133

Desolation 21, 141, 156, 159; chapter 13

Effort 179

Errors, False Prophets: 121 n 21, 263 ff, 278 n 108

Eucharist 3, 17, 21, 23-24, 33, 82, 88, 281, 289-290, 299, 307 n 78, chapter 12

Glory 11 n 19, 122 n 33, 139 ff, 142 (definition),242 n 58

God: - as Desire: 133; as Infinite Good: 51 n 7; as lost in Hell: 60; in the Exercises: 55 n 38; as Absolute Other but *not* wholly Other: 31, 288-289, 303 n 31;

as Patience: 43, 60

Grace:-intense: 287, 302 n 15

Heart of Jesus XXII, XXIII, 8, 88, 211 -215, 219 nn 3, 4

Holy Spirit 5, 41, 49, 54 n 29, 62, 70, 74, 76, 79 n 25, 85, 162, 283; - Fruits of the Holy Spirit: 170 n 32; - Prayers to the Holy Spirit: 65, 118-119, 145, 160-161

Indulgences 229 ff, 241 nn 37, 41-43, 258, 259, 265

Joseph, saint: 96-97, 98, 100, 102 n 18, 104 n 32

Joy, Happiness, Beatitude 47, 103 n 26, 160, 227, 291, 306 n 73

Judas 178 ff, 180, 187

Love: - for God: 171 n 38; - shown in revelation of Hell: 60; in fire of Hell 63; as recapitulative: 138, 281 ff , 289; as cyclical: 294; - as pure: 161, 297, 303 n 29; - reciprocity of love: 302 n 18; fraternal love: 304 n 54; 305 n 55; - prayer for love: 298

Marriage 94, 151 ff, 165, 168 n 9; 173 n 69; of Mary and Joseph: 97-98, 102 n 18; spiritual marriage: 306-307 n 77

Mary, Mariology 12 n 20, 16-17, 19, 22, 26 n 22, 27 n 34, 33, 48, 66 n 27, 76, 84-86, 91, 96-98, 100, 104 n 32, 116. 144, 201-203, 207-208, 215 ff, 233 ff, 238, 243-248; - prayers to Mary: 117, 132, 144, 160 - rosary: 66 n 27, 84-85, 218

Mediator 108, 121 n 22, 175

Papacy 112, 122 n 32, 254-255, 267, 271 n 31, 272 n 36
Purgatory 239 n 21, 240 nn 33, 34
Sacrifice 23, 24, 177 ff
Satan, devils, Lucifer: - Satan: 33, 50, 107 - 111, 117, 120 nn 17-20, 121 n 29, 124 n 60 - Lucifer: 105-108, 110, 115, 120 n 12
Suffering, Cross 144-145, 200-201, 203, 206, 221 n 37
Tears 38, 66 n 15, 98, 180, 185-187, 189 ff, 193, 203
Vow 124 n 57, 297
World 44-47, 57 n 74, 167

II

INDEX OF NAMES OF AUTHORS

A

Abercius, 188 n 45
Aldama, J. de, SJ, 247 n 77
Alszeghy, Z., SJ, 11 n 19
Ambrose, Saint, 238 n 7
Amselm, Saint, 188 n 41
Augustine, saint, XVIII, 11 n 7, 12 n 22, 27 n 41, 35, 45, 91 n 31, 102 n 18, 119 n 5, 209 n 29, 253, 254, 259, 270 nn 18, 20, 274 n 54, 277 n 94, 278 nn 107, 113, 284

B

Balthaser, H. Urs von, 26 n 31
Barreira, T., 65 n 8
Bartmann, B., 65 n 1
Bavaud, G., XXV n 15
Beeckx, SJ, XX, XXV n 14
Bellarmine, Saint Robert, SJ, 12, 221 n 37, 245 n 69
Bellecius, SJ, 103 n 28
Bernard-Maître, H., SJ, XIX, XXV nn 11, 12, 13
Bloy, L., 96
Bonaventure, Saint, XXI, XXVI n 26, 246 n 74, 304 nn 33, 36
Bonsirven, SJ, 121 n 21
Borgia, Saint Francis of, S.J., 170 n 30, 179, 187, 240 n 34, 306 n 68
Bossuet, J., 91 n 42, 102 n 7, 184 n 10, 207 n 11, 222 n 43
Bottereau, G., SJ, 173 n 64
Bourdaloue, L., 13, 240 n 35, 274 n 60
Bouyer, L., 44, 56 nn 62, 63; 57 nn 73, 74

Bover, J.M., SJ, 238 n 10, 242 n 50, 274 n 59
Bovon, XXVII n 37
Braun, F.M., O.P., 207 n 7, 221 n 34
Brou, A., SJ, 24 n 1, 25 n 3

C

Cafasso, St. Joseph, 212
Calveras, J., SJ, XXVII n 33, 185 n 26, 249 n 90
Calvin, J., 121 n 22
Câmara, 91 n 47
Canisius, Saint Peter, S.J., 147 n 20
Cantin, R., S.J., 139, 146 n 12
Casanovas, I, S.J., 171 n 40
Catherine of Siena, Saint, 221 n 30, 263, 276 n 79, 304 n 34
Certeau, M. de, S.J., 172 n 61
Cisneros, Garcia de, XIV n 6
Claret, Saint Anthony Mary, 90 nn 16, 19
Claudel, Paul, 221 n 32, 223 n 55
Clémence J., S.J., 169 n 26
Climachus, Saint John, 134 n 7
Clorivière, P. de, S.J., 77 n 6, 148 n 34
Coathalem, H., S.J., XXVII n 37, 65 n 6, 134 n 17, 169 n 25
Codina, A. de, S.J., XIV n 6, 119 n 1, 301 n 8
Colombini, Blessed J., 84
Congar, Y., O.P., 120 n 19
Courel, P., S.J., 25 n 11, 89 n 9, 133 n 2, 242 n 58
Cusson, G., S.J., XXVII n 37, 77, 301 n 6
Cyril of Alexandria, Saint, 196 n 7, 276

315

n 82
Cyril of Jerusalem, 242 n 54

D

Dalmases, C. de, S.J., 147 n 28
Daniélou, Cardinal J., S.J., 78 n 14
Desrumeaux, E., 133 n 5
Diepen, H.M., O.S.B., 91 n 37
Diez-Alegria, J.M., 301 nn 2, 4, 6, 12

E

Erasmus, 252, 259, 270 n 14, 273 nn 50, 51
Espinosa, C., XXV n 10
Eudes, Saint John, 221 n 33
Eymard, Saint Peter Julian, 17, 20, 25 n 12, 67 n 28

F

Fessard, G., S.J., 27 n 34, 269 nn 4, 10, 270 n 14, 271 nn 31, 32, 280, 302 n 19
Flick, M., S.J., 11 n 19
Foucauld, Charles de, 306 n 73
Francis de Sales, Saint, 151, 168 n 11, 285, 295, 305 n 59
Fulgentius, Saint, 188 n 52, 276 n 85

G

Gáetan du Saint Nom de Marie, 123 n 53
Gagliardi, S.J., 169 n 25, 184
Garrigou-Lagrange, R., O.P., 50, 67 n 31, 303 n 29
Gay, Monsignor Charles, 67 n 31
Gilleman, G., S.J., 26 n 25
Grandmaison, L. de, S.J., 91 n 41
Granero, J., S.J., 269 n 4
Gregory, Saint (Pope), XVIII
Gregory of Nyssa, 79 n 25
Grignon de Montfort, Saint Louis Mary, 76, 79 n 35, 104 n 30, 124 n 59, 148 n 33, 188 n 46, 208 n 16, 222 n 48, 223 n 54
Guibert, J. de, S.J., 11 n 19, 187, 301 nn 3, 5, 304 n 38
Guiges II, Carthusian, 25 n 5

H

Harrington, W., O.P., 90 n 30
Hoyos, Venerable Bernard of, S.J., 223 n 57
Hulst, Monsignor d', 240 n 23

I

Ignatius of Antioch, Saint, 91 n 45, 288, 304 n 32
Ignatius of Loyola, Saint, passim and 26 n 32, 169 n 26, 175, 188 n 42, 195 n 2, 207 n 2, 210 n 37, 220 n 27, 221 nn 28, 31, 37, 223 n 59, 241 n 37, 242 n 58, 272 n 34, 275 n 70, 305 n 43, 306 n 68
Ildefonso of Toledo, Saint, 217, 222 n 47
Iparraguirre, I., S.J., XXIV n 2, XXVI n 28, 140 n 8, 169 n 28, 171 n 39
Irenaeus, Saint, 11 n 20, 207 n 3, 210 nn 32, 38, 278 n 112

J

Jennesseaux, F., XXV n 14
Jerome, Saint, XVIII, 102 n 19
John VII, Pope, 217, 222 n 46
John XXII, Pope, 101 n 5
John XXIII, Pope, 102 n 13
John Chrysostom, Saint, 188 n 50, 197 n 28, 231-232, 242n 56, 244 n 68
John of the Cross, Saint, 11 n 16, 103 n 21, 112 n 33, 123 nn 52, 54, 133 n 5, 147 n 19, 249 n 90, 277 n 96, 293, 298, 304 n 47, 306 n 72, 307 n 77
John Damascene, Saint, XV n 16, 217, 221 n 37, 222 nn 46, 49, 223 n 58
Judde, C., S.J., 196 n 22

K

Kugelman, R., C.P., XV n 16

L

La Colombière, Blessed Claude, S.J., 5, 11 n 12, 13, 66 n 26, 134 n 13, 207 n 6
Lacordaire, O.P., 67 n 31
Lafont, G., O.S.B., 91 n 31
Lagrange, M.J., O.P., 243 n 64, 304 n 37
Lallemant, L, S.J., 185 n 15
Larranga, V., S.J., XXIV n 5, 168 n 19, 172 nn 52, 59
Laurentin, R., 245 n 69
Le Blond, J.M., S.J., 124 n 67
Lebreton, J., S.J., 221 n 39
Le Gaudier, A., S.J., 196 n 24
Lebreton, J., S.J., 221 n 39
Le Gaudier, A., S.J., 196 n 24
Leo the Great, Saint, Pope, 249 n 89
Leo XIII, Pope, 102 n 18, 185 n 20, 218, 221 n 35, 222 n 52, 242 n 49
Lépicier, Cardinal A.M., 222 n 44, 247 n 77

Leturia, P. de, S.J., XXIV n 2, 122 n 32, 269 nn 4, 7, 11
Libermann, Venerable, 305 n 54
Liguori, Saint Alphonsus, 1972, 306 n 73
Los Rios, B. de, XV n 16
Lubac, H. de, S.J., 91 n 34, 271 n 25
Ludolph the Carthusian, XIV n 6, 245 n 68
Lutgarde, Saint, 213
Luther, M., 46, 121 n 22, 241 n 43

M

Mainardi, 252 ff, 262
Manare, P., 119 n 1
Margaret Mary Alacoque, Saint, 76, 148 n 32, 191, 196 n 10, 203, 209 n 26, 220 n 13
Margerie, B. de, S.J., 78 nn 9, 20, 23, 89 nn 2, 7, 90 n 23, 91 nn 34, 42, 102 n 19, 135 n 22, 149 n 1, 185 n 20, 208 n 12, 210 n 35, 220 nn 8, 14, 21, 221 n 36, 306 nn 74, 76
Maritain, J., 65 n 2
Michel, A., 66 n 19
Mollat, 101 n 5
Musters, A., XV nn 16, 17

N

Nadal, J., XIX, XXIV notes 2, 5, 135 n 24, 171 n 43, 192, 196 n 18, 211, 220 nn 5-7, 18, 294, 301 n 10, 304 n 51
Nicolau, M., S.J., 26 n 25, 171 n 43, 220 n 6, 304 n 51
Nogales, G., 167 n 1
Nonnell, G., S.J., 79 n 29
Nouet, J., S.J., 219 n 4

O

Olivaint, P., S.J., 79 n 30
Orlandis, R., 78, 173 n 67

P

Passaglia, 66 n 19
Paul VI, XXI, XXIII, XXVI, XXVII, 102 n 20, 208 n 18, 210 n 34, 240 n 33, 241 n 41, 268 n 3, 277 n 90
Paul of the Cross, Saint, 217, 222 nn 40-43, 306 n 73
Peter Chrysologus, Saint, XV n 16, 102 n 18
Philip of the Trinity, 184 n 6
Pius IX, Pope, 208 n 17, 248 n 80
Pius X, Saint, Pope, 207 n 8, 238 n 9
Pius XI, Pope, XI, XXI, XXV n 19, XXVI

nn 20, 21, 22, 173 n 73, 196 nn 11, 21, 209 n 23, 223 n 56, 245 n 68
Pius XII, Pope, XVII, XXIV nn 1, 10 n 6, 11 n 14, 17, 25 n 13, 26 n 22, 27 nn 33, 35, 39, 66 n 27, 89 n 11, 91 n 35 146 n 18, 168 n 5, 172 n 55, 184 nn 7, 11, 185 n 20, 208 nn 15, 20, 210 n 36, 39, 220 n 8, 222 nn 48, 50, 238 n 9, 305 n 57, 306 n 71
Polanco, S.J., 169 n 23
Pozo C., S.J., 66 n 21
Puhl, S.J., 25 n 11, 168 n 10, 170 n 32

R

Rahner, Hugo, S.J., XVIII, 26 n 31, 69, 77 nn 3, 4, 119 n 4, 119 n 8, 122 n 32, 148 n 31, 171 n 43
Rahner, Karl, S.J., 46, 67 n 31, 212, 220 n 10, 294, 304 n 92
Ribadeneira, P. de, S.J., 147 n 28, 148 n 30
Richard, 67 nn 30, 31
Rodriguez, Saint Alphonsus, S.J., 16, 25 n 9, 148 n 34, 285
Roothaan, J., S.J., XXV n 14, 135 n 20
Roschini, G., 243 n 64, 246 nn 74, 75, 247 n 77, 248 n 79
Rouquette, R., S.J., 116, 124 n 56

S

Scheeben, M.J., 66 n 19
Schillebeeckx, E., O.P., 209 nn 21, 29, 218, 222 n 53
Schlier, H., 120 n 19
Soras, A. de, S.J., 78 n 19
Suárez, F., S.J., 120 n 20, 121 nn 28, 29, 245 n 68, 247 nn 77

T

Tertullian, 220 n 16
Theresa of Avilax, Saint, 21, 61, 235, 241 n 40
Thomas, J., S.J., 77 n 5

V

Van Steenberghe, E., 136 n 26
Vivès, L., 273 n 51
Vogt, E., S.J., XV n 16
Voragine, James of, O.P., XIV n 6, XV n 16, 245 n 68
Vries, P. De, XXIV n 2

Z

Zomparelli, B., 133 n 5

Letura, P. de, S.I., XXIV n 2, 122 n 32, 209 nn 4, 7, 11

Libermann, Venerable, 305 n 54

Liguori, Saint Alphonsus, 1972, 306 n 73

Los Rios, B. de, XV n 16

Lubac, H. de, S.I., 91 n 34, 271 n 25

Ludolph the Carthusian, XIV n 6, 245 n 68

Lutgarde, Saint, 213

Luther, M., 46, 121 n 22, 241 n 42

M

Mainarchi, 232 ff, 262

Manare, P., 119 n 1

Margaret Mary Alacoque, Saint, 76, 145 n 32, 191, 196 n 10, 203, 209 n 26, 220 n 13

Margerie, B. de, S.I., 78 nn 9, 20, 23, 89 nn 2, 7, 90 n 23, 91 nn 34, 42, 102 n 19, 135 n 22, 149 n 1, 155 n 20, 208 n 12, 210 n 35, 220 nn 8, 14, 21, 221 n 36, 306 nn 74, 76

Marsiain, J., 65 n 2

Michel, A., 66 n 19

Mollat, 101 n 3

Masters, A., XV nn 16, 17

N

Nadal, J., XIX, XXIV notes 2, 5, 135 n 24, 171 n 43, 192, 196 n 18, 211, 220 nn 5-7, 18, 296, 301 n 10, 304 n 51

Nicolaau, M., S.I., 26 n 25, 171 n 43, 220 n 6, 304 n 51

Nogazca, O., 167 n 1

Nonnell, G., S.I., 79 n 29

Nouet, J., S.I., 219 n 4

O

Olivaint, P., S.I., 79 n 30

Orlandis, R., 78, 173 n 67

P

Passaglia, 86 n 19

Paul VI, XXI, XXIII, XXVI, XXVII, 102 n 20, 208 n 18, 210 n 34, 240 n 35, 241 n 41, 268 n 3, 273 n 90

Paul of the Cross, Saint, 217, 222 nn 40-43, 306 n 73

Peter Chrysologus, Saint, XV n 16, 102 n 18

Philip of the Trinity, 184 n 6

Pius IX, Pope, 208 n 17, 248 n 60

Pius X, Saint, Pope, 207 n 8, 234 n 9

Pius XI, Pope, XI, XXI, XXV n 19, XXVI

nn 20, 21, 22, 173 n 73, 196 nn 11, 21, 209 n 23, 223 n 56, 245 n 68

Pius XII, Pope, XVII, XXIV nn 1, 10 n 6, 33, 35, 39, 66 n 27, 89 n 13, 26 n 22, 27 nn 146 n 16, 168 n 5, 172 n 55, 184 nn 7, 11, 185 n 20, 204 nn 15, 20, 210 nn 36, 39, 220 n 8, 222 nn 48, 50, 238 n 9, 305 n 57, 306 n 71

Polanco S.I., 169 n 23

Pavo C., S.I., 66 n 21

Puhl, S.I., 25 n 11, 168 n 10, 170 n 32

R

Rahner, Hugo, S.I., XVIII, 26 n 31, 69, 77 nn 3, 4, 119 n 4, 119 n 8, 122 n 32, 148 n 31, 174 n 43

Rahner, Karl, S.I., 46, 67 n 31, 212, 220 n 10, 294, 304 n 92

Ribadeneira, P. de, S.I., 147 n 28, 148 n 30

Richard, 67 nn 30, 31

Rodriguez, Saint Alphonsus, S.I., 16, 23 n 9, 148 n 34, 285

Roothaan, J., S.I., XXV n 14, 135 n 20

Roschini, G., 243 n 64, 246 nn 74, 75, 247 n 77, 248 n 79

Rouquette, R., S.I., 116, 124 n 56

S

Scheeben, M.J., 86 n 19

Schillebeeckx, E., O.P., 209 nn 21, 29, 218, 222 n 52

Schler, H., 120 n 39

Soras, A. de, S.I., 78 n 19

Suarez, F., S.I., 120 n 20, 121 nn 28, 29, 245 n 68, 247 nn 77

T

Tertullian, 220 n 16

Theresa of Avila, Saint, 21, 61, 235, 241 n 40

Thomas, J., S.I., 77 n 5

V

Van Steenberghe, E., 136 n 26

Vivès, I., 273 n 51

Vogt, F., S.I., XV n 16

Voragine, James of, O.P., XIV n 6, XV n 16, 245 n 68

Vries, P. De, XXIV n 2

Z

Zompatelli, B., 133 n 5

III

INDEX OF BIBLICAL REFERENCES

GENESIS

2, 17	54 n 29
2, 19	216
3, 4	54 n 29
3, 7	54 n 35
3, 15	117, 201
3, 16-20	55 n 36
3, 21	39
5, 5	55 n 36
47, 30	240 n 25

EXODUS

18, 20	184 n 12
33, 12-20	184 n 12

LEVITICUS

18,21	59

NUMBERS

16, 33	240 n 24

II SAMUEL

6, 3-7	180

II CHRONICLES

12, 20	160

II MACCHABEES

12, 46	230, 241 n 38

PSALMS

6, 3-6	10
31, 11	238 n 10
69, 22	204
144	77 n 6
149, 5	238 n 10

PROVERBS

3, 34	17

CANTICLE OF CANTICLES

2, 14	212
2, 16	290

WISDOM

5, 17-22	56 n 56
7, 14	51 n 3
9, 14-15	32
10, 1	53 n 16
11, 17	56 n 56
16, 24	56 n 56
19, 6	56 n 56

SIRAH (ECCLESIASTICUS)

7, 21	51 n 6
10, 15	53 n 15

319

ISAIAS

2, 4	181
6, 2-4	229
9	229
11, 2-5	112
11, 12	119 n 2
14, 4-21	112
14, 12	107
17, 10	51 n 3
44, 21	51 n 3
53, 6-12	229
53, 7	187 n 35

JEREMIAS

6, 13	121 n 21
26, 7-8	121 n 21
27, 16	121 n 21
28, 1	121 n 21
33, 8	51 n 3

ESECHIEL

20, 27	51 n 3

DANIEL

7, 10	55 n 44

ZECHARIAH

12, 10	57 n 81

MATTHEW

4, 2	136 n 25
5, 3	114, 123 n 48
5, 11-12	114
5, 22	592
5, 48	127
6, 1-8	136 n 25
6, 21	204
6, 22-23	151
6, 33	7
7, 7	20, 21
7, 13-14	90 n 18
7, 15	121 n 21
7, 21	302 n 17
9, 9	129
10, 15	59
10, 32-33	90 n 22
11, 12	188 n 38

11, 25-26	9
11, 29	59
11, 20	59
12, 32	62
12, 34	90 n 22
13, 1	10, 95
13, 24-30	124 n 69
13, 36-43	124 n 69
13, 41	205, 234
16, 18	205, 234
16, 26	138
18, 8	59
18, 15-17	262
19, 16-26	129
19, 21	95, 123 n 49
19, 23-26	101 n 6
20, 23	79 n 24
22, 21	97
22, 32	230
22, 37-38	285, 301 n 14
22, 39	173 n 77
23	180
23, 15	59
23, 33	59
24, 13	124 n 69
24, 35	103 n 23, 277 n 101
25, 30	59
25, 34-35	204, 230
25, 36	100
26, 28	176
26, 37-38	189
26, 38	193
26, 39	190, 193
26, 40-41	191
26, 42	190
26, 44	196 n 13
26, 52-53	187 n 33
26, 63	10, 187 n 35
27, 6	244 n 68
27, 46	204
27, 52-53	113, 247 n 75
27, 64	187 n 35
28, 1	244 n 68
28, 5	113
28, 20	251

MARK

1, 35	9
3, 29	278 n 112
6, 16	64
8, 17	233

9, 34	9	22, 15	133
9, 42-49	592	22, 19-20	9, 176, 178
10, 45	9, 10	22, 31-32	124 n 64
11, 6	10	22, 39	194
12, 24	176	22, 41	9
14, 21	60	22, 43	91 n 40, 193
14, 33	189	22, 44	190, 191
16, 18	124 n 64	23, 34	199
		23, 39	201
		23, 43	200
		23, 46	205
		24, 25	243 n 65

LUKE

JOHN

1-2	234, 245 n 69		
1, 27	XIV		
1, 28	248 n 80		
1, 28-35	84		
1, 37-38	84	1, 10	47
1, 42	248 n 80	1, 14	300
1, 45	248 n 77	1, 17	200
1, 48	248 n 77	1, 18	91 n 33
2, 7	93	1, 29	277 n 105
2, 19-51	245 n 69	1, 33	56 n 50
2, 26	238 n 7	1, 38	73
2, 34	208 n 14, 226	2, 14-16	10
2, 38	100	2, 19-21	289
2, 41-43	97	2, 22	200
3, 22	4	2, 25	194, 240 n 30
3, 34	228	3, 6-8	256
4, 1	269 n 13	3, 16	91 n 46, 99
4, 13	196 n 7	3, 19-20	32
6, 12-13	9	3, 21	157
7, 15	244 n 67, 248 n 80	3, 36	120 n 9
8, 3	95	4, 10	204
9, 31	229	4, 23-24	257
9, 51-58	95	4, 34	205
9, 58	10	4, 42	10, 257
10, 16	72	5, 24	72, 120 n 9, 232
10, 18	107	5, 29	60
11, 1	133	5, 44	140
11, 34-36	151, 153	6, 15	10
11, 35	153	6, 32-33	183
12, 4	64	6, 44	183
12, 4-5	59	6, 46	103 n 26
12, 33-34	94	6, 48	183
13, 28	59, 66 n 15	6, 51	183
14, 15-24	129	6, 53	60
14, 33	99	6, 53-55	204
15, 7	239 n 14	6, 68	277 n 101
15, 10	239 n 14	7, 16	113
16, 24	59	7, 37-39	204
18, 14	176	8, 10	85
18, 19	293	8, 12	196 n 17
21, 18	196 n 20	8, 21	184 n 12, 200

8, 21-55	180	17, 1-5	79 n 25
8, 26	72	17, 2	188 n 51
8, 26-29	10	17, 3	120 n 9, 302 n 19
8, 29	4	17, 4	205
8, 34	33	17, 9	47
8, 40	105	17, 13	226, 242 n 53
8, 44	85, 105, 108	17, 14-16	47
8, 49	188 n 51	17, 22	233
8, 56	10, 18	17, 23	91 n 33, 233
10, 18	231	17, 24	91 n 46, 233
10, 38	204	17, 25	47
11, 42	199	17, 27	47
12, 6	95	18, 6	187 n 33
12, 27	10	18, 11	79 n 24, 204
12, 32-33	242 n 53	18, 19	47
12, 41	229	18, 23	10
12, 42	115	19, 5	9
12, 49-50	72	19, 9	187 n 35
13, 1	184 n 4	19, 11	97
13, 20	83	19, 26	201, 234
13, 29	95, 99	19, 27	215
13, 31-32	146 n 14	19, 28	203
14	47	19, 30	205
14, 5	73	20, 9	211
14, 10	8, 73	20, 22-23	200, 221 n 19
14, 13	119		
14, 16-17	XXI	ACTS	
14, 17	74, 226		
14, 19-20	247 n 77	1, 3	234
14, 21	157	1, 11	251
14, 21-23	204, 226, 247 n 77	1, 14	234
14, 23	74, 188 n 77	1, 25	187 n 32
14, 24	72	2, 24	241 n 46
14, 26	248 n 80, 269 n 13	2, 37	57 n 81
14, 30	91 n 33	2, 42	199
15, 4	288	4, 4	199
15, 5	113, 234	7, 59	206
15, 9	204	13, 26	85, 122 n 34
15, 11	242 n 53, 290	20, 29-30	121 n 21
15, 13	146 n 6	20, 35	34, 100
15, 16	134 n 9		
15, 22	200		
15, 23-24	88	ROMANS	
15, 26	200, 277 n 105		
16, 8	47	1, 1	123 n 43
16, 14	5, 119, 188 n 51	1, 3-4	246 n 70
16, 20	47	1, 16	274 n 54
16, 27	204	1-3	78 n 22
16, 32	204	4, 25	231
16, 33	242 n 53	5, 2	238 n 10
16, 39	47	5, 5	11 n 18, 289
17, 1	5, 23, 146	5, 16-17	44
		5, 19	214

6, 12	45
7	45
7, 19-23	45
8, 6-8	44
8, 9	277 n 100
8, 9-11	70
8, 11	241 n 46
8, 15	11 n 18, 267
8, 22	98
8, 23	98, 168 n 8, 268
8, 26-27	292
8, 32	99, 222 n 45, 286
12, 2	160
13, 1-5	146 n 5
13, 1-7	257
13, 8-10	289
13, 10	138, 155
13, 14	44, 54 n 35
14, 7-9	292
15, 1-3	4
15, 31	95
16, 20	117

I CORINTHIANS

1, 8	163
1, 23	93
2-3	45
2, 2	213
2, 10-12	256
2, 14	273 n 43
2, 16	256
3, 11	1
3, 16	276 n 85
3, 18	293
3, 22-23	99, 291
5, 4-5	268
6, 17	266
6, 19	276 n 85
12, 7-10	105
12, 13	188 n 50
13, 7	20
13, 13	18
15, 6	233
15, 24-28	71, 73
15, 31	184 n 10
15, 43	282

II CORINTHIANS

3, 3	266
3, 16-17	266, 269 n 14
3, 23	266
4, 4	108
4, 6	266
4, 7-12	142
4, 10	255
4, 18	108
6, 10	99
8-9	95
8, 9	94
8, 14-15	242
9, 5	100
9, 7	100
11, 2-4	109, 253
11, 13-15	109
11, 14	50, 270 n 14
11, 18	107
12, 1-4	235
12, 7-9	192
12, 10	142

GALATIANS

1, 8-9	113
1, 9	268
1, 10	4
2, 19-20	199, 206
5, 26	45
5, 14	155
5, 17	136 n 24
5, 19-21	44, 51 n 6
5, 22	249 n 92
5, 24	176
6, 14	214

EPHESIANS

1, 6	8, 268, 277 n 93
1, 10	2, 289
1, 12	277 n 93
1, 18	88
1, 23	101 n 2
2, 2	52 n 11
2, 3	44
2, 10	8
2, 13-14	268
2, 14-18	216
2, 23	300
3, 8	93
3, 18-19	62
4	45
4, 2-3	258
4, 4-6	267
4, 15	181

4, 15-16	73
4, 16	8, 205, 251
4, 19	300
4, 22-29	79 n 24
4, 24	54 n 35
4, 30	XXIII
5, 5	51 n 6
5, 19	219
5, 22-27	254
6, 10-18	196 n 9
6, 11-12	120 n 19
6, 12	52 n 11, 107, 270

PHILIPPIANS

1, 9-11	160
2, 4	26 n 30
2, 8	214
2, 12	60
2, 13	134 n 10
3, 7-10	214
4, 4	249 n 92
4, 6	26 n 17

II THESSALONIANS

2, 7	54 n 31

I TIMOTHY

2, 1	18
4, 1	110, 120 n 18
6, 10	110
6, 20	268

II TIMOTHY

1, 6-7	267
1, 9-10	188 n 39
1, 12-14	268
2,5	46
4, 1-4	263

TITUS

1, 1	123 n 43
3, 6	160
3, 5-7	268

HEBREWS

2, 7	196 n 9
2, 14-15	33
2, 16	196 n 9

5, 7	10, 189, 193
7, 25	176
10, 5ff	86
10, 29	176, 200
12, 2	141, 277 n 95
12, 4	191
13, 8	194

JAMES

1, 19-22	103 n 22
2, 16	103 n 22
3, 2	51 n 6
3, 2-12	103 n 22
3, 15	108

I PETER

1, 8	226
2, 9	73
2, 21	101 n 4
4, 13-14	242 n 57
5, 5	52 n 11
5, 6	17
5, 8	121 n 20

II PETER

1, 19	176

I. JOHN

1, 8	51 n 6
2, 1	176, 248 n 84, 277 n 105
2, 15-17	47
3, 2	215
3, 16	241 n 36
3, 17-18	302 n 17
3, 20	294
4, 5	90 n 22
4, 14	232
4, 16	232
4, 18	116
5, 4	47, 232
5, 19	47

REVELATION (Apocalypse)

1, 15	72
2, 9	94
2, 26	200
3, 10	85

3, 17	94, 103 n 26	12, 12	117
3, 21	90 n 17, 200	12, 17	117
4, 2-10	90 n 17	13	121 n 29
5, 6	85	13, 1-5	84
6, 10	85	13, 8-12-14	85
7, 11	85	15, 13-14	52 n 11
8, 10	107	16, 9-11-21	84
8, 13	85	16, 13-16	109
9, 1	107	17, 2-8	85
11, 10	85	18, 3	108
12	42	20, 7-9	107, 119 n 6
12, 3	52 n 11	21, 1 ff	106
12, 4	109	21, 22	211
12, 7	109	22, 1	85, 90 n 17
12, 9	107, 109	22, 16-17-20	251

IV

INDEX OF SPIRITUAL EXERCISES

Ex. 1,   p. xiv n.5, 26 n.31, 149.

Ex. 2,   p. xiv n.5, 21, 176, 249 n.90, 269 n.11.

Ex. 3,   p. 22.

Ex. 4,   p. 39, 185 n.26.

Ex. 5,   p. 280, 297.

Ex. 7,   p. 160.

Ex. 10,   p. 33, 69, 152, 184 n.2, 236, 248 n.86, 281.

Ex. 12,   p. 25 n.4, 191.

Ex. 13,   p. 25 n.4, 192.

Ex. 14,   p. 55 n.42, 122 n.35, 124 n.57.

Ex. 15,   p. 55 n.42, 124 n.57, 152, 153, 161, 266, 297.

Ex. 16,   p. 131, 135 n.24, 163, 202, 204.

Ex. 17,   p. xix.

Ex. 18,   p. xxv n.10.

Ex. 19,   p. xix.

Ex. 20,   p. 17, 55 n.42, 165, 287, 307 n.77.

Ex. 21,   p. 26 n.31, 44, 149.

Ex. 22,   p. 252, 261.

Ex. 23,   p. 1, 4, 6, 22, 25 n.11, 63, 137, 142, 173 n.76, 175, 259, 274 n.55-, 297.

Ex. 24,   p. 15, 50.

Ex. 25,   p. 15,50.

Ex. 26,   p. 15, 50.

Ex. 27,   p. 15, 50.

Ex. 28,   p. 15, 50.

Ex. 29,   p. 15, 50.

Ex. 30,   p. 15, 50.

Ex. 31,   p. 15, 50.

Ex. 32,   p. 15, 50.

Ex. 33,   p. 15, 50, 55 n.42.

Ex. 34,   p. 15, 39, 50, 55 n.42.

Ex. 35,   p. 15, 39, 50, 51 n.42.

Ex. 36,   p. 15, 39, 50.

Ex. 37,   p. 15, 39, 50.

Ex. 38,   p. 15, 39, 50, 87.

Ex. 39,   p. 5, 15, 39, 50, 87, 274 n.55, 282, 300.

Ex. 40,   p. 5, 15, 39, 50, 55 n.42, 87.

Ex. 41,   p. 15, 39, 50, 87, 260-262, 275 n 69, 276 n 78.

Ex. 42,   p. 15, 39, 50, 159, 241 n.37, 273 n.45.

Ex. 43,   p. 15, 22, 50.

Ex. 44,   p. 39-, 55 n.42, 178, 185 n.13, n.18, 281.

Ex. 45,   p. xiv n.4, 15, 22.

Ex. 46,   p. 15, 16, 22, 43, 44.

Ex. 47,   p. xxiii, 15, 22, 23, 32, 52 n 11, 62.

Ex. 48,   p. 15, 22, 33, 90 n.18, 184 n.5, 185 n.21, n.23.

Ex. 49,   p. 15, 22, 50.

Ex. 50,   p. 15, 22, 34-, 52 n.12, 75, 184 n.5, 185 n.19.

Ex. 51,   p. 15, 22, 35-, 39, 55 n.36-, 90 n.18, 228, 255, 302 n.19.

Ex. 52,   p. 15, 22, 37-, 51 n.3, 90 n.18, 185 n.19.

Ex. 53,   p. xxii, 15, 22, 32, 37, 54 n.28, 61, 81, 181.

Ex. 54,   p. xxiii, 15, 22, 55 n.38, 296.

Ex. 55,   p. 25 n.7, 39, 40, 61, 66 n.15, 179.

Ex. 56,   p. 39.

Ex. 57,   p. 55 n.43, 297.

Ex. 58, p. 40, 62, 138, 163, 187 n.34.
Ex. 59, p. 22, 41, 176, 187 n.34, 255, 282.
Ex. 60, p. 42, 56 n.56, 187 n.34, 255, 302 n.22.
Ex. 61, p. 22, 42, 55 n.38.
Ex. 62, p. 25 n.7, 43-, 46.
Ex. 63, p. xiv n.2, n.8, xv n.16, 19, 43-, 47, 48, 56 n.59, 123 n.46, 148 n.29, 255.
Ex. 65, p. 25 n.7, 61, 62, 65 n.6, n.7, n.11-, 66 n.25, 90 n.18, 268.
Ex. 66, p. 62, 66 n.25, 75.
Ex. 67, p. 62, 66 n.16, n.25, 75, 83.
Ex. 68, p. 62, 66 n.25, 75.
Ex. 69, p. 62, 66 n.15, n.25, 75, 176
Ex. 70, p. 62, 63, 65 n 11, 66 n 25, 75, 159.
Ex. 71, p. 63, 66 n.23, n.25, 75, 90 n.18, 159, 228, 260.
Ex. 73, p. 25 n.6.
Ex. 74, p. 25 n.6, 57 n.72, 159, 176
Ex. 75, p. 17.
Ex. 78, p. 185 n.23.
Ex. 83, p. 186 n 27.
Ex. 84, p. 186 n.27.
Ex. 85, p. 186 n.27, 195 n.2.
Ex. 86, p. 186 n.27, 195 n.2.
Ex. 87, p. 39, 44, 45, 79 n.32, 185 n.26, 186 n.27-, 240 n.32.
Ex. 89, p. 185 n.26, 249 n.90.
Ex. 91, p. 25 n.7, 71, 72, 77 n.1, 78 n.16, 175.
Ex. 92, p. 78 n.11.
Ex. 93, p. 79 n.24.
Ex. 94, p. 74-, 79 n.27, 176.
Ex. 95, p. xxiii, 72-, 79 n.24, 113, 114, 123 n.45, 187 n.34, 233, 242 n.58-, 282, 302 n.20.
Ex. 96, p. 74, 75-, 79 n.32, 296.
Ex. 97, p. xxiii, 45, 74, 132, 159, 196 n.12.
Ex. 98, p. xiv n.14, 56 n.55, 74, 132, 139, 159, 163, 297.
Ex. 101, p. 15, 22, 81, 89 n.1.
Ex. 102, p. xiv n.10, n.13, 15, 81, 85, 87, 90 n.18.
Ex. 103, p. 15, 82, 89 n.9, n.10, 225.
Ex. 104, p. xxii, 15, 16, 22, 82-, 102 n.17.
Ex. 105, p. 15.
Ex. 106, p. 15, 52 n.11, 83, 85, 90 n.17, n.18, n.25, 10.
Ex. 107, p. 15, 52 n.11, 83, 84, 90 n.25, n. 18, n 25, 110

Ex. 108, p. xiv, n.13, 15, 52 n.11, 83, 85-, 86, 90 n.18, n.25, n.29, 110, 231.
Ex. 109, p. 15, 19, 86.
Ex. 110, p. 25 n.7.
Ex. 111, p. 96.
Ex. 112, p. 97.
Ex. 113, p. 97.
Ex. 114, p. xiv n.11, 97-, 100, 102 n.18-, 104 n.32-, 120 n.17.
Ex. 115, p. 98.
Ex. 116, p. 99, 103 n.24, n.25-.
Ex. 121, p. 15, 22, 207 n.1.
Ex. 122, p. 15, 22, 65 n.6, 207 n.1.
Ex. 123, p. 15, 22, 72, 207 n.1.
Ex. 124, p. 15, 22, 207 n.1, 248 n.78.
Ex. 125, p. 15, 22, 207 n.1.
Ex. 126, p. 15, 207 n.1.
Ex. 133, p. 249 n.90.
Ex. 135, p. 112, 153-, 276 n.89.
Ex. 136, p. 105, 107, 134 n.16.
Ex. 137, p. 106, 107.
Ex. 138, p. 106, 107, 108, 120 n.12.
Ex. 139, p. 107, 116, 119 n.7, 120 n.12, 260.
Ex. 140, p. 108, 120 n.12.
Ex. 141, p. 52 n.11, 107, 109, 116, 122 n.38, 260, 268 n.2.
Ex. 142, p. 110-, 116, 260, 302 n.19.
Ex. 143, p. 111-, 122 n.31.
Ex. 144, p. 112, 116.
Ex. 145, p. 109, 112-, 116, 120 n.18, 122 n.38, n.40, 252, 260, 274 n.59.
Ex. 146, p. 116, 302 n.20.
Ex. 147, p. xiv n.8, 19, 116, 124 n.58, 131, 148 n.29, 299.
Ex. 149, p. 125.
Ex. 150, p. 126.
Ex. 151, p. 127, 131, 160, 163.
Ex. 152, p. 128.
Ex. 153, p. 128, 129.
Ex. 154, p. 129-, 285.
Ex. 155, p. 129-, 130-, 132-, 134 n.12, 135 n.18.
Ex. 156, p. 131.
Ex. 157, p. 19, 45, 125, 131-, 134 n.17, 135 n.18-, n.24-, 204.
Ex. 158, p. 134 n.6.
Ex. 164, p. 120 n.18, 137.
Ex. 165, p. 137, 146 n.2.
Ex. 166, p. 128, 138, 146 n.4-.
Ex. 167, p. 75, 139.
Ex. 168, p. 19, 143, 147 n.22, n.24.

Ex. 169, p. 129, 151-, 152, 153, 160, 168 n.7, n.9, n.15.
Ex. 171, p. 152, 153.
Ex. 172, p. 45, 151, 152, 166, 168 n.7.
Ex. 173, p. 45, 152.
Ex. 174, p. 152.
Ex. 175, p. 134 n.12, 158, 161, 169 n.25, 170 n.33, n.34, 171 n.37, 173 n.65.
Ex. 176, p. 155, 157, 160.
Ex. 177, p. 156-, 163.
Ex. 178, p. 156, 159, 169 n.28.
Ex. 179, p. 156, 159-, 242 n.58.
Ex. 180, p. 156, 157, 158-, 159, 160, 161, 170 n.36-, 171 n.37.
Ex. 181, p. 156, 157, 159-, 160.
Ex. 182, p. 156, 157, 159, 160.
Ex. 183, p. 156, 159-, 161, 170 n.32, 171 n.45.
Ex. 184, p. 130, 134 n.12, 152, 155, 156, 158, 160-, 166, 285.
Ex. 185, p. 156, 166.
Ex. 186, p. 156, 159, 166.
Ex. 187, p. 156, 159, 166.
Ex. 188, p. 156, 159.
Ex. 189, p. 44, 45, 112, 154, 160, 165-, 116-, 167, 173 n.68, n.69-, n.76, 204.
Ex. 190, p. 184 n.4.
Ex. 191, p. 176.
Ex. 193, p. 175, 184 n.4.
Ex. 194, p. 176.
Ex. 195, p. 179, 180, 185 n.21, 187 n.36, 195 n.4.
Ex. 196, p. 180, 187 n.36.
Ex. 197, p. 181, 187 n.36.
Ex. 198, p. 182.
Ex. 199, p. 182.
Ex. 203, p. 189, 195 n.2, 199.
Ex. 208, p. xiv n.12, 215, 216, 221 n.37.
Ex. 209, p. 199.
Ex. 210, p. 55 n.39.
Ex. 211, p. 55 n.39.
Ex. 212, p. 55 n.39.
Ex. 213, p. 55 n.39.
Ex. 214, p. 55 n.39, 220 n.15.
Ex. 215, p. 55 n.39, 220 n.15.
Ex. 216, p. 55 n.39.
Ex. 217, p. 55 n.39.
Ex. 218, p. 238 n.1.
Ex. 219, p. 225, 227, 234, 235-, 239 n.21-, 241 n.44, 243 n.63, 246 n.73,

248 n.80.
Ex. 220, p. 89 n.12, 225.
Ex. 221, p. xv n.18, 226, 232, 242 n.58-.
Ex. 223, p. 231-.
Ex. 224, p. 229, 236.
Ex. 229, p. 248 n.85.
Ex. 230, p. 282, 284, 296-, 301 n.1, n.13.
Ex. 231, p. 282, 292, 296, 299.
Ex. 232, p. 283, 299.
Ex. 233, p. xxiv n.6, 283, 285, 287, 292-.
Ex. 234, p. xxiii, 79 n.32, 280-, 286, 287, 292, 296, 299, 305 n.55, n.65.
Ex. 235, p. 288.
Ex. 236, p. 118, 290.
Ex. 237, p. 171 n.38, 293.
Ex. 238, p. 22, 23, 25 n.2, 26 n.29, 40.
Ex. 239, p. 25 n.2, 40.
Ex. 240, p. 25 n.2, 40, 281-, 283.
Ex. 241, p. 25 n.2, 40.
Ex. 242, p. 25 n.2, 40.
Ex. 243, p. xiv n.10, 25 n.2, 40.
Ex. 244, p. 25 n.2, 40.
Ex. 245, p. 25 n.2, 40.
Ex. 246, p. 25 n.2, 40.
Ex. 247, p. 25 n.2, 40.
Ex. 248, p. xiv n.9, 25 n.2, 40, 209 n.24.
Ex. 249, p. 23.
Ex. 252, p. 249 n.90.
Ex. 253, p. xiv n.15, 23, 148 n.29.
Ex. 254, p. 249 n.90.
Ex. 258, p. xiv n.15, 15, 148 n.29, 307 n.78-.
Ex. 259, p. 15.
Ex. 260, p. 15, 307 n.78.
Ex. 264, p. 102 n.18.
Ex. 266, p. xiv n.12.
Ex. 267, p. 26 n.27.
Ex. 273, p. 244 n.67, 248 n.80.
Ex. 274, p. 26 n.27.
Ex. 281, p. 107.
Ex. 289, p. 178-, 184 n.3.
Ex. 290, p. 191.
Ex. 297, p. 201, 207 n.2-, n.5, 211, 219 n.1, n.2.
Ex. 298, p. xiv n.12, 214, 215, 221 n.37.
Ex. 299, p. 233, 243 n.65, 246 n.73.
Ex. 300, p. 246 n.73.
Ex. 301, p. 26 n.27, 246 n.73.
Ex. 302, p. 246 n.73.
Ex. 303, p. 243 n.65, 246 n.73.
Ex. 304, p. 246 n.73.
Ex. 305, p. 246 n.73.
Ex. 306, p. 246 n.73.

Ex. 307, p. 246 n.73.
Ex. 308, p. 233, 246 n.73.
Ex. 309, p. 246 n.73.
Ex. 310, p. 246 n.73.
Ex. 311, p. 221 n.31, 227, 235, 239 n.21-,
        246 n.72, n.73.
Ex. 312, p. 221 n.31, 268 n.1.
Ex. 313, p. 159.
Ex. 316, p. 22, 82, 120 n.10, 155-, 161,
        179, 185 n.23, n.26, 187 n.28,
        n.29, 236, 237, 243 n.59, 247-
        48 n.77-, 249 n.90, 282, 285,
        286, 287, 296, 3022 n.16.
Ex. 317, p. 243 n.59, 249 n.87.
Ex. 319, p. 192, 196 n.19, 249 n.90.
Ex. 320, p. 157, 192, 302 n.15.
Ex. 321, p. 193, 196 n.20, 249 n.90.
Ex. 322, p. 179, 185 n.22, n.26, 287-.
Ex. 323, p. 115.
Ex. 324, p. 115.
Ex. 325, p. 52 n.11.
Ex. 327, p. 23, 50, 69, 120 n.12, n.17.
Ex. 329, p. 159.
Ex. 330, p. 155, 169 n.25-, 193.
Ex. 331, p. 156, 159, 249 n.90, 270 n.14.
Ex. 332, p. 107, 109, 120 n.18, 156.
Ex. 333, p. xxiii, 127, 260, 306 n.71.
Ex. 335, p. 160, 193.
Ex. 336, p. 155, 169 n.27, 249 n.90.
Ex. 337, p. 55 n.39, 166.
Ex. 338, p. 55 n.39, 160, 166, 285.
Ex. 339, p. 55 n.39, 160, 166.
Ex. 340, p. 55 n.39, 166.
Ex. 341, p. 55 n.39, 166.

Ex. 342, p. 55 n.39.
Ex. 343, p. 55 n.39, 166.
Ex. 344, p. 55 n.39, 122 n.35, 166-, 167.
Ex. 351, p. 258.
Ex. 352, p. 252, 258.
Ex. 353, p. 253-, 255, 258, 277 n.92, 278
        n.112.
Ex. 354, p. 258, 277 n.92.
Ex. 355, p. 258, 265, 277 n.92, 296.
Ex. 356, p. 258, 260, 265, 276 n.89, 277
        n.92.
Ex. 357, p. 258, 260, 265, 276 n.89, 277
        n.92.
Ex. 358, p. 212, 230, 241 n.37, 258, 268
        n.3, 277 n.92.
Ex. 359, p. 258, 268 n.3, 277 n.92.
Ex. 360, p. 220, n.14, 258, 277 n.92.
Ex. 361, p. 253, 259, 277 n.92.
Ex. 362, p. 273 n.45, 275 n.70.
Ex. 363, p. xviii, xxii. 258, 260-, 274 n.55-.
Ex. 365, p. 123 n.48, 253-, 255, 262, 270
        n.14, 271 n.32, 307 n.77.
Ex. 366, p. 12 n.24, 260, 261-, 266, 268
        n.3.
Ex. 367, p. 12 n.24, 260-, 261, 266, 268
        n.3, 269 n.13, 274-75 n.60-.
Ex. 368, p. 12 n.24, 260, 261-, 266.
Ex. 369, p. 12 n.24-, 251, 260, 261-, 266,
        274 n.60-, 275 n.69.
Ex. 370, p. xxiii, xxiv n.6, 18, 65 n.11,
        118, 152, 155, 160, 165, 201,
        236, 261, 266, 268, 285, 295,
        303 n.29.

V

INDEX OF QUOTATIONS FROM ST. THOMAS

SUMMA THEOLOGICA
I.

12.7.3	55 n .45
12. 12	56 n .51
13. 8. 2.	56 n .51
18. 4	304 n .40
21. 4. 1	67 n .30
39. 7	242 n .49
43. 3	303 n .30
44. 4	10 n .3
62. 3	52 nn. 12, 13
63. 3	52 n .14
63. 8. 1, 2	120 n .17
93. 8, 9	304 n .33
109. 2 c, ad 3	120 n .17
114. 1	124 n .60
114. 2	120 nn. 17, 20

I.II

9. 1, 3	170 n .34
13.3	168 n .9
51. 2. 3.	168 n .14
68. 1	170 n .32
69-70	124 n .70
70. 1. 2	170 n .32
71. 6	51 n 1, 55 n 43
72. 5	51 n 6
72. 5. 1	51 n 7
77.4	53 n 15, 121 n 23
82. 3	56 n 65
84. 1	121 nn 25, 26
84. 1, 2	66 n 13

84. 3	53 n 15, 121 n 23
85. 1	55 n 45
85. 2	27 n 37
87. 3. 2	67 n 30
89. 3	56 n 66
102. 3	10 n 5
102. 3. 8	25 n 15
111. 2	134 n 11

II.II

8. 1. 2	172 n 53
13. 1. 3. 4.	66 n 17
19. 4, 6	66 n 12
19. 11	278 n 13
23. 1	302 n 18
23. 8	26 n 35
24. 8	284
25. 7	56 n 48
26. 4	173 n 77
26. 5	12 n 26
27. 2	305 nn 56, 61
27. 3	303 n 29
27. 4	283
27. 6. 3	284
28	249 n 86
33. 4. 2	276 n 78
34. 2	66 n 18
44. 2	284
44. 6	284
52. 1. 2	170 n 32
52. 2	170 n 32
66. 7	102 n 16
72. 3	146 n 10

81. 1. 1	27 nn 38, 40	52. 4. 1	246 n 73
81. 7	10	52. 5	239 n 21
83. 2	147 n 21	56. 2	146 n 16
83. 15. 2	123 n 47	60. 6	302 n 17, 305 n 63
83. 16	123 n 47	65. 3	242 n 51, 249 n 91
83. 17	26 n 20	72. 2. 1	172 n 54
118. 6	121 n 47	73. 3	242 n 51
161-162	146 n 8	79. 1 c, 1	249 n 91
161. 1. 5	123 n 55	86. 4. 2. 3	55 n 41
161. 2. 3, 3	123 n 55		
161. 3. 2. 6	56 n 46		SUPPL.
161. 6. 3	147 n 19		
162. 5	121 n 23	94. 3	67 n 30
175. 3	247 n 77	98. 5	66 n 18
180. 4	11 n 7	99. 1, 3	67 n 30
182. 2. 3	305 n 62		
183. 1	168 n 6		SUMMA CONTRA GENTILES
184. 2	287, 305 n 56		II
188. 6	169 n 22		
		55	54 n 23
	III.	79	54 n 23
1. 2. 2	54 n 34		III
3. 4	91 n 31		
3. 8 c	89 n 8	61	54 n 23
9. 1. 3	91 n 38	133	101 n 4, 102 n 10
18. 6	196 n 6	141	65 n 4
24. 3. 4	277 n 94	144	67 n 30
27. 1	247 n 77		
30. 1	89 n 11		IV
50. 6	146 n 16		
50. 6. c	220 n 25	39	91 n 31
50. 6. 1, 3	220 n 25	42	89 n 8
52, 2. 2. 4	240 n 31	90	66 n 19

VI

INDEX OF VATICAN II DOCUMENTS

Apostolicam Actuositatem (AA) (Decree on the Apostolate of the Laity), 11 n.13, 120 n.11, 122 n.39, 271 n.25, 275 n.61, 276 n.76.

Ad Gentes (AG) (Decree on the Church's Missionary Activity), 91 n.32, 271 n.25, n.26.

Christus Dominus (CD) (Decree on the Biships' Pastoral Office in the Church), 273 n.47.

Dignitatis Humanae (DH) (Declaration on Religious Freedom), 120 n.14, 167 n.2, 273 n.47, n.48, n,49-, n.51, 276 n.80, n.81, 277 n.106.

Dei Verbum (DV) (Dogmatic Constitution on Divine Revelation), xxiv n.3, 122 n.41, 270 n.17, 271 n.22, n.28, n.29, 275 n.62, n.63, 277 n.102, n.103, n.104-.

Gravissimum Educationis (GE) (Declaration on Christian Education), 167 n.2, 271 n.24.

Gaudium et Spes (GS)(Pastoral Constitution on the Church in the Modern World), 10 n.4, 11 n.6, 12 n.23, 53 n.16, 54 n.23, n.28, 55 n.43, n.45, 57 n.72, 65 n.5, 77 n.6, 91 n.44, 101 n.3, 102 n.8, n.9, n.11, n.12, n.13, n.16, 119 n.2, 120 n.14, n.15, 124 n.69, 133 n.4, 146 n.7-, 168 n.6, 173 n.71-, n.78, 174 n.81, 187 n.37-, 188 n.40, 209 n.27, 270 n.15, n.19, 272 n.37, n.38, n.41, 273 n.46, 276 n.75, n.80, 301 n.1, 304 n.44.

Lumen Gentium (GL) (Dogmatic Constitution on the Church), xxvi n.25, 11 n.13,

n.14, n.20, 27 n.39, 55 n.42, 66 n.21, 77 n.6-, n.7-, 78 n.10, n.17-, 79 n.34, 102 n.14, 104 n.32, 119 n.3-, 122 n.36, n.37, 123 n.50, 124 n.57, 142, 146 n.5, 168 n.17, 172 n.55, 184 n.9, 188 n.47, 207 n.9, n.10, 208 n.14, 209 n.29-, 210 n.35, 223 n.56, 238 n.9, 241 n.38, 244 n.66, 247 n.77-, 270 n.16, n.17, n.18, 271 n.21-, n.27, 272 n.36, n.38, 274 n.57, 275 n.61, n.73, 276 n.77, n.85-, n.89, 277 n.99, 278 n.109, n.112, 301 n.1.

Nostra Aetate (NA) (Declaration on the Relationship of the Church to Non-Christian Religions), 188 n.40.

Optatam Totius (OT) (Decree on Priestly Formation), xxvi n.23-, n.24, 54 n.29, 276 n.76.

Perfectae Caritatis (PC) (Decree on the Appropriate Renewal of the Religious Life), 102 n.15, 103 n.29, 173 n.79, 174 n.80.

Presbyterorum Ordinis (PO) (Drecee on the Ministry and Life of Priests), 185 n.14, n.18, 249 n.91.

Sacrosanctum Concilium (SC) (Constitution on the Sacred Liturgy), 11 n.9, n.21, 27 n.39, 119 n.2, 184 n.8, 185 n.18, 271 n.23, 273-74 n.52-, 277 n.90.

Unitatis Redintegratio (UR) (Decree on Ecumenism), 91 n.44, 199 n.2, 121 n.22, 209 n.31, 271 n.21, n.30, 272 n.39, n.40, 273 n.51, 275 n.72, 278 n.109, n.110, n.111.